D0049093

A Farewell to Alms

THE PRINCETON ECONOMIC HISTORY
OF THE WESTERN WORLD

Joel Mokyr, Editor

A Farewell to Alms

A BRIEF ECONOMIC
HISTORY OF THE WORLD

Gregory Clark

PRINCETON UNIVERSITY PRESS
Princeton and Oxford

Copyright © 2007 by Princeton University Press

Published by Princeton University Press, 41 William Street, Princeton, New Jersey 08540

In the United Kingdom: Princeton University Press, 3 Market Place, Woodstock, Oxfordshire OX20 1SY

Library of Congress Cataloging-in-Publication Data

Clark, Gregory, 1957–
    A farewell to alms : a brief economic history of the world / Gregory Clark.
      p.   cm. — (The Princeton economic history of the Western world)
    Includes bibliographical references and index.
    ISBN 978-0-691-12135-2 (cloth : alk. paper)
    1. Economic history.   I. Title.
    HC21.C63   2007
    330.9—dc22   2007015166

British Library Cataloging-in-Publication Data is available

This book has been composed in Adobe Garamond by Princeton Editorial Associates, Inc., Scottsdale, Arizona

Printed on acid-free paper. ∞

press.princeton.edu

Printed in the United States of America

10 9 8 7 6 5 4 3 2

To Mary, Maximilian, Madeline, and Innis

Contents

Preface

This book takes a bold approach to history. It discerns, within a welter of often sketchy and sometimes conflicting empirical evidence, simple structures that describe mankind's long history—structures that can accommodate the startling facts about human history and the present world detailed in these pages. It is an unabashed attempt at *big history*, in the tradition of *The Wealth of Nations, Das Kapital, The Rise of the Western World,* and most recently *Guns, Germs, and Steel.* All these books, like this one, ask: How did we get here? Why did it take so long? Why are some rich and some poor? Where are we headed?

Intellectual curiosity alone makes these compelling questions. But while the book is focused on history, it also speaks to modern economic policy. For the text details how economists, and the institutions they inhabit, such as the World Bank and the International Monetary Fund, have adopted a false picture of preindustrial societies, and of the eventual causes of modern growth. These fanciful notions underlie current policies to cure the ills of the poor countries of the world, such as those represented by the Washington Consensus.

Though the book is about economics, we shall see that in the long run economic institutions, psychology, culture, politics, and sociology are deeply interwoven. Our very nature—our desires, our aspirations, our interactions—was shaped by past economic institutions, and it now in turn shapes modern economic systems. This book thus also has much to offer readers interested in anthropology and political, social, and even cultural history.

Fortunately for the reader, a simple set of ideas can carry us a long way in explaining the evolution of the world economy through the millennia. No formal economics training is necessary to understand any of what follows. Thus—though the issues grappled with here are ones that remain on the agendas of the most technically oriented economists—they are issues that readers innocent of the elaborate theoretical apparatus can fully appreciate.

Doubtless some of the arguments developed here will prove over-simplified, or merely false. They are certainly controversial, even among my colleagues in economic history. But far better such error than the usual dreary academic sins, which now seem to define so much writing in the humanities, of willful obfuscation and jargon-laden vacuity. As Darwin himself noted, "false views, if supported by some evidence, do little harm, for every one takes a salutary pleasure in proving their falseness: and when this is done, one path towards error is closed and the road to truth is often at the same time opened."[1] Thus my hope is that, even if the book is wrong in parts, it will be clearly and productively wrong, leading us toward the light.

Underlying the book is a wealth of data I have assembled on the history of the English economy between 1200 and 1870. To make the book easier on the reader, figures and tables that rely on this data set are not individually referenced. Where a source is not indicated for a figure or a table, or for a portion of a figure or a table, the underlying data and its sources will be found in Clark (2007b).

This book is the product of twenty years of labor in a particularly obscure corner of the academic vineyard: quantitative economic history. I am fortunate that the economics and history professions both so lightly regard these vines that a single scholar can claim whole centuries as his personal garden, and tend it reflectively and unmolested. But I hope that the book will also interest professional economists and historians, and remind them that a constant diet of Gallo can dull the palate.

1. Darwin, 1998, 629.

Acknowledgments

In writing this book I have accumulated a list of debts that is Trumpian in scale. The first is to those who commented on the manuscript or related papers, saving me from countless embarrassments and suggesting important revisions: Cliff Bekar, Steven Broadberry, Bruce Charlton, Anthony Clark, Alexander Field, James Fulford, Regina Grafe, Eric Jones, Oscar Jorda, Madeline Mc-Comb, Mary McComb, Tom Mayer, Joel Mokyr, Jim Oeppen, Cormac Ó Gráda, Kevin O'Rourke, James Robinson, Kevin Salyer, James Simpson, Jeffrey Williamson, and Susan Wolcott. I owe a special debt to my editors—Joel Mokyr, the series editor for the Princeton Economic History of the Western World, and Peter Dougherty of Princeton University Press—for their patience and wise counsel in the face of significant provocation. Peter Strupp of Princeton Editorial Associates copyedited the manuscript with astonishing attention to both detail and content.

My second debt is to my colleagues at the University of California, Davis. The economics department here is an astonishingly lively and collegial place. Alan Olmstead made Davis a center for economic history. His leadership of the All-UC Group in Economic History helped make California the world center of economic history. Peter Lindert has ageless enthusiasm, energy, and generosity. Alan Taylor threatens to transform this neglected corner of the vineyard into a grand cru. My colleagues in economics—especially Paul Bergin, Colin Cameron, Kevin Hoover, Hilary Hoynes, Oscar Jorda, Chris Knittel, Doug Miller, Marianne Page, Giovanni Peri, Kadee Russ, Kevin Salyer, Ann Stevens, and Deborah Swenson—made every day fun, stimulating, and entertaining.

I am grateful to Gillian Hamilton, David Jacks, and Susan Wolcott, past co-authors whose work is incorporated in this book.

Several research assistants helped collect or code the data underlying much of this work: David Brown, Robert Eyler, Melanie Guldi, Peter Hohn, Eric Jamelske, David Nystrom, and Shahar Sansani. Shahar was diligent beyond duty in finding the correct citations for the many sources.

My fifth debt is to the Wissenschaftskolleg zu Berlin (Institute for Advanced Study) for a fellowship in 2005 06 that gave me the time and impetus to bring this project to completion. The library staff there, particularly Marianne Buck, were wonderfully helpful in tracking down sources and potential illustrations.

Three grants from the National Science Foundation (SES 02-41376, SES 00-95616, and SES 91-22191) over the past fifteen years funded much of the data collection underlying the book.

Another more general obligation of long standing is to the teachers of Holy Cross High School, Hamilton, Scotland. It would be hard to imagine a more ramshackle hodgepodge of buildings, and the discipline was at times medieval. But the teachers were dedicated, knowledgeable, and generous with their time for no reward beyond the satisfaction of a job well done.

My final debt is to my wife, Mary McComb. While struggling with the manuscript I largely abandoned any domestic responsibilities in Berlin from August 2005 to July 2006, and that neglect continued in Davis for the rest of 2006. Mary, while working full time at her own profession, took over as cook, councilor, tour guide, German translator, and domestic enforcer. In addition she read and commented on the entire manuscript. This debt, at least, I hope I can repay.

1 Introduction: The Sixteen-Page Economic History of the World

He may therefore be justly numbered among the benefactors of mankind, who contracts the great rules of life into short sentences, that may be easily impressed on the memory, and taught by frequent recollection to recur habitually to the mind. —Samuel Johnson, *Rambler* No. 175 (November 19, 1751)

The basic outline of world economic history is surprisingly simple. Indeed it can be summarized in one diagram: figure 1.1. Before 1800 income per person —the food, clothing, heat, light, and housing available per head—varied across societies and epochs. But there was no upward trend. A simple but powerful mechanism explained in this book, the *Malthusian Trap*, ensured that short-term gains in income through technological advances were inevitably lost through population growth.

Thus the average person in the world of 1800 was no better off than the average person of 100,000 BC. Indeed in 1800 the bulk of the world's population was poorer than their remote ancestors. The lucky denizens of wealthy societies such as eighteenth-century England or the Netherlands managed a material lifestyle equivalent to that of the Stone Age. But the vast swath of humanity in East and South Asia, particularly in China and Japan, eked out a living under conditions probably significantly poorer than those of cavemen.

The quality of life also failed to improve on any other observable dimension. Life expectancy was no higher in 1800 than for hunter-gatherers: thirty to thirty-five years. Stature, a measure both of the quality of diet and of children's exposure to disease, was higher in the Stone Age than in 1800. And while foragers satisfy their material wants with small amounts of work, the modest comforts of the English in 1800 were purchased only through a life of unrelenting drudgery. Nor did the variety of material consumption improve. The average forager had a diet, and a work life, much more varied than the

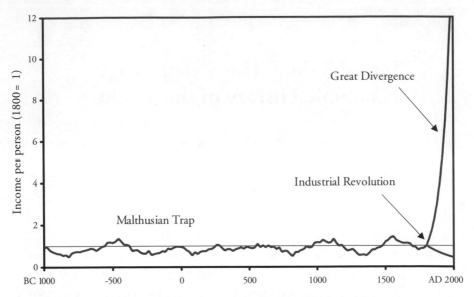

Figure I.I World economic history in one picture. Incomes rose sharply in many countries after 1800 but declined in others.

typical English worker of 1800, even though the English table by then included such exotics as tea, pepper, and sugar.

And hunter-gatherer societies are egalitarian. Material consumption varies little across the members. In contrast, inequality was pervasive in the agrarian economies that dominated the world in 1800. The riches of a few dwarfed the pinched allocations of the masses. Jane Austen may have written about refined conversations over tea served in china cups. But for the majority of the English as late as 1813 conditions were no better than for their naked ancestors of the African savannah. The Darcys were few, the poor plentiful.

So, even according to the broadest measures of material life, average welfare, if anything, declined from the Stone Age to 1800. The poor of 1800, those who lived by their unskilled labor alone, would have been better off if transferred to a hunter-gatherer band.

The Industrial Revolution, a mere two hundred years ago, changed forever the possibilities for material consumption. Incomes per person began to undergo sustained growth in a favored group of countries. The richest modern economies are now ten to twenty times wealthier than the 1800 average. Moreover the biggest beneficiary of the Industrial Revolution has so far been the unskilled. There have been benefits aplenty for the typically wealthy owners of land or capital, and for the educated. But industrialized economies saved their best gifts for the poorest.

Prosperity, however, has not come to all societies. Material consumption in some countries, mainly in sub-Saharan Africa, is now well below the preindustrial norm. Countries such as Malawi or Tanzania would be better off in material terms had they never had contact with the industrialized world and instead continued in their preindustrial state. Modern medicine, airplanes, gasoline, computers—the whole technological cornucopia of the past two hundred years—have succeeded there in producing among the lowest material living standards ever experienced. These African societies have remained trapped in the Malthusian era, where technological advances merely produce more people and living standards are driven down to subsistence. But modern medicine has reduced the material minimum required for subsistence to a level far below that of the Stone Age. Just as the Industrial Revolution reduced income inequalities *within* societies, it has increased them *between* societies, in a process recently labeled the *Great Divergence*.[1] The gap in incomes between countries is of the order of 50:1. There walk the earth now both the richest people who ever lived and the poorest.

Thus world economic history poses three interconnected problems: Why did the Malthusian Trap persist for so long? Why did the initial escape from that trap in the Industrial Revolution occur on one tiny island, England, in 1800? Why was there the consequent Great Divergence? This book proposes answers to all three of these puzzles—answers that point up the connections among them. The explanation for both the timing and the nature of the Industrial Revolution, and at least in part for the Great Divergence, lies in processes that began thousands of years ago, deep in the Malthusian era. The dead hand of the past still exerts a powerful grip on the economies of the present.

The focus on material conditions in this history will strike some as too narrow, too incidental to vast social changes over the millennia. Surely our material riches reflect but a tiny fraction of what makes industrialized societies modern?

On the contrary, there is ample evidence that wealth—and wealth alone—is the crucial determinant of lifestyles, both within and between societies. Income growth changes consumption and lifestyles in highly predictable

1. Pomeranz, 2000.

ways. The recent demise first of the American farmer and then of the manufacturing worker were already preordained when income began its upward march during the Industrial Revolution. Had we been more clear-sighted, we could have foreseen in 1800 our world of walk-in closets, his-and-her bathrooms, caramel macchiatos, balsamic reductions, boutique wines, liberal arts colleges, personal trainers, and $50 entrees.

There are surely many surprises ahead for mankind in the centuries to come, but for the most part the economic future is not an alien and exotic land. We already see how the rich live, and their current lifestyle predicts powerfully how we will all eventually live if economic growth continues.[2] Anyone who has visited the British Museum or the Sistine Chapel, for example, has had a foretaste of the relentless tide of tourism set to be unleashed on the world by another few decades of strong economic growth.[3] Even the high-income demand for unique and individualized travel and dining experiences is now catered to on an industrial scale.

Just as we can see the future through the lives of the rich, so the small wealthy elite of the preindustrial world led lives that prefigured our own. The delight of the modern American suburbanite in his or her first SUV echoes precisely that of Samuel Pepys, the wealthy London civil servant, on acquiring his first coach in 1668.[4] A walk through the reconstructed villas of Pompeii and Herculaneum, frozen in time on the day of the eruption of Vesuvius in AD 79, reveals homes that suburban Americans would happily move into: "Charming home with high ceilings, central courtyard, great room, finely detailed mosaics, and garden water feature—unobstructed Vesuvian views."

Thus I make no apologies for focusing on income. Over the long run income is more powerful than any ideology or religion in shaping lives. No God has commanded worshippers to their pious duties more forcefully than income as it subtly directs the fabric of our lives.

The Malthusian Trap: Economic Life to 1800

The first third of the book is devoted to a simple model of the economic logic of all societies before 1800, and to showing how this accords with historical

---

2. Thus when Bill and Melinda Gates were expecting a third child in 2002 they expanded their house, in light of their greater space needs, to its current 50,000 square feet.

3. The major export of New Zealand, for example, is now tourism services.

4. Pepys, 2000, November 28, 1668.

evidence. This model requires only three basic assumptions, can be explained graphically, and explains why technological advance improved material living conditions only after 1800.

The crucial factor was the rate of technological advance. As long as technology improved slowly, material conditions could not permanently improve, even while there was cumulatively significant gain in the technologies. The rate of technological advance in Malthusian economies can be inferred from population growth. The typical rate of technological advance before 1800 was well below 0.05 percent per year, about a thirtieth of the modern rate.

In this model the economy of humans in the years before 1800 turns out to be just the *natural* economy of all animal species, with the same kinds of factors determining the living conditions of animals and humans. It is called the Malthusian Trap because the vital insight underlying the model was that of the Reverend Thomas Robert Malthus, who in 1798 in *An Essay on the Principle of Population* took the initial steps toward understanding the logic of this economy.

In the Malthusian economy before 1800 economic policy was turned on its head: vice now was virtue then, and virtue vice. Those scourges of failed modern states—war, violence, disorder, harvest failures, collapsed public infrastructures, bad sanitation—were the friends of mankind before 1800. They reduced population pressures and increased material living standards. In contrast policies beloved of the World Bank and the United Nations today—peace, stability, order, public health, transfers to the poor—were the enemies of prosperity. They generated the population growth that impoverished societies.

At first sight the claim of no material advance before 1800 seems absurd. Figure 1.2 shows Nukak hunter-gatherers of the modern Amazonian rain forest, naked, with a simplicity of possessions. Figure 1.3 in contrast shows an upper-class English family, the Braddylls, painted in all their finery by Sir Joshua Reynolds in 1789. How is it possible to claim that material living conditions were on average the same across all these societies?

But the logic of the Malthusian model matches the empirical evidence for the preindustrial world. While even long before the Industrial Revolution small elites had an opulent lifestyle, the average person in 1800 was no better off than his or her ancestors of the Paleolithic or Neolithic.

The Malthusian logic developed in this book also reveals the crucial importance of fertility control to material conditions before 1800. All preindustrial

Figure 1.2   The Nukak, a surviving hunter-gatherer society in the Colombian rain forest.

societies for which we have sufficient records to reveal fertility levels experienced some limitation on fertility, though the mechanisms varied widely. Most societies before 1800 consequently lived well above the bare subsistence limit. That is why there has been plenty of room for African living standards to fall in the years since the Industrial Revolution.

Mortality conditions also mattered, and here Europeans were lucky to be a filthy people who squatted happily above their own feces, stored in basement cesspits, in cities such as London. Poor hygiene, combined with high urbanization rates with their attendant health issues, meant incomes had to be high to maintain the population in eighteenth-century England and the Netherlands. The Japanese, with a more highly developed sense of cleanliness, could maintain the level of population at miserable levels of material comforts, and they were accordingly condemned to subsist on a much more limited income.

Since the economic laws governing human society were those that govern all animal societies, mankind was subject to natural selection throughout the Malthusian era, even after the arrival of settled agrarian societies with the Neolithic Revolution of 8000 BC, which transformed hunters into settled agriculturalists. The Darwinian struggle that shaped human nature did not end

Figure 1.3 *The Braddyll Family,* Sir Joshua Reynolds, 1789. Wilson Gale-Braddyll was a Member of Parliament and Groom to the Bedchamber of the Prince of Wales.

with the Neolithic Revolution but continued right up until the Industrial Revolution.

For England we will see compelling evidence of differential survival of types in the years 1250–1800. In particular, economic success translated powerfully into reproductive success. The richest men had twice as many surviving children at death as the poorest. The poorest individuals in Malthusian England had so few surviving children that their families were dying out. Preindustrial England was thus a world of constant downward mobility. Given the static nature of the Malthusian economy, the superabundant children of the rich had to, on average, move down the social hierarchy in order to find work. Craftsmen's sons became laborers, merchants' sons petty traders, large landowners' sons smallholders. The attributes that would ensure later economic dynamism—patience, hard work, ingenuity, innovativeness, education—were thus spreading biologically throughout the population.

Just as people were shaping economies, the economy of the preindustrial era was shaping people, at least culturally and perhaps also genetically.[5] The Neolithic Revolution created agrarian societies that were just as capital intensive as the modern world. At least in England, the emergence of such an institutionally stable, capital-intensive economic system created a society that rewarded middle-class values with reproductive success, generation after generation. This selection process was accompanied by changes in the characteristics of the preindustrial economy, due largely to the population's adoption of more middle-class preferences. Interest rates fell, murder rates declined, work hours increased, the taste for violence declined, and numeracy and literacy spread even to the lower reaches of society.

The Industrial Revolution

The stasis of the preindustrial world, which occupied most of the history of mankind, was shattered by two seemingly unprecedented events in European society in the years 1760–1900. The first was the Industrial Revolution, the appearance for the first time of rapid economic growth fueled by increasing production efficiency made possible by advances in knowledge. The second was the demographic transition, a decline in fertility which started with the upper classes and gradually encompassed all of society. The demographic transition allowed the efficiency advance of the Industrial Revolution to translate not into an endless supply of impoverished people but into the astonishing rise of income per person that we have seen since 1800. The second third of the book examines these changes.

The Industrial Revolution and the associated demographic transition constitute the great questions of economic history. Why was technological advance so slow in all preindustrial societies? Why did the rate of advance

---

5. I first became interested in this idea in 1989. Clark and McGinley, 1989, argued through a simulation exercise that the logic of the Malthusian era implied that people evolved after the Neolithic Revolution toward greater patience and lower fertility. At the time these ideas seemed to conflict with the historical record and biological possibilities. My interest was reignited by a theoretical paper, making the same argument, by Oded Galor and Omar Moav; Galor and Moav, 2002.

increase so greatly after 1800? Why was one by-product of this technological advance a decline in fertility? And, finally, why have all societies not been able to share in the ample fruits of the Industrial Revolution?

There are only three established approaches to these puzzles. The first locates the Industrial Revolution in events outside the economic system, such as changes in political institutions, in particular the introduction of modern democracies. The second argues that preindustrial society was caught in a stable, but stagnant, economic equilibrium. Some shock set forces in motion that moved society to a new, dynamic equilibrium. The last approach argues that the Industrial Revolution was the product of a gradual evolution of social conditions in the Malthusian era: growth was endogenous. According to the first two theories the Industrial Revolution might never have occurred, or could have been delayed thousands of years. Only the third approach suggests that there was any inevitability to it.

The classic description of the Industrial Revolution has suggested that it was an abrupt transition between economic regimes, as portrayed in figure 1.1, with a change within fifty years from preindustrial productivity growth rates to modern rates. If this is correct then only theories that emphasize an external shock or a switch between equilibria could possibly explain the Industrial Revolution.

The classic description has also suggested that significant technological advances across disparate sectors of the economy contributed to growth during the Industrial Revolution, again pointing toward some economywide institutional change or equilibrium shift. This implies that we should be able to find the preconditions for an Industrial Revolution by looking at changes in institutional and economic conditions in England in the years just before 1800. And waves of economists and economic historians have thrown themselves at the problem with just such an explanation in mind—with spectacular lack of success.

The conventional picture of the Industrial Revolution as a sudden fissure in economic life is not sustainable. There is good evidence that the productivity growth rate did not experience a clean upward break in England, but instead fluctuated irregularly over time all the way back to 1200. Arguments can be made for 1600, for 1800, or even for 1860 as the true break between the Malthusian and modern economies.

When we try to connect advances in efficiency to the underlying rate of accumulation of knowledge in England, the link turns out to depend on many accidental factors of demand, trade, and resources. In crucial ways the classic Industrial Revolution in England in 1760–1860 was a blip, an accident, superimposed on a longer-running upward sweep in the rate of knowledge accumulation that had its origins in the Middle Ages or even earlier.

Thus, though an Industrial Revolution of some kind certainly occurred between 1200 and 1860 in Europe, though mankind crossed a clear divide, a materialist's Jordan at the gates of the Promised Land, there is still plenty of room for debate about its precise time and place, and hence debate about the conditions which led to it. An evolutionary account of gradual changes is a much more plausible explanation than has previously been appreciated.

Despite the dominant role that institutions and institutional analysis have played in economics and economic history since the time of Adam Smith, institutions play at best a minor direct role in the story of the Industrial Revolution told here, and in the account of economic performance since then. By 1200 societies such as England already had all the institutional prerequisites for economic growth emphasized today by the World Bank and the International Monetary Fund. These were indeed societies more highly incentivized than modern high-income economies: medieval citizens had more to gain from work and investment than their modern counterparts. Approached from the Smithian perspective, the puzzle is not why medieval England had no growth, but why today's northern European countries, with their high tax rates and heavy social spending, do not suffer economic collapse. The institutions necessary for growth existed long before growth itself began.

These institutions did create the conditions for growth, but only slowly and indirectly over centuries and perhaps even millennia. Here the book argues that the Neolithic Revolution, which established a settled agrarian society with massive stocks of capital, changed the nature of the selective pressures operating on human culture and genes. Ancient Babylonia in 2000 BC superficially possessed an economy remarkably similar to that of England in 1800. But the intervening years had profoundly shaped the culture, and maybe even the genes, of the members of agrarian societies. It was these changes that created the possibility of an Industrial Revolution only in AD 1800, not in 2000 BC.

Why an Industrial Revolution in England? Why not China, India, or Japan?[6] The answer hazarded here is that England's advantages were not coal,

6. Landes, 1998; Pomeranz, 2000; Mokyr, 2005.

not colonies, not the Protestant Reformation, not the Enlightenment, but the accidents of institutional stability and demography: in particular the extraordinary stability of England back to at least 1200, the slow growth of English population between 1300 and 1760, and the extraordinary fecundity of the rich and economically successful. The embedding of bourgeois values into the culture, and perhaps even the genetics, was for these reasons the most advanced in England.

Both China and Japan were headed in the same direction as England in 1600–1800: toward a society embodying the bourgeois values of hard work, patience, honesty, rationality, curiosity, and learning. They too enjoyed long periods of institutional stability and private property rights. But they were headed there more slowly than England. David Landes is correct in observing that the Europeans had a culture more conducive to economic growth.[7]

China and Japan did not move as rapidly along the path as England simply because the members of their upper social strata were only modestly more fecund than the mass of the population. Thus there was not the same cascade of children from the educated classes down the social scale.

The samurai in Japan in the Tokugawa era (1603–1868), for example, were ex-warriors given ample hereditary revenues through positions in the state bureaucracy. Despite their wealth they produced on average little more than one son per father. Their children were thus mainly accommodated within the state bureaucracy, despite the fixed number of positions. The Qing imperial lineage was the royal family of China from 1644 to 1911. They too were wealthy through the entitlements that fell to persons of their status. They produced more children than the average Chinese, but only modestly so.

Thus, just as accidents of social custom triumphed over hygiene, marriage, and reproduction to make Europeans richer than Asians in the Malthusian era, they also seem to have given Europe a greater cultural dynamic.

Whatever its cause, the Industrial Revolution has had profound social effects. As a result of two forces—the nature of technological advance and the demographic transition—growth in capitalist economies since the Industrial Revolution strongly promoted greater equality. Despite fears that machines would swallow up men, the greatest beneficiaries of the Industrial Revolution so far have been unskilled workers.

7. Landes, 1998.

Thus, while in preindustrial agrarian societies half or more of the national income typically went to the owners of land and capital, in modern industrialized societies their share is normally less than a quarter. Technological advance might have been expected to dramatically reduce unskilled wages. After all, there was a class of workers in the preindustrial economy who, offering only brute strength, were quickly swept aside by machinery. By 1914 most horses had disappeared from the British economy, swept aside by steam and internal combustion engines, even though a million had been at work in the early nineteenth century. When their value in production fell below their maintenance costs they were condemned to the knacker's yard.

Similarly there was no reason why the owners of capital or land need not have increased their shares of income. The redistribution of income toward unskilled labor has had profound social consequences. But there is nothing in the happy developments so far that ensures that modern economic growth will continue to be so benign in its effects.

The Great Divergence

The last third of the book considers why the Industrial Revolution, while tending to equalize incomes within successful economies, has at the same time led to a Great Divergence in national economic fortunes. How did we end up in a world where a minority of countries has unprecedented riches while a significant group has seen declining incomes since the Industrial Revolution? This disparity is reflected in ever-widening gaps in hourly labor costs across countries. In 2002, for example, apparel workers in India cost $0.38 per hour, compared to $9 in the United States (see figure 16.15). As the World Trade Organization labors to gradually dissolve remaining trade barriers, does this imply the end of all basic manufacturing activity in advanced economies? Do we face a future dystopia for rich societies in which the wages of the unskilled plummet to Third World levels?

The technological, organizational, and political changes spawned by the Industrial Revolution in the nineteenth century all seemed to predict that it would soon transform most of the world in the way it was changing England, the United States, and northwestern Europe. By 1900, for example, cities such as Alexandria in Egypt, Bombay in India, and Shanghai in China were all, in terms of transport costs, capital markets, and institutional structures, fully integrated into the British economy. Yet the growth in a favored few nations was followed haltingly in others, leading to an ever-widening income gap between societies.

This divergence in incomes is an intellectual puzzle on a par with that of the Industrial Revolution itself. And it provides a further severe test of theories of the Industrial Revolution. Can these theories be reconciled with the increasing divergence within the world economy?

A detailed examination of the cotton industry, one of the few found from the earliest years in both rich and poor countries, shows that the anatomy of the Great Divergence is complex and unexpected, and again hard to reconcile with economists' favorite explanations—bad institutions, bad equilibria, and bad development paths. In fact workers in poorly performing economies simply supply very little actual labor input on the job. Workers in modern cotton textile factories in India, for example, are actually working for as little as fifteen minutes of each hour they are at the workplace. Thus the disparity in hourly labor costs across the world is actually much less than it would appear from the differences in wage rates between rich and poor countries. Labor may cost $0.38 per hour in India, but its true cost per unit of work delivered is much higher. The threat to the living standards of unskilled workers in the United States from free trade with the Third World is less acute than hourly labor costs suggest. The new technologies of the Industrial Revolution could easily be transferred to most of the world, and the inputs for production obtained cheaply across the globe. But the one thing that could not be replicated so easily or so widely was the *social environment* that underpinned the cooperation of people in production in those countries where the technologies were first developed.

One reason why the social environment could not be replicated seems to be the comparatively long histories of various societies. In *Guns, Germs, and Steel* Jared Diamond suggested that geography, botany, and zoology were destiny.[8] Europe and Asia pressed ahead economically, and remained ahead to the present day, because of accidents of geography. They had the kinds of animals that could be domesticated, and the orientation of the Eurasian land mass allowed domesticated plants and animals to spread easily between societies. But there is a gaping lacuna in his argument. In a modern world in which the path to riches lies through industrialization, why are bad-tempered zebras and hippos the barrier to economic growth in sub-Saharan Africa? Why

8. Diamond, 1997.

didn't the Industrial Revolution free Africa, New Guinea, and South America from their old geographic disadvantages, rather than accentuate their backwardness? And why did the takeover of Australia by the British propel a part of the world that had not developed settled agriculture by 1800 into the first rank among developed economies?

The selection mechanisms discussed earlier can help explain how an initial advantage in establishing settled agrarian societies in Europe, China, and Japan, possibly from geography, was translated into a persistent cultural advantage in later economic competition. Societies without such a long experience of settled, pacific agrarian society cannot instantly adopt the institutions and technologies of the more advanced economies, because they have not yet culturally adapted to the demands of productive capitalism.

But history also teaches us that, even within societies of the same tradition and history, there can be regions and periods of economic energy and regions and periods of economic torpor. The economic fortunes of the north and south of England reversed after World War I; Ireland has become as rich as England after being significantly poorer for at least two hundred years; southern Germany has overtaken northern Germany.

These variations in the economic vitality of societies existed across the Malthusian era, and they continue to exist to this day. But in the Malthusian era the effects of these variations were dampened by the economic system. They mainly determined population densities. Polish farm workers in the early nineteenth century, for example, were allegedly slovenly, idle, and drunken compared to their British counterparts.[9] Yet living standards were little higher in England than in Poland. Instead Poland was very lightly populated. Since the Industrial Revolution such differences in the economic environment show up as variations in income levels.

Shifts in the nature of production technologies have further widened international income gaps. While Polish workers had low hourly outputs in farm tasks compared to workers in preindustrial England and the United States, the quality of their output was not markedly inferior. Polish wheat could still, after rescreening, be retailed at full price on the British market. When the majority of the tasks in agriculture consisted of such things as digging drainage ditches, spreading manure, and beating straw with a stick to extract the grain, the attitudes of the workers were not particularly important.

9. Jacob, 1826, 30, 65, 79–80.

However, modern production technologies, developed in rich countries, are designed for labor forces that are disciplined, conscientious, and engaged. Products flow through many sets of hands, each one capable of destroying most of the value of the final output. Error rates by individual workers must be kept low to allow such processes to succeed.[10] The introduction of such techniques in nineteenth-century England was accompanied by greater attention to worker discipline. When workers in poor countries lack these qualities of discipline and engagement, modern production systems are feasible only when little is demanded of each worker, to keep error rates as low as possible. This concept helps explain the dramatically lower observed work efforts of textile mill workers in such poor countries as India. It is cheaper to have frequently idle workers than idle machinery or defective output.

The Rise of Wealth and the Decline of Economics

Economics as a discipline arose in the dying decades of the Malthusian era. Classical economics was a brilliantly successful description of this world. But the torrent of goods unleashed by the Industrial Revolution not only created extremes of wealth and poverty across nations, it also undermined the ability of economic theory to explain these differences.

Thus there is a great irony in economic history. In most areas of inquiry —astronomy, archaeology, paleontology, biology, history—knowledge declines as we move away from our time, our planet, our society. In the distant mists lurk the strange objects: quasars, dwarf human species, hydrogen sulfide–fueled bacteria. But in economics the Malthusian era, however odd, is the known world. Preindustrial living standards are predictable based on knowledge of disease and environment. Differences in social energy across societies were muted by the Malthusian constraints. They had minimal impacts on living conditions. Since the Industrial Revolution, however, we have entered a strange new world in which economic theory is of little use in understanding differences in income across societies, or the future income in any specific society. Wealth and poverty are a matter of differences in local social interactions that are magnified, not dampened, by the economic system, to produce feast or famine.

The final great surprise that economic history offers—which was revealed only within the past thirty years—is that material affluence, the decline in

---

10. Kremer, 1993a.

child mortality, the extension of adult life spans, and reduced inequality have not made us any happier than our hunter-gatherer forebears. High incomes profoundly shape lifestyles in the modern developed world. But wealth has not brought happiness. Another foundational assumption of economics is incorrect.

Within any society the rich are happier than the poor. But, as was first observed by Richard Easterlin in 1974, rapidly rising incomes for everyone in the successful economies since 1950 have not produced greater happiness.[11] In Japan, for example, from 1958 to 2004 income per person rose nearly seven-fold, while self-reported happiness, instead of rising, declined modestly. It is evident that our happiness depends not on our absolute well-being but instead on how we are doing relative to our reference group. Each individual—by acquiring more income, by buying a larger house, by driving a more elegant car—can make herself happier, but happier only at the expense of those with less income, meaner housing, and junkier cars. Money does buy happiness, but that happiness is transferred from someone else, not added to the common pool.

That is why, despite the enormous income gap between rich and poor societies today, reported happiness is only modestly lower in the poorest societies. And this despite the fact that the citizens of poor nations, through the medium of television, can witness almost firsthand the riches of successful economies. It thus might be that there is no absolute effect of income on happiness, even at the lowest income levels. The people of the world of 1800, in which all societies were relatively poor and communities were much more local in scope, were likely just as happy as the wealthiest nations of the world today, such as the United States.

Since we are for the most part the descendants of the strivers of the preindustrial world, those driven to achieve greater economic success than their peers, perhaps these findings reflect another cultural or biological heritage from the Malthusian era. The contented may well have lost out in the Darwinian struggle that defined the world before 1800. Those who were successful in the economy of the Malthusian era could well have been driven by a need to have more than their peers in order to be happy. Modern man might not be designed for contentment. The envious have inherited the earth.

11. Easterlin, 1974; Blanchflower and Oswald, 2004.

PART I

The Malthusian Trap: Economic Life to 1800

2   The Logic of the Malthusian Economy

No arts; no letters; no society; and which is worst of all, continual fear, and dan-
ger of violent death: and the life of man, solitary, poor, nasty, brutish and short.
—Thomas Hobbes (1651)[1]

The vast majority of human societies, from the original foragers of the
African savannah through settled agrarian societies until about 1800, led an
economic life shaped and governed by one simple fact: in the long run births
had to equal deaths. Since this same logic governs all animal species, until
1800 in this "natural" economy the economic laws for humans were the same
as for all animal species. The break between the economics of humans and the
economics of the rest of the animal world occurred within the past two hundred years.

It is commonly assumed that the huge changes in the technology available to people and in the organizational complexity of societies, between our
ancestors on the savannah and those in England at the time of the Industrial
Revolution, must have improved material life even before modern economic
growth began. For example, Angus Maddison, the much-quoted creator of
preindustrial economic data, hazarded estimates of income per person for
millennia before 1820 on this basis.[2] But in this chapter I show that the logic
of the natural economy implies that the material living standard of the *aver-*
age person in the agrarian economies of 1800 was, if anything, worse than that
of our remote ancestors. Hobbes, in the quote that opens this chapter, was

---

1. Hobbes, 1651, 84.
2. Maddison, 2001, 28, for example, estimates that GDP per capita in western Europe
more than doubled from $450 in AD 1 to $1,232 by 1820 (in 1990 dollars), while for Japan the
rise was from $400 to $669.

profoundly wrong to believe that man was any worse off in the natural state than in the England of 1651.

This chapter develops a model of the preindustrial economy, the Malthusian model, from three simple and seemingly innocuous assumptions. This model has profound implications for how the economy functioned before 1800, which are then tested and explored in the following four chapters.

The Malthusian Equilibrium

Women, over the course of their reproductive lives, can give birth to twelve or more children. In some current societies the average woman still gives birth to more than six children. Yet in the world before 1800 the number of children per woman that survived to adulthood was always just a little above two. World population grew from perhaps 0.1 million in 130,000 BC to 770 million by 1800. But this still represents an average of 2.005 surviving children per woman before 1800. Even within successful preindustrial economies, such as those in western Europe, long-run rates of population growth were very small. Table 2.1 shows population in 1300 and 1800, and the implied numbers of surviving children per woman, for several western European countries. None of these societies deviated far from two surviving children per woman. Some force must have kept population growth rates within rather strict limits over the long run.

The Malthusian model supplies a mechanism to explain this long-run population stability. In the simplest version there are just three assumptions:

1. Each society has a *birth rate,* determined by customs regulating fertility, but increasing with material living standards.
2. The *death rate* in each society declines as living standards increase.
3. *Material living standards* decline as population increases.

The birth rate is just the number of births per year per person, for convenience normally quoted as births per thousand people. Maximum observed fertility levels have been 50–60. But the birth rate varies significantly even across preindustrial societies. Preindustrial England sometimes had birth rates of less than 30. As recently as 2000 in Africa, the area of highest birth rates, some countries had rates exceeding 50 per thousand: Niger, 55; Somalia, 52; Uganda, 51.

Table 2.1 Populations in Western Europe, 1300 and 1800

Location	Population ca. 1300	Population ca. 1800	Surviving children per woman
Norway[a]	0.40	0.88	2.095
Southern Italy[b]	4.75	7.9	2.061
France[c]	17.0	27.2	2.056
England[d]	5.8	8.7	2.049
Northern Italy[b]	7.75	10.2	2.033
Iceland[a]	0.084	0.047	1.930

Sources: [a]Tomasson, 1977, 406. [b]Federico and Malanima, 2004, table 4. [c]Le Roy Ladurie, 1981, 13.[d]Clark, 2007a, 120.

The death rate is again just deaths per year per person, also typically quoted per thousand people. In a *stationary* population, one of constant size, life expectancy at birth is the inverse of the death rate.[3] Thus if death rates are 33 per thousand, life expectancy at birth is thirty years. At a death rate of 20 per thousand, life expectancy would rise to fifty.

In a stationary population birth rates equal death rates. So in stationary populations, which were characteristic of the preindustrial world, life expectancy at birth is also the inverse of the birth rate. Thus in preindustrial society the only way to achieve high life expectancies was by limiting births. If preindustrial populations had displayed the fertility levels of modern Niger, life expectancy at birth would have been less than twenty.

The material living standard refers to the average amount of goods and services (e.g., religious ceremonies, barbers, servants) that people in a society consume. When new goods are introduced over time, such as newspapers, Wedgwood fine porcelain, and vacations at the seaside, it can be tricky to compare societies in terms of the purchasing power of their real wages. But for most of human history, and for all societies before 1800, the bulk of material consumption was food, shelter, and clothing, so their material living standards can be measured more accurately. In societies sophisticated enough to have a labor market, the material living standard for the bulk of the

3. Formally, if e_0 is life expectancy at birth and D is the death rate, $e_0 = 1/D$.

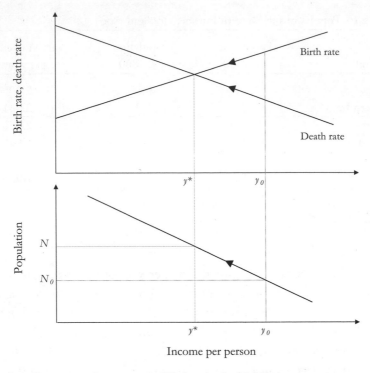

Figure 2.1 Long-run equilibrium in the Malthusian economy.

population will be determined by the purchasing power of the wages of unskilled workers.

Figure 2.1 shows graphically the three assumptions of the simple Malthusian model.[4] The horizontal axis for both panels is material income, the amount of goods and services available to each person. In the top panel birth and death rates are plotted on the vertical axis. The material income at which birth rates equal death rates is called the *subsistence income,* denoted in the figure as y^*. This is the income that just allows the population to reproduce itself. At material incomes above this the birth rate exceeds the death rate and population is growing. At material incomes below this the death rate exceeds the birth rate and population declines. Notice that this subsistence income is determined without any reference to the production technology of the society. It depends only on the factors that determine the birth rate and those that

---

4. The graphical exposition here follows that of Lee and Schofield, 1981.

determine the death rate. Once we know these we can determine the subsistence income and life expectancy at birth.

In the bottom panel population is shown on the vertical axis. Once we know population, that determines income and in turn the birth rate and death rates.

With just these assumptions it is easy to show that the economy will always move in the long run to the level of real incomes at which birth rates equal death rates. Suppose population starts at an arbitrary initial population, N_0 in the diagram. This will imply an initial income y_0. Since y_0 exceeds the subsistence income, births exceed deaths and population grows. As it grows, income declines. As long as the income exceeds the subsistence level population growth will continue, and income will continue to fall. Only when income has fallen to the subsistence level will population growth cease at the equilibrium level, N^*, and the population stabilize.

Suppose that instead the initial population had been so large that the income was below subsistence. Then deaths would exceed births and population would fall. This would push up incomes. The process would continue until income was again at the subsistence level. Thus wherever population starts from in this society it always ends up at N^*, with income at subsistence.

The term *subsistence income* can lead to the incorrect notion that in a Malthusian economy people are all living on the brink of starvation, like the inmates of some particularly nasty Soviet-era gulag. In fact in almost all Malthusian economies the subsistence income considerably exceeded the income required to allow the population to feed itself from day to day.

Differences in the location of the mortality and fertility schedules across societies also generated very different subsistence incomes. Subsistence for one society was extinction for others. Both 1400 and 1650, for example, fell within periods of population stability in England, hence periods in which by definition the income was at subsistence. But the wage of the poorest workers, unskilled agricultural laborers, was equivalent to about 9 pounds of wheat per day in 1650, compared to 18 pounds in 1400. Even the lower 1650 subsistence wage was well above the biologically determined minimum daily requirement of about 1,500 calories a day. A diet of a mere 2 pounds of wheat per day, supplying 2,400 calories per day, would keep a laborer alive and fit for work. Thus preindustrial societies, while they were subsistence economies, were not typically starvation economies. Indeed, with favorable conditions, they were at times wealthy, even by the standards of many modern societies.

The assumption that is key to the observation that income always re-turns to the subsistence level is the third one, of a fixed trade-off between population and material income per person. For reasons given below, this trade-off is called the *technology schedule.*

The justification for the decline in material incomes with higher popula-tion is the famous *Law of Diminishing Returns* introduced to economics by David Ricardo (and independently by Malthus). Any production system em-ploys a variety of inputs, the principal ones being land, labor, and capital. The Law of Diminishing Returns holds that, if one of the inputs to production is fixed, then employing more of any of the other inputs will increase output, but by progressively smaller increments. That is, the output per unit of the other input factors will decline as their use in production is expanded, as long as one input factor remains fixed.

In the preindustrial era land was the key production factor that was in-herently fixed in supply. This limited supply implied that average output per worker would fall as the labor supply increased in any society, as long as the technology of that society remained unchanged. Consequently average mate-rial income per person fell with population growth.

Figure 2.2 shows the assumed relationship between labor input and the value of output for preindustrial societies that underlies the third assumption of the Malthusian model. In economics the increase in the value of output from adding one more worker is called the *marginal product* of that person. In market economies this equals the wage.[5] As can be seen in the figure, the marginal product declines as more workers are added, and so does the wage. Average output per person also falls as the population rises. The additional output from the last person added to the economy is less than the output per person from existing workers.[6]

To appreciate concretely why this will happen, consider a peasant farmer with 50 acres of land. If he alone cultivates the land then he will maximize out-put by using low-intensity cultivation methods: keeping cattle or sheep which are left to fend for themselves and periodically culled for meat and hides, as with the Argentinean pampas in the early nineteenth century. With the labor

---

5. This is just the slope of the curve at any labor input.
6. Average output per person is the slope of the straight line drawn from the origin to the output curve at any given level of labor input.

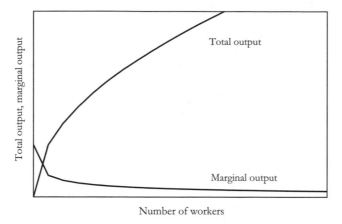

Figure 2.2 Labor input and output on a given area of land.

of an additional person milk cows could also be kept, increasing total output. With yet more labor the property could be cultivated as arable land with grain crops. Arable land requires much more labor input per acre than pasture, given the need for plowing, sowing, harvesting, threshing, and manuring. But arable land also yields a greater value of output per acre. With even more people the land could be cultivated more intensively as garden land, growing vegetables and tubers as well, thus increasing output yet further. Yields are increased by ever more careful utilization of manure, and by suppression of competing weeds by manual hoeing. With enough labor input the output of any acre of land can be very high. In the agricultural systems of coastal China and Japan around 1800, an acre of land was enough to support a family. In Ireland before the potato famine of 1845, an acre of potatoes, with careful spade husbandry, could supply to a family more than 6 tons of potatoes a year, 36 pounds a day, nearly enough to subsist on.[7] In the same period in England there were nearly 20 acres of land per farm worker.

We can also see in figure 2.1 that the sole determinants of the subsistence income are the birth rate and death rate schedules. Knowing just these we can determine the subsistence income. The connection shown in the lower panel between income and population level serves only to determine the population that corresponds to the subsistence income.

7. Ó Gráda, 1999, 227.

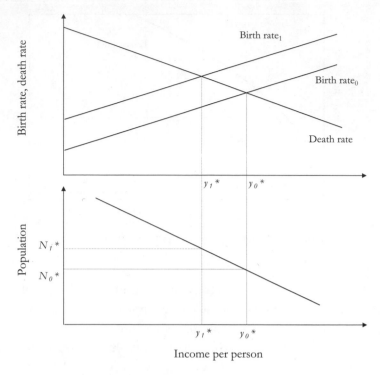

Figure 2.3   Changes in the birth rate schedule.

Changes in the Birth Rate and Death Rate Schedules

Different societies will have different *birth rate and death rate schedules,* that is, the birth and death rates at given incomes, and these schedules can change within a society over time. Suppose, for example, that the birth rate schedule increased, as in figure 2.3. It is then simple to see what happens to the death rate, material incomes, and the population. In the short run births exceed deaths. Population thus grows, driving down real income, and increasing the death rate until deaths again equal births. At the new equilibrium real income is lower and population is greater. Any increase in birth rates in the Malthusian world drives down real incomes. Conversely anything which limits birth rates drives up real income. Since life expectancy at birth in the Malthusian era was just the inverse of the birth rate, as long as birth rates remained high, life expectancy had to be low. Preindustrial society could thus raise both material living standards and life expectancy by limiting births.

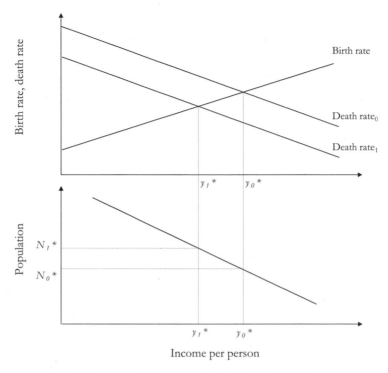

Figure 2.4 Changes in the death rate schedule.

Again if the death rate schedule moves down, as in figure 2.4, so that at each income there is a lower death rate, then at the current income births exceed deaths, so that population rises. This again drives down real income until the death rate once more equals the birth rate. At the new equilibrium population is higher and income lower. Given the now lower birth rate, however, life expectancy would be somewhat higher. So improvements in sanitation, or declines in violence and disorder, which reduce the death rate schedule in preindustrial societies, can raise life expectancy, but only at the cost of lower material living standards.

This Malthusian world thus exhibits a counterintuitive logic. Anything that raised the death rate schedule—war, disorder, disease, poor sanitary practices, or abandoning breast feeding—increased material living standards. Anything that reduced the death rate schedule—advances in medical technology, better personal hygiene, improved public sanitation, public provision for harvest failures, peace and order—reduced material living standards.

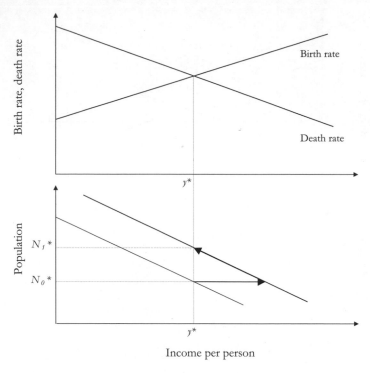

Figure 2.5   Effects of isolated technological advance.

Changes in Technology

The real income in Malthusian economies was determined from the birth rate and death rate schedules alone. Once this income was determined the population size depended just on how many people could be supported at this income level given the land area and technology of the society. For each society, depending on the land area and the production technology, there was a schedule connecting each population level with a given real income level. This is called the *technology schedule,* because the major cause of changes in this schedule has been technological advance. But other factors could also shift this schedule: the availability of more capital, improved trade possibilities, climate changes, or better economic institutions.

Figure 2.5 shows the path of adjustment from an isolated improvement in technology: a switch from an inferior technology, represented by curve T_0, to a superior technology, represented by curve T_1. Since population can change only slowly, the short-run effect of a technological improvement was an increase in real incomes. But the increased income reduced the death rate, births exceeded deaths, and population grew. The growth of population only ended when income returned to subsistence. At the new equilibrium the only effect of the technological change was to increase the population. There was no lasting gain in living standards.

The Malthusian Model and Economic Growth

In the millennia leading up to 1800 there were significant improvements in production technologies, though these improvements happened slowly and sporadically. The technology of England in 1800—which included cheap iron and steel, cheap coal for energy, canals to transport goods, firearms, and sophisticated sailing ships—was hugely advanced compared to the technology of hunter-gatherers in the Paleolithic, before the development of settled agriculture.

The degree of technological advance was revealed in the encounters between Europeans and isolated Polynesian islanders in the 1760s. The English sailors who arrived in Tahiti in 1767 on the *Dolphin,* for example, found a society with no metals. The Europeans' iron was so valuable to the Tahitians that a single 3-inch nail could initially be bartered for a 20-pound pig or a sexual encounter. Given the enthusiasm of the sailors for the sex trade, nail prices two weeks later had dropped by half, and "the Carpenter came and told me every cleat in the ship was drawn, and all the Nails carried off . . . most of the hammock nails was drawn, and two-thirds of the men obliged to lie on the Deck for want of nails to hang their Hammocks."[8] When Captain Cook arrived at a similarly isolated Hawaii the local inhabitants on a number of occasions stole ship's boats to burn them to retrieve the nails.

But, though technology was advancing before 1800, the rate of advance was always slow relative to that in the world after 1800. Figure 2.6, for example, shows the actual location of the technology curve of the Malthusian model for England from 1200 to 1800. The figure shows income per person by decade versus population. The observations for each decade are linked to show the movement of the population and income combinations over time. English population showed dramatic variation in the preindustrial period.

8. Robertson, 1955, 32, 78, 104. When Captain Cook arrived in 1769 he was shocked to find that the locals now demanded a hatchet for a pig; Banks, 1962, 252.

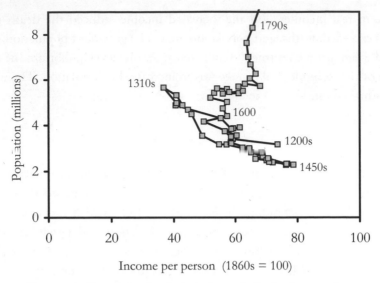

Figure 2.6 Revealed technological advance in England, 1200–1800.

There was growth in the medieval period from 1200 to 1316; at six million, the population in 1316 was as great as in the early eighteenth century. But the arrival from Asia of the bubonic plague (the so-called Black Death) in 1348 caused a long period of population decline from then to the 1450s.[9] By then England had barely two million people. Population grew again from 1540 to 1640 as the plague loosened its hold. From 1200 to 1650, as population changed under the influence of disease shocks, the income-population points lie along one downward-sloping line. This implies a completely stagnant production technology for 450 years. After 1650 the implied technology curve shifts upward, but not fast enough to cause significant increases in output per person. Instead technological advance, as predicted, resulted mainly in more people. In particular in the later eighteenth century all technological advance created only a larger population without generating any income gains. Before 1800 the rate of technological advance in all economies was so low that incomes could not escape the Malthusian equilibrium.

Because I want to show that the same economic model applies to all societies before 1800, even those with no labor market, and also to animal popula-

9. The popular term *Black Death* for the plague was introduced in England only hundreds of year after its onset.

tions, the Malthusian model has been developed in terms of material consumption per person. However, Thomas Malthus (1766–1834) and David Ricardo (1772–1823), who first formulated the Malthusian model and the associated economic doctrines now called classical economics, thought in terms of the wages of unskilled workers.[10] Thus Ricardo, using similar logic, argued that real wages (as opposed to income per person, which includes land rents and returns on capital) must always eventually return to the subsistence level.[11] Ricardo's proposition later became known as the *Iron Law of Wages*. Classical economics thus denied the possibility of other than transitory improvements in the living standards of unskilled workers. All the above reasoning about birth rates, death rates, population, and incomes can be carried out equivalently in terms of wages.

In light of subsequent events, the Iron Law of Wages may seem like an absurd proposition on which to found classical economics. But we shall see that the Malthusian model is an accurate description of all societies before 1800. The propositions of classical economics were developed at a time, 1798–1817, when real wages in England had been stationary or declining for generations. Though the innovations associated with the Industrial Revolution began appearing in the 1760s, their significance was not widely appreciated at the time. Technical progress in production technologies still seemed modest, sporadic, and accidental before 1820. Figure 2.7 shows the rural setting of Malthus's employment while working on his famous essay. Real wages did not begin the almost continual rise that characterizes the successful economies of the modern world until the 1820s. For some groups—such as the agricultural laborers in the south of England to whom Malthus ministered to as a parson while writing his *Essay on the Principle of Population*—real wages declined substantially between 1760 and 1820. Indeed one of the great social concerns of the years 1780–1834 in England was the rising tax burden on rural property owners created by payments to support the poor under the Poor Law.

Thus Malthus and Ricardo predicted that, as long as fertility remained unchanged, economic growth could not in the long run improve the human condition. All that growth would produce would be a larger population living at the subsistence income. China, for Malthus, was the embodiment of this type of economy. Though the Chinese had made great advances in agricul-

10. They did so in part because in the era in which they wrote there were scant available measures of income per person.
11. McCulloch, 1881, 50–58.

Figure 2.7 The church in Okewood, where Malthus earned his living as a curate while working on his essay. Malthus probably lived at his father's house in nearby Albury, whose population of 510 in 1801 had grown to 929 by 1831.

tural drainage and flood control, and had achieved high levels of output per acre, they still had very low material living standards because of the country's dense population. Thus, Malthus wrote of China, "If the accounts we have of it are to be trusted, the lower classes of people are in the habit of living almost upon the smallest possible quantity of food and are glad to get any putrid offals that European labourers would rather starve than eat."[12]

In the preindustrial world sporadic technological advance produced people, not wealth.

Human and Animal Economies

The economic laws we have derived in this chapter for the preindustrial human economy are precisely those that apply to all animal, and indeed plant,

12. Malthus, 1798, 115.

populations. Before 1800 there was no fundamental distinction between the economies of humans and those of other animal and plant species. This was also a point Malthus appreciated: "Elevated as man is above all other animals by his intellectual faculties, it is not to be supposed that the physical laws to which he is subjected should be essentially different from those which are observed to prevail in other parts of the animated nature."[13]

Thus the Malthusian model dominates in evolutionary ecology as well. For animal and plant species population equilibrium is similarly attained when birth rates equal death rates. Birth and death rates are both assumed to be dependant on the quality of the habitat, the analogue of the human level of technology, and population density. Ecological studies typically consider just the direct link between birth and death rates and population density, without considering the intermediate links, such as material consumption, as I have done above. But the Malthusian model for humans could also be constructed in this more reductionist way.

At least some ecological studies find that population density affects mortality in ways that are analogous to those we have posited for human populations, through the supply of food available per animal. Thus one study showed that over forty years wildebeest mortality rates depended largely on the available food supply per animal: "the main cause of mortality (75 percent of cases) was undernutrition."[14] Hence the Industrial Revolution after 1800 represented the first break of human society from the constraints of nature, the first break of the human economy from the natural economy.

Political Economy in the Malthusian Era

Malthus's essay was written in part as a response to the views of his father, who was a follower of the eighteenth-century Utopian writers William Godwin and the Marquis de Condorcet. Godwin and de Condorcet argued that the misery, unhappiness, and vice so common in the world were the result not of unalterable human nature but of bad government.[15] Malthus wanted to establish that poverty was not the product of institutions, and that consequently changes in political institutions could not improve the human lot. As

13. Malthus, 1830, 225.
14. Mduma et al., 1999, 1101.
15. Godwin, 1793; Condorcet, 1795.

we have seen, in a world of only episodic technological advance, such as England in 1798, his case was compelling.

Certainly one implication of the Malthusian model, which helped give classical economics its seemingly harsh cast, was that any move to redistribute income to the poor (who at that time in England were mainly unskilled farm laborers) would result in the long run only in more poor, perhaps employed at even lower wages. As Ricardo noted in 1817, "The clear and direct tendency of the poor laws is in direct opposition to these obvious principles: it is not, as the legislature benevolently intended, to amend the condition of the poor, but to deteriorate the condition of both poor and rich."[16] The poor laws would lower wages because they aided in particular those with children, thus reducing the costs of fertility and driving up the birth rate.

The arguments of Malthus and his fellow classical economists not only suggested the inability of government to improve the human lot through traditional methods, they also implied that many of the government policies that the classical economists attacked—taxation, monopolies, trade barriers such as the Corn Laws, wasteful government spending—would similarly have no effect on human welfare in the long run. But the classical economists did not see this.

Indeed, if we follow the logic laid out here, good government in the modern sense—stable institutions, well-defined property rights, low inflation rates, low marginal tax rates, free markets, free trade, avoidance of armed conflict—would either make no difference to material living standards in the Malthusian era or indeed lower living standards.

To take one example, suppose that the preindustrial king or emperor levied a poll tax on every person in the economy, equivalent to 10 percent of average income. Suppose also that, as was the wont of such sovereigns, the proceeds of the tax were simply frittered away on palaces, cathedrals, mosques, or temples; on armies; or to stock a large harem. Despite the waste, in the long run this action would have no effect on the welfare of the average person.

To understand why, refer back to figure 2.1. The tax would act like a shock to the technology of the economy, shifting the lower curve uniformly

16. McCulloch, 1881, 58. Thus classical economics was influential in creating the draconian reforms of poor relief in England in 1834. The most influential member of the Poor Law Commission set up to examine the workings of the old Poor Law was Nassau Senior, professor of political economy at Oxford University.

left by 10 percent. Initially, with the existing stock of people, the tax reduces incomes per person by 10 percent, thus driving up death rates above birth rates. But in the long run after-tax incomes must return to their previous level to stabilize population again. At this point population is sufficiently smaller that everyone earns a high enough wage that, after paying the tax, they have sufficient funds left over to equal their old pretax earnings. In the long run exactions by the state have no effect in the Malthusian economy on welfare or life expectancy. Luxury, waste, extravagance by the sovereign—all had no cost to the average citizen in the long run! Restrictions on trade and obstructive guild rules were similarly costless.

Thus at the time the *Wealth of Nations* was published in 1776, when the Malthusian economy still governed human welfare in England, the calls of Adam Smith for restraint in government taxation and unproductive expenditure were largely pointless. Good government could not make countries rich except in the short run, before population growth restored the equilibrium.[17]

So far we have considered only actions by government that shift the effective consumption possibilities for a society. Governments could also directly affect birth rates and death rates through their policies. War, banditry, and disorder all increased death rates at given levels of income (though war often killed more through the spread of disease than from direct violence). But all increases in death rates make societies better off in material terms. Here "bad" government actually makes people better off in material terms, though with a reduced life expectancy. Good governments—those that, for example, store grains in public granaries as a hedge against harvest failures, as in some periods in Imperial Rome and late Imperial China—just make life more miserable by reducing the periodic death rate from famines at any given average material living standard.[18]

It is thus ironic that—while the classical economists, and in particular Adam Smith, are taken as their intellectual fathers by modern proponents of limited government—their views made little sense in the world in which they were composed.

17. It is explained in chapter 5 that high incomes in eighteenth-century England probably owed more to bad personal hygiene than to advances in political economy.
18. In China state granaries in the eighteenth century routinely distributed grain to the poor. See Will and Wong, 1991, 482–83.

Income Inequality and Living Standards

Preindustrial societies differed in their degree of income inequality. Based on modern evidence, forager societies were egalitarian in consumption. In such communities there was no land or capital to own, while in settled agrarian societies as much as half of all income could derive from ownership of assets. Furthermore, forager societies were typically characterized by a social ethic that mandated sharing. Thus, for example, even the labor income of successful hunters was taxed by the less successful.

Agrarian societies from the earliest times were much more unequal. The richest members of these societies commanded thousands of times the average income of the average adult male. Aristocrats, such as the Duke of Bedford in England in 1798, resided in a state of luxury that the farm laborers on his extensive estates could hardly comprehend.

The Malthusian model takes no account of income distribution. But, by analogy with the discussion of the previous section on taxation and living standards, we can see that greater inequality will have little or no effect on the living standards of the landless workers, the mass of the population. The more equally land rents and capital income are distributed across the general population the more these rents will simply be dissipated in larger population sizes. If these rents were instead appropriated by an aristocratic elite, as they were in many preindustrial societies, then they could be enjoyed with little or no cost to the rest of the population. Thus while inequality could not make the median person better off in the Malthusian world, it could raise average income per person by raising the incomes of the propertied elite.

Thus it was possible that England, France, or Italy in 1800 could have a higher income per person than the original foragers. But perversely they would achieve this higher income only through their achievement of greater inequality than earlier societies. And the boost to income per person from inequality was limited. Land rents and capital income made up perhaps half of all income in settled agrarian societies. The expropriation of all these incomes by an elite would double income per person compared to a state of complete inequality.

In summary table 2.2 shows Malthusian "virtues" and "vices." But virtue and vice here are measured with reference only to whether actions raised or lowered material income per person.[19]

19. Chapter 3 explains why indolence is a virtue in Malthusian economies.

Table 2.2 Malthusian "Virtues" and "Vices"

"Virtues"	"Vices"
Fertility limitation	Fecundity
Bad sanitation	Cleanliness
Violence	Peace
Harvest failures	Public granaries
Infanticide	Parental solicitude
Income inequality	Income equality
Selfishness	Charity
Indolence	Hard work

The Neolithic Revolution and Living Standards

The great economic transformation of the preindustrial era was the Neolithic Revolution: the move from hunter-gatherer societies to those with economies based on cultivated crops and domesticated animals. Anthropologists and archaeologists have long debated what effect this transformation had on living standards, with many believing that farming reduced them. Jared Diamond has even gone so far as to argue that "Forced to choose between limiting population or trying to increase food production, we chose the latter and ended up with starvation, warfare, and tyranny."[20]

The empirical data are inconclusive. We shall see in chapters 3–5 that the evidence, on balance, is that living standards in the broadest sense—consumption, leisure, life expectancy—did decline after the spread of settled agriculture, but with significant variation across different agrarian societies. We will find in the following chapters that these modest declines are explained by the fact that the birth rates of forager and settled agrarian societies were likely the same, and death rates at a given income differed little. The ability to store food in settled agrarian societies, which allowed for survival of lean periods and so reduced death rates, would reduce living standards. On the other hand, increased disease mortality from greater population densities helped increase material living standards. The net result of these effects could go either way. Thus the effect of settled agriculture on living standards in a Malthusian world is inherently ambiguous.

20. Diamond, 1987, 66. See also Cohen, 1977; Kaplan, 2000.

The failure of settled agriculture to improve living conditions, and the possibility that living conditions fell with the arrival of agriculture, have led some economists, anthropologists, and archaeologists to puzzle over why mankind abandoned the superior hunter-gatherer lifestyle for inferior agrarian societies.[21] But within the framework of the Malthusian model there is no puzzle. Agriculture was adopted because it was initially a better technology, which generated higher incomes. But those higher incomes inevitably led to larger populations and a decrease of living standards to a new Malthusian equilibrium, seemingly one less favorable than that for the previous hunter-gatherer societies.

Material Conditions: Paleolithic to Jane Austen

This chapter explained the first claim made in the introduction, that living standards in 1800, even in England, were likely no higher than for our ancestors of the African savannah. Since preindustrial living standards were determined solely by fertility and mortality, the only way living standards could be higher in 1800 would be if either mortality rates were greater at a given real income or fertility was lower.

This conclusion may seem too powerful in the light of figures 1.1 and 1.2. But the upper class about whom authors such as Jane Austen wrote were a small group within English society. In *Sense and Sensibility* one of her characters says, of an income of £300 a year from a rectory, "This little rectory can do no more than make Mr. Ferrars comfortable as a bachelor; it cannot enable him to marry."[22] In contrast the mass of farm laborers in England in 1810 had an annual income of £36 or less per year.

Even though England was one of the richest economies in the world, its people lived by modern standards a pinched and straightened existence. If employed they labored three hundred days a year, with just Sundays and the occasional other day off. The work day in winter was all the daylight hours. Their diet consisted of bread, a little cheese, bacon fat, and weak tea, supplemented for adult males by beer. The diet was low in calories given their heavy manual labor, and they must often have been hungry. The monotony was relieved to some degree by the harvest period, in which work days were long

21. See, for example, Cohen, 1977, and Richerson et al., 2001.
22. Austen, 1957, 247.

but the farmers typically supplied plenty of food. Hot meals were few since fuel for cooking was expensive. The laborers generally slept once it got dark since candles for lighting were again beyond their means. They would hope to get a new set of clothes once a year. Whole families of five or six people would live in two-room cottages, heated by wood or coal fires.[23] Almost nothing they consumed—food, clothing, heat, light, or shelter—would have been unfamiliar to the inhabitants of ancient Mesopotamia. Had consumers in 8000 BC had access to more plentiful food, including meat, and more floor space, they could easily have enjoyed a lifestyle that English workers in 1800 would have preferred to their own.

In the following three chapters I show that all the major empirical implications of the Malthusian model hold true for the world in the years before 1800.

23. Eden, 1797; Clark, 2001b.

3   Living Standards

[Tierra del Fuego, 1832] These poor wretches were stunted in their growth. . . .
If a seal is killed, or the floating carcass of a putrid whale discovered, it is a feast;
and such miserable food is assisted by a few tasteless berries and fungi.
                                                                    —Charles Darwin (1839)[1]

[Tahiti, 1769] These happy people may almost be said to be exempt from the
curse of our forefather; scarcely can it be said that they earn their bread with the
sweat of their brow when their cheifest sustenance Bread fruit is procurd with no
more trouble than that of climbing a tree and pulling it down.
                                                                    —Joseph Banks (1769)[2]

The logic of the Malthusian economy is clear. There should be no systematic
gain in living standards on average across societies between earliest man and
the world of 1800 on the eve of the Industrial Revolution. Disease, war, infanticide, and customs regulating marriage and sex could elevate material living standards. But on balance the happy circumstances that made for Tahiti
in 1769, or the unhappy ones that made for Tierra del Fuego in 1832, were no
more likely in AD 1800 than in 100,000 BC. In this chapter I consider the
empirical evidence for this first crucial contention of the Malthusian model
of society. Were material living standards truly no better on average in 1800
than in 10,000 BC or even 100,000 BC?

Real Wages before 1800

Since the poorest half of any society typically lives on their wages alone, without any property income, measures of real wages provide a good index of living
standards in any society. Yet comprehensive measures of wages are available
for only a few societies before 1800, and only in rare cases can we get good
measures as early as 1200.

Preindustrial England, however, has a uniquely well-documented wage
and price history. The relative stability of English institutions after the Nor-

1. Darwin, 1965, 203.
2. Banks, 1962, 341.

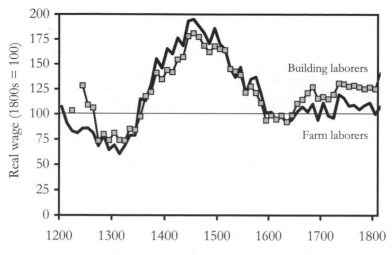

Figure 3.1 English laborers' real wages, 1209–1809.

man Conquest of 1066, and the early development of markets, allowed a large number of documents with wages and prices to survive. Using these we can estimate nominal wages, the prices of consumption goods, and thus real wages for England back to 1209. (To set this date in context, 1209 fell within the reign of the famously "bad" King John, just six years before he was forced by the barons to codify their rights in the Magna Carta of 1215.)

Figure 3.1 shows the real day wage of building laborers and farm laborers in England by decade from 1209 to 1809 as an index, with 1800–09, at the end of the Malthusian era, set at 100 for farm laborers. The real wage is just a measure of how many units of a standard bundle of goods these laborers could buy with one day's earnings through these sixty decades.[3]

The composition of that bundle of goods is shown in table 3.1. It was determined by expenditure studies for farm workers and others in the 1790s, a decade in which the poverty of these workers had become an issue, in part because of the growing burden of the Poor Laws.[4] These studies revealed that even around 1800 English farm workers spent three-quarters of their income on food, with starches such as bread accounting for the bulk of that expenditure at 44 percent of the entire budget. The other quarter of their expenditures

3. These real wages are drawn from the series derived in Clark, 2005, and Clark, 2007a. These series are the most comprehensive measures available for living standards in any preindustrial economy, including goods whose prices are typically not measurable, such as housing.

4. Clark, Huberman, and Lindert, 1995; Clark, 2001b.

Table 3.1 Expenditure Shares of
Laborers before 1800

Category of expenditure	Share (%)
Food and drink	75
Grains and starches	44
Dairy	10
Meat	9
Drink	8
Sugar and honey	3
Salt and pepper	1
Clothing and bedding	10
Housing	6
Heating	5
Light and soap	4

was devoted to the basics of shelter, heating, light and soap, and clothing and bedding. This despite the fact that by the 1790s English workers earned more than workers in most other European economies, and also significantly more, as we shall see, than workers in China, India, or Japan.

Real wages in England showed remarkably little gain in the six hundred years from 1200 to 1800. The fluctuations over that period are much more dramatic than any long-run upward trend. Thus in thirty-nine of the sixty decades between 1200 and 1800 real wages for farm workers are estimated to be above their level in 1800. The highest real wages are found in the interval 1400–1549, long before 1800. The years around 1300, before the onset of the plague in England in 1349, do show lower wages than in 1800. But wages in the early thirteenth century are close to their level in 1800.

It should be stressed that this wage index incorporates the arrival of new goods such as sugar, pepper, raisins, tea, coffee, and tobacco. Even allowing for the gains in real income from the decline in prices of all these new goods in the years 1500–1800, workers in the late Middle Ages were still much richer. They received extra rations of beef and beer as part of their wages, which more than covered any absence of tea or sugar.

The English experience also shows that, while the Malthusian economy displayed stagnant material living standards, these were not necessarily low

Table 3.2 Wages and Prices in Malawi, 2001–2002, and England, 1800

	England, 1800 (pence)	England, 1800 (units per day)	Malawi, 2001–02 (kwacha)	Malawi, 2001–02 (units per day)
Wage	23.9	—	69	—
Prices				
Flour (kilograms)	7.5	3.2	33	2.1
Bread (kilograms)	5.9	4.0	46	1.5
Potatoes (kilograms)	1.2	20.4	16	4.2
Beef (kilograms)	17.4	1.4	123	0.6
Eggs (dozen)	11.1	2.1	84	0.8
Milk (liters)	2.4	9.9	48	1.4
Sugar (kilograms)	26.3	0.9	42	1.7
Beer (liters)	4.1	5.8	93	0.7
Tea (kilograms)	219.5	0.1	248	0.3
Salt (kilograms)	9.1	2.6	24	2.8
Cost of English basket	23.9	1.0	178	0.4

Sources: England: Clark, 2007b. Malawi: International Labour Organization, Bureau of Statistics, 2006a.

standards of living, even by the measure of many modern economies. Though the consumption pattern of the preindustrial English worker around 1800 may seem primitive, it actually implies, from the shares devoted to different goods, high living standards by the measure of the modern Third World. Over 40 percent of the food consumption, for example, was for luxury goods like meats, milk, cheese, butter, beer, sugar, and tea (see table 3.1). All of these are very expensive sources for the calories and proteins necessary to work and to maintaining the body. Very poor people do not buy such goods.

The comparative affluence of the preindustrial worker in England can be illustrated in two ways. First we can compare the day wages of English farm workers and construction laborers before 1800 with those of some of the poorer countries of the current world.[5] Table 3.2 shows the wages of construction

---

5. These data are not so easy to obtain as might be assumed, since modern poor countries tend to have poor bureaucracies for gathering statistics.

laborers in Malawi in 2001–02, compared with the prices of some major items of consumption, along with the comparative data for construction laborers in England in 1800.

Only food prices are available for Malawi, but since these were 75 percent of English farm workers' expenditures they provide a fair approximation of living standards. The second column shows the day wage in England as well as prices in England. The fourth column gives the same data for Malawi in 2001–02. Columns 3 and 5 show how much of each item could be purchased with the day wage in each country. Thus the day wage in England in 1800 would purchase 3.2 kilograms of wheat flour, while the day wage in Malawi would purchase only 2.1 kilograms of inferior maize flour.

English workers of 1800 could purchase much more of most goods than their Malawian counterparts. The last row shows the cost of the English basket of foods in pence (assuming that all income was spent on food) and the equivalent cost in Malawian kwacha. If a Malawian had tried to purchase the consumption of the English worker in 1800 he would have been able to afford only 40 percent as much. Thus living standards in England in 1800 were possibly 2.5 times greater than those of current-day Malawi. Figure 3.2 shows a contemporary rural village in Malawi. Yet the meager wage in Malawi is still above the subsistence level for that economy in healthy modern conditions, since the Malawian population continues to grow rapidly.

For a much wider range of countries we have estimates of real national income per person in 2000. It is also possible to estimate national income per person for England back to 1200, so we can compare average income per person in preindustrial England with the range in the modern world. Table 3.3 shows the results of that comparison. England in 1200–1800 had an income per person as high as, or higher than, large areas of the modern world. Countries with an aggregate population of more than 700 million people in the year 2000 had incomes below the average of preindustrial England. Another billion people in India had average incomes only 10 percent above those in England before the Industrial Revolution. Some modern countries are dramatically poorer. Hundreds of millions of Africans now live on less than 40 percent of the income of preindustrial England.

The reductions in mortality from modern vaccines, antibiotics, and public health measures in these poor countries since 1950 have been rightly celebrated as a significant triumph of international aid efforts. Life expectancy

Figure 3.2   A rural village in Malawi, 1988.

was 40 in developing countries in 1950, but it had reached 65 by 2000.[6] Table 3.3 also shows modern life expectancies, which are much higher at a given income than in the preindustrial world. One side effect of these advances, however, has been that, even at wages well below those of preindustrial England, population in these countries is still growing with a rapidity never seen in the preindustrial world, as table 3.3 also shows. The subsistence wage, at which population growth would cease, is many times lower in the modern world than in the preindustrial period. This is one factor leading to the Great Divergence in incomes discussed in the last section of the book. Given the continued heavy dependence of many sub-Saharan African countries on farming, and a fixed supply of agricultural land, health care improvements are not an unmitigated blessing, but exact a cost in terms of lower material incomes.

In recent years the ravages of AIDS in sub-Saharan Africa have also, despite modern medical technologies, reduced life expectancy in some of these countries to levels that are little above those in the preindustrial world (as we shall see from table 5.2). Not only is Malawi dramatically poorer in material

6. Levine et al., 2004, 9.

Table 3.3 Comparative Incomes per Person, 2000

Country	Population, 2000 (millions)	Income per person (2005 $)	Relative income (%)	Population growth rate (%)	Life expectancy at birth, 2003
Tanzania	34	569	20	2.1	46
Burundi	7	717	25	2.9	44
Ethiopia	64	832	29	2.3	48
Sierra Leone	5	849	30	2.3	41
Malawi	10	935	33	2.4	40
Nigeria	127	956	34	2.4	43
Zambia	10	972	34	2.1	38
Madagascar	16	1,014	36	3.0	55
Rwanda	9	1,129	40	2.4	44
Burkina Faso	11	1,141	40	3.0	48
Mali	11	1,150	41	2.3	48
Benin	6	1,417	50	2.7	54
Kenya	30	1,525	54	2.6	47
Ghana	19	1,590	56	2.1	57
Nepal	23	1,809	64	2.2	62
Senegal	10	1,945	69	2.3	56
Bangladesh	131	2,052	73	2.2	63
Nicaragua	5	2,254	80	2.0	70
Côte d'Ivoire	16	2,345	83	2.0	46
Pakistan	138	2,497	88	2.2	63
Honduras	6	2,505	89	2.3	68
Moldova	4	2,559	90	0.3	68
Cameroon	15	2,662	94	2.0	46
England pre-1800	—	2,828	100	0.1	37
Zimbabwe	13	3,016	107	0.6	37
India	1,016	3,103	110	1.4	63
Bolivia	8	3,391	120	1.6	64
China	1,259	4,446	157	0.6	72

Sources: Income: Heston et al., 2006. Population: United Nations, 2006. Life expectancy: preindustrial England, table 5.2; others, United Nations, Development Program, 2005, 220–22.

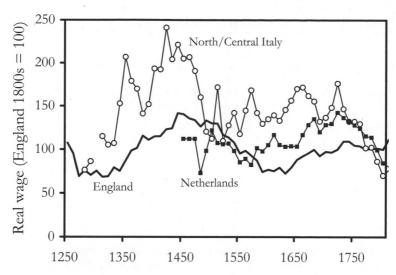

Figure 3.3 Comparative European real wages, 1250–1809. Northern and central Italian wages are from Federico and Malanima, 2004, appendix. Dutch wages are from de Vries and van der Woude, 1997, 609–28. The relative level of these wages to those in England in 1800 was fixed by assuming wages were proportionate to real GDP per person in each country relative to England in 1910 and 1810 respectively.

terms than preindustrial England, it also has a life expectancy barely above that of England before 1800: 40 versus 37. Indeed, given the patterns of mortality in sub-Saharan Africa, life expectancy at age 20 is lower in Malawi than it was in preindustrial England.

This information on English living standards before 1800 illustrates that within any society under the Malthusian constraints wages and living standards can fluctuate by large amounts. Societies subject to Malthusian constraints were not necessarily particularly poor, even by the standard of today.

Figure 3.3 shows long-run real English builders' day wages in comparison to those in northern and central Italy and those in the Netherlands. Wages in both Italy and the Netherlands were significantly higher in the years before 1800 than in 1800 itself. They were also typically even higher than wages in England. Again there is no secular increase in real wages.

Information on real wages for societies earlier than 1200 is more fragmentary. But table 3.4 shows a very simple measure of wages, the equivalent of the wage in pounds of wheat, for unskilled laborers in a variety of earlier societies all the way back to ancient Babylonia in the second millennium be-

Table 3.4 Laborers' Wages in Wheat Equivalents

Location	Period	Day wage (pounds of wheat)
Ancient Babylonia[a]	1800–1600 BC	15*
Assyria[b]	1500–1350 BC	10*
Neo-Babylonia[a]	900–400 BC	9*
Classical Athens[c]	408 BC	30
	328 BC	24
Roman Egypt[d]	c. AD 250	8*
England[e,f]	1780–1800	13
	1780–1800	11*

Sources: [a]Powell, 1990, 98; Farber, 1978, 50–51. [b]Zaccagnini, 1988, 48. [c]Jevons, 1895, 1896. [d]Rathbone, 1991, 156–58, 464–45. [e]Clark, 2005. [f]Clark, 2001b. *Note:* * denotes farm wage.

fore Christ. Wages on this same wheat basis are shown for England over the period 1780–1800. There is considerable variation in these earlier wages, but they are easily as high as in England on the eve of the Industrial Revolution, even those three thousand years before this.

Table 3.5 shows in the same terms wheat wages around the world in the late eighteenth century. Two things stand out. First is the great range of wage levels around 1800, of the order of 4 or 5 to 1. These variations, in the Malthusian framework, should have no relation to the technological sophistication of the society, and should instead be explained by differences in fertility and mortality conditions across societies. The wage quotes from 1780–1800 do seem to confirm that technological sophistication is not the determinant of wages. English wages, for example, are above average in the table, but not any higher than for such technological backwaters of 1800 as Istanbul, Cairo, and Warsaw.[7] English wages in 1800 on average were about the same as those for ancient Babylon and Assyria, despite the great technological gains of the intervening thousands of years. In the next two chapters we will ask whether fertility and

7. The limitations of the grain wage as a measure are, however, revealed in the comparison to Poland. Grain was the great export crop of eastern Europe and was much cheaper there than elsewhere in Europe. A more comprehensive wage measure would show lower eastern European wages.

Table 3.5 Laborer's Wages in Wheat Equivalents, circa 1800

Location	Period	Day wage (pounds of wheat)
Amsterdam[a]	1780–1800	21
Istanbul[b]	1780–1800	18
London[c]	1780–1800	16
Antwerp[a]	1780–1800	16
Cairo[b]	1780–1800	15
England[c]	1780–1800	13
Warsaw[a]	1780–96	13
Leipzig[a]	1780–1800	13
Danzig (Gdansk)[a]	1780–1800	11
England[d]	1780–1800	11*
Vienna[a]	1780–1800	10
Paris[e]	1780–1800	10
Madrid[a]	1780–99	9.0
Naples[a]	1780–1800	7.6
Valencia[a]	1780–85	6.8
China (Yangzi Delta)[f]	1750–1849	6.6*◊
Korea[g]	1780–99	6.0◊
Milan[a]	1780–1800	5.6
South India[f]	1750–90	5.1◊
Japan (Kyoto)[h]	1791–1800	4.5◊

Sources: [a]Allen, 2001, 411, note 1. [b]Pamuk, 2005, 224. [c]Clark, 2005. [d]Clark, 2001b. [e]Van Zanden, 1999, 181–85. [f]Broadberry and Gupta, 2006, 17, 19. [g]Ho and Lewis, 2006, 229. [h]Bassino and Ma, 2005, appendix table 1, assuming 45 pounds of wheat flour per 60 pounds of wheat.
Note: Silver wages in Europe 1780–1800 were deflated by the wheat prices in the Allen-Unger data set. * denotes farm wage. ◊ denotes the wheat equivalent of the rice wage, converting by the relative calorie content of wheat and rice.

mortality conditions are consistent with these wage variations. In particular, why were Asian societies such as Japan so poor compared to England in 1800?

The second noteworthy aspect of table 3.5 is that there is no sign of any improvement in material conditions for settled agrarian societies as we approach 1800. There was no gain between 1800 BC and AD 1800—a period of 3,600 years. Indeed the wages for east and south Asia and southern Europe for 1800 stand out by their low level compared to those for ancient Babylonia,

Table 3.6 Calories and Protein per Capita

Group	Period	Kilocalories	Grams protein
England, farm laborers[a]	1787–96	1,508	27.9
England, all[a]	1787–96	2,322	48.2
Belgium, all[b]	1812	2,248	—
Ache, Paraguay[c]	1980s	3,827	—
Hadza, Tanzania[d]	—	3,300	—
Alyware, Australia[d]	1970s	3,000	—
Onge, Andaman Islands[d]	1970s	2,620	—
Aruni, New Guinea[e]	1966	2,390	—
!Kung, Botswana[c]	1960s	2,355	—
Bayano Cuna, Panama[f]	1960–61	2,325	49.7
Mbuti, Congo[d]	1970s	2,280	—
Anbarra, Australia[d]	1970s	2,050	—
Hiwi, Venezuela[c]	1980s	1,705	64.4
Shipibo, Peru[g]	1971	1,665	65.5
Yanomamo, Brazil[h]	1974	1,452	58.1

Sources: [a]Clark et al., 1995, 223–34. [b]Bekaert, 1991, 635. [c]Hurtado and Hill, 1987, 183; Hurtado and Hill, 1990, 316. [d]Jenike, 2001, 212. [e]Waddell, 1972, 126. [f]Bennett, 1962, 46. [g]Bergman, 1980, 205. [h]Lizot, 1977, 508–12.

ancient Greece, or Roman Egypt. The evidence on preindustrial wages is consistent with the Malthusian interpretation of the previous chapter.

Calories, Proteins, and Living Standards

A proxy for living standards in the distant past is the living standard of surviving forager and simple agrarian societies. However, since these societies do not have labor markets with wages, we need another metric to compare their material conditions with those of preindustrial societies around 1800.

One such index of living standards is food consumption per person, measured as calories or grams of protein per person per day, as shown in table 3.6. As income rises in poor societies, calorie consumption per person characteristically also increases. How did calorie consumption in rich societies like England or Belgium in 1800 compare with that in earlier societies?

The evidence we have for England is from surveys of poorer families, mainly those of farm laborers, made in 1787–96 as part of a debate on the rising costs of the Poor Law.[8] The poor consumed an average of only 1,508 kilo-calories per day. The average income per head in these families, £4.6, how-ever, was only about 30 percent of the average English income per person of £15. We can estimate the average calorie consumption in England using the relationship between calorie and protein consumption and income derived from the survey data. This is also shown in the table.[9] The value for England as a whole is close to the average consumption calculated for Belgium in 1812.

The information we have for the likely consumption of earlier societies comes from studies of modern forager and shifting cultivation societies. These reveal considerable variation in calorie consumption across the groups surveyed, ranging from a modest 1,452 kilocalories per person per day for the Yanomamo of Brazil to a kingly 3,827 kilocalories per person per day for the Ache of Paraguay. Some of this is undoubtedly the result of errors in measuring food consumption. But the median is 2,340, implying that hunter-gatherers and sub-sistence agriculturalists ate as many calories as the median person in England or Belgium circa 1800. Primitive man ate well compared with one of the richest so-cieties in the world in 1800. Indeed British farm laborers by 1863 had just reached the median consumption of these forager and subsistence societies.

Furthermore, the English diet of the 1790s typically had a lower protein content than the diets of these technologically simpler societies. Since the me-dian forager ate as well as the English, foragers must have been eating much better than the poorer Asian societies in terms of both calories and protein.

Variety of diet is another important component of human material wel-fare. By 1800 the European diet had been enriched by the introduction of spices, sugar, tea, and coffee from Asia and potatoes and tomatoes from the New World. But for the typical European that enrichment was quite limited. In England in 1800 the daily diet had been supplemented on average by 0.85 ounce of sugar, 0.07 ounce of tea, 0.004 ounce of coffee, and 0.05 ounce of tobacco.[10] The overwhelming bulk of the diet was the traditional daily mo-notony of bread, leavened by modest amounts of beef, mutton, cheese, and beer. In contrast hunter-gatherer and subsistence cultivation diets were widely varied. The diet of the Yanomamo, for example, included monkeys, wild pigs,

8. Eden, 1797.
9. Clark et al., 1995, 223–24. Since the income elasticities would fall to almost zero for very high incomes, I assume the median consumer has an income of £12 per head.
10. Mokyr, 1988, 75.

tapirs, armadillos, anteaters, alligators, jaguar, deer, rodents, a large variety of birds, many types of insects, caterpillars, various fish, larvae, freshwater crabs, snakes, toads, frogs, various palm fruits, palm hearts, hardwood fruits, brazil nuts, tubers, mushrooms, plantains, manioc, maize, bananas, and honey.[11]

Engel's Law and Living Standards

When the Prussian statistician Ernst Engel (1821–96)—not to be confused with his rabble-rousing contemporary Friedrich Engels (1820–95)—undertook studies of German working-class budgets, he found a simple but powerful empirical relationship, now called Engel's Law. The poorer a family, the larger the share of its income that was spent on food. This relationship has been confirmed by numerous subsequent studies. For the poorest societies food can represent more than 80 percent or more of all expenditures, while for the richest spending on the actual food content of meals is a mere 5–10 percent of income.

Even within the food category of expenditures, there are further variants of the original Engel's Law. When people are very poor, so that hunger is ever present, they consume the cheapest forms of calories available—grains such as wheat, rice, rye, barley, oats, or maize, and beans or potatoes—consumed in the cheapest possible way as porridge, mush, or bread. Their diet is also extremely monotonous, with little spent on flavorings. Thus Irish farm laborers in the years before the famine lived on a diet that was composed almost entirely of potatoes. At the lowest incomes the cheapest calorie sources account for a very large share of income. But as incomes increase a larger and larger share of food consumption is devoted to more expensive calories—those provided by, for example, milk, cheese, butter, eggs, meat, fish, beer, and wine—or to spices and drinks of no calorific value, such as pepper, tea, and coffee.

For the ordinary people of the poorest societies meat seems to have been the preeminent luxury item. It was reported, for example, that the Sharanahua foragers of eastern Peru "are continually preoccupied with the topic of meat, and men, women and children spend an inordinate amount of time talking about meat, planning visits to households that have meat, and lying about the meat they have in their households." In this and a number of other forager societies meat would be traded by hunters for sexual favors

---

11. Chagnon, 1983, 57–58. In addition Yanomamo men were daily consumers of tobacco and a hallucinogenic snuff.

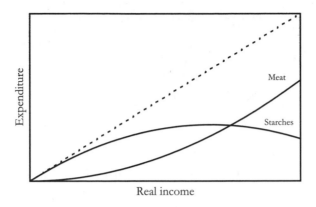

Figure 3.4 Engel curves.

from women. "The successful hunter is usually the winner in the competition for women."[12]

These consumption patterns can be portrayed using Engel curves, as in figure 3.4. An Engel curve shows how consumption of any good changes with income, with the implicit assumption that relative prices are kept constant. Goods such as food, called necessities, account for a much larger share of the consumption of poor people than of rich people. Indeed for many of these goods, such as basic starches, as income increases the absolute amount spent on the good will decline. Other goods are luxuries. Their share in consumption expenditure rises with income, at least for some range of incomes.

Differences in relative prices can induce deviations from the regularity of Engel's Law, but a good general index of living standards is thus either the share of income spent on food or the share of the food budget spent on basic starches as opposed to meats, alcohol, and refined sugars.

Table 3.7 shows the shares of food expenditures devoted to these categories for farm laborers in England in the 1790s. With only 61 percent of their food expenditures devoted to basic starches these workers reveal themselves to be living well, even compared to Indian farm laborers circa 1950. They also seem to have been much better off than Japanese laborers in the eighteenth century. For England we have evidence on the consumption patterns of agricultural workers back to the thirteenth century because of the custom of feeding harvest workers. The diets of those workers from 1250 to 1449 imply an

12. Siskind, 1973, 84, 95–96.

Table 3.7 Share of Different Products in Food Consumption of Farm Workers

Location	Period	Cereals and pulses (%)	Sugar (%)	Animal products, fats (%)	Alcohol (%)
England[a]	1250–99	48.0	0.0	40.2	11.8
	1300–49	39.7	0.0	43.0	17.0
	1350–99	20.8	0.0	55.3	24.0
	1400–49	18.3	0.0	46.4	34.3
England[b]	1787–96	60.6	4.7	28.4	1.3
Japan[c]	ca. 1750	95.4	0.0	4.6	0.0
India[d]	1950	83.3	1.6	5.4	0.8

Sources: [a]Dyer, 1988. [b]Clark et al., 1995. [c]Bassino and Ma, 2005. [d]Government of India, Ministry of Labour, 1954, 114, 118.

even higher standard of living for earlier centuries than for England in the 1790s. After the onset of the Black Death in 1348, which caused real wages to rise, harvest workers were fed a diet in which basic grains accounted for only about 20 percent of the cost. The rest was made up of dairy products, fish, and beer.

Engel's Law, though a simple empirical relationship, has profound importance in explaining world history. In the Malthusian era incomes were bound to remain low, and so food dominated expenditures. Apart from the effect this may have had on conversation, the high share of food expenditures before 1800 ensured that these early societies were largely dispersed and agrarian. If 80 percent of income in the preindustrial world was spent on food, then 80 percent of the population was employed in agriculture, fishing, or hunting.[13] Agricultural production also demanded a population that lived close to the fields, so preindustrial societies were rural, with small urban populations. The average parish in England in 1450 would have had 220 residents.[14] Unlike the situation in modern high-income economies, people would rarely encounter strangers.

13. This conclusion would not necessarily hold once countries began trading substantial quantities of foodstuffs. But such extensive trade was rare before 1800.

14. Assuming a population of 2.2 million from Clark, 2007a, and the same number of parishes as reported in the 1801 census.

If the great majority of income was spent on food then there was also little surplus for producing "culture" in terms of buildings, clothing, objects, entertainments, and spectacles. As long as the Malthusian Trap dominated, the great priority of all societies was food production.

But the link between consumption and production implies that another index of living standards, at least for societies in which trade possibilities were limited, was the proportion of the population engaged in agriculture. Again the comparative prosperity of early England shows up in the high shares of the population, even at early dates, occupied outside the agricultural sector, in areas such as clothing production or building. Thus in the county of Suffolk in England in 1620–35 only 63 percent of male testators were engaged in farming or fishing.[15] In comparison in Tanzania in 2000 83 percent of males were occupied in farming or fishing.[16]

Human Stature and Material Living Standards

Information on real day wages, food consumption, or occupations is available for only a small share of preindustrial societies. Wage labor was absent from very early societies, and later ones with labor markets have often left no records. To measure living standards for most of the preindustrial era we must resort to more indirect measures. One such index is average heights. The most obvious effect of better material living standards is to make people taller. If you travel even today to a poor country, such as India, you will immediately be struck by how short people are. Average heights of young males in rich contemporary societies of predominantly European origin are in the range 177–183 centimeters (70–72 inches). Young African-American males have an average height of 178 centimeters.[17] In contrast males in southern India in 1988–90 had an average height of only 164 centimeters (64.4 inches), a full 19 centimeters shorter than young Dutch males.[18] Poorer groups within modern India have even smaller heights. A group of tea plantation workers in West Bengal in 1994 had an average height of 161 centimeters.[19] Similarly males in

15. Evans, 1987; Allen, 1989.
16. International Labour Organization, Bureau of Statistics, 2006b.
17. United States heights from Ogden et al., 2004, table 14.
18. Brennan et al., 1997, 220. The states surveyed were Andhra, Karnataka, Kerala, Pradesh, and Tamil Nadu. Males were aged 25–39.
19. Roy, 1995, 695.

Figure 3.5   American traveler with Malawian porters, 2001.

rural Malawi in 1987 had an average height of 165 centimeters, 13 centimeters shorter than young African-American males in the United States.[20] Figure 3.5 illustrates the height gap between modern Americans and Malawians.

There is little sign in modern populations of any genetically determined differences in potential stature, except for some rare groups such as the pygmies of central Africa. Diet, however, does seem to influence height. Young men in rich East Asian countries are not so tall as in Europe (only 171 centimeters in Japan), probably because of dietary differences. But within societies the positive correlation between health and height is well documented.[21] Stature is determined by both childhood nutrition and the incidence of childhood illness. Episodes of ill health during growth phases can stop growth, and the body catches up only partially later on. But both nutrition and the incidence of illness depend on material living conditions.

There is evidence on the stature of the living from only a few preindustrial societies, and then typically not for much earlier than 1800. But through

20. Pelletier et al., 1991, 356.
21. Steckel, 1995.

Table 3.8 Estimated Average Height of Adult Males in Preindustrial Societies

Period	Location	Type	Ages	Height (centimeters)
1830s	Sweden[a]	Soldiers	Adult	172
1710–59*	England[b]	Convicts	23–60	171
		Indentured servants	23–60	171
1830s	England[a]	Soldiers	Adult	169
	Northern Italy[a]	Soldiers	25–40	167
	Bavaria[a]	Soldiers	Adult	167
	France[a]	Soldiers	Adult	167
	Netherlands[a]	Soldiers	Adult	167
1770–1815	England[c]	Convicts	23–49	166
1830s	Hungary[a]	Soldiers	Adult	166
	Austria[a]	Soldiers	Adult	164
1819–39	West Africa (Yoruba)[d]	Slaves	25–40	167
	Mozambique[d]	Slaves	25–40	165
	West Africa (Igbo)[d]	Slaves	25–40	163
1800–29*	Southern China[e]	Convicts	23–59	164
1843	Southern India[f]	Indentured servants	24–40	163
1842–44	Northern India (Bihar)[f]	Indentured servants	24–40	161
1883–92	Japan[g]	Soldiers	20	159

Sources: [a]A'Hearn, 2003, table 3. Adjusted to adult heights. [b]Komlos, 1993, 775. [c]Brennan et al., 1997, 220. [d]Eltis, 1982, 459–60. Slaves freed from ships transporting them. [e]Morgan, 2006, table 4a. [f]Nicholas and Steckel, 1991, 946. [g]Yasuba, 1986, 223. Adjusted from age 20 to adult heights. *Note:* * denotes birth years.

measurement of the long bones in skeletal remains we can get evidence on the stature of a much earlier set of preindustrial societies.

Table 3.8 shows a summary of this evidence on the stature of living males for the years around 1800 for a range of countries, given in order of average height. The heights were drawn from a variety of populations: soldiers, convicts, freed slaves, and indentured servants. Indian heights in 1843, for example, are those of indentured servants recruited for labor in Mauritius. But since these Indian workers were being selected for heavy manual labor abroad, there is no reason to expect they were smaller than the general population. These Indian indentured servants were significantly smaller than indentured servants recruited in England for service in North America in the eighteenth century. Similarly the

Chinese heights are for immigrants to Australia who were later imprisoned. But their heights were significantly less than those of eighteenth-century English convicts transported to America or Australia. The African heights are those of slaves freed en route to the Americas by British ships. Again there would be countervailing biases suggesting that they would be representative of the general population. Slaves would be expected to be poorer than average and thus smaller, but those shipped to plantation work in the New World would have been selected for strength and health, given the cost of transporting them.

Clearly at the onset of the Industrial Revolution the heights of European males were intermediate between those of males in the modern United States and Europe and those of modern India and Africa. Malthus himself, from his time as a country parson, knew that living conditions for the laboring classes in England around 1800 were poor enough that they resulted in stunting: "It cannot fail to be remarked by those who live much in the country, that the sons of labourers are very apt to be stunted in their growth, and are a long while arriving at maturity."[22]

Heights in preindustrial Asia seem to have been generally much lower than those in preindustrial Europe. As noted previously, dietary differences may explain some of this variation. But the gain of 12 centimeters in height for Japanese between the preindustrial world and today is greater than the gain of about 7 centimeters in England, suggesting that, even allowing for diet, pre-industrial Japan was poorer than preindustrial England. At 165 centimeters, heights for Africa, despite the presumably inferior technology there, were not far below the European average.

In tropical Africa, nature itself supplied high material living standards through high death rates from disease. For Europeans—and indeed almost as much so for native Africans—tropical Africa was deadly. Half of British troops stationed on the coast of West Africa in the eighteenth century died in their first year in station.[23] When the journalist Henry Morton Stanley made his famous journeys across equatorial Africa in the late nineteenth century, what allowed him to make his discoveries was not any particular skill with guns or languages, but his ability to withstand the many illnesses that killed all of his white companions.

22. Malthus, 1798, 94.
23. Black Americans who colonized Liberia after 1823 also had extraordinarily high death rates, suggesting that Africans had little genetic protection against the disease environment; McDaniel, 1992.

Table 3.9 Heights of Adult Males in Modern Foraging and Subsistence Societies

Period	Group	Location	Ages	Height (centimeters)
1892	Plains Indians[a]	United States	23–49	172
1970s	Anbarra[b]	Australia	Adults	172*
	Rembarranga[c]	Australia	Adults	171*
1910	Alaskan Inuit[d]	United States	Adults	170*
1890	Northern Pacific Indians[e]	United States	Adults	167*
1944	Sandawe[f]	Tanzania	Adults	167*
1891	Shoshona[g]	United States	20–59	166
1970s	Fox Basin Inuit[c]	Canada	Adults	166*
1880s	Solomon Islanders[h]	Solomon Is.	Adults	165*
1906	Canadian Inuit[d]	Canada	Adults	164*
1969	!Kung[i]	Bostwana	21–40	163
1980s	Ache[j]	Paraguay	Adults	163*
1970s	Hadza[c]	Tanzania	Adults	163*
1985	Hiwi[j]	Venezuela	Adults	156*
1980s	Batak[c]	Philippines	Adults	155*
	Agta[c]	Philippines	Adults	155*
	Aka[c]	Central African Republic	Adults	155*

Sources: [a]Steckel and Prince, 2001. [b]Kelly, 1995, 102. [c]Jenike, 2001, 223. [d]Hawkes, 1916, 207. [e]Boaz, 1891, 327. [f]Trevor, 1947, 69. [g]Boaz, 1899, 751. [h]Guppy, 1886, 267. [i]Truswell and Hansen, 1976, 172. [j]Hurtado and Hill, 1987, 180–82.
Notes: * denotes heights adjusted to ages 21–40. The heights of all !Kung males averaged 2 centimeters less than those aged 21–40.

How do these heights at the end of the preindustrial era compare with those in earlier societies? As a guide to likely living conditions before the arrival of settled agriculture we have average heights for modern foraging societies. Franz Boas in particular collected height observations from hundreds of Native American tribes in the late nineteenth century. As table 3.9 shows, the range of variation is similar to that in agrarian societies around 1800. Some hunter-gatherers were significantly taller than the nineteenth-century Chinese, Indians, and Japanese, and many Europeans. The median of the heights for these forager societies is 165 centimeters, very little less than that in Europe in 1800 and significantly above that in Asia circa 1800.

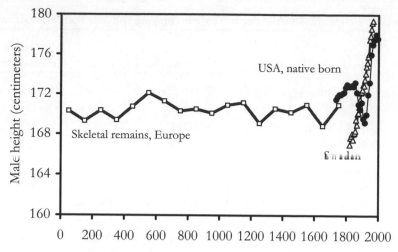

Figure 3.6 Male heights from skeletons in Europe, AD 1–2000. Data from Steckel, 2001, figures 3 and 4, and Koepke and Baten, 2005.

The Tahitians of the 1760s, still in the stone age, seem to have been as tall, or taller, than their English visitors with all their marvelous European technology. The explorers certainly thought them tall, remarkably enough that Joseph Banks, a scientist on the *Endeavour* expedition of 1769, measured the height of a particularly tall Tahitian at 75.5 inches (192 centimeters). In England in 1800 only one adult male in 2,500 would measure 192 centimeters or more.[24] Since he likely saw only a few hundred adult males, given the brevity of his stay and the low population densities of Tahiti, average heights in Tahiti were with strong probability greater than those in eighteenth-century England.

Thus the thousands of years of advance representing the difference between forager technology and that of agrarian societies around 1800 did not lead to any signs of a systematic improvement in material living conditions.

To look at living conditions in the actual historical past, as opposed to equivalent contemporary societies, we can use male heights inferred from skeletal remains. Figure 3.6 summarizes the published evidence available on average heights from skeletal remains in Europe from AD 1 to 1800, normalized to male heights. The century-long averages summarize data from 9,477 sets of remains. There is no trend before 1800. Also shown for comparison are

24. Banks, 1962, 334. The height range in England is calculated assuming the standard deviation of heights was the same as in modern Britain.

Table 3.10 Heights from Skeletal Remains by Period

Period	Location	Observations	Height (centimeters)
Mesolithic[a]	Europe	82	168
Neolithic[a,b]	Europe	190	167
	Denmark	103	173
1600–1800[c]	Holland	143	167
1700–1800[c]	Norway	1,956	165
1700–1850[c]	London	211	170
Pre-Dynastic[d]	Egypt	60	165
Dynastic[d]	Egypt	126	166
2500 BC[e]	Turkey	72	166
1700 BC[f]	Lerna, Greece	42	166
2000–1000 BC[g]	Harappa, India	—	169
300 BC–AD 250[h]	Japan (Yayoi)	151	161
1200–1600[h]	Japan (medieval)	20	159
1603–1867[h]	Japan (Edo)	36	158
1450[i]	Marianas, Taumako	70	174
1650[i]	Easter Island	14	173
1500–1750[i]	New Zealand	124	174
1400–1800[i]	Hawaii	—	173

Sources: [a]Meiklejohn and Zvelebil, 1991, 133. [b]Bennike, 1985, 51–52. [c]Steckel, 2001. [d]Masali, 1972. [e]Mellink and Angel, 1970. [f]Angel, 1971. [g]Houghton, 1996, 43–45. [h]Boix and Rosenbluth, 2004, table 6. [i]Dutta, 1984.

the heights of male conscripts by birth year for Sweden from 1820 on, and the heights of native-born U.S. males from 1710 on. The gains in income after 1800 show up clearly in the heights of the living.

Table 3.10 shows average male stature measured from skeletal collections from a broad range of preindustrial locations before 1800, back as far as the European Mesolithic (8000–5000 BC). The small size of many of these collections, their potentially unrepresentative economic status, and the errors in inferring stature from the lengths of long bones all imply large potential errors in inferring specific population heights from these samples. But the overall pattern is clear. In Europe, India, and Japan heights in the earlier millennia were as great or greater than those of 1800. In particular heights in the European

Mesolithic and Neolithic were slightly greater than even those of England and the Netherlands, the richest societies in the world in 1800.

Heights, and hence by implication living standards, did fluctuate somewhat before 1800. But the variations, as predicted in the Malthusian model, have no connection with technological advances.

Thus Europeans in parts of the medieval period seem to have been taller than those in the classical period, or in the eighteenth and early nineteenth centuries. Polynesians in the period before contact with the outside world were also tall by preindustrial standards, according well with the inference drawn above from the report by Banks. Yet there is no doubt that the technology of the Polynesians was far behind that of the Europeans. Polynesia was still a Neolithic economy without metals. Fishhooks were laboriously fashioned from bone or coral. The preferred weapon of war was a wooden club. Canoes had to be made from tree trunks using fire and stone axes. The canoes were sometimes fitted with sails, but these were not rigged in such a way that they could sail into the wind. Thus long ocean voyages were hazardous. There was little or no earthenware. There was no system of writing. Cloth was made from tree bark, but little clothing was required in the equatorial climate.

The natural environment of Polynesia was benign. The scourge of the tropics, malaria, did not exist on the islands until it was imported, along with the mosquito, by white mariners. Thus the British and French crews spent months ashore in Polynesia with few if any deaths from local diseases. But where nature failed them, the Polynesians seem to have supplied their own mortality. The reason for their high living standards, as we shall see in chapter 5, seems to have been high death rates from infanticide, internal warfare, and human sacrifice. Polynesia was paradise for the living—but a paradise with a cost.

The Industrious Revolution

Consideration of early forager societies through skeletons, and of contemporary remnant forager societies, suggests that material living conditions were if anything better for these societies than for the settled agrarian societies on the eve of the Industrial Revolution.

But another dimension of living conditions was how long people had to labor to earn their daily bread, and the types of labor they performed. Here the advent of settled agrarian societies probably reduced human welfare. A world

Table 3.11 Work Hours per Day of
English Builders

Period	Towns	Hours
1720–39	1	10.4
1740–59	1	8.3
1760–79	1	11.0
1780–99	2	11.1
1800–19	5	10.4
1820–39	9	10.1
1840–59	10	10.0
1860–69	8	10.0

Source: Clark, 2005.

of leisure for the original foragers had given way to a world of continuous labor by the eve of the Industrial Revolution. Not only was this labor continuous, it was also much more monotonous than the tasks of the foragers. But this change in the quantity and quality of work long preceded the arrival of modern technology.

In England on the eve of the Industrial Revolution the typical male worked 10 or more hours per day for 300 or more days per year, for a total annual labor input in excess of 3,000 hours. For building workers we know the length of the typical work day from the fact that employers charged for their services both by the hour and by the day. The ratio of daily to hourly wages suggests the typical hours per day. Table 3.11 shows this evidence. Average daily hours of paid labor for these workers over every day of the year would be over 8 per day. Agricultural workers seem to have had similarly long hours per year. Comparing the wages paid to workers hired by the day with those paid to workers hired for the year suggests that annual workers were putting in a full 300-day year.[25] Workers were kept in employment throughout the winter with such tasks as hand threshing of grains, ditching, hedging, and mixing and spreading manure.

Hans-Joachim Voth, in an interesting study of time use in Industrial Revolution England, used summaries of witness statements in criminal trials (which

25. Clark and van der Werf, 1998.

Table 3.12   Male Labor Hours per Day

Group or location	Group or activity	Hours
Tatuyo[a]	Shifting cultivation, hunting	7.6
Mikea[b]	Shifting cultivation, foraging	7.4
Ache[c]	Hunting	6.9
Abelam[d]	Subsistence agriculture, hunting	6.5
!Kung[e]	Foraging	6.4
Machiguenga[f]	Shifting cultivation, foraging, hunting	6.0
Xavante[g]	Shifting cultivation, hunting	5.9
Aruni[h]	Subsistence agriculture	5.2
Mekranoti[g]	Shifting cultivation, foraging, hunting	3.9
Shipibo[i]	Subsistence agriculture, fishing	3.4
Bemba[j]	Shifting cultivation, hunting	3.4
Hiwi[k]	Hunting	3.0
Yanomamo[a]	Shifting cultivation, foraging, hunting	2.8
Median		5.9
Britain, 1800[l,m]	Farm laborers, paid labor	8.2
	Building workers, paid labor	8.2
London, 1800[n]	All workers, paid labor	9.1
United Kingdom, 2000[o]	All workers aged 16–64	8.8

Sources: [a]Lizot, 1977, 514 (food only). [b]Tucker, 2001, 183. [c]Kaplan and Hill, 1992. [d]Scaglion, 1986, 541. [e]Gross, 1984, 526. [f]Johnson, 1975. [g]Werner et al., 1979, 311 (food only). [h]Waddell, 1972, 101. [i]Bergman, 1980, 209. [j]Minge-Klevana, 1980. [k]Hurtado and Hill, 1987, 178–79. [l]Clark and van der Werf, 1998. [m]Clark, 2005, 1322. [n]Voth, 2001. [o]United Kingdom, Office of National Statistics, 2003.

often contain statements of what the witness did for a living) to estimate annual work hours in 1760, 1800, and 1830. His results for London, for which the information is most complete, are shown in table 3.12. They suggest that men in London in 1800 worked 9.1 hours per day.[26] Thus a labor input of 8–9 hours per day of the year, for paid labor alone, seems to have been the norm in England by 1800.

To put these work efforts into context, time studies that include study, housework, child care, personal care, shopping, and commuting suggest that

26. Voth, 2001, 1074.

modern adult males (aged 16–64) in the United Kingdom engage in 3,200 hours of labor per year (8.8 hours per day). Thus work efforts in England by 1800 had reached modern levels.

The term *Industrious Revolution* was coined by Jan de Vries, who argued that the high labor hours of Industrial Revolution England were a new phenomenon, caused by the wider variety of available consumption goods.[27] Voth, in support, finds evidence that work hours in London were much lower in 1760. However, the summary of building workers' hours in table 3.11 shows no evidence of any rise in the length of the work day in the eighteenth century. Evidence from the English farm sector suggests a much slower and less dramatic increase in hours. Hours in agriculture were already high by 1770.[28] Despite popular images of the Industrial Revolution sentencing formerly happy peasants to a life of unrelenting labor in gloomy factories, this transition seems to have occurred significantly before the Industrial Revolution rather than as a result of it.

Anthropologists have long debated how much work people had to do to achieve subsistence in preindustrial societies.[29] The anthropological tradition prior to the 1960s assumed that hunter-gatherers lead hard lives of constant struggle to eke out a living. The Neolithic agricultural revolution, by increasing labor productivity in food production, reduced the time needed to attain subsistence, thus allowing for leisure, craft production, religious ceremonies, and other cultural expressions.

However, systematic time allocation studies of hunter-gatherer and subsistence cultivation groups undertaken from the 1960s onward revealed labor inputs in these societies to be surprisingly small. For example, the Hiwi, a foraging group from Venezuela, consumed a modest 1,705 kilocalories per day and often complained of hunger. Yet men would generally forage for less than 2 hours per day, even with high returns from each hour of work.[30]

Indeed work time in these societies is considerably less than that in settled agrarian societies. Table 3.12 also shows estimates of the total work input of males per day in modern societies in which foraging and hunting were still significant activities. For these societies median hours of work per day for males,

27. De Vries, 1994.
28. Clark and van der Werf, 1998.
29. See, for example, Gross, 1984.
30. Hurtado and Hill, 1987, 1990.

including food preparation and child care, were just 5.9, or 2,150 hours per year. Thus males in these subsistence societies consume 1,000 hours more leisure per year than in affluent modern Europe.

Such low work inputs need not be maladaptive for foragers. Ecologists have calculated for how many hours a day various bird and mammal species engage in "work"—foraging, moving, defending territory, or even socializing— as opposed to resting. If we take the just species closest to man—apes and monkeys—work hours per day averaged only 4.4.[31]

The typical low work effort of subsistence societies helps explain why Polynesia appeared such an idyll to European sailors, and why Captain Blyth had trouble getting his sailors on board again after their stay in Tahiti. The main food supplies in Polynesia were from breadfruit trees and coconut palms, supplemented by pig meat and fish. But all the labor that was required for the breadfruit trees and the palms was to plant the tree, tend it until it grew to sufficient height, and then harvest the fruits when ripe. Like the subsistence societies of table 3.12 the Polynesians apparently labored little.

The Industrious Revolution and Welfare

Suppose a Malthusian economy in which workers work 2,100 hours per year experiences an "industrious revolution" which increases labor inputs to the 3,000 hours per year typical of English workers during the Industrial Revolution. What is the long-run effect of this development on living standards? Figure 2.5, showing the effects of a technological advance in the Malthusian era, also covers this situation. Higher labor inputs would generate higher annual material output, and thus a short-run situation in which births exceeded deaths, hence population growth. Eventually with enough population growth the economy would again attain equilibrium, with the same annual real income as before, but with workers now laboring 3,000 hours per year for this annual wage as opposed to the previous 2,100 hours.

Indeed a community that had cultural norms which prevented people from working more than 2,100 hours per year would be better off than one in which people were allowed to work 3,000 hours. The prohibitions of work on Sundays and holy days by the Catholic church, or of work on the sabbath

31. Winterhalter, 1993, 334. Chimpanzees, the hardest working of the ape and monkey families, did work as much as modern man at 9 hours per day.

in Judaism, improved welfare in the preindustrial era. More enforced holidays would have made living conditions even better.

In comparing forager living standards with those on the eve of the Industrial Revolution we need to correct for this difference in hours. Another way to measure the real living standards of people in 1800 relative to those of the predocumentary past is to consider the number of kilocalories such societies generated per hour of labor when producing their major food staples. This is a measure of their consumption possibilities as opposed to their realized consumption, which also depends on hours of work.

The surprise here is that while there is wild variation across forager and shifting cultivation societies, many of them had food production systems which yielded much larger numbers of calories per hour of labor than English agriculture in 1800, at a time when labor productivity in English agriculture was probably the highest in Europe. In 1800 the total value of output per man-hour in English agriculture was 6.6 pence, which would buy 3,600 kilocalories of flour but only 1,800 kilocalories of fats and 1,300 kilocalories of meat. Assuming English farm output was then half grains, one-quarter fats, and one-quarter meat, this implies an output of 2,600 calories per worker-hour on average.[32] Since the average person ate 2,300 kilocalories per day (table 3.6), each farm worker fed eleven people, so labor productivity was very high in England.

Table 3.13 shows in comparison the energy yields of foraging and shifting cultivation societies per worker-hour. The range in labor productivities is huge, but the minimum average labor productivity, that for the Ache in Paraguay, is 1,985 kilocalories per hour, not much below England in 1800. The median yield per labor hour, 6,042 kilocalories, is more than double English labor productivity.

Some of the reported labor productivities are astonishing, such as that for shifting cultivation of maize by the Mikea of Madagascar. These societies, many of them utilizing the most primitive of cultivation techniques, thus typically had greater potential material outputs, at least in food production, than England on the eve of the Industrial Revolution. For example, the Peruvian Shipibo's staple crop, providing 80 percent of their calorie intake, was bananas cultivated in shifting patches of forest land. The technique of cultivation was extremely simple. The land was burned and the larger trees felled. Banana

32. Clark, 2002b, tables 2 and 12.

Table 3.13 Calories Produced per Worker-Hour, Forager and Shifting Cultivation Societies versus England, 1800

Group	Location	Staple foods	Kilocalories per hour
Mikea[a]	Madagascar	Maize	110,000
		Tuber foraging	1,770
Mekranoti[b]	Brazil	Manioc, sweet potato, banana, maize	17,600
Shipibo[c]	Peru	Banana, maize, beans, manioc	7,680
Xavante[b]	Brazil	Rice/manioc	7,100
Machiguenga[d]	Peru	Manioc	4,984
Kantu[e]	Indonesia	Dry rice	4,500
Hiwi[f]	Venezuela	Game (men)	3,735
		Roots (women)	1,125
Ache[g]	Paraguay	Palm fiber, shoots (women)	2,630
		Game (men)	1,340
England, 1800		Wheat, milk, meats	2,600

Sources: [a]Tucker, 2001, 183. [b]Werner et al., 1979, 307. [c]Bergman, 1980, 133. [d]Johnson, 1975. [e]Dove, 1984, 99. [f]Hurtado and Hill, 1987, 178. [g]Kaplan and Hill, 1992.

seedlings were planted among the fallen trees and stumps. The land was periodically weeded to prevent weeds choking out the banana trees. Yet in these tropical conditions the yield was more than 60 pounds of bananas (15,000 kilocalories) per labor hour. This is just another illustration of the Law of Diminishing Returns. With a vast land area at their disposal even foragers with a very primitive agricultural technology can have very high outputs per worker.

Had work hours been as high as those in England in 1800, these foraging and shifting cultivation societies would have had much greater outputs per person than England. Whatever material prosperity the English had in 1800 was wrested from the soil by hard work and long hours. The evidence seems to be that Marshall Sahlins was substantially correct when he controversially claimed that foraging and shifting cultivation societies had a form of "primitive affluence," which was measured in the abundance of leisure as opposed to goods.[33]

33. Sahlins, 1972.

Thus if anthropologists are correct about the low labor inputs of hunter-gatherer societies then, while we would expect material living standards to be the same between 10,000 BC and AD 1800, real living conditions probably declined with the arrival of settled agriculture because of the longer work hours of these societies. The Neolithic Revolution did not bring more leisure, it brought more work for no greater material reward.

That still leaves a puzzling question. Why as the Industrial Revolution approached had labor inputs in some societies increased so much? This issue is addressed in chapter 9.

Asia versus Europe

European travelers of the seventeenth and eighteenth centuries routinely reported that Chinese and Indian living conditions were below those of northwestern Europe. This is assumed in the writings of both Smith and Malthus. While a recent collection of historians, called oddly enough the California School, has argued that living conditions in Asia were just as good as those in northwestern Europe, the evidence presented above contradicts this.[34] In terms of wages, stature, diet, and occupations Japan, China, and India seem much poorer in 1800 and earlier than Europe. This conclusion is backed by evidence on the incidence of famines in England versus Japan. The last significant nationwide famine to strike England was in 1315–17, when the grain harvest across northern Europe failed for two years in a row. After that, though there were local dearths, famine deaths on a national scale were negligible, even though the central government did little to promote grain storage for scarce years. In contrast Japan in the Edo period (1603–1868) witnessed at least seven nationwide famines. Those of 1783–87 and 1833–37 are both estimated to have killed more than 4 percent of the population.[35]

There are suggestions in the genetic data that this disparity in living standards between Europe and East Asia may go back over thousands of years. Hunter-gatherers consume meat but not milk. Thus the arrival of settled agriculture with animal domestication created the possibility of large-scale consumption of milk from animals for the first time. However, people at very low income levels do not typically consume many dairy products. Milk, butter,

34. See, for example, Pomeranz, 2000.
35. Jannetta, 1992, 428–29.

and cheese are all expensive ways of getting calories, favored only by the rich. Grains and starches are much cheaper calorie sources. Geographic factors that affect the relative cost of production of animals and arable crops also play a role, but in general only richer preindustrial agrarian economies consumed milk regularly.

Consequently populations that never developed settled agriculture, such as Australian Aboriginals, almost all lack a genetic mutation that permits adults to digest lactose, a sugar found in milk. In contrast most people from northwestern Europe have this mutation. However, Chinese adults, despite their very long history of settled agriculture and the variety of climate zones within China, generally lack the ability to absorb lactose, suggesting that milk was never a large part of the Chinese diet, and that by implication Chinese living standards were generally low in the preindustrial era.[36]

The Success of the Malthusian Model

There is ample evidence in the historical and skeletal record to support the key contention of the Malthusian model. Living conditions before 1800 were independent of the level of technology of a society. But living standards did vary substantially across societies before 1800. Medieval western Europe, for example, in the period between the onset of the Black Death in 1347 and renewed population growth in 1550, was extraordinarily rich, rich even by the standards of the poorest economies of the world today. Polynesia before European contact also seems to have been prosperous. In contrast China, India, and Japan in the eighteenth and nineteenth centuries appear to have been very poor. Chapters 4 and 5 consider the causes of these variations, which lay in the determinants of fertility and mortality.

36. Stinson, 1992.

4 Fertility

In almost all the more improved countries of modern Europe, the principal check which keeps the population down to the level of the actual means of subsistence is the prudential restraint on marriage. —Thomas Malthus (1830)[1]

Given that societies before 1800 were Malthusian, the only ways human agency could improve living standards were by reducing fertility or increasing mortality. Reducing fertility had two effects in a Malthusian economy. First it would increase living standards. Second it would increase life expectancy. If the birth rate was at the biological maximum of 60 per thousand, life expectancy at birth would be a mere 17 years. If the birth rate could be reduced to 25 per thousand, life expectancy would rise to 40.

The demography of northwestern Europe before 1800 has been intensively researched. Parish records of baptisms, burials, and marriages in both England and France allow historical demographers to establish fertility and mortality rates back to 1540. From the earliest records birth rates in northwestern Europe were well below the biological possibilities. In England in the 1650s, for example, when fertility was at its preindustrial minimum, the birth rate was 27 per thousand, less than half the biological maximum. The average English woman then gave birth to only 3.6 children.[2]

It used to be thought that fertility limitation of this magnitude was unique to northwestern Europe and helped explain the prosperity of these European areas compared to other preindustrial economies in the seventeenth and eighteenth centuries. The northwestern European marriage pattern was unique for societies before 1800: women married late and large numbers of

---

1. Malthus, 1830, 254.
2. Wrigley et al., 1997, 614.

them never married.[3] Indeed Malthus himself in the second and subsequent editions of his *Essay on the Principle of Population* argued that the prosperity of northwestern Europe was based on its exercise of the *preventive check* through marriage choices. It was also thought that the fertility limitation of northwestern Europe reflected a more individualistic, rational society in which men and women realized the costs of high fertility and took steps to avoid it. Europe's eventual experiencing of the Industrial Revolution was thus foreshadowed hundreds of years earlier by its adoption of a modern marital pattern and family structure, a structure emphasizing individual choice and restraint.[4]

More recent research, however, suggests most societies before 1800 limited fertility as strictly as did northwestern Europe, though by very different mechanisms. It also suggests that the reasons for fertility limitation in northwestern Europe had little to do with rational individual calculation and much more to do with social customs.

European Fertility

The marriage pattern that kept fertility in northwestern Europe well below the biological possibilities is a curious one. There is no sign in these countries before 1800 that contraceptive practices were consciously employed.[5] Fertility levels within marriage were always high. Table 4.1, for example, shows marital fertility for a variety of countries in northwestern Europe before 1790 compared to the Hutterite standard.[6]

Birth rates within marriage were lower than for the Hutterites, but by different amounts across countries. English fertility was the lowest, Belgian and French the highest. A woman married from ages 20 to 44 had an average of 7.6 children in England in the years before 1790, but 9.1 in Belgium or France. In comparison a Hutterite woman would have an average of 10.6 children in these twenty-five years. But these European differences from Hutterite levels

3. Hajnal, 1965.
4. Macfarlane, 1978, 1987.
5. France just before the French Revolution is a possible exception, though any fertility limitation there in the late eighteenth century was limited.
6. The Hutterites are communal Anabaptists of German origin, now mainly located in Canada, with good health but early marriage and no fertility limitation within marriage. They thus provide a reference on the possibilities of unrestricted fertility.

Table 4.1 Annual Birth Rate, Married Women, Europe before 1790

Country or group	Birth rate at age:					All births (20–44)
	20–24	*25–29*	*30–34*	*35–39*	*40–44*	
Hutterites	0.55	0.50	0.45	0.41	0.22	10.6
Belgium	0.48	0.45	0.38	0.32	0.20	9.1
France	0.48	0.45	0.40	0.32	0.16	9.1
Germany	0.45	0.43	0.37	0.30	0.16	8.6
Switzerland	0.45	0.38	0.34	0.22	0.16	7.8
Scandinavia	0.43	0.39	0.32	0.26	0.14	7.7
England	0.43	0.39	0.32	0.24	0.15	7.6

Source: Flinn, 1981, 86.

stemmed mostly from health and nutrition differences and from adherence to different social practices, rather than individual targeting of fertility.

Part of the evidence against conscious contraceptive practices is the absence of fertility patterns that would be expected if there had been conscious fertility control. With conscious control birth rates should be relatively lower compared to the Hutterite standard for older women. For by then many would have achieved their target family size and would have stopped having children. As table 4.1 shows, however, the relative birth rate in early Europe compared to Hutterite rates is instead about the same at all ages.

Similarly if there were a target number of children, then we might observe that women with many children by a given age would show lower subsequent fertility.[7] Or, with targets, the death of a child would increase the chances of a birth in the following years, since the family would now be falling farther below its target. Yet such targeting patterns do not occur within European marriages before 1800.

The other source of evidence about fertility control comes from diaries, letters, and literature. The diaries of Samuel Pepys, for example, give an extraordinary insight into the habits and mores of the upper classes in London in 1660–69. Pepys was having extramarital sexual relationships, even

7. Both these tests unfortunately run into one problem: people have different targets for family size. The ones who want lots of children may then marry earlier and so still have high fertility levels at later ages.

abusing his stewardship of the Navy Office to obtain sexual favors from the spouses of naval workers and contractors. Yet though he feared getting his companions pregnant, he made no use of contraception. Instead he preferred relationships with married women whose pregnancy could be attributed to their husbands. Or, to his intense frustration, he refrained from penetration in his amorous encounters.[8]

Yet despite the apparent absence of contraceptive practices, the birth rate in most preindustrial western European populations was low, at only thirty to forty births per thousand, because of the other features of the *European marriage pattern*. These were as follows:

1. A late average age of first marriage for women: typically 24–26.
2. A decision by many women to never marry: typically 10–25 percent.
3. Low illegitimacy rates: typically 3–4 percent of births.

The low illegitimacy rates imply large-scale abstinence from sex outside marriage, since the majority of women of reproductive age were unmarried.

These features avoided more than half of all possible births simply from marriage patterns, as is illustrated in figure 4.1. The horizontal axis is the number of women, the vertical their ages. The area of the rectangle gives the total number of reproductive years per hundred women, assuming women are fertile from 16 until 45.

Delayed marriage avoided nearly a third of possible births. Eschewing marrying avoided 10–25 percent of the remaining births. Thus fertility was reduced by a third to a half by the marriage pattern. In addition, since the years 16–25 are those of higher fertility for women, the proportion of births avoided is even higher than this exercise would suggest.

Table 4.2 shows the mean age at first marriage of women in various European countries before 1790. Also shown is the number of children a women married at the average age of first marriage would have if she lived to age 45. Finally the total fertility rate, the number of children born to the average woman who lived to age 50, is roughly calculated, taking into account the il-

---

8. See, for example, his affair with one Mrs. Bagwell, the wife of a navy carpenter; Pepys, 2000, July 9, 1663, May 31, 1664, October 20, 1664, January 23, 1665, and May 16, 1666. Once, when he feared he had impregnated the wife of a naval officer who was then at sea, Pepys frantically used his official position to recall the husband in time for the pregnancy to be attributable to him.

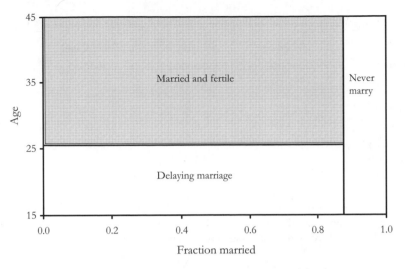

Figure 4.1 The European marriage pattern and fertility.

legitimacy rate and the likely fraction of women never marrying. Before 1790 women in northwestern Europe who survived to age 50 gave birth to between 4.5 and 6.2 children, with a median of 4.9. The median corresponds to a crude birth rate of about 32 per thousand. By implication birth rates in Belgium and France were about 40 per thousand.

East Asian Fertility

When Malthus wrote his various editions of the *Essay on the Principle of Population* he assumed that China represented the full misery of the Malthusian Trap, and that oriental life was miserable as a result of high fertility. Research over the past thirty years, however, suggests that, like preindustrial western Europe and like many forager societies, both China and Japan avoided many potential births. Indeed Asian fertility rates, though arrived at through completely different mechanisms, were likely as low as those in northwestern Europe.

In Asia, as Malthus knew, the norm for women was early and nearly universal marriage. Recent studies of family lineages and local population registers suggest that first marriage for Chinese women around 1800 took place on average at age 19. A full 99 percent of women in the general population

Table 4.2 Age of Marriage of Women and Marital Fertility in Europe before 1790

Country or group	Mean age at first marriage	Births per married women	Percentage never married	Total fertility rate
Belgium[a]	24.9	6.8	—	6.2*
France[a,b]	25.3	6.5	10	5.8
Germany[a]	26.6	5.6	—	5.1*
England[a]	25.2	5.4	12	4.9
Netherlands[c]	26.5	5.4*	—	4.9*
Scandinavia[a]	26.1	5.1	14	4.5

Sources: [a]Flinn, 1981, 84. [b]Weir, 1984, 33–34. [c]De Vries, 1985, 665.
Note: * denotes values inferred assuming missing values at European average.

married.[9] Men also married young, first marriage occurring on average at 21. But the share of men marrying was much lower, perhaps as low as 84 percent. Chinese males were no more likely to marry than their northwestern European counterparts. This was because female infanticide created a surplus of males, and men were more likely than women to remarry after the death of a spouse.[10] There is similar evidence that in nineteenth-century Japan marriage was earlier than in preindustrial northwestern Europe and that it was nearly universal for women.

But in both Japan and China fertility rates within marriage were lower than in northwestern Europe. Table 4.3 shows the estimated age-specific birth rates for married women averaged across various Chinese groups, and in Japan, compared to those in northwestern Europe. At all ages within marriage Chinese and Japanese women had fewer births per year. As a result a Chinese or Japanese woman married from ages 20 to 45 would give birth to only about 5 children, as opposed to 8 in northwestern Europe. Across both upper and lower classes the mean age of last birth was about 34 in China, compared to nearly 40 in Europe.[11]

It is not known why marital fertility in East Asia was so low. As in preindustrial northwestern Europe there is no sign of an early curtailment of fer-

9. Lee and Feng, 1999, 67–68.
10. Ibid., 70–73, 89.
11. Because of female infanticide some of these birth rates are estimated from male births alone, appropriately inflated; Lee and Feng, 1999, 87.

Table 4.3 Age-Specific Marital Fertility Rates outside Europe

Country or group	Fertility rate at age: 20–24	25–29	30–34	35–39	40–44	All (20–44)
Hutterite[a]	0.55	0.50	0.45	0.41	0.22	10.6
Northwestern Europe[a]	0.45	0.42	0.35	0.28	0.16	8.3
China[b]	0.24	0.25	0.22	0.18	0.10	5.0
Japan[b]	0.29	0.25	0.22	0.15	0.12	5.2
Roman Egypt[c]	0.38	0.35	—	—	—	7.4

Sources: [a]Table 4.1. [b]Lee and Feng, 1999, 87. [c]Bagnall and Frier, 1994, 143–46.

tility that would clearly indicate family planning. Fertility rates within China and Japan were uniformly about half those of the Hutterites at all ages. Possibly the very low incomes of preindustrial Asia played a role, for reasons given below. Alternatively low fertility might result from adherence to social customs that caused low fertility, rather than conscious individual fertility control.[12]

These patterns imply that, despite early and nearly universal marriage, the average woman in China or Japan around 1800 gave birth to fewer than 5 children, less than half the biological possibility, resulting in a birth rate similar to that for eighteenth-century Europe.

An additional factor driving down birth rates (and also of course driving up death rates) was the Chinese practice of female infanticide. For example, based on the imbalance between recorded male and female births an estimated 20–25 percent of girls died from infanticide in Liaoning. Evidence that the cause was conscious female infanticide comes from the association between the gender imbalance of births and other factors. When grain prices were high, more girls are missing. First children were more likely to be female than later children. The chance of a female birth being recorded for later children also declined with the numbers of female births already recorded for the family. All this suggests female infanticide that was consciously and deliberately practiced.[13]

12. Lee and Feng, 1999, 90–91, cite as contributors to low Chinese fertility rates both extended breast feeding and cultural beliefs that sexual activity was damaging to health.
13. Lee and Campbell, 1997, 64–75.

Female infanticide contributed to limiting the overall birth rate in later generations by changing the adult sex ratio. Female infanticide meant that, while nearly all women married, almost 20 percent of men never found brides. Thus the overall birth rate per person, which determines life expectancy, was reduced. The overall birth rate for the eighteenth century is unclear from the data given in this study, but by the 1860s, when the population was stationary, it was around 35 per thousand, about the same as in preindustrial Europe, and less than in many poor countries today. Earlier and more frequent marriage than in northwestern Europe was counteracted by lower marital fertility and by female infanticide, resulting in equivalent overall fertility rates.

Japan had a similar "Asian" pattern of fertility control. Measured birth rates were as low as in northwestern Europe. One source of demographic information for Japan is Buddhist temple death records. These records, documenting the memorial services for persons affiliated with the temple, suggest that circa 1800 villages in the Hida region of Central Japan had a birth rate of only 36 per thousand, little higher than in preindustrial England.[14] These low rates were the consequence of marriage and fertility patterns similar to those in Liaoning.

Roman Egyptian Fertility

The one even earlier society for which we have demographic data is Roman Egypt in the first three centuries AD. As in preindustrial China and Japan female marriage was early and universal. The estimated mean age at first marriage for Egyptian women was even lower, at 17.5.[15] Marital fertility rates, however, were lower than in northwestern Europe, but higher than in China and Japan: about two-thirds the Hutterite standard.

This early and universal marriage, and relatively high fertility rates within marriage, would seem to imply high overall fertility rates. After all, at these rates Egyptian women married from 17.5 until 50 would give birth to 8 or more children. But in fact birth rates were 40–44 per thousand, implying a life expectancy at birth of 23–25 years. In comparison French birth rates in 1750

14. Jannetta and Preston, 1991, 426.
15. Bagnall and Frier, 1994, 114.

were about 40 per thousand. So Roman Egypt, despite early marriage, had fertility levels only slightly higher than those in eighteenth-century France.[16]

The intervening factor that kept Egyptian birth rates lower than we would expect was again social custom. In northwestern Europe younger widows commonly remarried, but not in Roman Egypt. Furthermore, divorce was possible in Egypt. But while divorced husbands commonly remarried younger women, divorced women typically did not remarry. Thus while in Egypt almost all the women got married, the proportion still married fell steadily from age 20. Consequently women surviving to age 50 typically gave birth to only 6 children rather than 8.[17] Thus, for all the settled agrarian societies for which we have good demographic data for the years before 1800, fertility rates were well below the biological possibilities.

Forager Society Fertility

Forager societies also typically restrained their fertility, though in a pattern more reminiscent of Asia than of northwestern Europe. Table 4.4 shows some measures of fertility for modern forager groups: the average number of births per woman per year, the average age of women at first birth, the average age at last birth, and the total fertility rate (the number of births per woman who lived to the end of her reproductive life). For the groups in table 4.4, the median total fertility rate was 4.5. The numbers of births per year in these hunter-gatherer societies are thus again far below the biological possibilities. These birth rates are as low as, or even lower than, those of preindustrial northwestern Europe. In England before 1790, for example, the average woman similarly gave birth to 4.9 children across her entire reproductive life. Thus fertility rates in England on the eve of the Industrial Revolution were likely no lower than those for the earliest forager groups. This is one reason why living standards did not show any upward tendency before the Industrial Revolution. In Malthusian societies some kind of fertility control was the norm rather than the exception. Only the sources of these controls varied widely.

16. Weir, 1984, 32–33.
17. Average births per adult woman would be lower than this number because not all women would live to age 50.

Table 4.4   Fertility in Modern Forager Societies

Group	Births woman per year	Mean age at first birth	Mean age at last birth	Total fertility rate
Ache[a]	0.32	20	42	8.0
Yanomamo[a]	0.34	18	38	6.9
James Bay Cree[b]	0.37	22	39	6.3*
Cuiva (Tiiwi)	—	—	—	5.1
Arnhem Land (monogamous)[b]	0.30	19	34	4.5*
Kutchin, pre-1900[b]	0.30	23	35	4.4
!Kung[b]	0.31	20	36	4.4
Batak[b]	0.44	18	26	3.8
Arnhem Land (polygamous)[b]	0.18	19	34	2.8*
Median	0.32	20	36	4.5

Sources: [a]Hill and Hurtado, 1996, 262. [b]Kelly, 1995, 246. [c]Hurtado and Hill, 1987, 180.
Note: * denotes values estimated from columns 2–4.

Explaining Preindustrial Fertility

Fertility was limited in almost all preindustrial societies. But, with rare exceptions such as France on the eve of the French Revolution, there is no evidence that this was a conscious individual decision. Nor is there any indication that control was exercised at the community level. People exhibited individual behaviors that limited fertility, but with scant evidence of an explicit objective. This stark conclusion will be controversial among demographic historians, but it can be amply supported by consideration of the details of people's behavior.[18]

Fertility control was absent within marriage in preindustrial northwestern Europe. But were the delay and avoidance of marriage aimed, at the individual or the community level, at reducing fertility? In later editions of the *Principles* Malthus seems to assume that postponing or eschewing marriage was

18. Thus Macfarlane, 1987, argues that marriage decisions in preindustrial England were individualistic, prudential, and calculating.

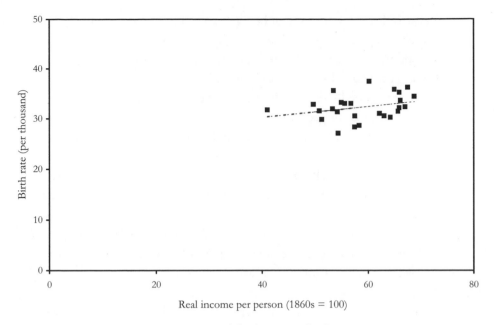

Figure 4.2 Income and fertility in England, 1540–1799.

the only way to limit fertility. (He himself did not get married till age 38, and then to a woman of 27, who gave birth to only 3 children.)[19]

The case for marriage behavior as a planned limitation of fertility is strengthened by the fact that the European marriage pattern prevailed to different degrees in different epochs. In England, for example, it was most marked in the seventeenth century; fertility limitations were so severe that population sometimes declined. In the eighteenth century the average age of first marriage by women declined, so that by 1800–50 it was 23.4 compared to nearly 26 in the seventeenth century. The percentage of women never marrying also declined, to 7 percent. Did fertility increase at the time of the Industrial Revolution because of the enhanced job opportunities?

Yet the increase in birth rates in the eighteenth century occurred in a context in which real wages and real incomes, from the 1730s to the 1790s, were stagnant or declining. Figure 4.2 shows the birth rate plotted against real income per person in England by decade from the 1540s to the 1790s. In

19. Ironically only two of Malthus's children survived to marry, and neither of them had children. So Malthus himself has no descendants.

preindustrial England there was at best a modest link over time between birth rates and aggregate living standards. Shifts in birth rates owing to factors other than income levels are more important than income-induced shifts in explaining the decade-by-decade variations.

In addition the increase in fertility in the eighteenth century occurred in all settings across England, not just places with enhanced industrial employment opportunities: rural parishes, industrial parishes, urban parishes. Furthermore, if delayed marriage was a conscious attempt by individuals to reduce the numbers of children they had, then it has inexplicable features. The first is that not marrying seems to have involved, at least for the woman, a lifetime of sexual abstinence, since illegitimacy rates were so low. Given that large numbers of women were prepared to eschew sexual pleasures for life, or delay them for a decade or more, it is mysterious that once they married they abandoned themselves wantonly to sexual passions.[20]

Once a woman married no control was exercised, no matter how many children had already been born and were still alive. The randomness of births and deaths in the preindustrial world meant that the numbers of surviving children varied enormously across families. A sample of 2,300 English married men's wills from the early seventeenth century shows, for example, that, while 15 percent died with no surviving children, 4 percent died with 8 or more surviving children. If delaying marriage was about consciously controlling fertility then why did those with the abundance of children show no signs of abstinence within the later years of their marriages, compared to their less fecund compatriots?

Another difficulty emerges if we consider the "marriage market." In looking for a spouse people were looking not just for affection but also for a partner who would be an economic asset. Both wives and husbands in the poorer classes had to work, for example, and a good worker would add substantially to the comfort of the partner. Surviving descriptions of courtship behavior in the seventeenth and eighteenth centuries have a fairly unromantic caste; the focus of the parties was as much or more on the character and energy of the prospective spouse as on his or her physical attractiveness. Younger women would be less desirable as marriage partners, it was argued, because

---

20. Selective abstinence is practiced in many foraging societies through, for example, social customs that forbid sexual relations between a married couple for a period after the birth of each child.

they had more potential childbearing capacity. That is why they tended to get married later.

But this would imply that the age of marriage for women would be pushed up in this society beyond the age of marriage for men. The age at which men marry has no effect on the number of children they would have to support. But the age of marriage of men was always two to three years higher than that for women, as it is in modern western countries. When the age of first marriage fell in England in the eighteenth century, it fell equally for men and women.

Finally once a woman has delayed marriage until age 30 or 35, the expected number of children she would bear falls to a small number under preindustrial conditions. In England the average woman marrying at 35 would give birth to fewer than 1.9 children, and even one marrying at 30 would give birth to fewer than 3.5 children.[21] So by age 30 the number of children that a woman would expect to have who would survive to adulthood would be close to 2. Thus there was no reason to delay marriage beyond 30 if fertility limitation was the issue. Yet many women remained celibate their entire lives, and many did not marry until their mid-thirties or later.

Nor is there any sign that the marital pattern in northwestern Europe was the result of community controls. For communities had very limited means to prevent marriages. In preindustrial England, for example, by age 21 children could marry without parental consent. The authorities in England did attempt to raise the age of marriage in many places by requiring apprentices to trades not to marry and by making them complete long apprenticeships (as long as seven years). But since apprenticeships began at age 14, this would not explain the much higher average age of marriage for men, 26–28.

Ministers and parishioners also sometimes explicitly tried to stop marriages by refusing to read the bans (the required announcement of the intention to marry, to be read for three weeks prior to the marriage date) or to allow a ceremony.[22]

But such tactics, which were of dubious legality anyway under both canon and common law, were likely to prevent or delay relatively few marriages, and those only in the more rural parishes. In a large city such as London,

21. Based on the fertility rates in table 4.2 the numbers would be 1.9 and 3.5 *if the woman survived to age 45.* Not all women would, so these numbers are upper bounds.
22. Ingram, 1985, 145.

which by the seventeenth century had swelled to over half a million people, a tenth of the population of England, such tactics would be futile. For even if the local parish refused to marry the couple, there was a cheap and easy alternative. Preindustrial England before 1753 had its own equivalents of Las Vegas wedding chapels.

Because of the arcane and involved nature of ecclesiastical authority, at a number of places in London free-lance chaplains, who made their living from the fees paid by couples, were able to legally marry couples without the formal posting of bans and a public marriage ceremony. These marriages were valid if they did not violate other church rules concerning marriages. The most popular place was the Fleet Prison and its "rules."[23] Between 1694 and 1754 an average of four thousand such marriages were performed yearly.[24] Since in these same years there were only six thousand marriages per year in London, the Fleet prison was a huge purveyor of weddings. The marriage registers suggest that people also traveled from counties near London for a Fleet wedding. There were other lesser London marriage emporiums, such as the Southwark Mint and the King's Bench prison rules. Thus in London there was no effective control over marriage by local parishes. Yet the average age of marriage and the percentage of the populace not marrying do not seem to have been any lower in London and its environs than in remote rural areas where communities might exert more informal controls.

Consequently social controls do not seem plausible as an explanation for the late age and low frequency of marriage before 1700. Individual choice was the determining element. But, as noted, such choices seemed to be centered on factors other than conscious control of fertility.

The Birth Rate and Income

There has been much debate by historical demographers as to whether in the Malthusian era the adjustment of population to resources was ensured

---

23. The "rules" of a prison were the area around a prison house in which prisoners imprisoned for debt were allowed, after giving enough security to clear their debts if they fled, to live and continue in their normal work where possible.

24. The prison was surrounded by public houses where chaplains had established wedding chapels and where the newly wed couple could celebrate their union; Brown, 1981.

primarily by changes in death rates or changes in birth rates. When population got so large that incomes fell, for example, was the population reduced mainly by increased mortality or by declining fertility? A world in which adjustment was mainly through changes in fertility was somehow seen as a "kindler and gentler" Malthusian world than one in which variations in death rates did the work.

So what was the slope of the curve that connected birth rates and income levels in the preindustrial world? We saw that the aggregate data for England by decade from the 1540s to the 1790s suggest that this curve might be quite flat. But if both the birth and death rate schedules were shifting up and down from decade to decade, then the points we observe in figure 4.2 might reveal little of the true relationship between income and fertility.

A better picture of the role of income in fertility potentially comes from comparing the fertility of rich and poor people at any one time. Because the parish sources that provide evidence of fertility rates in preindustrial northwestern Europe do not indicate the income or even the occupation of the parents, this subject has previously been investigated only on a limited scale and by a mere handful of studies.[25]

For England, however, we can derive a fairly good estimate of the economic position of men by studying their wills. In the seventeenth century at least wills were drawn up by a wide variety of people, from the poor to the rich. Here is a will typical except for its brevity:

> JOHN WISEMAN of Thorington, Carpenter [signed with an X], 31 January 1623.
>
> To youngest son Thomas Wiseman, £15 paid by executrix when 22. Wife Joan to be executrix, and she to bring up said Thomas well and honestly in good order and education till he be 14, and then she is to bind him as apprentice. To eldest son John Wiseman, £5. To son Robert Wiseman, £5 when 22. To daughter Margery, £2, and to daughter Elizabeth, £2. To son Matthew Wiseman, £0.25. Rest of goods, ready money, bonds, and lease of house where testator dwells and lands belonging to go to wife Joan. Probate, 15 May 1623.[26]

25. For example, the village of Nuits in France during the period 1744–92, studied by Hadeishi, 2003.

26. Allen, 1989, 266.

Wills could bequeath very small amounts, such as the following:

WILLIAM STURTENE of Tolleshunt Major, Husbandman, 14 November 1598.

　　To Francis my son 10s. To Thomas Stonard my son-in-law 1 cow in consideration of money which I owe him. To William and Henry his sons and Mary his daughter each a pewter platter. To Elizabeth my wife the rest of my goods. Probate, 3 February 1599.[27]

Wills were not made by a random sample of the population; they were made more often by those who had property to bequeath. But the custom of making wills seems to have extended well down the social hierarchy in pre-industrial England. In Suffolk in the 1620s perhaps as many as 39 percent of males who lived past age 16 made a will that was probated.[28] Higher-income individuals were more likely to leave a will, but there are plenty of wills available for those at the bottom of the economic hierarchy, such as laborers, sailors, shepherds, and husbandmen.

The estimated wealth of testators was constructed from the information in wills by adding together cash bequests and the estimated value of houses, land, animals, and grain bequeathed by the testator. Average wealth equaled £235 in 1630s prices.[29] But the median was only £100. This would generate an annual income of about £6 at the return on capital typical of this period. The yearly earnings of a carpenter in this period would be about £18, and those of a laborer £12. The wills thus covered men across a wide range of wealth.

These wealth measures correlate well with literacy, as measured by whether the person signed the will, and with the occupation or social status of the person. Table 4.5 shows this by dividing testators into seven broad occupational categories. Members of the gentry at the top of the scale were mostly literate and had average bequests of more than £1,200. Laborers at the bottom were mostly illiterate and had average bequests of £42. But within each social rank there were huge wealth variations. There were laborers wealthier than some of the gentry. Indeed knowing someone's occupation explains only about one-fifth of the wealth variation across testators.

27. Emmison, 2000, 171.
28. To probate a will means to register it in the appropriate court. Since probate had a cost others would have made wills that were never probated.
29. The breakdown was as follows: 1.1 houses, £44; 9.9 acres of land, £99; goods, £4; and cash, £88.

Table 4.5   Testators by Social Rank, 1585–1638

Social group	Number of wills	Fraction of testators literate	Average value of bequests (£)	Maximum value of bequests (£)
Gentry	94	0.94	1,267	8,040
Merchants/ professionals	116	0.88	267	1,540
Farmers	824	0.53	376	6,352
Traders	116	0.46	124	1,226
Craftsmen	340	0.42	78	600
Husbandmen	377	0.26	82	1,898
Laborers	111	0.17	42	210

Source: Clark and Hamilton, 2006.

For about a fifth of these three thousand men we have information from the parish baptism records on the number of children to whom their wives gave birth. Figure 4.3 shows the estimated total number of births to 645 men in England, mainly those who died in the years 1620–38, by the size of the bequest they left. This shows a clear and strong association between wealth and births. The richer half of male testators fathered 40 percent more children than the poorer half.

We can gain some insight into the reasons for that association if we divide men into "rich," those with wealth at death of more than £100, and "poor," those with less than £100. This differentiation is shown in table 4.6. Richer men were more likely to be married and lived slightly longer than poor men. But the major reason for their greater numbers of births was that, per year of marriage, richer men fathered more children. A richer man married for twenty or more years fathered 9.2 children, while a poorer man would have only 6.4, an advantage to the rich man of over 40 percent. The rich of preindustrial England thus had fertility rates within marriage that fully equaled Hutterite levels.[30] This again illustrates the absence of fertility control within marriage

30. An exact comparison is not possible, since some wives would have died before age 45, reducing apparent fertility rates. Some of the men would then have remarried, and if they married younger women it would have increased the apparent fertility rates.

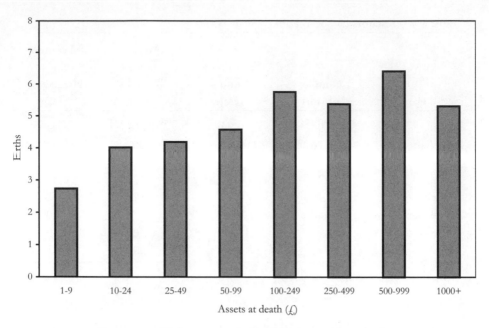

Figure 4.3   Births per man in England, by wealth at death.

Table 4.6   Fertility and Wealth in England, 1620–1638

Variable	Number of observations	Poorer	Richer
Average births	642	4.2	5.8
Average bequest	642	£44	£534
Percent never married	642	9%	5%
Average age at death	499	53.6	56.1
Age at first marriage	128	27.5	27.4
Age of wife at marriage	51	25.0	23.6
Births, married 20+ years	304	6.4	9.2

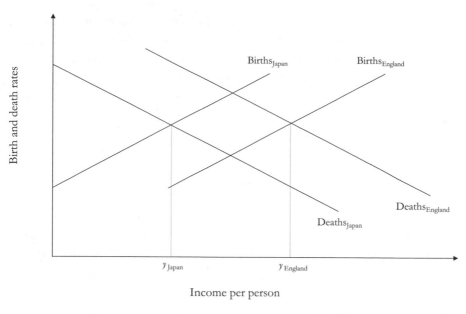

Figure 4.4   Fertility and mortality: England versus Japan.

in preindustrial northwestern Europe. Testators with wealth of less than £25 at death, who had been married twenty or more years, had only 5.4 births.

Europe versus Asia

Given that the gross fertility rate was about the same in northwestern Europe as in East Asia, why were living standards so low in Asia? The observation above that fertility within marriage increased with income in England suggests that the low fertility within marriage in Asia may in part be just a product of poorer nutrition. Figure 4.4 shows the apparent difference in the Malthusian equilibrium in preindustrial England and East Asia. If fertility within marriage also increased with income in Japan and China, then the observed similarity in birth rates implies that at a given income fertility was higher in Japan and China. So Europe did apparently have a low fertility regime compared to Asia, and in this respect Malthus seems correct in his suppositions.[31]

31. In preindustrial China, however, gross fertility among high-status lineage groups in the Beijing nobility was lower than for peasants in Liaoning. Total marital fertility was higher in the lower-status community, and the percentage of women marrying was somewhat higher; Lee and Feng, 1999, 68, 85.

But if the only difference between northwestern Europe and Asia was fertility rates at a given income, then the birth rate should have been higher in Japan (assuming a declining death rate schedule) and life expectancy consequently lower. To get the same aggregate birth rate at lower income levels seems also to imply that mortality rates for a given income were lower in Asia. Europe seems to have gained twice over: from both lower fertility and higher mortality.

Thus living standards stayed well above the physical subsistence minimum in the preindustrial world, because most societies had customs and social mores that kept fertility well below the biological possibilities. The way these customs operated, however, varied greatly across societies. If modern foragers are any guide to the distant past, our ancestors of the savannah probably limited fertility as much as did settled agrarian societies around 1800.

The empirical finding in the previous chapter of the absence of any sign of improving living conditions before 1800, even for technologically advanced societies, is explained in part by the probable absence of any fertility decline before 1800. Mortality rates, however, were also crucial in the Malthusian era in determining living standards. What happened to mortality as man moved from a forager lifestyle into settled agrarian society? Chapter 5 considers this question.

5 Life Expectancy

*Oh happy people of the future, who have not known these miseries and per-
chance will class our testimony with the fables. We have, indeed, deserved these
[punishments] and even greater; but our forefathers also have deserved them,
and may our posterity not also merit the same.*
—Letter from Petrarch to his brother at the onset of the Black Death in Italy (1348)[1]

In this chapter we consider two main questions. The first is whether, as assumed in the Malthusian model, preindustrial mortality was a declining function of income. In England, for example, in the years 1540–1800, just as for
birth rates, there is no sign of any association between national mortality rates
and national income levels, as would be expected in the Malthusian model.
Did England, and perhaps also the Netherlands, escape the Malthusian constraints long before 1800?

The second question involves the role of differences in mortality rates (at
a given income level) in explaining income differences across societies before
1800. There were substantial variations in incomes across preindustrial societies. England and the Netherlands, for example, had comparatively high incomes in the eighteenth century, while Japan had a very low income. Part of
this difference can be attributed to differences in fertility rates. But, as discussed
above, part also would have to come from mortality differences. Can we find
evidence of such differences?

Life Expectancy

Since in the preindustrial world, even with various mechanisms for limiting
births, fertility levels were high by modern standards, mortality rates had to
be high as well. As we have seen, in the stationary populations typical of the

1. Deaux, 1969, 94.

preindustrial world life expectancy at birth was just the inverse of the birth rate. Life expectancy at birth in England averaged only 37 years between 1540 and 1800. Life expectancy at birth, at 28 in the latter half of the eighteenth century, was even lower in preindustrial France (which also had a higher birth rate).[2]

These low life expectancies are often misinterpreted in popular writings to mean that few people survived into their forties. But though the chances of living to the biblical three score and ten were much less than today, there were plenty of elderly people in the preindustrial world. Fully 15 percent of the English men making wills in the seventeenth century died at age 70 or above. Those who lived long enough to become famous had even better prospects of getting to their biblical entitlement. The mean age at death of a sample of 1,064 notable scientists and philosophers born between 1500 and 1750 was 66: Berkeley was 67; Goethe, 83; Hume, 65; Kant, 80; Leibniz, 70; Locke, 72; Molière, 51; Newton, 85; Adam Smith, 68; Voltaire, 83.[3]

These considerable ages reflect the fact that life expectancy at age 20 was as high, or even higher, than life expectancy at birth. Natal life expectancy was so low because infant and child mortality were so high. In England from 1580 to 1800 18 percent of infants died within the first year. Only 69 percent of newborns made it to their fifteenth birthday. But those lucky enough to celebrate a fifteenth birthday could then expect to celebrate thirty-seven more.

Tables 5.1–5.3 show indicators of mortality and life expectancy for a variety of societies: life expectancy at birth and at 20 years of age, as well as the fraction of people dying within one year and fifteen years of birth. Table 5.1 shows these measures for modern forager societies. Since these are small populations of innumerate people, individual estimates of life expectancy for these groups are subject to considerable error. Life expectancy at birth in these groups ranged from 24 to 37, with a median of 32.5 years: less than that for eighteenth-century England, but as good or better than life expectancies for all the other agrarian societies listed in table 5.2.

Table 5.2 shows life expectancy for settled agrarian societies in the Malthusian era. Preindustrial England stands out as having relatively good life expectancies. There was, however, no trend toward improved life expectancy in England from 1550 to 1800. The other settled agrarian societies before 1800—

2. Weir, 1984, 32.
3. Mokyr, 2006.

Table 5.1 Life Expectancy for Modern Foragers

Group	Life expectancy at birth (e_0)	Life expectancy at age 20 (e_{20})	Infant mortality (%)	Deaths at ages 0–15 (%)
Ache, Paraguay[a]	37	37	12	34
Kutchin, Yukon[b]	35*	—	17	35
Hadza, Tanzania[b]	33	39	21	46
!Kung, Ngamiland, Botswana[b]	32*	—	12	42
!Kung, Dobe, Botswana[b]	30	40	26	44
Agta, Philippines[b]	24	47	37	49

Sources: [a]Hill and Hurtado, 1996, 196. [b]Pennington, 2001, 192.
Note: * denotes values estimated from share of population dying by age 15.

China, Egypt, France, Italy, and Japan—generally had lower life expectancies. Thus on average life expectancy in settled agrarian societies was no higher, and possible a bit lower, than for modern foragers.

Death rates were typically much higher in towns and cities than in the countryside. Urban mortality was indeed so high that, were it not for continual migration from the countryside, the cities would have faded from the earth. In London from 1580 to 1650, for example, there were only 0.87 births for every death. Without migration the population would have declined by a half percent every year.

Early towns were generally crowded and unsanitary, so that infectious diseases such as plague, typhus, dysentery, and smallpox spread quickly. Life expectancy at birth in London in the late eighteenth century, a mere 23 years, was thus lower than for most preindustrial societies, even though London then was perhaps the richest city in the world. As late as 1800 Londoners were not able to reproduce themselves: 30 percent of all infants died in the first year of life. Indeed urban dwellers in Roman Egypt had a better life expectancy than eighteenth-century Londoners.

The greater mortality rates of towns shows in the data from the English male testators, though there we have evidence only from smaller towns such as Bury St. Edmonds, Colchester, and Ipswich and not from London itself. While life expectancy at age 25 was 56 in the countryside, it was only 50 in the towns. And while 67 percent of children born in the country survived to

Table 5.2 Life Expectancy in Agrarian Economies

Group	Life expectancy at birth (e_0)	Life expectancy at age 20 (e_{20})	Infant mortality (%)	Deaths at ages 0–15 (%)
Western Europe				
Italy (medieval Pistoia)[a]	29	25	21	56
England, 1550–99[b]	38	33	18	30
England, 1650–99[b]	35	31	18	32
France, 1750–89[c]	28	—	21	—
England, 1750–99[b]	38	34	17	30
East Asia and Africa				
Egypt (rural), 11–257[d]	28	21	—	45
China (Anhui), 1300–1880[e]	28	33	—	—
China (Beijing), 1644–1739[e]	26	30	—	—
China (Liaoning), 1792–1867[e]	26	35	—	—
Rural Japan, 1776–1815[f]	33	37	25	50
Urban				
Egypt (urban), 11–257[d]	24	17	—	48
London, 1750–99[g]	23	—	30	—

Sources: [a]Herlihy, 1967, 283–88. [b]Wrigley et al., 1997, 224, 256, 614. [c]Weir, 1984; Flinn, 1981, 92. [d]Bagnall and Frier, 1994, 334–36. [e]Lee and Feng, 1999, 54–55. [f]Jannetta and Preston, 1991, 427–28. [g]Landers, 1993, 136, 158, 170–71.
Note: Life expectancy at age 0 is assumed to be three years less than life expectancy at age 6 months. One-quarter of girls are assumed to have died at birth from infanticide. Life expectancy at 20 is estimated from life expectancy at 15.

appear in their fathers' wills, in the towns it was only 64 percent. Surprisingly, though, the lower reproduction rate of those in the towns was due mainly to differences in fertility. The average testator in the countryside fathered 5.1 children, while the average town dweller fathered only 4.3.

For the years before 1540 it is generally possible to estimate only adult life expectancy. Table 5.3 shows these estimates. The Roman Empire outside Egypt provides just two reliable pieces of evidence. The first is a list of the hundred town councilors at Canusium, in southern Italy, in AD 223. From the regular succession of office holding it is possible to estimate that life expectancy for town councilors at age 25 was 32–34. This is upper-class male life

Table 5.3   Preindustrial Life Expectancy at Age 20

Group	Age	Life expectancy at 20
Magistrates, Canusium, Italy, AD 223[a]	25	33
Ex-slaves, Italy, ca. AD 200[a]	22.5	28
England		
1300–48 (tenants)[b]	20+	28
1350–1400 (tenants)[b]	20+	32
1440–1540 (monks)[c]	20	27
1600–1638 (testators)	20	35
England, 1750–99[d]	20	34
Rural Japan, 1776–1815[d]	20	37
Rural China (Liaoning), 1792–1867[d]	20	35
Modern foragers[d]	20	40

Sources: [a]Duncan-Jones, 1990, 94–97. [b]Razi, 1980. [c]Harvey, 1993, 128. [d]Tables 5.1 and 5.2.

expectancy. The second piece of evidence is a table constructed by a jurist, Ulpian. This was a guide to the length of time that bequests of life annuities, typically to freed slaves, would be a burden on testators' estates. Life expectancy at age 22 was 28 in Ulpian's table. These data, if correct, show lower-class life expectancy.

In England life expectancies in the medieval period can be estimated for male tenants of land and cottages on medieval manors, and for members of monastic communities. Zvi Razi used the court records of Halesowen to determine the interval between male tenants' first acquiring property and their death. Since the minimum legal age was 20, the average age at first property holding must be 20+. The estimated life expectancy of males in their early twenties was 28 years before the onset of the Black Death, and 32 years in the 50 years after the first outbreak. This is close enough to life expectancy in England at age 20 in the years 1580–1800 that we cannot be sure, absent additional evidence on medieval infant and child mortality, that life expectancy in England was in fact any lower in 1300 than in 1800.

In both China and Japan life expectancies at age 20 were as high or higher than those in England in 1800. These societies had a different pattern of mortality, with infant mortality relatively greater than in Europe, probably as a result of infanticide, and adult mortality consequently lower.

It would be nice to directly compare the life expectancies for Europe in the years after 1300 with those of communities before 1300, to test further the claim made above that living conditions did not improve between the Neolithic and 1800. Unfortunately, while it is possible to estimate the age at death from skeletal remains, no reliable way has been found to translate these estimates into estimates of life expectancy at a given age. Skeletal material from the very young and the very old does not survive so well in the ground as that of prime age adults, so that the surviving remains are unrepresentative.

However, modern foragers had a higher life expectancy at age 20 than any other group in table 5.3, and this suggests that in the Stone Age life prospects at 20 were better than for the much more technologically advanced societies of Asia and Europe in 1800. Thus, as with material living conditions and fertility, there was probably little change in life expectancy in the preindustrial world all the way from the original foragers to 1800. Since fertility was likely similar between forager and settled agrarian societies, the mortality rate must also have been similar.

Income and Mortality

There is no correlation decade by decade in England from 1540 to 1800 between income levels and death rates. Figure 5.1, for example, shows decadal infant mortality rates as a function of income levels. If anything infant mortality is higher in high-income periods. After 1540 temporary income shocks, such as bad harvests, also had little apparent impact on mortality, and this observation has led some to conclude that England escaped the grip of the Malthusian economy long before 1800.[4] However, as the figure shows, this pattern may just reflect shifts over time in the death rate schedule.

Infant mortality rates in eight London parishes in the years 1538–1653 can be compared with the percentage of the households in each parish that were "substantial" according to the tax listings of 1638. Figure 5.2 shows that the infants of the rich had much better survival chances. Indeed the crude measure of household income used here explains 62 percent of the variation in infant mortality rates in London. Furthermore, though London had notoriously high mortality rates, with the population maintaining itself only through

---

4. "The results question the usefulness of Malthusian models for early modern European economic history"; Weir, 1984, 27.

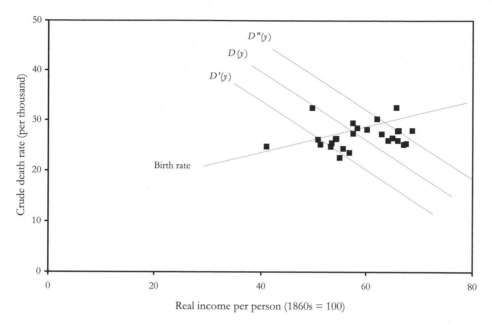

Figure 5.1 English death rates and real incomes by decade, 1540–1800. Death rates from Wrigley et al., 1997, 614.

constant immigration from the countryside, the infant mortality rates of the richer parishes were better than those for England as a whole in these years.[5]

The wills used above to estimate birth rates by income can also give some insight into mortality rates by income. Figure 5.3 shows the life expectancy of male testators at age 25 in England in the early seventeenth century. The effects of income on adult life expectancy are modest but still significant. Testators with £500 or more as a bequest had a life expectancy at 25 of 32 years, compared to 26 years for those with a bequest of £25 or less.

Figure 5.4 shows the fraction of children born to testators by bequest class who survived to be mentioned in the will. Again the effects of income are modest but clear. While only 63 percent of the children of poorer testators survived, 69 percent of the children of the richer testators survived.

The failure of the aggregate data for England to show any relationship between income or wages and the death rate thus seems to be merely the product of shifts of the death rate schedule over time caused by changes in the

5. The overall infant mortality rate for England in 1580–1649 was 169; Wrigley et al., 1997, 219.

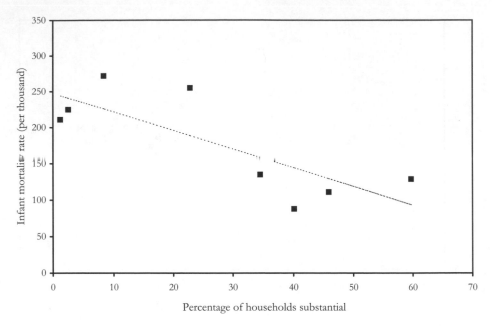

Figure 5.2   Household wealth and infant mortality in England, 1538–1653. Data from Landers, 1993, 186–88.

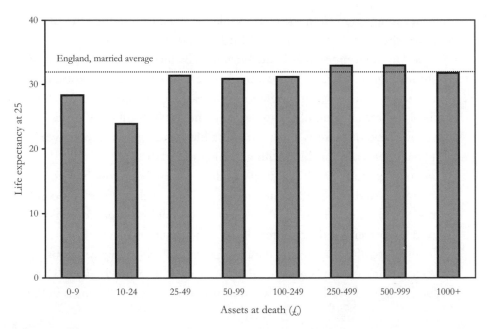

Figure 5.3   Life expectancy at 25 for male testators in England, 1620–38. Mortality rates from Wrigley et al., 1997, 614–15.

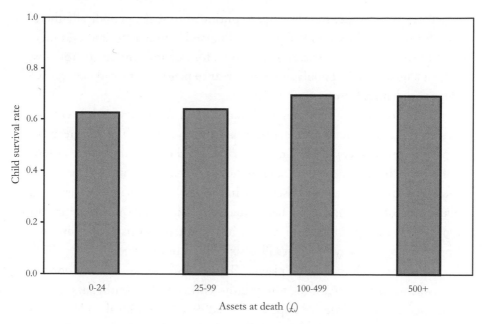

Figure 5.4 Survival rates for the children of richer and poorer testators.

disease environment, changes in the degree of urbanization (which drove up mortality rates), and improvements in sanitation and medical practices. So overall it seems safe to assume that even up until 1800 there was in all societies an inherent, but shifting, trade-off between income and mortality rates that tied long-run incomes to the level which balanced fertility with mortality.

Mortality and Living Standards

Fertility rates did not seemingly vary much across the preindustrial world, at least where we can observe fertility. Fertility rates in England in 1800 were no lower than those in eighteenth-century Japan or in forager societies. Living standards did vary considerably across preindustrial societies, however. Referring, for example, to figure 3.1, living standards of English laborers in 1450 were three times as high as in 1300, and nearly double the levels of 1800. This variation in living standards would seem to be explained mostly by variation in mortality rates at given levels of income.

Thus the explanation for the very high living standards of Europeans in the years 1350–1600 was undoubtedly the arrival of the Black Death in 1347. Its first onslaught in the years 1347–49 carried away 30–50 percent of the population of Europe. But the plague continued to strike periodically thereafter for the next three hundred years. In England between 1351 and 1485 there were thirty plague outbreaks. As late as 1604, for example, the city of York lost at least a quarter of its population in one year to plague. Paris had twenty-two plague epidemics from 1348 to 1596.[6]

Plague outbreaks mysteriously diminished in frequency and severity in western Europe from the late seventeenth century onward. The last great European plague epidemics were in 1657 in Italy, in the 1660s in France, in 1663 in Holland, in 1665 in London, and in the 1670s in Austria and Germany. Yet the plague did not disappear elsewhere in the world; it remained endemic in many parts of Asia. Plague had been present in Hunan in China since at least 1792, but in the late nineteenth century it spread to other parts of China and from there to Bombay, where it killed six million in the 1890s.[7]

The bacterium that causes plague, *Yersinia pestis,* seemed to lose none of its virulence with time. In the nineteenth-century Indian outbreak from 60 to 90 percent of the infected population died. In a late outbreak in Marseilles in 1721, 78 percent of those infected died, as did 80 percent of the infected in Noja, Italy, in a small outbreak in 1815. Thus the London outbreak of 1665 killed perhaps 16 percent of the city's population. The 1657 outbreak in Italy killed 44 percent of the populations of the afflicted cities.[8]

The continued virulence of the disease in these later outbreaks is one of the reasons its disappearance from Europe remains a medical mystery.

We know a considerable amount about preindustrial plagues because of the later Asian outbreak. In the course of this late-nineteenth-century outbreak the plague bacterium, as well as the means of transmission, was discovered independently by French and Japanese investigators. If the medieval plague was similar to this later outbreak, it was transmitted not from person to person but through the bites of infected fleas. The fleas' preferred host is rats, but when rats die from the disease the fleas move on to people, spreading the plague bacterium.[9]

6. Cipolla, 1993, 132; Galley, 1995, 452.

7. Benedict, 1988. The plague spread from Bombay to England through rats on grain ships, but it was contained there with the loss of only six people. An even more recent outbreak in India in 1994 infected at least seven hundred people.

8. Cipolla, 1993, 133.

9. The British performed experiments, such as suspending guinea pigs at different heights above plague-infested fleas, to see just how high the fleas could jump.

Bubonic plague was so called because of the "buboes" or boils, caused by swelling of the lymph nodes, which appear in the groin and armpits of the afflicted. The plague was particularly loathsome because of the appearance of the sick and because they exude an unbearable stench. Agonizing pain accompanies the boils, and sufferers normally die four to seven days after symptoms appear.

In line with modern beliefs on how the disease was transmitted, epidemics were reported sometimes to be preceded by the appearance of large numbers of dying rats. Since rats do not move great distances the plague would thus spread at a slow pace from one district of a town to another.

Yet in preindustrial Europe no one made the connection between rats and the plague. Instead all kinds of absurd theories as to the cause and transmission of the disease were put forward, even as late as the London outbreak of 1665. It was widely believed both that people were infectious and that the plague came from a poisonous cloud called a "miasma" being exuded from the earth in certain localities.[10] Thus a further horror of the disease was that the afflicted were often abandoned to their fate. Sometimes the city or commune would order that their houses be sealed with the sick inside. In the 1665 London outbreak attempts to control the disease included such useless measures as killing large numbers of cats and dogs, shutting up the infected in their homes, sniffing herbs to ward off bad air, and burning fires in the streets to dispel the supposedly poisonous air.

The plague years from 1347 to the 1660s are often taken by historians as a period when Europe was sadly afflicted. If we understand the Malthusian model we see that the plague was not the harsh judgment of a vengeful Old Testament God on a sinful Europe, but merely a mild reproof by a beneficent New Age–style deity. We saw that the plague, by increasing death rates at any given material living standard, raised living standards all across Europe in these years. Since birth rates were a function of income, these should have increased with the income gains of the plague years, so reducing life expectancy.

But table 5.3 suggests that any reductions in adult life expectancy after the onset of the plague were modest. The life expectancies of tenants and monks at age 20 in the plague years were no worse than those for tenants before the onset of the plague. After the initial onset the plague offered Europeans a

10. Special tight-fitting garments were made for those who administered to the sick and dying, to protect them from the miasma.

greatly enhanced material lifestyle at small cost in terms of the average length of life. In the Malthusian world gifts from God took surprising forms!

Dutch and English Mortality

The plague explains the high incomes of many European societies in the medieval period. The eventual disappearance of the plague from Europe—because of its dependence for transmission on a sufficiently large rat popula tion in close proximity to people—is probably due to improvements in standards of cleanliness in Europe in the seventeenth century. The result for many European societies was, of course, lower incomes. But incomes in both England and the Netherlands remained high compared to those in most preindustrial societies, particularly those of South and East Asia. Why were England and the Netherlands comparatively wealthy in the eighteenth century?

Some see this as the first breaking of the Malthusian trap, a break that first occurred in the Netherlands around 1600.[11] But even though both the Netherlands and England witnessed productivity advances in the seventeenth century that were unusually rapid by preindustrial standards, the rates of these advances were too low to raise incomes much above subsistence, given the continued link of population with income.

Figure 5.5, for example, shows real wages in the Netherlands versus the population by decade from the 1500s to the 1810s. In the early sixteenth century the Dutch experienced the same real wage declines as the rest of Europe as populations everywhere grew. But from the 1570s to the 1670s the Dutch were able to expand their production possibilities and experience both rising population and increasing wages. However, the efficiency advance that appears between the 1570s and 1670s, in the so-called Dutch Golden Age, was followed by a period of technological stagnation, characteristic of Malthusian economies, from then until the 1810s. During that 140-year period of stasis, when the population had plenty of time to adjust to the subsistence level, real wages remained high by preindustrial standards in the Netherlands (see figure 3.2 and table 3.4).

High Dutch real wages seem to stem from bad health conditions in the Netherlands in two ways. First, given the effects we observe in England of income on gross fertility, Dutch fertility remained surprisingly constrained

11. See, for example, de Vries and van der Woude, 1997, 687–89.

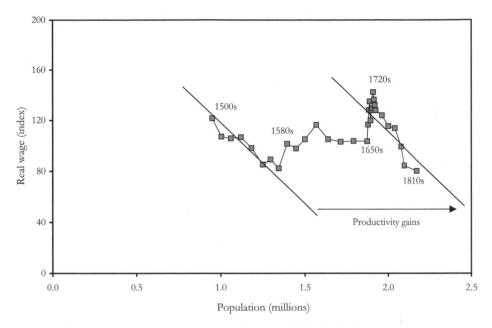

Figure 5.5   Real wages versus population in the Netherlands, 1500s–1810s.

given the high wages. High Dutch wages did not produce the abundance of children that would be expected. Despite these high real living conditions Dutch fertility rates were seemingly no higher than those in East Asia. Second, the high wages in the Netherlands did not reduce mortality as much as might be expected.

In England, where efficiency gains were modest or nonexistent between the 1700s and the 1790s, the ability to sustain relatively high real wages must again stem from unusually low fertility and high mortality.

One factor that helped keep eighteenth-century incomes high in the Netherlands and England was the increasingly urban character of these societies. Figure 5.6 shows the percentage of the population in towns in northern Italy, England, and the Netherlands at fifty-year intervals from 1500 to 1800 (and at hundred-year intervals before that) on the vertical axis compared to real wages. The observations for each location are linked to show the movement of these urbanization–real wage pairs for each place over time. The figure shows two things. The first is that in Europe before 1800 real wages and urbanization were poorly linked, even at the national level. In northern Italy urbanization was always about 20 percent, even while real wages varied by a

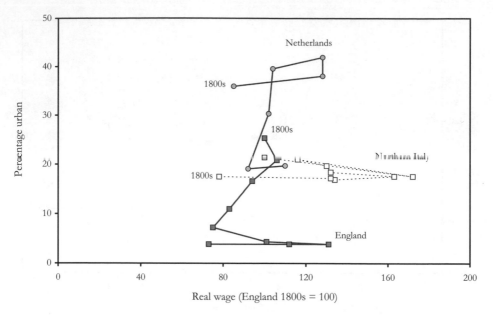

Figure 5.6 Urbanization rates, 1300–1800. Urbanization rates for northern Italy from Federico and Malanima, 2004, table 1. Urbanization rates for the Netherlands and England from de Vries, 1984, 39 (adjusted upward to be comparable to northern Italy).

factor of 2:1. In England in 1400 urbanization rates were less than 5 percent, even though wages were significantly higher than in 1800, when urbanization rates were more than 25 percent. Factors other than real wages were driving urbanization.

The second feature revealed by the figure is that by 1800 the Netherlands and England were the most urbanized parts of Europe. The evidence from testators and from parish records is that high urbanization rates helped keep down fertility and helped drive up death rates, maintaining high incomes. For example, in late-eighteenth-century England, death rates were about 23 per thousand in the countryside compared to 43 per thousand in London. The existence of London alone pushed up the death rate schedule in England by about 10 percent. Thus the development of trade in the years 1600–1800, which fostered greater urbanization in metropolitan centers such as those in the Netherlands and England, also allowed living standards to rise, but by purely Malthusian mechanisms.

In the Dutch case another factor driving up mortality was colonial adventures. From 1602 to 1795 the Vereenigde Oostindische Compagnie (VOC;

the Dutch East Indies Company) recruited about a million men, of whom half died in service. The annual losses from this service counterbalanced the half million immigrants drawn by high wages to the Netherlands from elsewhere in Europe in the same years. In a society with about the equivalent of 35,000 male births per year, counting immigrants, the VOC was annually consuming the equivalent of about 5,000 of these! But since these losses were almost all men, they also skewed the sex ratio in the Netherlands. In Amsterdam in 1795 there were 1.3 adult women per adult male. In Delft in 1749 the ratio of adult women to men was 1.5. The skewed gender ratio drove down the percentage of women marrying in Dutch cities. Thus the 1829 census revealed that 24 percent of Amsterdam women aged 40–55 had never married.[12]

Another factor favoring high living standards for Europeans compared to Asians is that throughout the preindustrial era Europeans were—by modern standards and also those of preindustrial China and Japan—a filthy people, living in dirt and squalor. The low standards of personal and community hygiene are everywhere apparent in preindustrial Europe. Indeed the travel diaries of European visitors to Japan in the years 1543–1811 frequently stressed the extreme cleanliness of the country by contemporary European standards.[13] This is true even in the account of the Dutchman Engelbert Kaempfer, who resided in Japan in 1690–92, despite the fact that the seventeenth-century Dutch were reputed to be the most fastidious among the Europeans.[14]

One crucial economic problem for hygiene in preindustrial Europe was that human waste had little or no market value, because it was not socially acceptable to use it as the valuable fertilizer it was for farm and garden purposes. As Alan Macfarlane notes, "where in Japan, night soil could be used in lieu of rent, in England one had to pay to have it taken away."[15] Its disposal was thus a major social problem in Europe. Samuel Pepys, for example, complains in his diary in October 1660 that "Going down to my cellar . . . I put my feet into a great heap of turds, by which I find that Mr. Turner's house of office is full and comes into my cellar."[16] Neighbors' overflowing turds were apparently nothing more than an everyday nuisance in seventeenth-century London!

---

12. De Vries and van der Woude, 1997, 72–75.
13. Alam, 1987, 238.
14. Schama, 1987, 375–97.
15. Macfarlane, 2003, 173.
16. Pepys, 2000, October 20, 1660. It took five days after this complaint for the neighbor to clean out the overflowing privy.

In contrast in China and Japan human waste, urine as well as feces, was a valuable property which householders sold to farmers, and which various groups competed for the right to collect. Waste was not dumped into cesspits, sewers, and streams, contaminating water supplies. Instead in cities such as eighteenth-century Osaka contractors found it profitable even to provide public containers on street corners in order to profit from the waste deposits.[17] In China and Japan the waste also seems to have been carried away daily, as opposed to being stored in cesspits below houses which were only periodically emptied.

Human waste poses dangers as a fertilizer, but the Japanese at least, aware of this, stored the waste in pits and tubs for months before use, allowing fermentation the time to destroy many of the infectious organisms.

The Japanese and Chinese also had a more highly developed sense of personal hygiene. Bathing was not popular in England and indeed was regarded as an indulgence in the early modern period. Even as late as 1811–17 Jane Austen's novels, otherwise full of domestic incident, contain not a single reference to bathing.[18] But in Japan bathing in hot water was popular and frequent. The Chinese also bathed whenever possible, and they employed plenty of soap.[19] The Japanese washed their hands after urinating or defecating, and they kept privies clean. In the ten years during which Pepys kept his diary, only once does he mention his wife having a bath: "My wife busy in going with her woman to the hot house to bathe herself. . . . she now pretends to a resolution of being hereafter clean. How long it will hold I can guess." This bath seems to have indeed been a dramatic event, since he records the next day, "Lay last night alone, my wife after her bathing lying alone in another bed." His newly clean wife seemingly objected to his coming to bed dirty, since three days later he notes, "at night late home, and to clean myself with warm water; my wife will have me, because she do herself, and so to bed."[20] But, as Pepys expected, bathing did not become a regular habit and the subject disappears for the next four years of the diary.

17. Hanley, 1997, 104–29.

18. Dr. Robert Willan, the famous London dermatologist, writing in 1801, noted that "most men resident in London and many ladies though accustomed to wash their hands and face daily, neglect washing their bodies from year to year"; quoted in Razzell, 1994, 164.

19. Lee and Feng, 1999, 45.

20. Pepys, 2000, February 21, 22, 25, 1665.

Data on soap production in eighteenth-century England support the idea that washing of people and clothing was not a frequent activity. In the 1710s, when England's population was 5.7 million, taxed soap output was 25 million pounds, less than 0.2 ounce per person per day for all uses of the product.[21] To illustrate how meager a use of soap this is, note that the Southern Africa Food Security Operation currently aims to supply to its destitute clients 0.4 ounce of soap per day, that transported convicts in Australia in the mid-nineteenth century got a ration of 0.5 ounce of soap per day, and that the ration of soap for both the Union and Confederate armies at the beginning of the U.S. Civil War was 0.64 ounce per day.[22]

The low attention paid by the English to personal hygiene was expressed in their primitive toilet arrangements. While in Japan toilets were built at some distance from living quarters, the English upper classes seemed to prefer the convenience of adjacent toilets, even with the attendant problem of odors.[23] Or they dispensed with toilet arrangements altogether. When the Globe Theater was constructed on the south banks of the Thames in London in 1599, not one toilet was provided for the 1,500 audience members that the theater could accommodate. Spectators, even those in the 5-pence boxes above the stage (the equivalent of nearly a day's wage for a laborer), did their toilet in the yard outside, or more likely in the stairways and passages of the theater itself.

Furthermore, in Japan the living spaces were kept much cleaner. Houses had raised wooden floors, and outside shoes were taken off at the entrance. The Japanese watered the streets outside their houses to keep dust down. In contrast in England the majority of people, until quite close to 1800, lived in dwellings with beaten earth floors covered by rushes that were only infrequently renewed. Into these rushes went deposits of waste food, urine, and spit. Indeed the effluvium deposited on floors from ordinary household business was so rich that, when saltpeter men were empowered in the late sixteenth and early seventeenth centuries to dig out the earth floors as rich sources of saltpeter (potassium nitrate), they allegedly dug up not just barn floors but also the floors of houses. The English also lived with a much more extensive

21. Deane and Cole, 1967, 72.
22. See, for example, Shannon, 1927, 479.
23. Hanley, 1997, 19.

domestic menagerie of dogs and cats, who made their own contributions of fecal material to dwelling spaces and streets.

Thus the relative wealth of the English—expressed also in their comparatively greater physical stature then versus now, matched against the Chinese or Japanese in 1800—probably stemmed mostly from the relative filth in which they wallowed. For in the Malthusian economy the traditional virtues of cleanliness and hard work gave no reward to a society at large, and indeed just made life harder and incomes lower.

Infanticide

Polynesia was a healthy place before Europeans arrived. The climate was mild, there were no mosquitoes to carry malaria, and the isolation of the islands protected them from many diseases, such as the plague. The healthiness of island living shows in the fates of the wives and children of the Bounty mutineers from HMAV *Bounty*. After the 1789 mutiny Fletcher Christian, eight other mutineers, and six Tahitian men settled in 1790 with twelve Tahitian women (some probably kidnapped) on the tiny mischarted island of Pitcairn, two miles long and one mile wide. By 1800 fourteen of the fifteen men were dead, twelve having been murdered by their companions and one having committed suicide.[24] But the women had borne 23 children by 1808, all of whom survived. So that, despite the murderous violence among the men, the population of 27 in 1790 had grown to 34. By 1823 there were 66 people on Pitcairn. Thus in one generation the population doubled. By 1856 there were 196 people on Pitcairn, an island with 88 acres of flat land and, by then, a serious population problem.

The healthiness of the Pacific islands is confirmed by the death rates of European troops stationed abroad in the early nineteenth century, which are given in table 5.4. The death rates in the table for British and French troops in the Pacific are lower than those in the same period for troops stationed in their own countries. Notice also that the death rates for European troops stationed in tropical Africa or the Caribbean were extremely high in comparison to the Pacific. Nearly half of British troops stationed in Sierra Leone in West Africa died each year.

24. Once conflict broke out, there was no retreat for any of the participants, and no one could sleep soundly at night until he had dispatched his enemies; Nordhoff, 1934.

Table 5.4 Healthy and Unhealthy Locations as Evidenced by Troop Mortality, circa 1800

Location	Troop nationality	Period	Death rate per thousand
New Zealand	British	1846–55	9
Tahiti	French	1845–49	10
Cape Colony	British	1818–36	16
Canada	British	1817–36	16
Gibraltar	British	1817–36	21
Bombay	British	1830–38	37
Bengal	British	1830–38	71
Martinique	French	1819–36	112
Jamaica	British	1817–36	130
Senegal	French	1819–38	165
East Indies	Dutch	1819–28	170
Sierra Leone	British	1819–36	483

Source: Curtin, 1989, table 1.1.

Fertility was also probably high among the precontact Polynesians. Sexual activity among women was early and universal. Why then was Tahiti such an apparent paradise to the visiting English sailors, rather than a society driven to the very subsistence margin of material income, as in Japan? The answer seems to be that infanticide was widely practiced before European Christian missionaries, who first arrived in 1797, changed local practices.[25] Unfortunately since our sources on this practice are the missionaries themselves, who had every incentive to portray pre-Christian practices as abhorrent, we will never be certain of these reports.[26]

The estimates from the early nineteenth century are that between two-thirds and three-quarters of all children born were killed immediately.[27] The

25. Oliver, 1974, 424–26.
26. The first Christian mission in Tahiti was not a success, and the missionaries had limited influence until after 1809, when the social disruption caused by contact with Europeans led many Tahitians to turn to Christianity.
27. This seems extraordinary, but it is what the missionary accounts record. Captain James Cook mentions the practice in his journal, but with no estimate of its incidence. The

alleged methods used included suffocation, strangulation, and breaking of the neck. All the observers agree that the act was performed immediately after birth. If the child lived for any length of time he or she would then be treated with great care and affection. One sign of the practice of infanticide was the agreement by most visitors that there were more men than women on the islands. The reasons for this Tahitian practice are surprisingly unclear. The paradise of the noble savage seemingly had its savage underside.[28]

The Europeans may have been a dirty people, but they did have a horror of infanticide, and there is no evidence of this practice in preindustrial Europe, either as a deliberate strategy or as the result of differential care for girls and boys.

But infanticide was common enough in other Malthusian economies that European abstinence from the practice may indeed be regarded as an aberration. In both Roman Italy and Roman Egypt parents exposed unwanted children in the marketplaces and the streets, though at least some of these unfortunates were rescued and raised as slaves. In preindustrial China and Japan the gender ratio of the population shows that there was significant female infanticide. In these Malthusian economies infanticide did raise living standards.

The White Death

In 1347, as we have seen, Europe was invaded by a bacterium from the East that caused the Black Death, which by raising mortality rates increased living standards in Europe for the next three hundred years. In 1492 when Columbus, perhaps the luckiest man in history, stumbled upon a continent whose existence he had no right to expect, the local peoples were visited by death from the West in the form of numerous new diseases. The four major diseases constituting this White Death were cholera, measles, smallpox, and typhus. All these had developed relatively recently under the crowded conditions of the Eurasian landmass and were novel to the Americas, which had been cut

---

journals of Captain William Bligh, Sir Joseph Banks, and others contain little information on infanticide.

28. "I thought I was transported into the garden of Eden. . . . A numerous people there enjoy the blessings which nature showers liberally down upon them. . . . Every where we found hospitality, ease, innocent joy, and every appearance of happiness amongst them"; Bougainville, 1772, 228–29, writing of Tahiti in 1768.

off from contact with Eurasia for millennia. Similarly the inhabitants of Australia, New Zealand, and the Pacific islands made acquaintance with these four diseases and others only with the arrival of Europeans.[29]

By analogy with the earlier experience of Europeans with the Black Death, the spread of the White Death to the New World in the years 1492 and later should have both reduced the native population of the Americas and also substantially improved living standards for Native Americans. There are some indications of groups in the New World for whom exposure to European diseases may have had the expected beneficial effects on living standards. Studies by Boas in 1892 of Great Plains Indians, who were born mainly between the 1830s and the 1860s, reveal that, despite substantial suffering from exposure to European diseases such as smallpox, they were very tall by the standards of the preindustrial world.[30] But the bulk of the native populations seemingly derived no material benefits from contact with European diseases. This would be a challenge for the Malthusian model to explain, except that the White Death was typically accompanied by Europeans expropriating native lands and resources, thus preventing higher mortality rates from exerting their normal Malthusian effects.

A Hundred Thousand Years of Stasis?

The Malthusian equilibrium held all societies in its grip before 1800. This would seem to imply a world of complete economic stasis, at least from the arrival of settled agriculture eight thousand years ago in the Neolithic Revolution. However, we shall see in the next chapter that there was a surprising source of dynamism in this Malthusian world. The population was changing, in ways that have hitherto escaped attention, in at least some of the preindustrial economies in the grip of the Malthusian vise. Chapter 6 explores this change.

29. McNeill, 1976.
30. Steckel and Prince, 2001.

6   Malthus and Darwin: Survival of the Richest

Man accumulates property and bequeaths it to his children, so that the children of the rich have some advantage over the poor in the race for success.

—Charles Darwin (1871)[1]

As has been emphasized, in the Malthusian era the economic laws that governed human society were the same as those that govern all animal societies. Indeed Charles Darwin proclaimed in his autobiography that his inspiration for *On the Origin of Species* was Malthus's *Essay on the Principle of Population*.[2] Then in *The Descent of Man* Darwin employed his theory of natural selection to explain how humans evolved from earlier progenitors. He even went so far, in the conclusion of that work, to endorse the theory that came to be known as social Darwinism: "Man, like every other animal, has no doubt advanced to his present high condition through a struggle for existence consequent on his rapid multiplication; and if he is to advance still higher, it is to be feared that he must remain subject to a severe struggle."[3]

While this affirmation of social Darwinism was misguided, Darwin's insight that, as long as population was regulated by Malthusian mechanisms, mankind would be subject to natural selection was profoundly correct.

In the Malthusian era on average every woman could have only two surviving offspring. But these two had to be selected by some mechanism from the average of four or five children each women had in the preindustrial era. And as long as mothers and fathers varied in their characteristics this survival process favored some types of individuals over others. The Darwinian struggle

1. Darwin, 1998, 139.
2. Darwin, 1969.
3. Darwin, 1998, 642.

that shaped human nature did not end with the Neolithic Revolution but continued right up to 1800.

In this chapter we will see that there is very good evidence of differential survival of types in preindustrial England in the years 1250–1800. In particular economic success translated powerfully into reproductive success, with the richest individuals having more than twice the number of surviving children at death as the poorest.

Indeed the evidence is that the poorest individuals in the Malthusian era would typically not reproduce themselves at all. Instead preindustrial England was a world of constant downward mobility. Given the static nature of the economy and of the opportunities it afforded, the abundant children of the rich had to, on average, move down the social hierarchy. The craftsmen of one generation supplied many of the laborers of the next, merchants' sons became the petty traders, large landowners' sons ended up as the smallholders.

The downward nature of social mobility in the Malthusian era is in stark contrast to the modern world, in which the lower fertility of the rich for most of the years since 1870, and the expansion of upper-level economic opportunities, have created a world of constant upward mobility, in which parents on average see their children move up the social hierarchy.

Survival of the Richest

The first two basic Malthusian propositions, shown again in figure 6.1, imply that reproductive success, the number of offspring a person leaves on his or her death, increases with income. This curve is drawn for society as a whole. But within any settled agrarian society there are huge variations in income across families at any time. The existence of land and capital as assets that generate rents allows some individuals to command much greater shares of output than others. The same Malthusian logic thus implies that those who are successful in economic competition in settled agrarian societies, those who acquire and hold more property, or develop skills that allow for higher wages, would also be more successful reproductively.

The wills of the men in England discussed in chapter 4 seem, at least by 1585, to mention nearly all surviving children. One way this can be demonstrated is through the ratio of sons to daughters. Daughters were much more likely than sons to be excluded from wills, because they had married and were given their share of the inheritance in dowry or because they were simply given

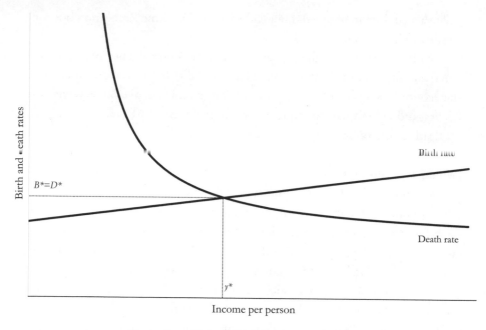

Figure 6.1 Birth rate and death rate schedules.

no bequest. John Hynson of Fordham, Cambridge, left to his two unmarried daughters Margaret and Mary £30 each. His three married daughters, whose names were not even given, were described thus: "To my 3 daughters who are married 10s [£0.5] each." Even bequests to unmarried daughters were generally smaller. For example, John Pratt of Cheveley, Cambridge, left each son £5, but each daughter only £2.[4]

Hence the ratio of boys to girls named in wills can be used as a measure of how many daughters were omitted. The expected ratio will be 1.03 if boys and girls had equal chances of being mentioned in wills.[5] The actual ratio, as table 6.1 shows, averaged 1.04. Probably only 1 percent more girls than boys are omitted from these wills. But given that girls were so much more likely to be excluded, if anyone was, the overall omission rate for children must have been very low.

4. Evans, 1993, 108, 217.
5. Based on estimated relative male and female mortality rates by age in 1580–1649; Wrigley et al., 1997, 296, 303.

Table 6.1 Surviving Children per Male Testator in England, 1585–1638

Location	Number of wills with information on children	Children per testator	Sons per testator	Ratio sons/daughters
London	177	1.96	0.83	0.77
Towns	344	2.39	1.19	1.02
Rural	2,210	2.92	1.50	1.06
Total	2,731	2.79	1.42	1.04

Source: Clark and Hamilton, 2006.

We can thus use these wills to investigate the connection between wealth and reproductive success in preindustrial England. Since we are interested in the reproductive success of testators, dead children were counted as surviving offspring if they themselves had produced living offspring. Thus William Cooke of Great Livermere in Suffolk, who died at about age 74, left four living children, but also two dead sons who each had two surviving children.[6] He was counted as having six children.

As can be seen in table 6.1 the average numbers of children per testator were modest. For a population to be just reproducing itself the numbers of children surviving each male at time of death would have to exceed two. This is so because some of these children would be minors who would die before they would reach the age (16 or more) at which they would potentially be writing wills. For the average testator in our sample to have two children who survived at least to age 16, he would need to have left 2.07 children when he died. Thus London testators circa 1620 were definitely not reproducing themselves. Those outside London in smaller towns, with 2.39 surviving children per testator, were experiencing a population growth of less than 15 percent per generation. Rural testators, however, were growing by 40 percent per generation.

Figure 6.2 shows the estimated numbers of children per male of each of eight bequest classes revealed by the wills. The bottom four income groups

6. Evans, 1987, 359.

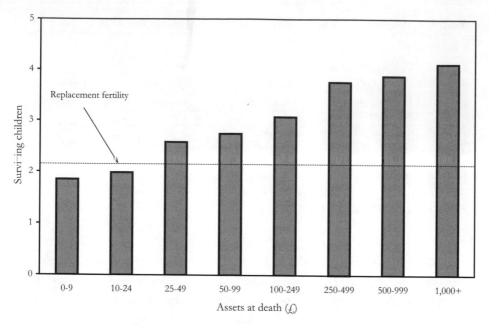

Figure 6.2   Surviving children by assets of the testator.

cover the bottom half of testators. Someone with less than £25 in bequests would typically have fewer than two children, while someone with £1,000 or more would typically have more than four children. The link between wealth and surviving children was thus extremely strong.[7]

The link shown here between wealth and children cannot be an artifact created by poorer testators omitting some children because they had nothing to bequeath them. This is evident in a number of ways. We know, for example, from the work of Anthony Wrigley and his associates that the typical male testator in England in these years would leave 2.58 surviving children.[8] So the richest testators with more than four children per family must have been producing substantially more surviving children than the general population, and by inference than the poorest testators as well. In addition the frequency of either no child being named as an heir or no male heir being named was higher for the poor. Even if poorer testators omitted some children from their

7. Given that the wealth of testators can be inferred from the wills only with a large amount of error, the true relationship between wealth and children is most likely even stronger than what is shown in the figure.

8. Wrigley et al., 1997, 614.

wills because they had few assets, or chose to leave everything to one child, they would certainly not omit all their children for this reason. Furthermore, given the preference for males as heirs, while they might have left assets only to the oldest son, they would not have omitted all their surviving sons from a will.[9] Poorer men simply had very few surviving children at the time of their deaths.

Interestingly wealth predicted reproductive success much better than social status or literacy. Economic status rather than social class is what mattered for reproductive success in England in these years. Presumably this was because the occupational labels used to form people into status classes were imprecise. There were husbandmen who were literate and wealthier than yeomen who were illiterate. There were carpenters who worked for others and owned nothing, and there were carpenters who were employers and engaged in building and leasing property.

It could be that economic success was an idiosyncratic element, created by luck or by personality factors that were nonheritable. In this case, while survival of the richest would have the social consequences illustrated below, it would have no long-run effects on the characteristics of the population.

However, the children of the rich had one significant advantage over those of the poor: the significant amount they inherited from their parents. One thing that stands out in these wills is that the major concern of the writers was to ensure that their assets passed to their biological children, and absent these to others genetically related to them: nephews, nieces, brothers, sisters, or cousins. Where wives were young enough to have children by another husband the fear was that the children of another man would benefit from the testators' assets. Wives were sometimes forbidden to remarry, or were required to surrender bequests on remarriage. Even though the early seventeenth century was a time of relatively heightened religiosity, and in fact the wills came from an area of England which produced many of the early Puritan settlers in New England, the amounts bequeathed to the poor were extremely small. Little also was left to the many servants the rich would have. Figure 6.3 illustrates the dominance of transmission of assets to those genetically related to the testator.[10] Bequests to the poor were typically less than 0.5 percent of the

9. Clark and Hamilton, 2006, give the evidence for this assertion.
10. Wives were counted as genetically related since the assets bequeathed to them were typically to raise children, or would pass on to children on their deaths.

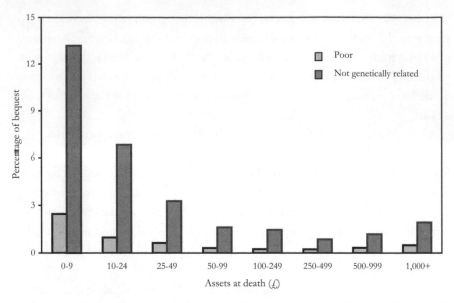

Figure 6.3 Share of bequests to the poor and those not genetically related by size of bequest.

testator's wealth. Bequests to those not genetically related were between 1 and 12 percent. The greater frequency of such bequests by poorer testators probably reflects the fact that they more often had no genetic relatives to whom to leave property.

Thus the sons of the rich would typically end up inheriting, counting the dowry their brides would bring, about half their fathers' bequests. They started life with an advantage over the children of poor men. And there is evidence that they too were more successful reproductively.

The first piece of this evidence is the number of grandchildren mentioned in the wills of richer and poorer testators. Only some grandchildren were mentioned in these wills. But if omissions were equally likely for the poor as for the rich, then, if the children inherited some of the reproductive success of their parents, the ratio of grandchildren to children should be greater for the children of the wealthy. If there was no inheritance of reproductive advantage the ratio should be the same for the children of the rich and the poor. Figure 6.4 shows this ratio for a subsample of the wills. It is clearly higher for the children of the rich. However it is only about 50 percent

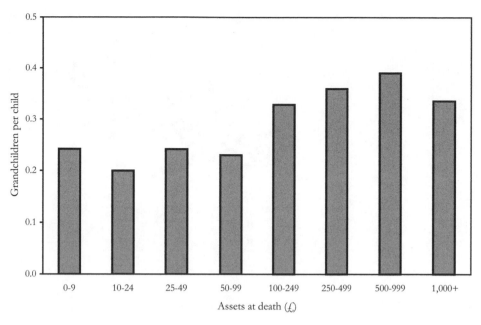

Figure 6.4 Grandchildren per child by bequest class.

higher for the children of the two richest groups of testators than for the children of the poorest. So clearly this advantage is not perfectly heritable, or this ratio would have been close to double for these groups.

A second check on the heritability of these differences in reproductive success is to look at the correlation of wealth between fathers and sons, since the size of the bequest is so closely linked to reproductive success. Figure 6.5 shows this relationship for 147 father-son pairs, where the bequest size has been transformed into units roughly equivalent to the intervals used in figures 6.2 and 6.3. Clearly there was a correlation between the wealth of fathers and sons when they both left wills. Rich fathers tended to have rich sons and vice versa. The dotted line shows the best fit of the relationship.

There are some problems with these data that limit what they can demonstrate, since the chances of a man making a will were much greater if he had a larger bequest to make. But if that was all that was happening we would expect poorer fathers, for example, those who left less than £100, to have significantly richer sons in cases where their sons left wills. In practice the twenty poorest fathers in this group, whose average bequest was only £51, left sons

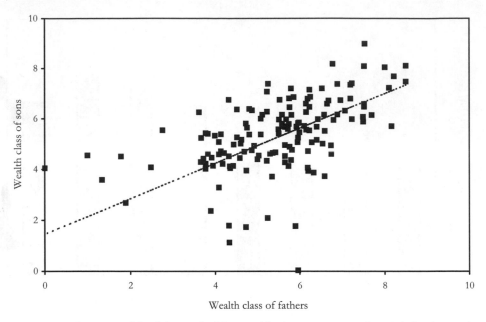

Figure 6.5 Bequests of the father and of the son. The bequest measure here is ln(1 + bequest).

whose average bequest was just slightly higher at £123. The correlation between fathers and sons cannot be purely from such selection. Economic status was indeed inherited.

The information from these linked father-son pairs also suggests that the advantage the sons had in accumulating wealth was not purely, or even largely, from the bequests they received. The number of children the 72 fathers had at time of death varied from one to eleven. If the advantage of the sons lay only in the bequests they received, then sons from large families should have done much less well than their fathers. The assets in such cases would have been dissipated among many children. In fact the number of brothers and sisters had little influence on how rich sons were at death. Fathers rich at the time of their deaths tended to have sons who were also rich at the time of their deaths, even when the sons received a small share of the fathers' wealth because there were many surviving children. The principal advantages the fathers were transmitting to their sons were thus either cultural (the sons learned how to succeed economically) or even genetic (the sons shared innate characteristics with their fathers that made them economically successful).

There is evidence that the pattern uncovered here, of much higher net fertility by richer groups, existed in England at least by 1250. Medieval kings

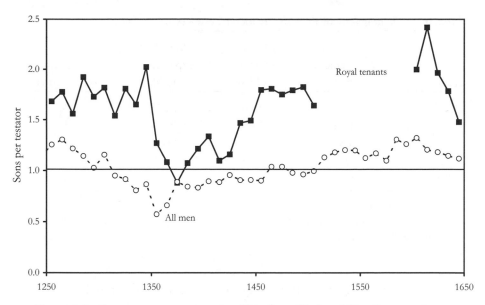

Figure 6.6 Sons per testator, 1250–1650. Data from Clark and Hamilton, 2006, 733.

had a financial interest in the deaths of their tenants in chief, those who held land directly from the crown under the feudal system. These individuals were mostly an economically privileged group, and they included the highest nobility of the land. Thus from 1250 on the king's officials conducted *inquisitiones post-mortem* on the deaths of these tenants, which are preserved in the Public Record Office. These inquisitions, however, record only the following information about surviving children: the oldest surviving son or his descendants or, failing a male heir, all daughters or their descendants.

The evidence of the wills in 1585–1638 provides a way to infer total numbers of surviving children from measures such as the fraction of times there was an heir, or the fraction of times there was a male heir, for wealthy groups such as royal tenants before 1500. Figure 6.6 shows two series by decade from the 1250s to the 1640s. The first is the average number of males per adult inferred for the whole population of England by decade from data on the aggregate movement of the population. As can be seen, except for the phase of population growth up to 1315, this number before 1500 was 1 or below 1. The second is the implied average number of adult male children produced by royal tenants. This was calculated by using the proportions revealed for 1585–1638 between total male surviving children and the fraction of testators leaving a son or leaving some child.

Table 6.2 Demography of English Aristocrats, 1330–1829

Period	Net replacement rate	Male life expectancy at birth	Male life expectancy at 20	Fraction of deaths from violence
1330–1479	—	24.0	21.7	26
1480–1679	1.04	27.0	26.3	11
1680–1729	0.80	33.0	30.0	7
1730–1779	1.51	44.8	39.9	3
1780–1829	1.52	47.8	42.7	4

Source: Hollingsworth, 1965, 8–11.
Note: Hollingsworth considers only legitimate children, but he argues that illegitimate children were few, less than 10 percent of these totals.

In the two periods in medieval England during which the population was stable or growing, 1250–1349 and 1450–1500, tenants in chief were producing an average of 1.8 surviving sons, nearly double the average for the population as a whole. Even in the years of population decline from 1350 to 1450, though the number of implied surviving sons per tenant in chief declined, it remained at or above the replacement rate in most decades. Thus, as later in medieval England, the rich seem to have been out-reproducing the poor.

In England the reproductive success of the class that engaged in warfare on a large scale in the preindustrial era, the aristocracy, was much poorer than for economically successful commoners, and it was probably less than that of the average person. Table 6.2 shows for the English aristocracy (kings, dukes, and duchesses) the net reproduction rate, as well as life expectancy at birth for males by period from 1330 (when dukes were first created). Medieval manorial tenants, for example, had a life expectancy at age 20 of about 30, compared to about 22 for the aristocracy.[11]

These excess deaths at relatively young ages contributed to the low net fertility of aristocrats. Thus in the earliest period for which we observe fertility, 1480–1679, the aristocracy, despite its privileged social position, was barely reproducing itself. Only after 1730, when death rates from violence declined to levels not much above those for the general population, did aristocratic life

11. Razi, 1980, 130.

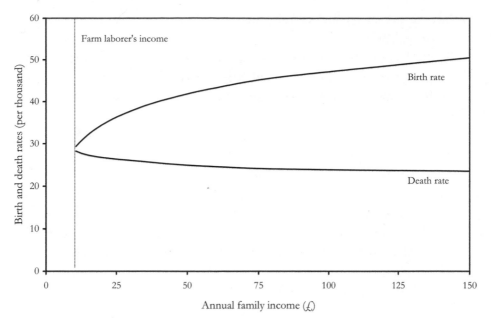

Figure 6.7 Birth rate and death rate schedules in England, circa 1630.

expectancy come to exceed that of the average person. And it was only in this latter period that aristocrats finally enjoyed more reproductive success than the average person.

Thus from the earliest times we can observe in the preindustrial era reproductive success in a settled agrarian economy like England seemingly went to those who succeeded in the economic sphere and avoided occupations in which violent death was a hazard. Ever since the arrival of institutionally stable agrarian societies, with private ownership of land and capital, and secure transmission of assets between generations, those who were economically successful—and in particular those who accumulated assets—were likely also reproductively successful.

The Malthusian Scissors

The data from the wills on wealth and occupations, combined with information from parish registers, allow us to portray the birth rate and death rate schedules of seventeenth-century England as a function of income over a large range of the income distribution, though excluding the very poorest families.

Income for each testator was calculated as his likely wage income from his occupation, combined with asset income. Figure 6.7 shows these curves for England around 1630. The Malthusian "scissors" are evident. At the income level of a farm laborer, the birth rate barely exceeded the death rate. Implied birth rates are low for the preindustrial era, at 29 per thousand. For those in the highest-income group, with average implied incomes of about £150 per family per year, more than five times the national average, implied birth rates were nearly 50 per thousand, close to the highest levels observed for preindustrial populations as a whole. Since the implied death rate of this high-income group was only 24 per thousand, the implied population growth rate of this group was nearly 2.6 percent per year.

Thus there is no sign that even preindustrial England in the period 1600–1800 had escaped the grip of the Malthusian trap. The curves displayed in figure 6.3 imply that any significant increase in average incomes would have led immediately to rapid population growth.

Sources of Mortality

The likelihood that reproductive success was determined by very different means in settled, institutionally stable agrarian societies than in hunter-gatherer and shifting cultivation communities is reinforced by studies of mortality in modern forager and nonmarket societies. These suggest that deaths from accidents—to use the old legal terminology, deaths from *misadventure*—and homicide formed a surprisingly high proportion of all deaths compared to settled agrarian societies, and to modern societies.

This was partly due to the way of life in early societies. In the mobile forager societies there were heightened risks of death from encounters with dangerous animals, drowning, thirst, and falls. But homicide was an even more common killer than such accidents. Despite romantic notions of the noble savage, violent conflict within and between bands of foragers seems to be frequent.

Table 6.3 shows for some modern hunter-gatherer societies the male death rates per thousand males per year overall and from accidents and homicide. Forager societies for which we have a complete breakdown of causes of death are few. And the small size of these groups implied much random variation in the causes of death in the observation periods. But these observations

Table 6.3 Causes of Male Deaths in Forager and Subsistence Societies

| | Death rate (per thousand) | | |
Group	Overall	Accident	Homicide
Neolithic France, 5500–2200 BC[a]	—	—	1.4
Ache, forest period, 1900–70[b]	27	3.5	15.0
Yanomamo, 1970–74[b]	—	2.1	3.6
!Kung, before 1973[b]	32	4.4	
New Guinea (Gebusi)[c]	—	0.6	6.9
New Guinea (Goilala, Hewa)[c]	—	—	6.6*
Agta[c]	42	—	3.3*
United Kingdom, 1999[d]	12	—	0.01
United States, 1999[d]	12	—	0.07

Sources: [a]Guilaine and Zammit, 2005, 133, 241–49 (very rough estimate). [b]Hill and Hurtado, 1996, 174. [c]Knauft, 1987. [d]World Health Organization, 2002, table A.8.
Note: * denotes male and female deaths.

FYI to next reader: in 2016, in AL, gun death rate was 0.23 per thousand. AK 0.23.3 US overall 0.118. (Guns only, not counting other homicides)

suggest that homicide, including intergroup conflicts, was the source of death for 7–55 percent of men in such communities, averaging 21 percent of deaths. The reason for these high rates of violent death among men in forager societies is not clear. In part it may stem from the absence of supervening legal authorities which could settle disputes without resort to violence. But we shall see that there is also the possibility that the people of long-established forager societies were inherently, maybe even genetically, more violent.

Jean Guilaine and Jean Zammit estimate the numbers of people who died violently in Neolithic France from skeletal evidence. Figure 6.8 shows the kind of graphic evidence of violence that can be found in skeletal remains. Though there must be many caveats about their estimate, they conclude that 3 percent of the dead were killed or injured by violence. Assuming, based on their appendix tables, that the ratio of killed to injured was 2:1, that these were all male, and that life expectancy was 35 at birth gives the estimate in the table, 1.4 deaths per thousand from homicide. This suggests a rate much lower than that for modern foragers, but much higher than that for modern high-income societies.

Figure 6.8 Copper dagger blade lodged in a vertebra, third millennium BC.

In most modern societies deaths from violence occur at a low rate. In typical modern western European societies, such as the United Kingdom, the rate of male deaths from violence is only 0.01–0.02 per thousand per year. There seemingly was a transition from early societies, in which interpersonal violence was a major contributor to death rates, to modern ones, in which violence is not an important source of mortality. When did that transition occur?

In England we can trace sources of mortality all the way back to the late twelfth century. Since in medieval England the property of anyone who killed unlawfully reverted to the king, the king had an incentive to discover all murders. English kings thus established early on a system of coroners' inquests for all accidental and violent deaths. These inquests establish the numbers of homicides and accidental deaths per year for various counties in England back to the late twelfth century.[12]

Figure 6.9 shows the trend in these various local estimates of homicide rates as well as later national homicide rates, per thousand people. Though there was a steady decline in homicide rates between 1200 and 1800, medieval England was already very peaceable compared to modern forager societies. Death rates per year from unorganized violence in England even circa 1200 averaged 0.2 per thousand. But this figure shows only the toll from unorganized violence. War deaths, the result of organized violence, must be added in to arrive at the overall losses from homicide.

12. Hair, 1971; Hanawalt, 1976, 1979; Cockburn, 1977, 1991; Given 1977.

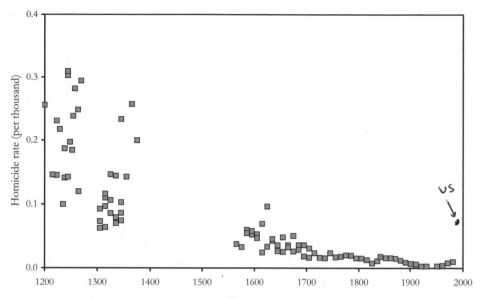

Figure 6.9 Homicide rates for males in England, 1190s–2000.

Figure 6.10 shows estimated English male death rates from the various external and internal wars by decade from the 1170s to the 1900s.[13] Here the average losses were surprisingly small, of the order of 0.12–0.15 per thousand people for most of the period 1150–1800. Thus even in medieval England before 1350 the average annual death rate from all violence was 0.4 per thousand. Even allowing for the fact that the death rates for forager societies were calculated for men, this is an order of magnitude less than the rate currently observed for forager societies. It is also less than the estimated Neolithic rate.

Early European wars produced few casualties because the size of armies before 1700 was typically small. In the 1290s, when Edward I assembled the largest armies of his long reign, before he was severely constrained by financial problems, his army to suppress the Welsh rebellion of 1294–95 was 31,000 at its maximum. This was about 0.6 percent of the English population. When the locus of the fighting switched to France during the Hundred Years War, the size of armies was even smaller because of the development of more professional and better-equipped forces, and the cost of moving troops to France.

13. There is a good historical record of all the battles and campaigns of the English, many with casualty estimates. For the earlier battles casualty numbers were estimated from those conflicts for which a count was available.

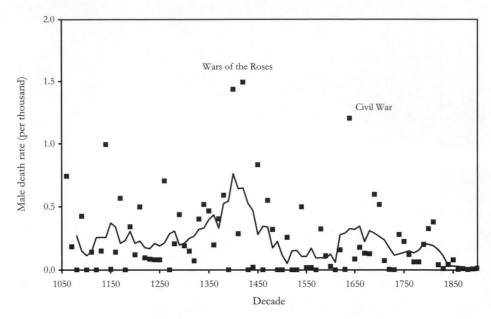

Figure 6.10 Death rates from military conflicts in England, 1170s–1900s. The line shows a fifty-year moving average of combat death rates in England.

When Henry V invaded France in 1415 he had only about 10,000 men. And casualties from violence in war were limited because battles were infrequent and the battles themselves did not always produce large numbers of casualties. Edward I, who reigned for thirty-five years from 1272 to 1307, and who led armies in Wales, Scotland, Flanders, and the Holy Land, took part in only one full-scale battle, at Falkirk in Scotland in 1298.[14] Thus one reason that forager living standards were probably as high as those in Europe by the eighteenth century was the relatively low rates of death from violence in these settled agrarian economies—though England was a particularly stable and peaceable preindustrial society.

Reproductive Success in Earlier Societies

The Malthusian assumptions imply that in all societies those who command more income will have greater reproductive success. We shall soon see, when we look at preindustrial China and Japan, that this relationship may have been

14. Prestwich, 1996, 116–18, 305–11.

particularly strong for England. Yet it seems probable, given the Malthusian model, that such a connection existed in all settled, institutionally stable agrarian economies before 1800. In these environments men could more effectively translate income into reproductive advantage.

Thus anthropologists have demonstrated that among pastoralists in modern Kenya ownership of cattle correlates strongly with reproductive success through marrying more and younger wives.[15] The Ache of Paraguay, hunter-gatherers, moved every day in search of game, so property ownership was minimal, limited to what a person could carry. Reproductive success in this group was still correlated with economic success. But it was the success of males in bringing meat into camp each day. All the adult males hunted, and Ache hunters who brought home more meat had higher fertilities. The most successful hunters at the mean age of 32 had 0.31 children per year compared to 0.20 for the least successful. Survival rates were about the same for the children of successful and unsuccessful hunters.[16]

But some of the mechanisms by which people commanded more income seem to have been very different in hunter-gatherer societies than in the settled agrarian economies that preceded the Industrial Revolution.

As we saw for the case of the upper classes in England, violence was not a successful reproductive strategy. Rates of violent death were very low. This finding contrasts with conditions in modern hunter-gatherer or shifting cultivation societies in which accidents and violence are a much more important source of mortality. There mortality rates from accidents and violence for males were typically 3–18 per thousand males per year. At the extreme, among the Ache violence was the cause of most male deaths.

In these societies violence was a way of gaining more resources and hence more reproductive success. Thus Napoleon Chagnon, in a famous study of the warlike Yanomamo society, found that a major predictor of reproductive success was having killed someone. Male Yanomamo sired more children at a given age if they had murdered someone than if they had not.[17] Table 6.4 shows the numbers of children male Yanomamo had fathered as a function of age and of their status as killers or nonkillers.

15. Borgerhoff-Mulder, 1987; Cronk, 1991.
16. Hill and Hurtado, 1996, 316–17.
17. Of course this raises the question of whether murder is a successful reproductive strategy for males, since some of those who fail in the attempt will die themselves.

Table 6.4 Reproductive Success of Male Yanomamo, 1987

Age	Number of killers	Killers' average offspring	Number of nonkillers	Nonkillers' average offspring
20–24	5	1.00	78	0.18
25–30	14	1.57	58	0.86
31–40	43	2.83	61	2.02
41+	75	6.99	46	4.19

Source: Chagnon, 1988.

Social Mobility with Survival of the Richest

England in the years 1585–1638 was still a relatively static society, with little change in income per person. It was, as noted, a society still in the grip of the Malthusian Trap, in which economic change was slow or nonexistent. Consequently the relative numbers of occupations, the wage rates for different occupations, and the stock of housing per person changed little. The amount of land per person fell, but land values were increasing with the growth of the population, so the value of land per person also changed little. The great reproductive success of richer testators thus meant that their children were on average moving down the social ladder in terms of wealth and occupations— and moving down reasonably rapidly.

Table 6.5 illustrates this for Suffolk in 1620–38. The second column of the table shows the sample of males from Suffolk who made wills, arranged by wealth class. Added to the observed wills are the appropriately sized group of males who made no will, assumed to have zero assets, as well as an appropriately sized group of testators whose wills were approved in higher courts and whose wealth is assumed to have exceeded £1,000. The next column shows the share of each class of males in the population in the first generation. The next column gives the observed numbers of male children from each asset class who reach at least age 16. We assume those who did not make wills had the same numbers of children as those making wills whose assets were £0–9. For those whose wills were proved in higher courts we assume they had the same numbers of children as those of the highest observed asset class. This implies that of a population of 3,613 wills in the first generation we end up with 4,266 adult male successors in the next generation, an increase of 18 per-

Table 6.5 Intergenerational Mobility in Suffolk, 1620–38

Assets	Males in first generation	Share of first generation (%)	Male adult children	Share of second generation (%)
0 (no will)	2,204	61.0	(2,125)	49.8
0–10	140	3.9	135	3.2
500–999	116	3.2	220	5.2
1,000+	168	4.7	338	7.9
All	3,613	100	4,266	100

Source: Clark and Hamilton, 2006.
Note: The number in parentheses in column 4 is an estimate from the observed reproductive success of the highest and lowest group of those who made wills in the archdeaconry courts.

cent per generation. This is close to the 21 percent gain per generation found by Wrigley et al. for England in this period.

The last column of the table shows the shares of the children of each wealth class in the next generation. Testators with wealth of less than £10 and those who left no will were 65 percent of the first generation. But their sons constituted only 53 percent of the next generation. Testators with wealth of more than £500 were 8 percent of the initial generation. Their sons were 13 percent of the next generation. Given that wealth per person probably stayed constant over this interval, there must have been considerable net downward mobility in the population. Nearly half of the sons of higher-class testators would end up in a lower wealth class at death. Indeed net mobility would be downward for testators in all the groups with a wealth of £25 or more.

Zvi Razi's evidence from the court rolls of Halesowen for 1270–1348 is consistent with the suggestion of the *inquisitiones post-mortem* that the rich were much more successful in reproducing themselves in medieval England. Table 6.6 shows the percentage of families showing up in the court rolls of 1270–82 who had direct descendants holding land in the manor in 1348. All the families with the largest holdings in 1270–82 still had direct descendants holding land. But only 25 of the 70 families holding the smallest amounts of land had a descendant holding land.

However, the distribution of the sizes of these holdings had not become more unequal. Families with larger holdings in 1270–82 on net acquired more

Table 6.6 Survival of Landowners in Halesowen, 1270–1348

Family type in 1270–82	Numbers of families	Number with descendants holding land in 1348	Percentage with descendants holding land in 1348
Rich	40	40	100
Middling	64	58	91
Poor	70	25	36
All	174	123	—

Source: Razi, 1981, 5.

land. But they also often had more heirs, and so divided up their holdings more often between multiple heirs, keeping the overall land size distribution in balance. Since Ravi's data do not allow us to know whether the small land-holders were in fact suffering demographic collapse, or whether they simply either disappeared from the court rolls or left the manor, the data do not demonstrate that medieval England was experiencing the same population dynamics as occurred in later years.[18] But they are consistent with that interpretation.

This story of the reproductive advantage of the rich is also found in a collection assembled by Joerg Baten of surveys of communicants in villages in Austria and southern Germany for the seventeenth to nineteenth centuries. Villagers of higher social status and those revealed to be more likely literate had at the time of the surveys more surviving children.[19]

Thus economic orientation had a dynamic of its own in the static Malthusian economy. Middle-class values, and economic orientation, were most likely being spread through reproductive advantage across all sections of stable agrarian societies. The next two chapters consider the dynamic elements of the economy before 1800. Chapter 7 examines technological advance, and chapter 8 explores the implications of these Darwinian selection processes for people's economic behaviors.

18. Inhabitants without land were less likely to appear in court rolls since they do not show up in land transactions or as pledges.
19. Joerg Baten, personal communication.

7   Technological Advance

There be dayly many things found out, and dayly more may be which our Fore-
fathers never knew to be possible in Nature.

—Sir Robert Filmer (1653)[1]

Despite the sluggishness of preindustrial technological advance, there was over time—agonizingly slowly, incrementally—significant technological progress. Europe of 1800 was technologically significantly advanced over Europe of 1300. And Europe of 1300, surprisingly, had a much better technology than the ancient Romans or Greeks. Even the supposedly technologically stagnant eras of the Dark Ages and the Middle Ages saw many innovations.[2]

Thus the list of basic technologies which were unknown or unused in the ancient world is surprisingly long. None of the Babylonians, Egyptians, Persians, Greeks, or Romans, for example, managed to discover the stirrup for horse riders, simple as this device seems. Ancient horse riders held on with their knees. The stirrup was introduced in China only in the third century AD, and in Europe not until the early Middle Ages.[3] The Romans and Greeks also used horse harnesses which wound around the belly and neck of the horse. Experiments in the early twentieth century by a retired French cavalry officer, Richard Lefebvre de Noëttes, suggest that horses harnessed in this way lose up to 80 percent of their traction power, since the neck strap

---

1. Filmer, 1653, 8.
2. Many of these same innovations were made earlier and independently in China.
3. Temple, 1986, 89–90. Lynn White, 1962, famously argued that the introduction of the stirrup to western Europe in the ninth century led to the dominance of the heavily armored knight in warfare.

compresses both the windpipe and the jugular vein. Only in the eighth century in Europe were efficient harnesses, which sit on horses' shoulders, discovered.[4] Horseshoes to protect hooves were also unknown in the Roman and Greek world.

Looking just at Europe, the Greeks and Romans also lacked windmills (first documented in Yorkshire, England, in 1185), buttons for clothing (first found in Germany, 1230s), spinning wheels (France, by 1268), mechanical clocks (England, 1285), spectacles (Italy, 1285), firearms (Spain, 1331), and movable-type printing (Germany, 1453).[5] Though the Romans had learned how to make at least primitive soaps, it was not used for cleaning bodies. That was accomplished by rubbing oil onto the body and removing it with a scraper. A Swedish windmill, the successor to a medieval innovation, is shown in figure 7.1.

Similarly China between AD 1 and 1400 saw the introduction of porcelain, matches, woodblock printing, movable-type printing, paper money, and spinning wheels.[6] The technology of the preindustrial world was not completely static.

What was the rate of improvement of technology compared to the modern world? And how did it vary over time? Can we reduce all the complex changes in technology to a single number, the rate of advance of technology per year? How do we compare the invention of the bow for hunting, for example, with the introduction of the personal computer? How much technological progress is represented by the introduction of the mechanical clock in Europe in 1285, compared to the knitting frame of 1589?

Economists measure the rate of technological advance in a particular way. The lower curve in figure 7.2 shows the typical preindustrial connection between land per person and output per person, the *production function* of the society. Technological change in this measure is an upward shift in the production possibilities at any given amount of land per person, again shown in figure 7.2. If A is the measure of the level of technology, the rate of technological advance, g_A, is the percentage upward movement per year of the production function at any given amount of land per person. For example,

4. Mokyr, 1990, 36. Again such harnesses are claimed to have appeared in China much earlier, before 300 BC; Temple, 1986, 20–21.

5. Mokyr, 1990, 31–56.

6. Temple, 1986, 75–122.

Figure 7.1 A windmill, unknown in the world of Plato, Aristotle, and Euclid but introduced in the Middle Ages (Faro, northern Gotland, Sweden).

if g_A is 1 percent per year, at a given land-labor ratio the society is able to produce 1 percent more output per year.

This measure of the rate of technological advance has the property that

$$g_A = \theta_1 g_{A_1} + \theta_2 g_{A_2} + \cdots + \theta_n g_{A_n},$$

where the θs are the values of the output of each industry of the economy divided by the total value of the final outputs, and the g_{A_i}s are the growth rates of efficiency within each industry.

Economists use this weighting because it measures how much technical changes matter to the average consumer. It measures efficiency by looking at the changes in the efficiency of production of each good within the economy weighted by how much of each good is consumed. This productivity measure effectively takes a poll of consumers and asks "How much more efficiently are things being done for *you* this year as opposed to last year?"

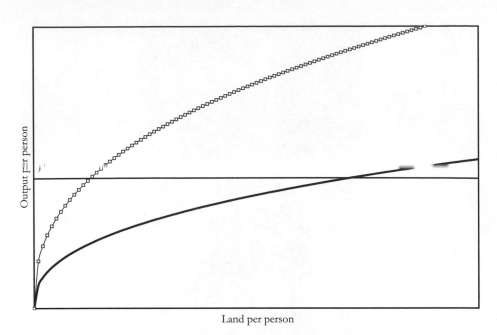

Figure 7.2   Effects of technological advance before 1800.

Measuring Technological Advance from Population

In figure 7.2 the Malthusian mechanism stabilizes population at the level at which the land per person produces just the subsistence income y^*. Technological change in this world showed up as an upward shift in the production possibilities.[7] But as long as income was constrained to return to the subsistence level, y^*, population would grow after technological advance until land per person fell sufficiently so that output per person was again y^*.

For one preindustrial society we can actually plot this curve over a wide range of acres per person. That is England during the period 1240–1600, when production technology seems to have been static but population varied by a factor of nearly 3 because of losses from the plague after 1348. The data points in figure 7.3 show output per person for each decade from the 1240s to

7. Here *technology* is used in the broadest possible sense to include any element of invention or social organization that affects output per acre. Thus legal innovations that increase output through better defining property rights will be included in the technology of a given period.

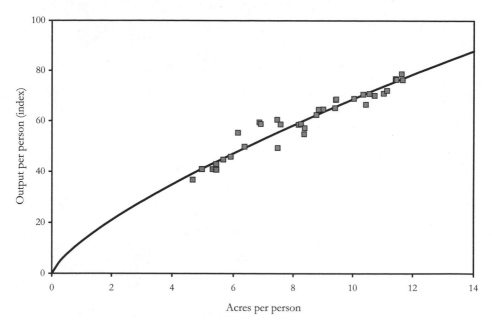

Figure 7.3 Output per person versus land per person in England, 1240s–1590s.

the 1590s. Also shown is the single production function that best fits these data. The static nature of the technology over these years is well illustrated by how well this single curve fits all these observations.

If we can represent aggregate technological advance in this way, as the upward shift in the production function, then measuring technological advance over long periods using population data becomes easy.

Let N be population and g_N the population growth rate. If c is the share of land rents in income in preindustrial society, then

$$g_N = \left(\frac{1}{c}\right) g_A.$$

The detailed derivation of this relationship is provided in the technical appendix.

This simple formula says, for example, that if the share of land rents in income was one-fifth, then a 1 percent improvement in the technology will increase population by 5 percent. To use this formula to measure the rate of preindustrial technological advance all we need is some estimate of the share of land rents in all sources of income and of the rate of population growth.

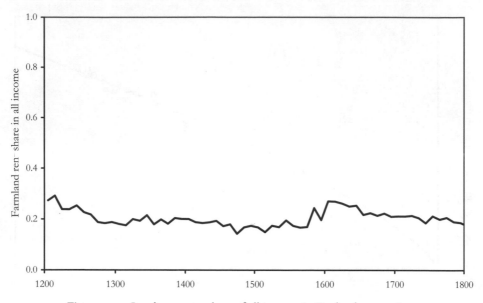

Figure 7.4   Land rents as a share of all income in England, 1200–1800.

Preindustrial England again supplies estimates of the share of land rents in national income all the way from 1200 to 1800. Figure 7.4 shows this share by decade. Though the share varied somewhat it was remarkably stable over time at an average of 20 percent of income. The constancy of the share of rent in all income allows us to infer simply how much technological progress would change the population. (To be precise, the production function is Cobb-Douglass.)

In preindustrial England the rent share in agriculture (as opposed to the economy as a whole) was 30–40 percent.[8] In comparison in Sichuan, China, in the eighteenth century sharecroppers paid 50 percent of farm output as rent.[9] Evidence from Babylonia in the time of Hammurabi (1792–50 BC) suggests a share of one-third for farmland rents.[10] So the share of land rents in national income could vary between 0.2 and 0.4, taking into account that farm output was 60–80 percent of all output. But for our purposes the exact number hazarded makes little difference in estimating the rate of preindustrial technological advance.

8. Clark, 2007b.
9. Zelin, 1986, 518.
10. Harris, 1968, 728.

Table 7.1 Population and Technological Advance, 130,000 BC to AD 1800

Year	Population (millions)	Population growth rate (%)	Technology growth rate (%)
130,000 BC	0.1	—	—
10,000 BC	7	0.004	0.001
AD 1	300	0.038	0.009
AD 1000	310	0.003	0.001
AD 1250	400	0.102	0.025
AD 1500	490	0.081	0.020
AD 1750	770	0.181	0.045

Source: Durand, 1977, 285.
Note: The estimate for 130,000 BC was made based on the idea that the range of animals man could hunt expanded greatly in this era. See Stiner, 2001, 2005.

What is the history of world population up until 1800? The second column of table 7.1 shows rough estimates of world population from 130,000 BC, when anatomically modern humans first appeared, to 1750. There is huge error in these estimates. For example, the population in 10,000 BC before the onset of the Neolithic Revolution is estimated using the observed densities of modern foraging populations. We know from archaeological evidence that in the years leading up to the Neolithic Revolution humans were steadily expanding the range of foods they consumed from hunting and foraging, allowing for greater population densities.[11] In the table I guess at a population of 100,000 people in 130,000 BC, but the time scale is so long here that the exact number matters little.

The last two columns of table 7.1 show the implied rate of population growth, and the implied rate of technological advance according to the formula above, with the assumption that land rents constituted a quarter of all income before 1800.[12] The low rate of technological advance before 1750 is

11. See Stiner, 2001, 2005.
12. The crudeness of these estimates is illustrated by the fact that there is tremendous uncertainty about even the population of Italy in AD 14. Estimates of seven million and seventeen million both have supporters. See Brunt, 1971.

immediately apparent. Since the Industrial Revolution rates of technological progress for successful economies have typically been 1 percent or greater. For the preindustrial era, at the world scale, rates of technological advance over long periods never exceeded even 0.05 percent per year. At a rate of 0.05 percent the production possibilities curve, shown in figure 7.2, shifts upward by 5 percent every hundred years. Thus the Industrial Revolution was an abrupt shift in the character of the economy, represented in the first instance by the rate of technological advance seemingly shifting abruptly upward.

Another suggestion that emerges from the table is that within the Malthusian era the rate of technological advance increased over time. The Malthusian era was not completely static, and indeed it showed signs of greater dynamism as it approached its end. But even at these higher rates of technological change, things happened very slowly. In the 1,750 years between the birth of Christ and the eve of the Industrial Revolution the technology improved by a total of 24 percent, based on these population estimates. That is, on aggregate economies in 1750 produced only 24 percent more output per acre of land, at a given level of people per acre, than in AD 1. That was why the world was trapped in the Malthusian era for so long.

The Locus of Technological Advance

Just as we can use population densities to measure roughly the rate of technological advance before 1800, we can also use them to measure which societies had the most advanced production technologies. Figures 7.5 and 7.6 give the numbers of people per square mile of farmland in the various regions of the world circa 1500 and 1800. Four regions show up as having high populations per acre: central Europe, the Middle East, India, and East Asia, particularly Korea and Japan. Though population densities had increased everywhere by 1800, as the result of technological advance, the world shows a very similar pattern of densities. As in the modern era a large share of world population is found in Europe, India, and East Asia.

In particular, there is little sign of any great difference in the implied technological sophistication of Europe and either the Indian subcontinent or East Asia on the eve of the Industrial Revolution. If living standards were the same across these societies than there is nothing that would highlight Europe in 1800 as having a more advanced technology than any number of eastern societies, including China, India, Korea, and Japan.

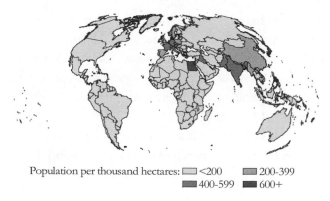

Population per thousand hectares: □ <200   ▨ 200-399
■ 400-599 ■ 600+

Figure 7.5 World population densities, circa 1500. The figure is drawn using the admittedly wildly speculative numbers of McEvedy and Jones, 1978, for population. Farmland areas are those for modern times as reported by the Food and Agriculture Organization (FAO).

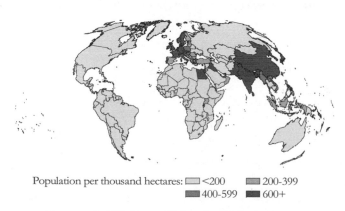

Population per thousand hectares: □ <200   ▨ 200-399
■ 400-599 ■ 600+

Figure 7.6 World population densities, circa 1800.

The population density figures show aggregate population densities for large areas. If we concentrate on smaller regions and subregions, such as the Yangzi Delta in China, population densities circa 1800 were dramatic by European standards. In 1801 England, then just moderately densely populated by European standards, had 166 people per square mile. In contrast Japan as a whole was supporting about 226 people per square mile from 1721 to 1846, and the coastal regions of China attained even higher population densities: Jiangsu in 1787 had an incredible 875 people per square mile. It may be objected that these densities were based on paddy rice cultivation, an option not open to most of Europe. But even in the wheat regions of Shantung and Hopei Chinese population densities in 1787 were more than double those of England and France. Thus in terms of the major production activity of these societies, agriculture, if there was any technological advantage in 1800 it likely lay with the coastal regions of East Asia.

However, as we saw, at least in the cases of India, China, and Japan there are indications that material living standards were far behind those in England, and indeed were likely lower than those of most Malthusian economies.

Technological Regression

Before 1800 there were also long periods in which technology either showed no advance at all or even regressed. Australian Aboriginals, for example, are believed to have arrived in that country between forty and sixty thousand years ago, long before people first arrived in the Americas. But technology seemingly remained frozen on the Australian continent throughout the long period up to the arrival of British colonizers in 1788, judging by the technology of the Aboriginals at first contact.

Furthermore, there are signs of actual technological regression. The Aboriginals are presumed to have reached Australia by sea. Yet by 1788 they no longer had seaworthy craft in most of Australia. In Tasmania, where a community of about 5,000 Aboriginals was cut off from the mainland by rising sea levels for about twelve thousand years, the technological regression was even more dramatic. When encountered by Europeans in the late eighteenth century, the Tasmanians had a material culture at the level of the early Paleolithic, more primitive than that with which they had been endowed by their ancestors. Despite the cold they had no clothing, not even animal skins. They had no bone tools, and no ability to catch the fish abounding in the sea around them. Yet archaeological evidence shows that they had once had such bone tools, and that fish was once an important part of their diet. The gap between their technology and that of the English in 1800 was, as illustrated above, reflected in the respective population densities of the societies. Tasmania, about half the area of England, had an estimated five thousand inhabitants at a time when England had eight million.[13]

13. Jones, 1977, 1978.

The statues of Easter Island similarly pay mute testimony to a technological and organizational ability that the inhabitants had once had but no longer possessed by the time of European contact. The inhabitants of Hawaii had arrived there by sea voyages they were no longer capable of undertaking. Allegedly they had lost the knowledge of where they had come from and so were surprised to find that any other people existed in the world.[14]

In Artic Canada the Inuit, on first contact in the nineteenth century, had a material culture considerably less complex than that of their ancestors the Thule of five centuries before. The Thule were able to hunt large sea mammals in open water, and they wintered in permanent houses that were stocked with ingenious and elegant artifacts, including games and children's toys, harpoons, boats, and dogsleds. Sometime between the sixteenth and eighteenth centuries the Inuit lost much of their material culture. Hunting of sea mammals in open water disappeared, or was restricted to smaller species. Winter was now spent in transient snow-houses, since the Inuit were unable to procure sufficient food supplies to winter in one location. Artifacts were simpler, and decorated or ornamental objects were produced in only a few areas. So marked was this difference that it took archaeologists a long time to accept that the Inuit were indeed the descendants of the Thule.[15]

It is even claimed that China, which led the world in technological sophistication as late as 1400, also went into a technological decline. When Marco Polo visited China in the 1290s he found that the Chinese were far ahead of the Europeans in technical prowess. Their oceangoing junks, for example, were larger and stronger than European ships. In them the Chinese sailed as far as Africa. The Portuguese, after a century of struggle, reached Calicut, India, in the person of Vasco da Gama in 1498 with four ships of 70–300 tons and perhaps 170 men. There they found they had been preceded years before by Zheng He, whose fleet may have had as many as three hundred ships and 28,000 men.[16] Yet by the time the Portuguese reached China in 1514, the Chinese had lost the ability to build large oceangoing ships.

Similarly Marco Polo had been impressed and surprised by the deep coal mines of China. Yet by the nineteenth century Chinese coal mines were

14. The Hawaiians thus regarded Cook on first encounter as one of their gods; Beaglehole, 1974, 649–60.
15. McGhee, 1994.
16. Finlay, 1992, 225–26.

primitive shallow affairs which relied completely on manual power. By the eleventh century AD the Chinese measured time accurately using water clocks, yet when the Jesuits arrived in China in the 1580s they found only the most primitive methods of time measurement in use, and amazed the Chinese by showing them mechanical clocks. The decline in technological abilities in China was not caused by any catastrophic social turmoil. Indeed in the period after 1400 China continued to expand by colonizing in the south, the population grew, and there was increased commercialization.[17]

Why Was Technological Advance So Slow before 1800?

This is one of the great puzzles of world history, in the light of what came after 1800. What makes it so puzzling in part is that preindustrial societies differed from each other in every conceivable way socially and institutionally. Christian Europe had a horror of incest. In Roman Egypt the preferred marriage partner was a sibling. Christian Europe embraced alcohol with fervor and relish, and in good times its people consumed enormous quantities. The Muslim world abhorred it. Animal flesh was eaten with gusto in Europe. In Hindu India all but the sinful and debased avoided it. The Europeans in turn were horrified by the Aztec practice of eating the flesh of dead enemies.

Yet despite the bewildering variety of cultures and institutions, all these societies had one thing in common: the production technology improved very slowly. Indeed there were periods of regression as well as advance. But in general the drift was inexorably upward, so that cumulatively, over millennia, enormous advances occurred. A growing world population was a powerful and direct testament to these changes, as much as the written and archaeological remains of machines and devices.

But why was a society like England able to achieve modern rates of technological advance only after so many millennia? We will not address this puzzle fully until we discuss the Industrial Revolution itself. There is a common misapprehension that must be corrected first—that before 1800 the institutional framework of societies removed all incentive for people to invest in better technology.

17. Mokyr, 1990.

8   Institutions and Growth

*Give a man the secure possession of a bleak rock, and he will turn it into a gar-
den. . . . The magic of* PROPERTY *turns sand to gold.*

—Arthur Young (1787)[1]

The popular misconception of the preindustrial world is of a cowering mass
of peasants ruled by a small, violent, and stupid upper class that extracted
from them all surplus beyond what was needed for subsistence and so gave no
incentives for trade, investment, or improvement in technology. These exclu-
sive and moronic ruling classes were aided in their suppression of all enterprise and innovation by organized religions of stultifying orthodoxy, which
punished all deviation from established practices as heretical. The trial and
condemnation of Galileo Galilei by the Holy Inquisition in 1633, for defending the Copernican view that the earth revolved around the sun (figure 8.1),
seems an exemplar of the reign of superstition and prejudice that was responsible for the long Malthusian night.

There may have been societies before 1800 that fit this popular stereotype.
There were frequent attempts by religious authorities to impose fallacious
dogmas about the natural world. But we shall see that, as an explanation of
the slow technological advance of the world as a whole before 1800, the prevailing view makes no sense. It is maintained only by a contemporary variety
of dogmatism—that of modern economics and its priestly cast.

The central vision of modern economics, the key message of Adam Smith
in 1776 and of his followers, is that people are the same everywhere in their
material preferences and aspirations. They behave differently only because of
differences in incentives. Given the right incentives—low tax rates on earnings,

1. Young, 1792, July 30, 1787, and November 7, 1787.

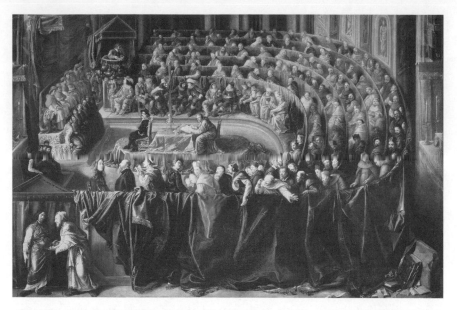

Figure 8.1 The trial of Galileo before the Inquisition, 1633, as portrayed in an anonymous seventeenth-century painting.

security of property and of the person, free markets in goods and labor—growth is guaranteed. The long Malthusian night persisted because of the inability of all societies before 1800 to create such institutions.

This vision of progress permeates the potted history of the world contained in the *Wealth of Nations* of 1776. Smith repeatedly explains the poor economic performance of the preindustrial world as a consequence of institutions that offered poor incentives. His vision permeates contemporary economics, from the practical councils of the International Monetary Fund and the World Bank to the theorists of university economics departments. The so-called *Washington Consensus* of the 1990s on the institutional prerequisites for growth in underdeveloped economies was an elaboration of the Smithian program, one that could have been penned by the master himself. It called for limited taxes and spending, low tax rates, private enterprise wherever possible, liberalized goods and capital markets, and security of property.

In economic history as well, the Smithian vision is the dominant intellectual tradition. Indeed much of modern quantitative economic history has been a search for empirical confirmation of his vision of growth. These empirical studies of past societies, however, rather than confirming Smith's hypothesis, systematically find that many early societies had all the prerequisites for economic growth, but no technological advance and hence no growth. While all societies before 1800 displayed slow rates of technological advance, some had institutions as favorable to economic growth as any the current World Bank could wish for.

Economic historians thus inhabit a strange netherworld. Their days are devoted to proving a vision of progress that all serious empirical studies in the field contradict. Trapped in this ever-tightening intellectual death spiral, they can maintain the vision only though a strange intellectual dissonance, appealing to more and more elaborate conceptions of how early institutions could unwittingly have provided poor incentives.[2]

We shall see below that private property institutions do play an important role in the escape from the Malthusian Trap, but only in a much more long-run and indirect fashion. But first we must clarify that there were preindustrial societies that had most, if not all, of the institutional prerequisites for growth hundreds, and probably thousands, of years before the Industrial Revolution.

Medieval England as an Incentivized Society

Medieval England in the years 1200–1500 experienced little or no overall technological advance, as we saw in figure 7.2. Yet medieval England had extraordinary institutional stability. Most individuals enjoyed great security both of their persons and of their property. Markets for goods, labor, capital, and even land were generally free. Indeed if we were to score medieval England using the criteria typically applied by the International Monetary Fund and the World Bank to evaluate the strength of economic incentives, it would rank much higher than all modern high-income economies—including modern England.

Table 8.1 gives a rough scoring of England on these criteria in 1300 and 2000, the details of which are supplied below. For five of the twelve criteria, the medieval economy had better institutions than the modern. For another five they were equivalent. There were only two out of twelve criteria according to which the medieval economy may have been worst.

2. See, for example, Greif, 2006.

Table 8.1 The Incentives of Medieval versus Modern England

Economic desiderata	1300	2000
Low tax rates	Yes	No
Modest social transfers	Yes	No
Stable money	Yes	No
Low public debt	Yes	No
Security of property	Yes	Yes
Security of the person	?	Yes
Social mobility	Yes	Yes
Free goods markets	Yes	Yes
Free labor markets	Yes	Yes
Free capital markets	Yes	Yes
Free land markets	Yes	No
Rewards for knowledge creation	?	Yes

Taxation

Preindustrial societies were generally low-tax societies. England, in particular, was an extremely lightly taxed nation. Figure 8.2 shows all government expenditures, both central and local, by year as a function of GNP from 1285 to 2000.[3] Before the Glorious Revolution of 1688–89, which established the modern constitutional democracy of Britain, government expenditures of all types were extremely modest. In the years 1600–88 these averaged just 2.2 percent of national income. Before the sixteenth century these expenditures were typically less than 1.5 percent of national income.

Before 1689 attempts by the king to increase his take were vigorously resisted. Thus the Poll Tax of 1380—which triggered a brief but widespread rebellion in which the rebels captured London and killed the archbishop of Canterbury and the king's chancellor—was a temporary war tax on all adult

---

3. Expenditures, rather than taxes, are used since the government in the years 1720–1815 resorted to large-scale issue of debt to fund itself. But debt is just deferred taxes and so should have the same disincentive effect.

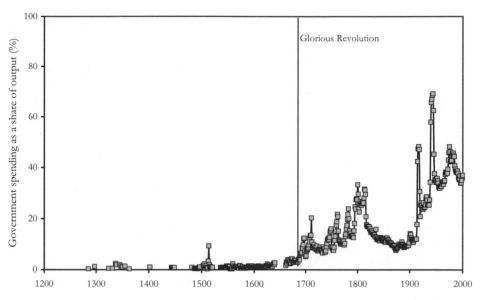

Figure 8.2 Government command of output as a percentage of GNP in England, 1285–2000.

males in England, equivalent to 1 percent of a laborer's annual earnings.[4] After this reaction no English government attempted a poll tax again, until the similarly ill-fated venture of Prime Minister Margaret Thatcher in 1990.

The Glorious Revolution had an immediate negative effect in raising government taxes and expenditures. Expenditures quickly rose to more than 10 percent of output, a level they have exceeded ever since. This spending was almost all for warfare. The share of government expenditures in national income has continued, with fluctuations, to rise to the present day. By the 1990s government expenditures constituted 36 percent of U.K. national income.

Yet the citizens of the United Kingdom are modestly taxed relative to those in other modern, high-income economies. A measure of the tax burden that is more directly geared to the disincentives to work implied in the tax system is the marginal total tax rate: the share of the last dollar in wages taken by the government, counting all forms of taxation including employers' contributions and sales taxes. Table 8.2 shows this rate for the average wage earner in a selection of economies in 2000, arranged in decreasing order of the take. This tax rate varied from 66 percent in Belgium to 32 percent in Japan.

4. The tax was 12 pence, about three times a farm laborer's day wage.

Table 8.2 Taxes and Government Spending by Country

Country	Marginal tax rate, 2000 (%)	Social spending as percentage of GNP, 1995	Hours of market employment per adult, 2000
Belgium	66	32	954
Germany	65	29	1,010
France	56	33	1,003
Italy	55	28	1,159
Ireland	53	23	1,240
Netherlands	51	30	1,037
Sweden	49	40	1,189
Denmark	49	37	1,220
Spain	46	25	1,146
United Kingdom	41	27	1,245
United States	34	19	1,364
Japan	32	16	1,312

Sources: Social spending from Lindert, 2004, 177–78, 236–37. Marginal tax rates from Organisation for Economic Co-operation and Development, Tax Database. Hours worked and population aged 20–64 from Organisation for Economic Co-operation and Development, Productivity Database.

Most of the money collected in taxes is used either to provide goods and services available to all, regardless of their income, or for transfers to those with low earnings.[5] The publicly provided common goods include complete or partial support for highways, law and order, defense, child care, education, health care, and the component of old age pensions not indexed to earnings. The third column of table 8.2 shows such social spending as a share of GDP in the same economies in 1995.

A system of high taxes on economic activity, combined with generous provision of income and services independent of effort, is precisely what the Washington Consensus would fear as a barrier to effort and initiative. The rational, self-interested individuals of the Smithian conception, facing such high marginal tax rates, should have produced significant declines in work hours. Indeed, based on the Smithian conception, it is not clear why economic

---

5. Some of the taxes on wages do fund pensions that are dependent in size on the earnings of the recipient, but this is less common.

Figure 8.3   Inland Revenue inquiry center, Mill Hill, London.

activity has not completely ground to a halt. The taxation systems of preindustrial economies like medieval England—which typically returned none of the income collected to consumers in the form of social services or transfers—should have discouraged individual initiative to a lesser extent than modern tax and transfer schemes.[6] Modern Europe may have no equivalent of the Inquisition, such as Galileo faced, yet it does have taxation systems that intrude just as shockingly into the lives of its citizens (figure 8.3).

These data suggest two things: If incentives are the key to growth, then some preindustrial societies like England had better incentives than modern high-income economies. And incentives may be much less important to explaining the level of output in economies than the Smithian vision assumes.

The last column of table 8.2 shows hours worked per person aged 20–64 in the same economies. Figure 8.4 shows how this correlates with the marginal tax rate for a larger group of economies within the Organisation for Economic Co-operation and Development (OECD), in which currently reported marginal tax rates vary between 20 and nearly 80 percent. There is a

6. A government that taxes wages and wastes the gains simply reduces the wages of everyone. But there is little sign within societies that work hours decline when wages are lower. A government that taxes and then redistributes the gains to all, regardless of work input, can eventually tax sufficiently to induce lower work hours.

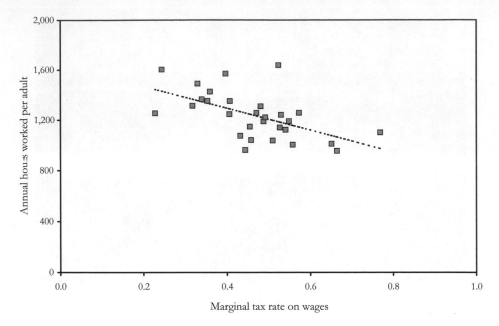

Figure 8.4 Hours worked per person aged 20–64 versus the marginal wage tax rate. Sources as for table 8.2.

negative correlation of hours and tax rates, but the effect is surprisingly modest. Average hours per adult are about 1,400 at a marginal tax rate of 20 percent on wages and 1,000 at a marginal tax rate of 70 percent.[7] In addition the effect on actual hours worked may be much less than on hours reported. High marginal tax rates have the effect of pushing workers into the undocumented "black" economy. The correlation between documented hours and tax rates may just reflect this substitution.[8]

Thus if for this same group of economies we graph marginal tax rates against income per adult, as is done in figure 8.5, we actually find a positive correlation. This has been dubbed by Peter Lindert the "free lunch paradox."[9] Surprisingly there is no evidence that the heavy taxes and transfers of modern states have any effect on output.

7. Edward Prescott, looking at changes over time in hours worked and tax rates, finds a much more significant effect; Prescott, 2004.

8. A recent survey estimated that such economic activity now constitutes as much as 18 percent of output in high-tax European economies. For example, 24–30 percent of Italian GDP was estimated to be produced in this way in 1990–93; Schneider and Enste, 2000, 80.

9. Lindert, 2004.

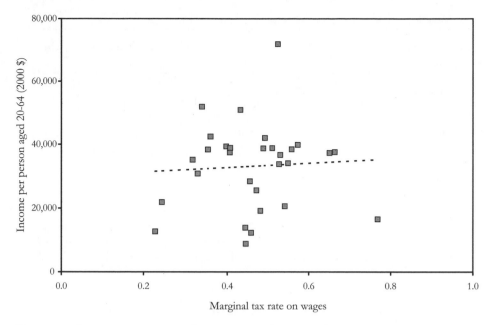

Figure 8.5 Income per person aged 20–64 versus the marginal wage tax rate. Income is GDP given in 2000 dollars in the Penn World Tables.

The expenditure shares for England before 1837 in figure 8.2 report just the activities of governments at various levels. In the preindustrial period in Europe the church was another important extorter of income, in the form of the tithe.

The tithe was theoretically 10 percent of gross output. If it had been collected in full the church would have received as much as 15 percent of the net agricultural income in the years before 1800, since some of the grain output had to be used as seed for the next year. However, the difficulties of collecting the tithe in kind, particularly on animal products, led to tithe owners collecting at a much lower rate. Tithe collections before 1800 averaged only 11 percent of land rents or 4 percent of farm output. So tithe income in preindustrial England was likely less than 4 percent of national income.[10]

Thus even allowing for the additional taxing power of the church, all taxes collected in preindustrial England before the Glorious Revolution were typically less than 6 percent of income.

10. Clark, 2002a.

Table 8.3 Share of Preindustrial Income Collected in Taxes

Country	Period	All taxes (including church) (%)
England	1285–1688	6
	1689–1800	14
China[a]	Ming, ca. 1550	6–8
	Qing, ca. 1650	4–8
	Qing, ca. 1750	8
Ottoman Empire[b]	1500–99	3.5
	1600–99	3.5
	1700–99	4.5

Sources: [a]Feuerwerker, 1984. [b]Pamuk, 2005, graph 1, central government only.

England is typical of other preindustrial societies in which we can estimate the share of taxes in all income. As table 8.3 shows, estimates for late Imperial China and for the Ottoman Empire suggest similarly low tax rates.

One reason why taxes were so light in preindustrial agrarian societies was that the ruling class had a rich source of income without resorting to taxation: land ownership. As figure 7.4 showed for England land rents accounted for about 20 percent of income. In England by 1300 most of the land owned by the ruling class was either leased out to tenants on a commercial basis or held by tenants on fixed-rent leases with hereditary rights.

Price Stability

Money, the use of tokens that carry value, is an institution of great value to any society. The percentage cost of holding a given stock of money per year is the nominal interest rate, which is the real interest rate plus the inflation rate. If you hold an average of $100 in your wallet, the real interest rate is 3 percent, and the inflation rate is 2 percent, then the annual cost of holding money, as opposed to some real asset like land, is $5. This cost leads people to economize on how large a cash balance they hold, and reduces the value of money in facilitating transactions and storing value. As the inflation rate rises the cost of holding cash becomes greater and so the real size of cash balances declines.

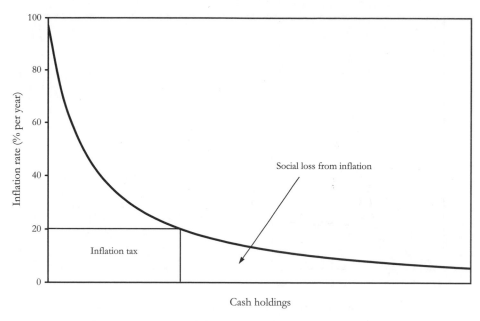

Figure 8.6 Demand for money and social costs of inflation.

Since token monies cost little to create, the optimal inflation rate from a social perspective is always zero or less. That is when money has its maximum value as a medium of exchange and a store of value. However, by printing more money and creating inflation, governments can extract an inflation tax from the economy. Thus from a revenue perspective the government would favor a relatively high level of inflation, to the cost of society as a whole.[11] Figure 8.6 shows the disjuncture between a revenue-maximizing government's incentives and the socially best outcome.

The figure shows the demand curve for cash balances as a function of the annual cost of holding money. The *inflation tax* is the area of the rectangle. When the revenue from this tax is maximized there is substantial inflation. This would create a significant social cost, called the *deadweight loss,* from all the uses of money that are now abandoned because of the cost the government has imposed.

11. If the government maintains an inflation rate of π and r is the real interest rate, then the issue of fiat money generates a revenue for the government per year of $(r + \pi)M$, where M is the real (constant value) money stock. rM is what it would cost per year for the government to borrow an amount M. But when $\pi > 0$, the public also has to acquire πM units of new cash each year to maintain their real cash balances.

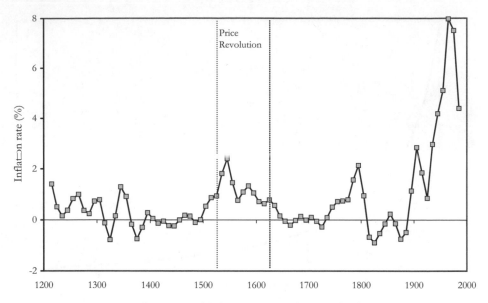

Figure 8.7   Inflation rates by forty-year periods in England, 1200–2000.

Weak modern governments rely heavily on the inflation tax, and many poor countries have been subjected to high inflation rates in recent decades. Inflation rates have also been high in even the richest economies during some periods over the past fifty years. However, in preindustrial England, and indeed in many preindustrial economies, inflation rates were low by modern standards. Figure 8.7 shows the English inflation rate from 1200 to 2000 over successive forty-year intervals. Before 1914 inflation rates rarely exceeded 2 percent per year, even in the period known as the *Price Revolution,* when the influx of silver from the New World helped drive up prices. In a country such as England, which had a highly regarded currency in the preindustrial era, the crown did not avail itself of the inflation tax, despite the close restrictions Parliament placed on its other tax revenues. Only in the twentieth century did significant inflation appear in England. By the late twentieth century annual inflation averaged 4–8 percent per year. Thus there has been a decline, not an improvement, in the quality of monetary management in England since the Industrial Revolution.

Even though there were periods of substantial inflation in some other preindustrial societies, other societies achieved long-run price stability. Thus in Roman Egypt wheat prices roughly doubled between the beginning of the first century AD and the middle of the third.[12] But that reflects an inflation rate of less than 0.3 percent per year.

Public Debt

Another macroeconomic success forced on preindustrial economies by their low tax bases was the general avoidance of extensive public debt. Before the Glorious Revolution English public debt, for example, was minuscule since the government could service with current revenues a debt of, at maximum, less than 10 percent of GDP.

An immediate consequence of the greater taxing power of the government after 1689, however, was an increase in public debt. Figure 8.8 shows the ratio of public debt to GNP for England from 1688 to 2000. The fiscal stresses of the "Second Hundred Years War" with the French saw debt rise by the 1820s to record levels of nearly 2.5 times GNP. Peace and economic growth had reduced the debt relative to GNP by 1914. But the stresses of the wars of the early twentieth century again inflated the debt to 2.5 times GNP by 1950. Since then the debt has declined. But at more than 40 percent of GNP it still substantially exceeds that of England before the Glorious Revolution.

Assuming the public has a limited perception of the level and significance of public debt, it will crowd out private investment, reducing the capital stock, and thus reduce the overall output of societies. An unaware public will not respond when governments finance current expenses with debt, as it would if it were aware and rational, by increasing its savings by the amount of the debt in anticipation of a future greater tax burden. Thus public debt will drive up interest rates and drive out private investments. Jeffrey Williamson, for example, argues that the huge accumulated debt of Britain during the period of the French wars was a major economic policy disaster that substantially slowed growth during the Industrial Revolution.[13]

The average OECD economy now has a public debt of 50–60 percent of GNP—another sign that modern growth has been associated with poorer macroeconomic performance.

12. Duncan-Jones, 1990, 145–55.

13. Williamson, 1984. Since the capital output ratio was typically 4 in the nineteenth century, if the debt of the 1820s reduced private capital on a 1:1 basis, then the capital stock in England would have been half its level in the absence of the public debt.

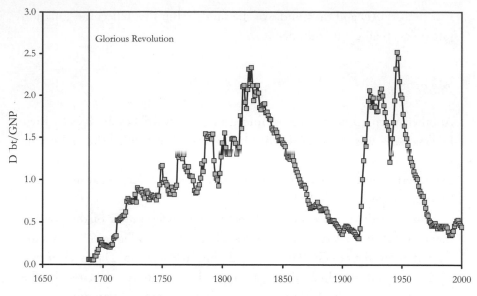

Figure 8.8 Ratio of debt to GNP in England, 1688–2000.

Security of Property

An indicator of the security of property in medieval England, and of the general stability of institutions, is the modest fluctuation in property values over time. Figure 8.9 shows the average real price of farmland per acre in England by decade from 1200 to 1349 relative to the price of farm output.[14] There is remarkably little variation in the real price by decade. Medieval farmland was an asset with little price risk. This implies few periods of disruption and uncertainty within the economy, for such disruption typically leaves its mark on the prices of such assets as land and housing.

In comparison the figure also shows the decadal average of the real price of arable land in the district of Zele, near Ghent, in Flanders from 1550 to 1699, which shows dramatically greater variation. The reason for this is easy to infer from the narrative history of Flanders. In 1581–92 Flanders was the setting for the battle over Dutch independence. Ghent was recaptured from the rebels in 1584 after fierce fighting. Flanders from then was mostly Spanish, but the Dutch continued to raid the countryside until 1607. The fight-

14. The property sales are recorded in the cartularies of religious foundations and private families.

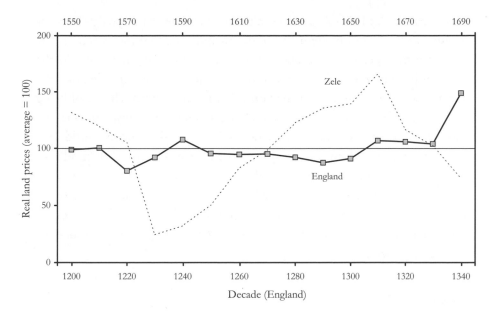

Figure 8.9 Real farmland prices in England, 1200–1349, and in Zele, 1550–1699. Prices for Zele from Clark, 1996.

ing is reflected in the huge depreciation in land values in Zele: by the 1580s they had sunk to less than 20 percent of their level in the 1550s. There was also warfare in Flanders in 1672–97 during the wars of the Dutch and the Habsburgs against Louis XIV. Land values then also declined sharply relative to the peaceful years of the 1660s.

Thus the sometimes turbulent nature of high politics in England in the medieval period—there were armed conflicts between the king and the barons during 1215–19, 1233, 1258–65, and much of 1312–26—had no impact on the average person. At the local level property rights were stable and secure.

Personal Security

A second aspect of the security and stability of medieval England was the comparatively low threat from physical violence, discussed in chapter 6. From the thirteenth century onward, the typical Englishman died in his bed. This was no Hobbesian world of plundered, burning villages strewn with the unburied dead.

In day-to-day life violence rates in the medieval period were high by comparison with those in modern England, but not such that they would interfere with the operation of economic incentives. Even at their worst in the thirteenth century, homicide rates, at 0.2 per thousand, still implied that the average person over his lifetime had only about a 0.7 percent chance of being murdered.[15] By the fourteenth century these rates were down to 0.12 per thousand. Such murder rates are at the high end for the modern world. But most travelers would not be afraid to visit modern societies with similar or higher homicide rates today: Trinidad and Tobago (0.12), Estonia (0.15), the Philippines (0.14), Bahamas (0.15), Mexico (0.16), Puerto Rico (0.21), Brazil (0.23).[16] And, as figure 6.8 shows, most of the decline in homicide rates toward modern levels had occurred by 1550, long before the onset of modern economic growth.

Social Mobility

Property and person might be secure, the objection will be voiced, but in a society in which there was a strict division between the noble class at the top and a mass of undifferentiated servile peasantry at the bottom, this security was that of a stultified social order, not that of an economy pregnant with the possibilities of progress. This is yet another caricature of the preindustrial world. Case after case, study after study, shows that even medieval England was a highly fluid society in which people lived at every possible economic level, from landless wage laborers to wealthy, and in which movement between conditions was frequent.

Taxation records and manorial court rolls reveal from the earliest years enormous income and wealth disparities. Records of the 1297 Subsidy (a tax on movables), for example, suggest huge variations in wealth, even above the minimum value of possessions (about a quarter of the annual wage of a laborer) that made households liable to the tax.[17]

Even at the lowest level, the laborers and peasants, there was an active land market from at least the early thirteenth century, which transferred even

15. Since people lived on average 35 years, and had a 0.00021 chance of being murdered in each year, 0.7 out of every 100 were murdered over their lifetimes.

16. World Health Organization, 2002, table A.7. Rates are for the latest available year in the 1990s.

17. Biddick, 1987.

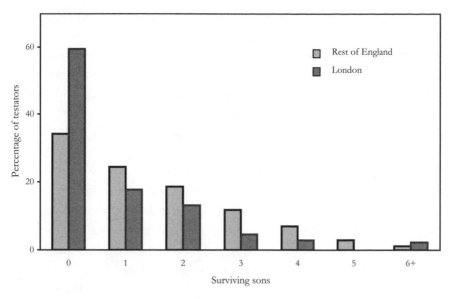

Figure 8.10 Sons per male testator in England, circa 1620.

land notionally held by nonfree tenants to unrelated individuals. Thus peasants or even laborers who were energetic and frugal could accumulate land and
move up the rural social hierarchy. This fact shows up, even from the earliest
years, in the great inequalities in landholdings. A survey of the royal manor
of Havering in 1251, for example, reveals that, while four tenants held more
than 200 acres of land each, forty-one held less than an acre and forty-six held
between 1 and 3 acres.[18]

Another factor responsible for the great social mobility and fluidity in
Malthusian societies like medieval England was the accidents of demography.
Figure 8.10 illustrates the distribution of the numbers of surviving sons for
male testators in England, both outside London and in London itself, from
the wills discussed in chapter 6. The distributions shown here would have
been characteristic for the whole Malthusian era. Outside London one-third
of males leaving wills had no surviving son, while 11 percent had four or more.
Few fathers had just one son to whom all their property and position de-
volved. Instead collateral inheritance was frequent, as were cases in which, to
retain their social position, the sons of larger families would have to accumulate

18. MacIntosh, 1980.

property on their own. This meant that accidents of birth and inheritance were constantly moving people up and down the social ladder.

The data also illustrate the well-known fact that in the preindustrial era cities such as London were deadly places in which the population could not reproduce itself and had to be constantly replenished by rural migrants. Nearly 60 percent of London testators left no son. Thus the craft, merchant, legal, and administrative classes of London were constantly restocked by socially mobile recruits from the countryside.

Medieval England may have been a static society economically. But the overall stasis should not blind us to the churning dynamism of the social fabric, with individuals headed up and down the social scale, sometimes to an extraordinary extent. A substantial fraction of the landed aristocracy of England, even in the medieval period, actually had its foundation not in long aristocratic lineage or in military success, but in successful merchants and lawyers who from the twelfth century onward were using their profits to buy land and enter the aristocracy.[19] High church positions were even more open to the lower orders. In the medieval period only 27 percent of English bishops, the clerical aristocracy, came from the nobility. The rest were the sons of lesser gentry, farmers, or merchants and tradesmen.[20]

The social fluidity of medieval England was probably more the norm, rather than an exception, for the Malthusian era. Thus in Ming and Qing China, all the way from 1371 to 1904, commoners typically accounted for 40 percent or more of those recruited by way of examination into the highest levels of the imperial bureaucracy. And in China those with money, at least from the 1450s onward, could alternatively buy official ranks and titles.[21] In *ancien régime* France the ranks of the nobility were similarly stocked from financially successful merchants and government officers from earlier generations.[22]

Markets

Markets in medieval England were relatively complete and competitive. Labor, for example, was not immobile and fixed to the land or traditional occupa-

19. Wasson, 1998.
20. Chibi, 1998, table 1.
21. Ho, 1959.
22. Kalas, 1996. However, Japan's samurai class in the Tokugawa era (1603–1868) does seem to have been a closed elite; Moore, 1970.

tions. Medieval Europe in general had a surprising degree of geographic mobility. Given the low reproductive success of the urban population there had to be a constant flow of labor from the country to the city. Thus the records of a 1292 tax levied by Philip the Fair on the commoner households of Paris show that 6 percent were foreigners: 2.1 percent English, 1.4 percent Italian, 0.8 percent German, 0.7 percent Flemish, 0.6 percent Jewish, and 0.4 percent Scottish.[23] A poll tax levied on aliens in England in 1440 revealed about 1,400–1,500 non-naturalized alien males in London at a time when the total adult male population of the city would be only about 15,000: nearly 10 percent of the population.[24]

Goods markets were similarly open. The grain trade in medieval London was so well developed that private granary space was available for hire by the week.[25] From 1211 onward local yields had no effect on the prices at which manors sold wheat. The national price was the only thing that mattered in predicting local prices.[26]

The earliest surviving records of transactions in property from the twelfth century already show an active land and house market. Manorial court records, which survive in quantity from the 1260s, also reveal a very active land market among the peasantry, trading small pieces of farmland back and forth between families.[27] The land market was certainly much less restricted than in modern England, where the decisions of planning authorities can change the value of an acre of land by millions of dollars.

Intellectual Property Rights

The one area of property rights in which medieval England may have been lacking compared to the modern world was intellectual property rights. In most early societies innovators had relatively poorly defined rights. Such societies lacked the legal notion that one could own property in ideas or innovations. Thus in both the Roman and Greek worlds, when an author published a

---

23. Sussman, 2005, 18, 20.

24. Thrupp, 1957, 271. This assumes a total population for London of 50,000. The tax lists show few merchants, suggesting that the tax was targeted only to artisans and laborers.

25. Campbell et al., 1993, 101–3.

26. Clark, 2001a.

27. This is one of the reasons Alan Macfarlane, 1978, famously argued that by the Middle Ages England was no longer a peasant society.

book there was no legal or practical way to stop the pirating of the text. Copies could be freely made by anyone who acquired a version of the manuscript, and the copier could amend and alter the text at will. It was not uncommon for a text to be reissued under the name of a new "author."[28] Such pirating of works or ideas was frequently condemned as immoral, but writings and inventions were simply not viewed as commodities with a market value of their own.[29] There was no equivalent to the modern patent system before its introduction in Venice some time before 1416.

But institutions, as we shall see, often respond to economic circumstances rather than determine them. Societies with very low rates of technological innovation, such as those in most of the preindustrial world, would feel little need to establish institutions protecting the property rights of innovators. The establishment of institutions such as patent rights in northern Europe in the sixteenth century arose from the desire of countries to attract foreign artisans with specialized production knowledge. These workers would not emigrate without legal guarantees that their knowledge would be protected.

Other institutions that should have promoted innovation existed in societies like medieval England. Producers in many towns were organized into guilds that represented the interests of the trade. These guilds could tax members to facilitate lump-sum payments to innovators as an incentive to explain productive new techniques to the members. They also fostered competitions (based more on pride and status than on monetary rewards) between members to demonstrate new techniques.[30]

As long as we can find examples of Malthusian societies, like medieval England, which were fully incentivized yet witnessed only the glacially slow preindustrial pace of technological advance, then formal institutions cannot be the cause of the long Malthusian era in the simple way that most economists routinely imagine. If formal institutions are the key, it must be because somehow Malthusian economies provided little or no specific incentive for technological advance. But we shall see later when we come to study the Industrial Revolution itself that, while innovation lay at its core, the transition to higher rates of advance in efficiency was accomplished before there was any

28. This problem persisted into at least the seventeenth century in England, where publishers freely pirated the works of authors.

29. Long, 1991, 853–57.

30. Epstein, 1998.

significant improvement in incentives to innovate. Thus there must have been informal, self-reinforcing social norms in all preindustrial societies that discouraged innovation.

The next chapter explores why these norms might have been present in all preindustrial societies, but were loosened over time by the formative power of Malthusian mechanisms on the culture, and perhaps even the genetic makeup, of long-established agrarian societies.

9   The Emergence of Modern Man

We see, therefore, how the modern bourgeoisie is itself the product of a long course of development, of a series of revolutions in the modes of production and of exchange.
                                                    —Karl Marx and Friedrich Engels (1848)[1]

The Malthusian era was one of astonishing stasis, in terms of living standards and of the rate of technological change. It was thus an economy in which we would expect that only one economic feature, land rents, would change across the ages. Wages, returns on capital, the capital stock per person, hours of work per person, skill premiums—all should have remained the same on average from the dawn of market economies to the end of the Malthusian era. This only reinforces the puzzle of how the economy ever escaped the Malthusian Trap. How did stasis before 1800 transform itself into dynamism thereafter?

The era's static living standards have been amply proven by the empirical evidence cited in previous chapters, as has the slow aggregate rate of efficiency advance. Yet there were, despite this evidence, profound changes in basic features of the economy within the Malthusian era. Four in particular stand out. Interest rates fell from astonishingly high rates in the earliest societies to close to low modern levels by 1800. Literacy and numeracy went from a rarity to the norm. Work hours rose from the hunter-gatherer era to modern levels by 1800. Finally there was a decline in interpersonal violence. As a whole these changes show societies becoming increasingly *middle class* in their orientation. Thrift, prudence, negotiation, and hard work were becoming values for communities that previously had been spendthrift, impulsive, violent, and leisure loving.

1. Marx and Engels, 1967, 81.

A plausible source of this apparent evolution of human preferences is the survival of the richest that is evident in preindustrial England. The arrival of institutionally stable agrarian economies with the Neolithic agricultural revolution of 6000–7000 BC gradually molded human behavior, probably culturally but also potentially genetically.[2] Evidence from animal populations shows that, in cases in which a trait has previously been neutral in terms of survival, so that it exists in varying frequencies in populations, strong selective pressures can change the characteristics of the population within a few generations.[3]

The people of the settled agrarian economies who launched the Industrial Revolution around 1800, though they lived no better than their grandfathers of the Paleolithic, were systematically different in attitudes and abilities. The exact date and trigger of the Industrial Revolution may remain a mystery, but its probability was increasing over time in the environment of institutionally stable Malthusian economies. Technology, institutions, and people were interacting in an elaborate dance in the long eight- to ten-thousand-year preindustrial agrarian era.

Interest Rates

One of the most profound prices in any economy, along with land rents and wage rates, is the interest rate for the use of capital. Capital, the stored-up output that is used to aid current production, exists in all economies. Its principal form in the settled agrarian economies that preceded the Industrial Revolution was housing and land improvements. But another important element in temperate regions was the stored-up fertility of the land, which constituted a bank that farmers could make deposits into and withdrawals from depending on the urgency of their needs. There was thus as much capital per unit of output in medieval Europe, India, or China as there is in modern economies.

Because capital allows for the production of more output when combined with labor and land, it commands a rent just like land, and that rent, when

2. Galor and Moav, 2002, construct a theoretical model of such a process.
3. I owe this point to Oded Galor. Recent experiments in domesticating foxes and rats, for example, suggest that, with sufficiently strong selection, powerful changes can be made in the behavior of animals within as few as eight generations; Trut, 1999.

we measure it as percentage return on the value of the capital, we call the *interest rate* or the *return on capital*. The real interest rate is simply the number of dollars of rent the lender of a $100 worth of capital will receive each year, net of allowances for the depreciation of the value of the capital from physical decay or from loss of value through inflation in the case of financial capital. Such implicit interest rates can be measured in any society in which land or housing is both sold and rented.

Measuring real interest rates is not easy in the modern world of relatively high and variable inflation rates and rapidly changing asset prices. But rapid inflation, as we saw for the case of England, is a modern problem generally absent from the Malthusian era. So typically in England the nominal return on assets, the annual payment to the owner divided by the price, provided a good measure of the real return on capital before 1800. For England we have two measures of the rate of return that stretch back with relatively few interruptions from the modern era to 1200. The first is the return on ownership of farmland, the major asset before 1800. The second is the return on *rent charges*. Rent charges were perpetual fixed nominal obligations secured by land or houses. The ratio of the sum paid per year to the price of such a rent charge gives the interest rate for another very-low-risk asset, since the charge was typically much less than the rental value of the land or house.

Both of these returns have an additional attraction as a measure of return on capital for the preindustrial era in Europe: they were each excused from any taint of usury under Catholic doctrine. Since land and houses were productive assets it was not considered usurious to collect a return on the ownership of them, and there were no limitations on the amount of this return. Such an exemption was fortunate, since all across medieval Europe the church was the greatest owner of land and rent charges.

Figure 9.1 shows the percentage return on farmland and rent charges by decade in England from 1170 to 2003. Medieval England had real rates of return typically 10 percent or greater. By the eve of the Industrial Revolution rates of return had fallen to 4–5 percent.

The rates of return for medieval England were in fact typical of Europe in this period. Table 9.1 shows the returns on land purchases and rent charges for other areas in Europe between 1200 and 1349. There is surprisingly little variation across the different countries. The decline in interest rates in England was also echoed across the rest of Europe. Rates of return by 1600

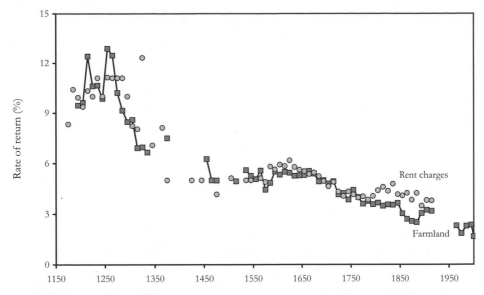

Figure 9.1 Return on land and on rent charges by decade in England, 1170–2003. For the years before 1350 the land returns are the moving average of three decades because in these early years this measure is noisy.

had fallen from these medieval levels in Genoa, the Netherlands, Germany, and Flanders.[4]

All societies before 1400 for which we have sufficient evidence to calculate interest rates show high rates by modern standards.[5] In ancient Greece loans secured by real estate generated returns of close to 10 percent on average all the way from the fifth century to the second century BC. The temple of Delos, which received a steady inflow of funds in offerings, invested them at a standard 10 percent mortgage rate throughout this period.[6] Land in Roman Egypt in the first three centuries AD produced a typical return of 9–10 percent. Loans secured by land typically earned an even higher return of 12 percent.[7]

4. De Wever, 1978; Clark, 1988; Cipolla, 1993, 216–17; de Vries and van der Woude, 1997, 113–29.

5. Hudson, 2000.

6. Compound interest was not charged, so since some of the loans ran for a number of years the actual rate charged was somewhat lower than 10 percent. See Larsen, 1938, 368–79.

7. Calculated from the ratio of rents to land sale prices given in Johnson, 1936, 83–173, using wheat prices from Duncan-Jones, 1990, 146.

Table 9.1 Rate of Return on Capital across
Europe, 1200–1349

Country	Land	Rent charges
England[a]	10.0	9.5
Flanders[a]	—	10.0
France[a]	11.0	—
Germany[a]	10.2	10.7
Italy[b]	10.1	10.7

Sources: [a]Clark, 1988, table 3. [b]Herlihy, 1967, 123,
134, 138, 153 (Pistoia).

Medieval India had similarly high interest rates. Hindu law books of the
first to ninth centuries AD allow interest of 15 percent of the face amount of
loans secured by pledges of property, and 24–30 percent of loans with only
personal security. Inscriptions recording perpetual temple endowments from
the tenth century AD in southern India show a typical income yield of 15 percent of the investment.[8] The return on these temple investments in southern
India was still at least 10 percent in 1535–47, much higher than European interest rates by this time. At Tirupati Temple at the time of the Vijayanagar
Empire the temple invested in irrigation improvements at a 10 percent return
to the object of the donor. But since the temple only collected 63 percent on
average of the rent of the irrigated land, the social return from these investments was as high as 16 percent.[9]

While the rates quoted above are high, those quoted for earlier agrarian
economies are even higher. In Sumer, the precursor to ancient Babylonia,
between 3000 and 1900 BC rates of interest on loans of silver (as opposed to
grain) were 20–25 percent. In Babylonia between 1900 and 732 BC the normal rates of return on loans of silver were 10–25 percent.[10] In the sixth century BC the average rate on a sample of loans in Babylonia was 16–20 percent,
even though these loans were typically secured by houses and other property.
In the Ottoman Empire in the sixteenth century debt cases brought to court
revealed interest rates of 10–20 percent.[11]

8. Sharma, 1965, 59–61.
9. Stein, 1960, 167–69.
10. Homer and Sylla, 1996, 30–31.
11. Pamuk, 2006, 7.

When we consider forager societies the evidence on rates of return becomes much more indirect. There is no explicit capital market, and lending may be subject to substantial default risks given the lack of fixed assets with which to secure loans. However, one important element underlying the existence of interest rates in any society is a behavior called *time preference*. Time preference is simply the idea that, everything else being equal, people prefer to consume now rather than later. The *time preference rate* measures the strength of this preference. It is the percentage by which the amount of consumption of a good next year must be higher than consumption this year for people to be indifferent between consuming now or later.

Time preference rates are very high in young children and decline as they age. Experiments suggest that American 6-year-olds have time preference rates on the order of 3 percent per day. That is, they will delay collecting a reward only if they are offered the equivalent of an interest rate of at least 3 percent per day, or a monthly interest rate of 150 percent.[12] Time preference rates also vary across people within a society. They are higher among the poor and less educated. Children with high time preference rates in preschool in California did less well academically later and had lower SAT scores.[13]

Anthropologists have devised ways to measure time preference rates in premarket societies. They look, for example, at the relative rewards of activities whose benefits occur at different times in the future: digging up wild tubers or fishing with an immediate reward, as opposed to trapping with a reward delayed by days, as opposed to clearing and planting with a reward months in the future, as opposed to animal rearing with a reward years in the future.

A recent study of Mikea forager-farmers in Madagascar found, for example, that the typical Mikea household planted less than half as much land as was needed to feed themselves. Yet the returns from shifting cultivation of maize were enormous. A typical yield was a minimum of 74,000 kilocalories per hour of work. Foraging for tubers, in comparison, yielded an average return of 1,800 kilocalories per hour. Despite this the Mikea rely on foraging for a large share of their food, consequently spending most of their time foraging. This implies extraordinarily high time preference rates.[14] James Woodburn

12. Krause and Harbaugh, 1999, 13.

13. Mischel et al., 1989.

14. Tucker, 2001, 299–338. Maize and manioc cultivation had higher yield variances, and so were riskier than foraging.

claimed that the Hadza of Tanzania showed a similar disinterest in distant benefits: "In harvesting berries, entire branches are often cut from the trees to ease the present problems of picking without regard to future loss of yield."[15] Even the near future mattered little. The Pirahã of Brazil are even more blind to future benefits. Daniel Everett, a linguistic anthropologist who has studied their language and culture for many years, concluded that future events and benefits were of almost no interest to them.[16]

Why Did Interest Rates Decline?

The real rate of return, r, can be thought of as composed of three elements: the time preference rate, ρ, a default risk premium, d, and a premium that reflects the growth of overall expected incomes year to year, ψg_y. Thus

$$r \approx \rho + d + \psi g_y.$$

The existence of time preference in consumption cannot be derived from consideration of rational action. Indeed it has been considered by some economists to represent a systematic deviation of human psychology from rational action, in which there should be no absolute time preference. Economists have thought of time preference rates as being hard-wired into people's psyches and as having stemmed from some very early evolutionary process.[17]

The "growth premium" in interest rates reflects the fact that if all incomes are growing it is harder to persuade people to lend money and defer consumption. Suppose everyone knows that in twenty years their income will have doubled, which has been the case in a number of modern economies. They will all prefer to borrow from the future to enjoy better consumption now, rather than save money when they are poor to spend when they are rich. Only if interest rates rise to high levels can sufficient numbers of people be persuaded to save rather than consume now. Since sustained income growth appeared in the economy only after 1800, the income effect implies an increase in interest rates as we move from the Malthusian to the modern

15. Woodburn, 1980, 101.
16. Everett, 2005.
17. Rogers, 1994, gives an evolutionary argument for why positive time preference would exist, deducing, however, that the time preference rate would always be the 2.5 percent or so observed in high-income modern societies.

economy—an increase which of course we do not observe. We should be the high-interest-rate society, not England in the Malthusian era.

Default risks also cannot explain high early interest rates. The default risk premium, d, reflects the fact that all investment involves some risk that the capital invested will not result in future consumption but will be lost. The loss could come from the death of the investor, although if the investor has altruism toward his or her children this will reduce the compensation needed for this risk. However, the risk of the death of the investor, we know from the evidence presented above on mortality in the Malthusian era, was unchanged over time and thus cannot explain any of the decline in interest rates before 1800.

The extra 6–8 percent return that capital offered in medieval England, if it came from default risks, had to stem from the risk of expropriation of the asset. But in the previous chapter I emphasized that in fact medieval England was a very stable society, and that investments in land in practice carried a very low risk. Confiscation or expropriation was extremely rare, and real land prices were stable over the long run.

The medieval land market offered a practically guaranteed 10 percent or more real rate of return with almost no risk. It was a society in which anyone could significantly change his social position just by saving and investing a modest share of his income. Suppose, for example, that a landless farm worker in thirteenth-century England, at the bottom of the social ladder, were to start at age 15, invest 10 percent of his annual wage earnings in land, and reinvest any rents received. By age 50 he would have accumulated 85 acres to pass on to his children or support them in comfort in their old age, making him among the largest peasant proprietors in most medieval villages.

One other source of risk in purchasing land does exist in any society: the risk that another claimant with a prior title will appear. Was it that the medieval legal system was so imperfect as to make all property purchases highly insecure?

A problem with any such interpretation is that different parts of England in the Middle Ages had very different jurisdictions and legal structures. Sometime before 1200, for example, London had secured from the crown a large set of privileges. The first of these was that the city was allowed to pay a lump sum for taxes to the king, "the farm of the city," and to arrange its own collection within the city of this annual sum. The town was also allowed to appoint its own judges, even in cases before the crown courts, so that Londoners would only ever be judged by Londoners. Land cases were to be settled according to the law of the city, even in the king's courts. Londoners were free from trial by battle, the Norman tradition that resulted in some property cases being determined by armed combat as late as the 1270s.

In the reigns of Richard I and John (1189–1216) the kings' fiscal problems led them to sell off to many other towns rights and privileges similar to those of London. Thus by 1200 or soon thereafter there were a host of local legal jurisdictions in urban areas in England under which property could be held. If the high returns on land and rent charges were the result of deficiencies in property laws and their enforcement, then we would expect some of these jurisdictions to have performed much better than others. In those with the best-defined property rights returns would be lowest. In the sample of rent charge returns I have for the years before 1349 I have enough data on a small group of cities and towns to compare their average rate of return with the national average. The results are shown in table 9.2. There is little difference between rates of return in the six specific locations and the national average. If insecurity in property rights explains high medieval rates of return, different jurisdictions, amazingly, created systems with roughly the same degree of insecurity.

The third problem with an interpretation relying on insecure property rights is that even if property rights were generally insecure in early societies, there would have been periods of greater and lesser security. Thus if the risk of confiscation was the source of high early interest rates we would expect that interest rates would fluctuate from period to period, and would be connected to political developments. Yet not only were average rates of interest very high, they tended to be high and relatively stable over time where they can be measured reasonably well, as with rent charges. Thus in figure 9.1 note that the rate of return on rent charges in the decades from the 1180s to the 1290s all fall within about 1 percent of the average rate of 10.4 percent. If these returns are so high because of the radical insecurity of property, why did they not show any substantial deviations between decades, despite the huge changes in political regimes in this era?

In the thirteenth century, for example, the reigns of John (1199–1216) and Henry III (1216–72) were times of greater turmoil in England. There was open rebellion by the barons in the last years of John's reign and again in the 1260s under Henry III. Edward I (1272–1307) ushered in nearly forty years of stability and strong central government. But his son Edward II (1307–27) was again a weak ruler who was eventually deposed and murdered by his wife

Table 9.2 Rent Charge Returns by Location, 1170–1349

Location	Number of observations	Mean return (%)	Median return (%)
National average	535	11.0	10.1
Canterbury	30	11.8	12.2
Coventry	48	11.4	10.0
London	84	10.3	10.0
Oxford	68	10.2	10.0
Stratford-upon-Avon	8	11.7	12.3
Sudbury	8	11.1	12.3

Note: In calculating the mean returns twenty-one observations implying rates of return below 4 percent or above 25 percent were dropped. The mean for the entire sample without dropping these observations would be 11.5 percent.

and her lover and replaced as ruler by his son. But there is no correspondence between the periods of calm and stability, as under Edward I, and the prevailing interest rate. It is always high before 1300, whatever the politics, but shows signs of declining in the turbulent years 1307–27 (see figure 9.1).

The implied return on investments in land in Zele in Flanders, an area that suffered greatly from war and civil strife in the years 1580–1720, is shown in figure 9.2. These returns again show the influence of the war years, with much higher returns on land purchases in the years 1581–92. But notably, despite the problems of war, the average return on land is only about 4 percent. The Netherlands and Belgium were the first areas in Europe to come close to modern rates of return in the preindustrial era. And even in the worst years of the Spanish reconquest in 1581–92, when many Protestants were fleeing from areas like Zele to the Dutch Republic, the average return on capital invested in land was still below the steady rate of 10 percent found even in the most secure circumstances in medieval Europe.

Literacy and Numeracy

At the same time as we see interest rates decline, there were significant increases in the basic literacy and numeracy of societies as we approach the Industrial

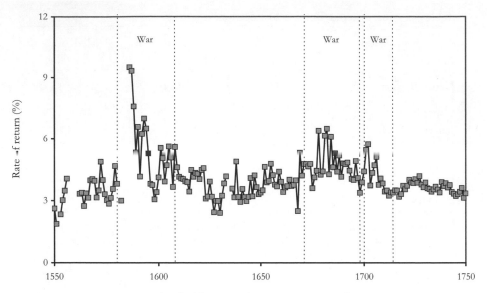

Figure 9.2 Returns on landholding in Zele, 1550–1750. Data from De Wever, 1978.

Revolution. The average numeracy and literacy of even rich people in the classical and medieval eras in Europe was surprisingly poor. Table 9.3, for example, shows five age declarations of a prosperous landowner, Aurelius Isidorus, in Roman Egypt in the third century AD. No two of the declarations are consistent. Clearly Isidorus had no clear idea of his own age. Within two years' time he gives ages that differ by eight years. Other sources show that Isidorus was illiterate.

Isidorus's age declarations show a common pattern for those who are innumerate and illiterate. That is a tendency to round the age to one ending in a 0 or a 5. In populations in which ages are recorded accurately, 20 percent of the recorded ages will end in 5 or 0. We can thus construct a score variable *H*—which measures the degree of "age heaping," where

$$H = \frac{5}{4}(X - 20)$$

and *X* is the percentage of age declarations ending in 5 or 0—to measure the percentage of the population whose real age is unknown. This measure of the percentage of people who did not know their true age correlates moderately well with literacy rates in modern societies.

Table 9.3 Age Reporting by Aurelius Isidorus

Date	Declared age	Implied birth year
April 297	35	262
April 308	37	271
August 308	40	268
Pre-June 309	45	264
June 309	40	269

Source: Duncan-Jones, 1990, 80.

A lack of knowledge of their true age was widespread among the Roman upper classes as evidenced by age declarations made by their survivors on tombstones, which show a high degree of age heaping (table 9.4). Typically half had ages unknown to their survivors. Age awareness did correlate with social class. More than 80 percent of officeholders' ages were known to relatives. When we compare this with death records for modern Europe we find that by the eve of the Industrial Revolution age awareness in the general population had increased markedly. In the eighteenth century in Paris only 15 percent of the general population had unknown ages at the time of death, in Geneva 23 percent, and in Liege 26 percent.[18]

We can also look at the development of age awareness by examining censuses of the living. Some of the earliest of these are for medieval Italy, including the famous Florentine *catasto* of 1427, a wide-ranging survey of wealth for tax purposes. Even though Florence was then one of the richest cities of the world and the center of the Renaissance, 32 percent of the city's population did not know their ages. In comparison a census in 1790 of the small English town of Corfe Castle, with a mere 1,239 inhabitants, most of them laborers, shows that all but 8 percent knew their age. The poor in England around 1800 had more age awareness than office holders in the Roman Empire, as table 9.4 demonstrates.[19]

18. Duncan-Jones, 1990, 90.

19. The exception to this trend is ages recorded in the censuses of Roman Egypt, taken every seven years. Here age heaping is modest, and the age structure is much more plausible than the tombstone ages (or mummy inscription ages in Egypt). But this accuracy may be explained by the census procedures. If children first enter the census at an accurate age, and then

Table 9.4 Age Heaping over Time

Location	Date	Type	Group	Z
Rome[*a]	Empire	Urban	Rich	48
Roman Africa[*a]	Empire	Both	Rich	52
Carthage[*a]	Empire	Urban	Rich	38
England[b]	ca. 1350	Both	Rich	61
Florence, Italy[a]	1427	Urban	All	32
Pistoia, Italy[a]	1427	Urban	All	42
Florentine territory[a]	1427	Rural	All	53
Corfe Castle, England[c,d]	1790	Urban	All	8
	1795	Urban	Poor	14
Ardleigh, England[e]	1796	Rural	All	30
Terling, England[f]	1801	Rural	Poor	19
Cotton operatives, England[g]	1833	Both	Workers	6

Sources: [a]Duncan-Jones, 1990, 84–90. [b]Russell, 1948, 103–11. [c]Hutchins et al., 1796, xc–xciii. [d]Dorset Record Office, P11/OV197. [e]Essex Record Office, D/P 263/1/5. [f]Essex Record Office, D/P 299/12/3. [g]Parliamentary Papers, 1834, 21–31.
Note: * denotes ages of the dead. Since age heaping is more evident with the elderly, the table was constructed for ages 23–62.

Another feature of the Roman tombstone age declarations is that many ages were greatly overstated. We know that life expectancy in ancient Rome was perhaps as low as 20–25 at birth. Yet the tombstones record people as dying at ages as high as 120. In North Africa, 3 percent allegedly died at 100 or more.[20] Almost all these great ages must be complete fantasy. In comparison, a set of 250 relatively prosperous testators in England circa 1600, whose ages can be established from parish records, had a highest age at death of 88. Yet the children and grandchildren who memorialized richer Romans did not detect any implausibility in recording these fabulous ages.

For literacy the earliest measure we have is the ability of people to sign their name on various legal documents, shown in figure 9.3. For England these

---

have their ages updated from the previous census by the census takers every seven years, accuracy will be preserved, even if the individuals themselves have little idea of their own ages; Bagnall and Frier, 1994.

20. Hopkins, 1966, 249.

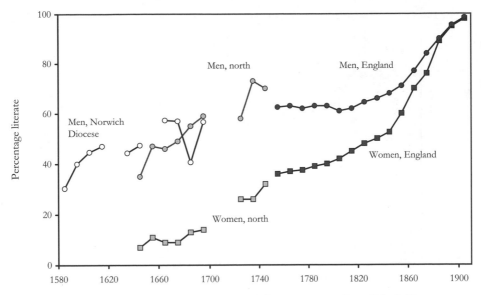

Figure 9.3 Literacy in England, 1580–1920. Data for 1750s–1920s from Schofield, 1973, men and women who sign marriage resisters; for the north, 1630s–1740s, from Houston, 1982, witnesses who sign court depositions; for Norwich Diocese, 1580s–1690s, from Cressy, 1980, witnesses who sign ecclesiastical court declarations.

proxy measures for literacy go back to the 1580s: such things as the percentage of grooms who signed the marriage register or the percentage of witnesses in court cases who signed their depositions. These measures similarly show a long upward movement in implied literacy rates as England approached the Industrial Revolution.

It is hard to define measures of actual literacy before 1580, but we know that literacy rates must have been extremely low in medieval Europe. In England, for example, after the Norman Conquest of 1066 clergy had the privilege of being tried only in ecclesiastical courts, the so-called benefit of clergy. The test for whether an accused in secular courts could assert benefit of clergy became the ability to read a passage from the Bible. By 1351 this was established as the test in law. In the medieval period the number of people outside those with clerical training who could read was so low that this ability was regarded as a sufficient test.

The low levels of literacy and numeracy in early societies go along with what has been called the "chronic vagueness" of early mentalities. Fabulous numbers are quoted in accounts and chronicles, when even the most cursory

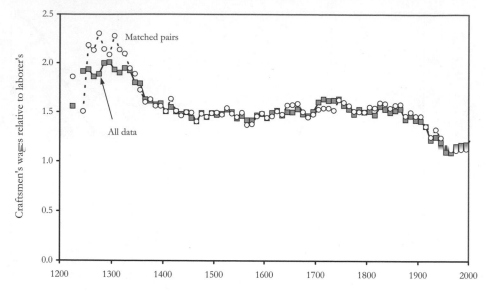

Figure 9.4 Wage of craftsmen relative to that of laborers in England, 1200–2000. The relative wage looks different in the earlier years depending on whether it is calculated using all the wage data or only data for matched pairs of craftsmen and their helpers.

inquiry would have shown how fallacious they were. Gervaise of Canterbury, for example, writing a contemporaneous account of the campaign of Henry II of England against the Count of Toulouse in 1159, notes that the king funded the war with a special tax of £180,000. English Treasury records suggest the actual sum was about £8,000. Roger of Wendover, a leading scholar of the age, notes that in 1210 there were three thousand masters and scholars in Oxford. The actual figure would not have been above three hundred, based on later histories of the university. Tacitus, the great Roman historian, describes an incident at a private gladiatorial contest in the small town of Fidenae, near Rome, during which a wooden stand collapsed, killing fifty thousand people. More recent experience with such collapses at large sporting events suggests a likelier figure would be fewer than a hundred deaths.[21]

The rising standards of numeracy and literacy do not seem to have been driven by any market signals from within the Malthusian economic system. There is no sign, for example, that the rewards to numeracy and literacy were any higher in England in 1800 than they were in 1200. We cannot measure

21. Ramsay, 1903.

this directly, but certainly the premium for other skills in the labor market seems to have actually declined over the long run. Thus if we measure the wage of building craftsmen against that of the laborers who assisted them during the interval 1200–2000, as in figure 9.4, we find that the skill premium was at its highest in the earliest years, before the onset of the Black Death in 1349. Then a craftsman earned nearly double the wage of a laborer. If there was ever an incentive to accumulate skills it was in the early economy. Thereafter the skill premium declined to a lower but relatively stable level from about 1370 until 1900, a period of over five hundred years, before declining further in the twentieth century. Thus the greatest reward for skills and training was bestowed in the marketplace long before the Industrial Revolution.

Nor, in places like England, was higher numeracy or literacy before 1800 the result of any kind of government regulation or intervention. The education that people were acquiring was largely privately funded (though aided by growing numbers of charitable foundations).

Work Hours

We saw in chapter 3 that work hours were very high in England by 1800 compared to forager and shifting cultivation societies. When exactly the transition to longer work hours took place is hard to establish, given the nature of preindustrial records. It is clear that the transition in England had largely occurred before the onset of the Industrial Revolution. But work hours in medieval England were probably already high by forager standards.[22]

Thus despite the static living conditions of the preindustrial world we have seen that somehow a very different society had emerged by 1800, at least in some parts of Europe. Returns on capital had fallen close to modern levels, work effort was much higher than in forager societies, skill premiums decreased, interpersonal violence rates declined, literacy and numeracy rose. Places like England were becoming more stereotypically middle class at all levels of society.[23]

22. Clark and van der Werf, 1998; Clark, 2005.
23. Mokyr argues in an analogous way that the stock of *useful knowledge*, meaning the knowledge economic agents had about their physical environment, in Europe had been expanded greatly by 1800. The practice of performing experiments to establish relationships between causes and effects, for example, had by then spread widely. He ascribes this to the intellectual developments of the Age of Reason and the Enlightenment; Mokyr, 2002, 28–77; 2005, 286.

Judicial Violence

We have already noted the declining homicide rates in preindustrial England, the only preindustrial society for which we can derive such measures, in the years 1190–1800. Along with these declines in interpersonal violence went a general decline in the taste of the public for blood, torture, and mayhem. Earlier societies—the Babylonians, Greeks, Romans, Incas—seem remarkably similar to ours in many of the details of their daily life, except for one thing: the apparently insatiable blood lust of the ancients. The Romans seem the most depraved. Criminals were executed for sport in the Coliseum and smaller town amphitheaters, often after being burned, raped, gouged, mangled, or mutilated. Captives from Roman wars were made to fight to the death for the amusement of easily bored crowds. Wild animals were set on each other, or on humans, just to warm the crowd up.

Even in the medieval period England was never the scene of such viciousness. But cock fighting, bear and bull baiting, public executions, and the public display of the decaying bodies of the executed were all still popular entertainments into the eighteenth century. Pepys, a man of refined musical and literary tastes, records the events of October 13, 1660, wryly and dispassionately in his diary: "Out to Charing Cross, to see Major-general Harrison hanged, drawn, and quartered; which was done there, he looking as cheerful as any man could do in that condition. He was presently cut down, and his head and heart shown to the people, at which there was great shouts of joy. . . . From thence to my Lord's, and took Captain Cuttance and Mr. Sheply to the Sun Tavern, and did give them some oysters."[24] What he is describing so blithely is seeing someone partially strangled, then disemboweled and castrated, then watching his organs being burned in front of him, before finally being beheaded. Gradually this delight in pain faded. The last such execution for treason in England was in 1782. Women who murdered their husbands or counterfeited the coinage were no longer burned at the stake after 1789.[25] Riotous behavior by visitors viewing the lunatics in Bedlam, a popular entertainment in eighteenth-century London, forced its governors in 1764 to hire four constables and four assistants to patrol the galleries on holidays.[26]

24. Pepys, 2000, October 13, 1660.
25. By the eighteenth century such women were normally first strangled by the executioner before being burned.
26. Hunter and Macalpine, 1963, 427–29.

In 1770 visits were finally restricted to those with admission tickets issued by one of the governors. The gibbeting of the bodies of executed criminals ended by 1832. Cock fighting and bear and bull baiting were all outlawed in 1835. Finally public executions were ended in 1869.

Selection Pressures

Why was Malthusian society, at least in Europe, changing in this way as we approached the Industrial Revolution? Social historians may invoke the Protestant Reformation of the sixteenth century, intellectual historians the Scientific Revolution of the seventeenth century or the Enlightenment of the eighteenth. Thus "The Enlightenment in the West is the only intellectual movement in human history that owed its irreversibility to the ability to transform itself into economic growth."[27]

But a problem with these invocations of movers from outside the economic realm is that they merely push the problem back one step. Like invoking God to explain the creation of the world, it necessarily invites the question of the creation of God.

Protestantism may explain rising levels of literacy in northern Europe after 1500. But why after more than a thousand years of entrenched Catholic dogma was an obscure German preacher able to effect such a profound change in the way ordinary people conceived religious belief? The Scientific Revolution may explain the subsequent Industrial Revolution. But why after at least five millennia of opportunity did systematic empirical investigation of the natural world finally emerge only in the seventeenth century?[28] And, had the unexpected and inexplicable Scientific Revolution never occurred, would the world have forever remained in the grip of the Malthusian Trap? Ideologies may transform the economic attitudes of societies. But ideologies are themselves also the expression of fundamental attitudes in part derived from the economic sphere.

There is, however, no need to invoke such a deus ex machina in the Malthusian era, given the strong selective processes identified in chapter 6. The forces leading to a more patient, less violent, harder-working, more literate,

27. Mokyr, 2005, 336.
28. Mokyr, in a personal communication, argues that the Scientific Revolution and subsequent Enlightenment were themselves by-products of the development of commercial capitalism in early modern Europe. But that, of course, merely creates another regress.

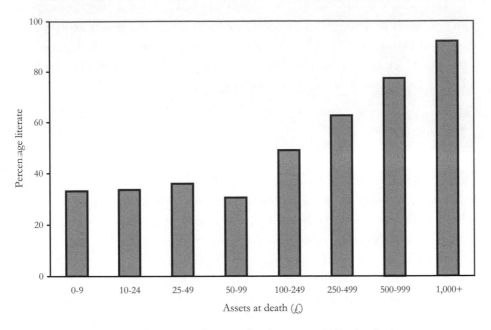

Figure 9.5   Literacy and assets of male testators in England, 1630.

and more thoughtful society were inherent in the very Malthusian assumptions that undergird preindustrial society. Figure 9.5, for example, shows literacy rates for men circa 1630 as a function of wealth. As was shown in chapter 6, the wealthiest testators, who were almost all literate, left twice as many children as the poorest, of whom only about 30 percent were literate. Generation by generation the sons of the literate were relatively more numerous than the sons of the illiterate.

Agrarian societies differed in two crucial ways from their forager predecessors. Agriculture allowed for much higher population densities, so that, instead of living in communities of twenty to fifty, people now lived in communities of hundreds to thousands. By 2500 BC the cities of Sumeria are estimated to already have been as large as forty thousand people.[29] Agrarian societies also had large stocks of assets that were owned by specific people: land, houses, and animals. The sizes of these societies allowed the extensive use of money as a medium of exchange. Their size, and the importance of the income streams from these assets, created a need for enduring records of property ownership and property transfers. Thus a mass of clay tablets record-

29. Gat, 2002.

Figure 9.6   Cuneiform tablet account of cattle in Mesopotamia in the Ur III period (2112–04 BC).

ing leases, sales, wills, and labor contracts survive from ancient Sumeria and Babylonia. Figure 9.6 shows the most common type of cuneiform tablet, a receipt for delivery of goods.

In the institutional and technological context of these societies, a new set of human attributes mattered to accumulate the only currency significant in the Malthusian era—reproductive success. Literacy and numeracy, previously irrelevant, were now both helpful for achieving economic success in agrarian preindustrial economies. And because reproductive success was linked to economic success, facility with numbers and words was pulled along in its wake. Patience and hard work had found a new reward in a society with large amounts of capital; thus these characteristics were now also favored.

Trade and production in turn also helped stimulate innovations in arithmetic and writing systems designed to make calculations and recording easier. The replacement of Roman numerals by Arabic numerals in Europe, for example, was aided by the demands of trade and commerce. In medieval Europe "the needs of commerce formed one important stimulus to the spread and growth of arithmetic." In Europe religious bodies and the state, insulated from market pressures, were the slowest to adopt these innovations. The English Treasury was still employing Roman numerals in its accounts in the sixteenth century. But from the thirteenth century onward Arabic numerals increasingly dominated commerce, and many treatises on arithmetic were clearly aimed at a commercial audience.[30]

So the market nature of settled agrarian societies stimulated intellectual life in two ways. It created a demand for better symbolic systems to handle commerce and production. And it created a supply of people who were adept at using these systems for economic ends. While living standards were not changing, the culture, and perhaps even the genes, of the people subject to these conditions were changing under the selective pressures they exerted. All Malthusian societies, as Darwin recognized, are inherently shaped by survival of the fittest. They reward certain behaviors with reproductive success, and these behaviors become the norm of the society.

What were societies like at the dawn of the settled agrarian era with the Neolithic Revolution of circa 8000 BC? Based on observation of modern forager and shifting cultivation societies we would expect that the early agriculturalists were impulsive, violent, innumerate, illiterate, and lazy. Ethnographies of such groups emphasize high rates of time preference, high levels of interpersonal violence, and low work inputs. Abstract reasoning abilities were limited.

The Pirahã, a forager group in the Brazilian Amazon, are an extreme example. They have only the number words *hói* (roughly one), *hoí* (roughly two), and *aibaagi* (many). On tests they could not reliably match number groups beyond 3. Once the number of objects reached as large as 9, they could almost never match them.[31] Yet the Pirahã perform very well as hunters and in tests of spatial and other abilities. Similarly the number vocabulary of many surviving forager societies encompasses only the numbers 1, 2, and "many." Forager society must thus have had no selective pressures toward the kinds of attitudes and abilities that make an Industrial Revolution.

The New World after the Neolithic Revolution offered economic success to a different kind of agent than had been typical in hunter-gatherer society: Those with patience, who could wait to enjoy greater consumption in the future. Those who liked to work long hours. And those who could perform

30. Murray, 1978, 167–91; quotation on page 191.
31. Gordon, 2004.

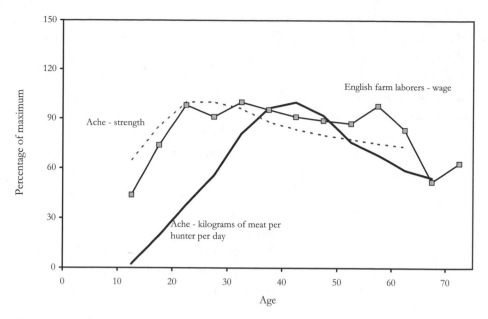

Figure 9.7 Lifetime output for hunter-gatherer versus agrarian societies. Data on hunting success and strength from Walker et al., 2002, 653; English farm wages from Burnette, 2006.

formal calculations in a world of many types of inputs and outputs—of what crop to profitably produce, how many inputs to devote to it, what land to profitably invest in. And we see in England, from at least the Middle Ages on, that the kind of people who succeeded in the economic system—who accumulated assets, acquired skills, became literate—were increasing their representation in each generation. Thus it is plausible that through the long agrarian passage leading up to the Industrial Revolution man was becoming *biologically* better adapted to the modern economic world.

This is not in any sense to say that people in settled agrarian economies on the eve of the Industrial Revolution had become "smarter" than their counterparts in hunter-gatherer societies. For, as Jared Diamond points out, the skills that ensure the survival and reproduction of hunter-gatherers are many and complex.[32] This is illustrated by figure 9.7, which shows the

32. Diamond even goes so far as to argue that selection in agrarian economies would be based on resistance to epidemic diseases that arise with more concentrated populations, so that the people of forager societies were more intelligent than those of long-settled agrarian economies; Diamond, 1997, 18–22.

earnings profile of a group of agricultural laborers with age in England in the 1830s, alongside the earnings profile of Ache hunters (measured in kilograms of meat per hunter per day). An English farm laborer reached peak earnings around age 20, while for an Ache hunter the peak did not come until the early 40s. This was so despite the fact that the Ache reached the peak of their physical strength in their 20s.[33]

Clearly hunting, unlike agricultural labor, was a complex activity that took years to master. The argument is not that agrarian society was making people smarter. For the average person the division of labor that agrarian society entailed made work simpler and more repetitive. The argument is instead that it rewarded with economic and hence reproductive success a certain repertoire of skills and dispositions that were very different from those of the pre-agrarian world, such as the ability to perform simple repetitive tasks hour after hour, day after day. There is nothing natural or harmonic, for example, in having a disposition to work even when all the basic needs of survival have been achieved.

The strength of the selection process through survival of the richest also seems to have varied depending on the circumstances of settled agrarian societies. Thus in the frontier conditions of New France (Québec) in the seventeenth century, where land was abundant, population densities low, and wages extremely high, the group that reproduced most successfully was the poorest and the most illiterate.[34] The more stable a society was, the less reproductive success could be attained by war and conquest, the better chance these mechanisms had to operate.

Thus it is no real surprise that China, despite nearly a generation of extreme forms of Communism between 1949 and 1978, emerged unchanged as a society individualist and capitalist to its core. The effects of the thousands of years of operation of a society under the selective pressures of the Malthusian regime could not be uprooted by utopian dreamers.

We saw in chapter 8 that economics is founded on the idea that different economic outcomes across societies are the product of the incentives created by different social institutions. Given the same incentives and information everyone will act the same way—economically. This chapter established that,

33. This pattern of a late peak in maximum hunting ability is common for male subsistence hunters.
34. Hamilton and Clark, 2006.

in terms of the history of the preindustrial, world this assumption is untenable. People's basic preferences were changing as the world approached the Industrial Revolution, shaped by Malthusian pressures.

In the chapters that follow we shall consider how these selective pressures, and their differential strength across societies, might help explain the timing, location, and nature of the Industrial Revolution.

PART II

The Industrial Revolution

10 Modern Growth: The Wealth of Nations

Behold, I make a covenant. Before all your people I will do marvels, such as have not been wrought in all the earth or in any nation.

—King James Bible, Exodus 34:10

Around 1800, in northwestern Europe and North America, man's long sojourn in the Malthusian world ended. The iron link between population and living standards, through which any increase in population caused an immediate decline in wages, was decisively broken. Between 1770 and 1860, for example, English population tripled. Yet real incomes, instead of plummeting, rose (figure 10.1). A new era dawned.

The seemingly sudden and unpredictable escape from the dead hand of the Malthusian past in England around 1800, this materialist crossing of the Jordan, was so radical that it has been forever dubbed the Industrial Revolution.

The *Industrial* part of the label is, however, unfortunate and misleading. It was conferred mainly because the most observable of the many changes in England was the enormous growth of the industrial sector: cotton mills, potteries, foundries, steel works. Most Malthusian economies had 70 or even 80 percent of the population employed in agriculture. By 1861 that share had dropped to 21 percent in England. But that switch to industry, as we shall see, was due to the idiosyncrasies of England's geography and demography. There is, in fact, nothing inherently *industrial* about the Industrial Revolution. Since 1800 the productivity of agriculture has increased by as much as that of the rest of the economy, and without these gains in agriculture modern growth would have been impossible. We have to resign ourselves to the fact that one of the defining events in human history has been mislabeled.

Material well-being has marched upward in successful economies since the Industrial Revolution to levels no one in 1800 could have imagined. Figure 10.2

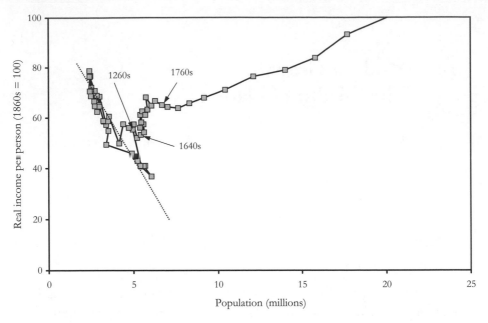

Figure 10.1 Real income per person and population in England by decade from the 1260s.

shows, for example, income per capita in England by decade from the 1260s to the 2000s. After six hundred years of stasis, income has increased nearly tenfold since 1800. It continues its inexorable rise. Note, however, that though the conventional date for the onset of the Industrial Revolution in Britain is given as the 1760s there is little sign of rapid growth of income per person until the decade of the 1860s.

As a result of the Industrial Revolution the citizens of the economically successful countries—such as Britain, the United States, France, and Japan—are enormously richer than their Malthusian ancestors.

Another unusual feature of the modern economy, however, is that the gap between the living standards of people in rich and poor economies today is an enormous chasm, compared to that in the era before 1800. In the pre-industrial epoch societies with the most favorable demographic factors could attain incomes perhaps three to four times those of societies with the least favorable demographic regimes. They looked down on their less favored brethren from a modest knoll. Now the richest countries stand on a mountain compared to the poorest. The gap between rich and poor in the modern world is on the order of 40:1.

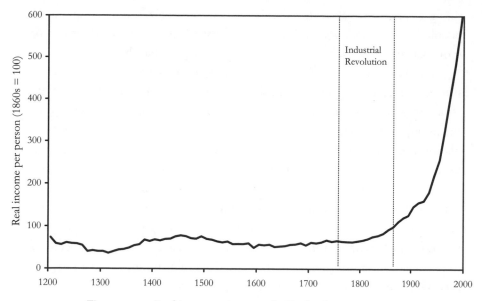

Figure 10.2   Real income per person in England, 1260s–2000s.

Most of the change in the structure of economic life in the advanced economies can be traced directly to one simple fact: the unprecedented, inexorable, all-pervading rise in incomes per person since 1800. The lifestyle of the average person in modern economies was not unknown in earlier societies: it is that of the rich in ancient Egypt or ancient Rome. What is different is that now paupers live like princes, and princes live like emperors.

As incomes increase, consumers switch spending between goods in very predictable ways. We have already seen that the increase in demand with income varies sharply across goods. Most importantly, food consumption increases little once we reach high incomes. Thus in Germany real incomes per person rose by 133 percent from 1910 to 1956, while food consumption per person rose by only 7 percent, calorie consumption per person fell by 4 percent, and protein consumption fell by 3 percent. Indeed the calorie content of the modern European diet is little higher than that of the eighteenth century, even though people are ten to twenty times wealthier.[1] The character of

1. People in the eighteenth century engaged in heavy manual labor, walked to work and market, and lived in poorly heated homes, so they easily burned off these calories without the modern problem of obesity.

the diet, however, has switched toward more expensive calorie sources. As people become sated with calories their demand for variety, in the form of more expensive foods, becomes insatiable: goodbye bread, hello sushi.

Thus as income marched upward the share of farm products in consumption treaded downward, and the share of farmers among producers declined in step. In preindustrial economies farmers made up 50–80 percent of the population. Today, if we had a free market in food, 2 percent of the population could feed everyone. The farm population share in the United States, for example, is 2.1 percent. Half of these people are kept in farming by government subsidies that futilely try to stem the inexorable exodus from the land and from rural communities. A mountain of European Union subsidies keeps 3.3 percent of the French in their beloved *campagne*. The less sentimental British, with a more efficient agriculture, employ only 1.2 percent of the population in farming.[2] The Industrial Revolution looks peculiarly industrial largely because of the switch of population and production out of agriculture and into industry thanks to higher incomes.

The switch of labor out of agriculture has profoundly affected social life. In Malthusian societies most of the population lived in small rural settlements of a few hundred souls. They had to be close to the daily grind of their work in the fields, since they walked to work. In the southeast of England, for example, villages in the eighteenth century were on average only two miles apart. Typically they had fewer than a hundred residents. The countryside was densely settled because of all the labor required in inefficient preindustrial agriculture: plowing, reaping, threshing, hauling manure, tending animals.

With an ever-dwindling proportion of the population tied to the land through agriculture, modern populations are footloose. People can locate anywhere, but they have concentrated increasingly in urban centers because of the richer labor market and the social amenities they offer. In particular the rise of the two-wage-earner family makes denser urban labor markets attractive to people, despite the costs associated with huge agglomerations. The urbanization of rich economies has, in turn, produced the many social changes we associate with industrial society. Income—the unending, inexorable rise in income—drives all this change. Why are we on the march to endless wealth?

2. Data for the year 2000 are from the Food and Agriculture Organization of the United Nations. Densely populated Britain does, however, import about half its food requirements.

Explaining Modern Growth

Modern economies seem on the surface to be breathtakingly complex machines whose harmonic operation is nearly miraculous. Hundreds of thousands of different types of goods are sold in giant temples of consumption. The production, distribution, and retailing of these products, from paper cups to personal espresso machines, involves the integration and cooperation of thousands of different types of specialized machines, buildings, and workers. Understanding why and how economies grow would seem to require years of study and Ph.D.-level training. But in fact understanding the essential nature of modern growth, and the huge intellectual puzzles it poses, requires no more than basic arithmetic and elementary economic reasoning.

For, although modern economies are deeply complex machines, they have at heart a surprisingly simple structure. We can construct a simple model of this complex economy and in that model catch all the features that are relevant to understanding growth.

The model reveals that there is one simple and decisive factor driving modern growth. Growth is generated overwhelmingly by investments in expanding the stock of production knowledge in societies. To understand the Industrial Revolution is to understand why such activity was not present or was unsuccessful before 1800, and why it became omnipresent after 1800.

The simple model collapses the immense complexity of all economies down to just five summary variables: output Y, labor L, physical capital K, land Z, and the level of efficiency A. In this picture of the economy it is a giant machine that receives inputs of physical capital, labor, and land and turns them into a single sausage-like output, with A indexing how much output is received per unit of input. Since we will be thinking in terms of output per worker, capital per worker and so on, lowercase letters will denote a "per worker" quantity. Thus K is capital, and k is capital per worker.

We need to specify how these quantities are related. And here again we find that, despite the huge variety of economies in our world, there is a simple relationship that holds for all time and in all places, the *fundamental equation of growth:*

$$g_y = a g_k + c g_z + g_A,$$

where g_y, g_k, g_z, and g_A are, respectively, the growth rates of output per worker, capital per worker, land per worker, and efficiency.[3] When we are looking at long-run growth the efficiency term measures overwhelmingly the sophistication of the technology of the society; a and c are the shares of output received by the owners of capital and land.

This equation shows the percentage change in output per worker resulting from a 1 percent change in either capital per worker, land per worker, or efficiency. It is a matter of only a brief formal argument, given in the technical appendix to this book, to demonstrate this basic connection.

Some of the elements of this equation are obvious and intuitive. If the efficiency of the economy grows by 1 percent, then so does output per person. Less intuitive, but nevertheless clear, is the effect of more capital per person. If we increase the capital stock per person by 1 percent we only increase output per person by the amount a, the share of capital in national income. Since that share is typically about 0.24, this implies that, if we expand the capital stock per person by 1 percent, we increase output by only 0.24 percent.

This implies that growing faster by investing in more capital is costly. The ratio of physical capital to output in richer modern economies averages about 3:1. To increase the capital stock per person by 1 percent requires switching 3 percent of current output from consumption to investment. But for that switch is purchased an increase in income in future years of only 0.24 percent.

The first surprising implication of this fundamental growth equation is that, in the modern world, land per person, which had completely dominated income determination before 1800, no longer matters in economic growth. This is because land rents have fallen to only a few percent of total output in modern high-income economies. Figure 10.3 shows this trend for England. Farmland rents, which were 23 percent of national income in 1760, fell to 0.2 percent by 2000. In part this decrease was offset by a rise in the site rental value of urban land. But by 2000 urban land rents represented only 4 percent of national income, even in crowded England with its very high housing costs. Thus, although population growth tends to make g_z negative in modern economies, this drag on income is inconsequential at present. Indeed so unimportant is land in the current economy that for most purposes economists simplify the fundamental equation of growth to the even more stark

3. Robert Solow first derived this result in Solow, 1956, though he had predecessors, as discussed in Griliches, 1996.

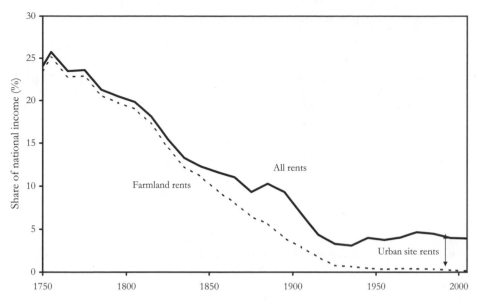

Figure 10.3   Land rents as a share of income in England, 1750s–2000s. Income from Clark, 2007b. Urban land rents 1845–1913 from Singer, 1941, 224. Urban land rents 1947–2004 estimated from the difference between the asset value of dwellings and structures in the United Kingdom and the net capital stock embodied in these, assuming a 3 percent return on land until 1997, when the rent was estimated from dwelling rent trends. Urban land rents in other years estimated from the value of the housing stock; data from Clark, 2007b.

$$g_y \approx ag_k + g_A.$$

Whereas in the preindustrial world the amount of land per person was a crucial determinant of the wealth of a society, now it is largely irrelevant, except for a few resource-abundant economies. Countries like Singapore and Japan, with very little land per person, can be just as rich as those, like Australia, with huge amounts.

Thus, despite all the complexities of economies since the Industrial Revolution, the persistent growth we have witnessed since 1800 can be the result of only two changes: more capital per worker and greater efficiency of the production process. At the proximate level all modern growth in income per person is that simple!

This conclusion has been derived for an economy with only one output, one type of labor, one type of land, and one type of capital (which is just stored-up output). But it generalizes easily into an analogous expression for realistic economies, as the technical appendix details.

Table 10.1   Modern Economic Growth, 1960–2000

Country	Growth rate of y (%)	Growth rate of k (%)	Share of capital in income, a	Percentage of output growth from capital
New Zealand	1.18	1.55	0.27	35
United States	1.75	1.59	0.20	18
Australia	1.97	1.65	0.30	25
United Kingdom	2.40	2.87	0.23	27
Germany	3.29	3.07	0.25	23
Ireland	4.20	3.98	0.15	14
Japan	4.47	5.34	0.27	32

Sources: Capital and output from Kamps, 2004. Work hours 1970–2000 from OECD. Labor force 1961–70 from Earth Trends. Capital share in income 1985–2000 from OECD productivity database.

Note: y is output per worker-hour, k is capital per worker-hour.

The second surprising implication of the fundamental equation is that physical capital accumulation directly explains only a quarter of the growth of output per person since the Industrial Revolution. Efficiency advance explains the other three-quarters.

To see this we note that the physical capital stock of economies since the Industrial Revolution has grown at roughly the same rate as output. Thus the ratio of capital to output has remained surprisingly unchanged. For the OECD economies it is estimated at 2.93 in the 1960s compared to 2.99 in 2000–01.[4] Table 10.1 shows the figures for the growth rate of output per work hour and capital per work hour for 1960 to 2000 for a group of these economies. On average for a group of twenty-two OECD economies the growth rates were the same in this interval.

Since on average the share of capital rental payments in income was only 0.24 for these economies, this implies that only about a quarter of the growth of output per work hour stems from physical capital investments. The bulk of the growth is explained by advances in efficiency.

The efficiency term in the above equation, g_z, is frequently referred to as the *residual*. This is because, while the other terms in the equation can be di-

4. Kamps, 2004.

Table 10.2 Replacement Cost of the Human Capital Stock in the United States, 2000

Education	Period	Cost per person) ($)	Labor force (millions)	Direct social cost ($ billions)	Foregone earnings ($ billions)
Less than high school	10	77,000	11	879	0
High school	12	122,000	63	5,963	1,767
Some college	14	199,000	32	4,167	2,155
Some postgraduate	16	312,000	35	7,075	3,727
Labor force		183,000	141	18,084	7,650

Source: United States, Census Bureau, 2002, tables 198, 199, 210, and 211.
Note: The foregone earnings per year are assumed for each level of education to be 70 percent of the average wage and salary compensation earned by a person aged 25–29 with education at the next lowest level. (This is assuming that students take classes or study for 1,350 hours per school year—undoubtedly an overestimate.)

rectly measured and calculated, efficiency growth is simply a balancing quantity thrown in to make the sides equate. It is, in the famous phrase of Moses Abramovitz, merely a "measure of our ignorance."[5] It is the difference between what we see and what economists can account for. For the typical successful economy the measured efficiency with which inputs are translated into outputs has risen at 1 percent or more per year since the Industrial Revolution.

The residual can be reduced a little by expanding the measure of capital to also include human capital, the investments made in the education and training of workers. Unskilled, uneducated workers produce much less than skilled, educated ones. Part of this gain in productivity is attributable to the investment in skills and education.

Table 10.2 shows a rough estimate of the value of the human capital stock per worker, and for the economy as a whole, in the United States in 2000. The labor force is divided into four broad education categories—less than high school, high school, some college, and some postgraduate training—and the associated capital cost of each type of worker is listed. These costs include both direct expenditures for teachers and classrooms and the indirect expenditures of wages sacrificed by spending time in schooling. The average U.S.

5. Abramovitz, 1956.

worker now embodies as much as $183,000 in capital. In the economy as a whole there was about $26 trillion of human capital.

The stock of physical capital per worker in the United States in 2000 was still somewhat greater at $210,500, but the calculation here shows the importance of human capital in modern economies. The share of income derived from this human capital investment per worker, assuming a 10 percent return on the investment, was 26 percent, compared to 20 percent for physical capital.[6]

Thus the true share of income earned by capital in the modern United States might be 46 percent of all income. But it is also evident that accounting for human capital alone, while it reduces the size of the residual, does not eliminate increased efficiency as an important source of growth. Thus if we estimate the fundamental equation of growth for the United States in the years 1990–2000, even with human capital included, residual productivity growth was 1.36 percent per year, which was still a full 72 percent of the growth of output per worker-hour.[7]

In earlier times, such as in England during the Industrial Revolution, the stock of human capital was much smaller, since most people had not even completed grade school. Thus counting it reduces the size of the residual, but the residual is still the major direct explanator of growth.

What generates the residual? It stems from a largely unmeasured form of capital accumulation: innovation. This comprises the myriad of investments, small and large, made by producers each year to try to improve the efficiency of their production processes.

Knowledge that is proprietary, that is legally owned, is counted in the modern capital stock, since it is an asset of firms that earns them a return. Table 10.3 shows the capital stock in the United Kingdom in 1990, separated into structures, plants and machinery, vehicles, and intangible capital (which includes patent rights and other forms of proprietary knowledge). But such

6. George Psacharopoulos calculated the social rate of return to education in the richer economies in 1993 as 14.4 percent per year for primary education, 10.2 percent for secondary education, and 8.7 percent for higher education; Psacharopoulos, 1994. But this probably exaggerates the true return to capital, since Psacharopoulos attributed all the increase in wages of the more highly educated to their education.

7. Income per worker-hour grew at 1.9 percent per year. Growth in physical capital, at 1.3 percent per year, explained 0.36 percent of this. Human capital grew at 0.7 percent, explaining another 0.18 percent.

Table 10.3   U.K. Capital Stock, 1990

Type of capital	Share in stock (%)	Share in rental payments (%)
Structures	72	54
Plants and machinery	17	31
Vehicles	10	12
Intangibles	1	3

Source: Oulton, 2001.

knowledge constitutes only a tiny share of the modern capital stock, even if we measure capital by how much rent it earns (which is higher in the case of intangible capital).

The legal system gives protection only to certain classes of new ideas, and then only for a limited period. After that they enter the common pool of knowledge available to all. But most of the knowledge capital of the modern economy is not owned by anyone; it is available free for all to use and so would not get counted in this way. It cannot be kept private by its creators and so is utilized for free by others.

The difficulty of profiting from the creation of knowledge is revealed, for example, by the emblematic industry of the Industrial Revolution, cotton textiles. In the next chapter we will learn that about half the measured efficiency gains of the Industrial Revolution stemmed from textile innovations. Yet the typical earnings of the entrepreneurs in textiles—who were remaking the world in which they lived—were no higher than those in such stagnant sectors as retailing or boot and shoe making. The gains from their innovations were instead flowing to consumers in England and across the world in the form of lower prices for textile products.

The time and energy that innovators invested in new methods thus yielded a much higher social return than the meager private return they reaped. To eliminate the appearance of free efficiency growth external benefits must be added into the private return on capital in calculating *a*.

Thus the fundamental equation of growth actually reduces, for the world since the Industrial Revolution, to the approximate expression

$$g_y <\approx a^* g_{k^*},$$

where k^* is an augmented measure of capital, which includes all the capital stock of the economy—physical capital, human capital, and knowledge capital—and a^* is an augmented expression for the share of income in the economy that would flow to capital, were all the spillover benefits from investment in knowledge directed to the investors.

Note, however, that when we arrive at this final truth as to the nature of modern growth we have lost all ability to empirically test its truth. It is a statement of reason and faith, not an empirical proposition. Physical capital can be measured, as can the share of capital income in all income in the economy. But the generalized spillovers from innovation activities are not in practice measurable. Nor is the total amount of activity designed to improve production processes measurable. Investments in innovation occur in all economies. But unknown factors speed and retard this process across different epochs and different economies.

Innovation Explains All Modern Growth

The fundamental equation of growth seems to suggest that growth since the Industrial Revolution has had two independent sources. Most important is efficiency growth fueled by investment in knowledge capital, which has large social external benefits that show up in the residual. But there is also a substantial contribution from investments in physical capital and human capital, which explains 30–50 percent of the growth in income per person.

But the efficiency growth from innovation is actually the true source of all growth, and it also explains the growth of physical capital. The apparently independent contribution of physical capital to modern growth is illusory.

If efficiency advances and physical capital were truly independent sources of modern income growth, then there would be economies with rapid growth of physical capital per person, but no efficiency gains, and economies with rapid efficiency gains but little growth of physical capital per person. In practice, both across time and across countries at any given time, the growth of the capital stock and efficiency growth are always closely associated in free market economies.[8]

---

8. Command economies such as the old USSR were characterized by rapid capital accumulation but slow efficiency advance.

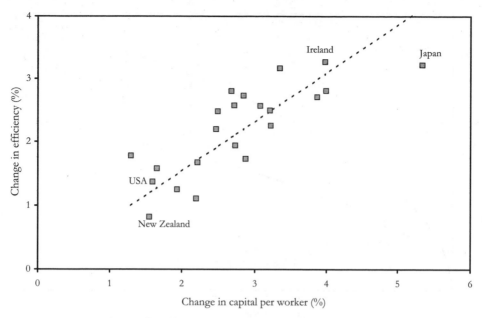

Figure 10.4 Growth rates for efficiency versus growth rates for capital per worker, 1960–2000. Capital and output from Kamps, 2004. Work hours 1970–2000 from OECD. Size of labor force 1961–70 from Earth Trends.

Figure 10.4, for example, shows for a group of OECD countries at different income levels their efficiency growth rates from 1960 to 2000 compared to their capital growth rates per worker. Even though capital stocks are notoriously difficult to measure, the correlation between capital growth and efficiency growth is close.

When two variables are so closely correlated one must cause the other.[9] The growth in efficiency must also be driving up the stock of capital per worker. The process through which this occurs is shown in figure 10.5.

The lower curve in the figure shows the output in an economy of given efficiency level as a function of the stock of physical capital employed per worker, k. Adding more capital always increases output, but at a smaller and smaller rate as the capital stock per worker increases. Investors will expand the stock of capital to the point k_0 where the net additional output created from

9. Or there could be a single independent cause for both.

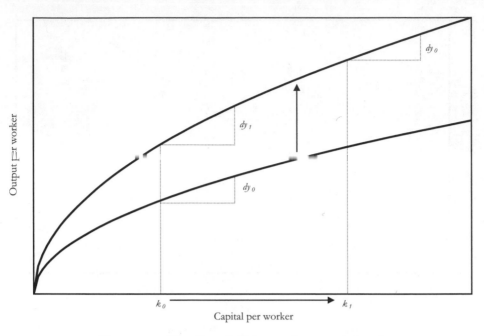

Figure 10.5 The effect of efficiency gains on capital stock.

another \$1 of capital, dy_0, equals the real interest cost of \$1. Thus the real interest rate, the price of capital, determines the capital stock in any economy.

An increase in efficiency moves the production curve upward everywhere, as figure 10.5 shows. It also increases the net additional output from adding more capital, to dy_1 in the diagram. Thus investors buy more capital until once again the return equals the interest rate at the new capital stock k_1. At the new capital stock once again addition of a unit of capital increases output by dy_0. So as long as interest rates do not change, innovation induces physical capital investment.

Thus a 1 percent increase in the efficiency of the economy though innovation leads to an increase in output of more than 1 percent because it induces more physical capital accumulation.

The shape of the production function in modern economies, depicted in figure 10.5, is such that the ratio of physical capital to output has changed little since the Industrial Revolution, as a result of these induced investments from technological advance. That implies that the growth of the physical capital stock has been as fast as the growth of output. In that case the direct effect of technological advance, plus the indirect effect from induced investment, makes a 1 percent gain in efficiency create about a 1.3 percent gain in output. Thus

$$g_y \approx g_k \approx \frac{g_A}{(1-a)} \ .$$

Thus investments in knowledge capital that generate efficiency growth not only explain most modern economic growth at a proximate level, they explain all modern growth.

The Agenda

Enhanced production of knowledge capital, seemingly starting around 1800, generated great external benefits throughout the economy. This increased the measured efficiency of the economy, and with it the stock of physical and human capital. Thus the path to explaining the vital event in the economic history of the world, the Industrial Revolution, is clear. All we need explain is why in the millennia before 1800 there was in all societies—warlike, peaceful, monotheist, polytheist—such limited investment in the expansion of useful knowledge, and why this circumstance changed for the first time in Britain some time around 1800. Then we will understand the history of mankind. The next chapter details some approaches to this problem and considers why the timing of the Industrial Revolution remains so difficult to explain.

11 The Puzzle of the Industrial Revolution

So the Industrial Revolution was the only significant event that happened in all world economic history. And you have no explanation for the Industrial Revolution. What kind of theory is this?

—Irad Kimhi (personal communication, 2006)

The mystery of why the Industrial Revolution was delayed until around 1800 is the great and enduring puzzle of human history. In this chapter I outline what makes explaining the Industrial Revolution an almost impossible challenge and describe various attempts to resolve this challenge.

We have seen that economic growth after 1800 was the product of small, but highly productive, investments in expanding the stock of useful knowledge in societies. Since most of the benefits of these investments did not flow to the investors, the result was a seemingly costless expansion of the efficiency of the economy. These gains in efficiency in turn induced more investment in physical capital. We also saw that the average rate of expansion of technology before 1800 was extremely slow.

What makes the Industrial Revolution so difficult to understand is the need to comprehend why—despite huge variation in the customs, mores, and institutions of preindustrial societies—none of them managed to sustain even moderate rates of productivity growth, by modern standards, over any significant time period. What was different about *all* preindustrial societies that generated such low and faltering rates of efficiency growth? What change to such a stable nongrowth configuration generated the Industrial Revolution?

Theories of the Industrial Revolution

This book adopts a particular view of the Industrial Revolution: that it emerged only millennia after the arrival of institutionally stable economies in societies such as ancient Babylonia, because in the interim institutions themselves interacted with and changed human culture. Millennia of living in stable societies, under tight Malthusian pressures that rewarded effort, accumulation, and fertility limitation, encouraged the development of cultural forms—in terms of work inputs, time preference, and family formation—which facilitated modern economic growth.

In part I argue that, given the nature of the question, there is no other explanation which can meet the exacting standards required of any theory of the Industrial Revolution. For the existing theories, offered by a variety of historians, economic historians, economic theorists, and sociologists, end up falling into three basic types, each of which faces characteristic difficulties.

Exogenous Growth Theories. Some feature outside the economy, such as the legal institutions of the society or the relative scarcities of different inputs in production, changed. This change induced investment in expanding production techniques by potential innovators within economies. Such a change would include, for example, changes in the institutions governing the appropriability of knowledge or the security of all property. Thus Douglass North and Barry Weingast argue that the arrival of the constitutional monarchy in England in 1689 was a key political innovation that ushered in modern economic growth.[1] These theories would predict that we will find in England in 1760 or soon before, or perhaps more widely in Europe, institutional forms or other social innovations not seen in earlier societies. An example of such a theory might be Joel Mokyr's view that the Enlightenment in Europe was a key stimulant of the Industrial Revolution, though Mokyr would argue that the Enlightenment itself had its roots in the earlier commercial expansion of the European economy.[2]

Multiple Equilibrium Theories. Some shock—disease, war, conquest of new lands—led the economy to jump from the bad, stagnant equilibrium to the good, dynamic equilibrium of the modern world. A particular class of theories that has recently attracted adherents in economics is one in which families switch from an equilibrium under which everyone has large numbers of children (each of whom they invest little time in) to one under which families have small numbers of children (on whom they lavish much attention).[3]

1. North and Weingast, 1989.
2. Mokyr, 2005.
3. Lucas, 1988, 2002; Becker et al., 1990.

Endogenous Growth Theories. Some feature internal to the economic system evolved over time in the long preindustrial era to eventually create the preconditions for modern economic growth. The Industrial Revolution was thus predetermined from the time the first human appeared on the African savannah. It was just a matter of time before the economic conditions for rapid technological progress were created. The question then is: What is different about the economy of England in 1760, compared to Florence in 1300, China in 500, Rome at the time of Christ, or Athens at the time of Plato? Posited internal drivers of the economic system that eventually created the Industrial Revolution have included the size of the population itself and an evolution of the characteristics of the population.[4]

This chapter reviews the major variants of these three theories before we examine the Industrial Revolution in detail, to consider whether it conforms with or contradicts any or all of them.

Exogenous Growth Theories

For economists the great exogenous force that is continually invoked as shaping the lives of men and the fates of economies is the institutions that govern society—determining who owns what, how secure property is, and how property gets transferred. The preferred assumption is that the desires and rationalities of people in all human societies are essentially the same. The medieval peasant in Europe, the Indian coolie, the Yanomamo of the rain forest, the Tasmanian Aboriginal, all share a common set of aspirations and a common ability to act rationally to achieve those aspirations. What differs across societies, however, are the institutions that govern economic life. If sustained rapid productivity advance is not observed before 1800 in any society, it must be because all these societies were even worse at rewarding innovation than our own. Thus

> Institutions form the incentive structure of a society, and the political and economic institutions, in consequence, are the underlying determinants of economic performance.[5]

4. Kremer, 1993b; Galor and Weil, 2000.
5. North, 1994, 359.

Consider how the . . . economy would behave in the absence of property rights. In this case, innovators would be unable to earn the profits that encourage them to undertake research in the first place, so that no research would take place. With no research, no new ideas would be created, technology would be constant, and there would be no per capita growth in the economy. Broadly speaking, just such a situation prevailed in the world prior to the Industrial Revolution.[6]

Studying institutions sheds light on why some countries are rich and others poor. . . . The quality of these institutional foundations of the economy and the polity is paramount in determining a society's welfare.[7]

The advantage of a theory which relies on an exogenous shock to the economic system is that it can perhaps account for the seemingly sudden change in the growth rate of measured efficiency around 1800. Institutions can change suddenly and dramatically—witness the French Revolution, the Russian Revolution, or the 1979 Iranian Revolution that overthrew the Shah.

The sophisticated proponents of such theories among economic historians realize, however, that the difference in institutions between technologically static preindustrial societies and modern growth economies, as we have seen, must be relatively subtle.[8]

Yet this approach exerts its powerful hold over the economics profession in part because of the limited historical knowledge of most economists. The caricature many modern economists have of the world before the Industrial Revolution is a mixture of all the bad movies ever made about early societies: Vikings pour out of long ships to loot and pillage defenseless peasants and burn the libraries of monasteries. Mongol hordes thunder out of the steppes on horseback to sack Chinese cities. Clerical fanatics burn at the stake those who dare to question arcane religious doctrines. Peasants groan under the heel of rapacious lords, whose only activities are feasting and fighting. Aztec priests wielding obsidian knives cut out the hearts of their screaming, writhing victims. In such a world, who has the time, the energy, or the incentive to develop new technology?

6. Jones, 2002, 121.
7. Greif, 2006, 3–4.
8. See, for example, Greif, 2006.

Two considerations, however, suggest that exogenous growth theories face almost insurmountable problems despite their grip on both economic history and economists.

First, we shall see that there is no sign of any improvement in the appropriability of knowledge until long after the Industrial Revolution was well under way.

Second, there is no evidence that institutions can, in the long run at least, be a determining factor in the operation of economies, that is, independent of the economic system. For there is another view of how institutions affect economic life, that over the long run they adapt to the technology and relative prices of economies and play a secondary role in economic history. Interestingly enough this was the view of Douglass North in 1973 in *The Rise of the Western World*, before he converted to the view that institutions are exogenous determinants of economic performance.[9] Let us call this the "efficient institutions" hypothesis.

The argument for such endogeneity of institutions is as follows. Economic institutions, being just a set of rules about who owns what and how ownership is determined, can be changed at little cost in terms of resources. It typically costs no more to have efficient institutions, those that maximize the potential output of a society, than to have inefficient institutions. If an institution impeded the production of the maximum potential output from a society, there would be pressure to change it into one promoting greater efficiency. Many people would gain from the change, and their net gains would be bigger than the losses of the losers. They will thus find a way to compensate the losers in order to persuade them to accept the change. Even preindustrial people are not insensitive to material gain. Institutions destructive of output will be reformed. Thus institutions vary across time and place mainly because differences in technology, relative prices, and people's consumption desires make different social arrangements efficient.[10]

In this view institutions play no role in explaining long-run economic development. Their evolution is interesting, but it is driven by more fundamental economic forces. Their history is also not important for explaining

9. North and Thomas, 1973.
10. This view in many ways echoes Marx's famous statement that "The totality of these relations of production constitutes the economic structure of society, the real foundation, on which arises a legal and political superstructure and to which correspond definite forms of social consciousness"; Marx, 1904, 11.

Figure 11.1 Fallen Lenin statue, Riga, Latvia. The weak economic performance of Soviet-style economies helped ensure the end of the Soviet regime in Latvia in 1991, forty-six years after its imposition.

current outcomes, since their origins will have little bearing on their current functioning. Where you started from makes no difference: there is no path dependence, at least in the long run, from institutional history.[11]

This "efficient institutions" view can accept, especially in dealing with long-run history, that there may be periodic ideological pushes to adopt inefficient institutions as a result of episodes of religious fervor or social turmoil. Examples of religious fervor would be the arrival of Christianity circa AD 30 in the Mediterranean, of Islam in AD 622 in the Middle East, or of Khomeinism in 1979 in Iran. Incidents of social turmoil would include the French Revolution of 1789, the Russian Revolution of 1917, and the subsequent Communist takeovers of North Korea in 1946 and China in 1949. But if the new institutions are economically inefficient they will quickly (by historical time) evolve toward efficiency.

11. Acemoglu et al., 2001, 2002, assert empirically that the past of societies really does predict the future.

History is full of instances of institutions that were over time subverted and refashioned because they were inefficient. One example is the method of deciding legal cases in medieval England by "wager of battle." The Norman conquerors of 1066 imported the right of a defendant in legal cases, including property disputes, to prove his case in this way. In this procedure the defendant would duel with the plaintiff in a ritualized combat that could be fought to the death of one of the parties. The practice grew out of the warrior origins of Norman society and their belief that God would intervene to favor the combatant in the right.[12]

From the earliest records, we know that the parties named champions to fight these duels for them.[13] The great religious houses—those with much land and hence many territorial disputes—even kept champions in training. Thus in 1287 the Abbey of Bury St. Edmunds fought a duel for possession of two manors. The Abbey's chronicle records that "The abbot paid a certain champion called Roger Clerk . . . 20 marks in advance from his own money. After the duel Roger was to receive 30 marks more from him. The champion during the whole time of waiting [for the battle] stayed with us, accompanied by his trainer. . . . On St. Calixtus's day our enemies were victorious and our champion slain in judicial combat in London. And so our manors of Semer and Groton were lost without hope of any recovery."[14]

Since the annual wages of a laborer at this time would be less than 3 marks, the champion who was to receive 50 marks if successful was a highly skilled worker. Unlike Roger Clerk in the example above, the men who fought for pay generally did not fight to the death, and typically one would yield before fatal injury.[15] Wager of battle, it could be argued, was not an institution that ensured productive land use or encouraged investment in land.[16]

But as early as 1179 a tenant whose possession of land was challenged could, for a price, apply to the royal courts for a "writ of peace" prohibiting

12. Von Moschzisker, 1922, 160; Russell, 1959, 242.

13. Until 1275 champions had to swear that they personally knew the facts of the case, thus in many cases committing obvious perjury. This illustrates the elasticity of concepts like truth when they prove institutionally inconvenient.

14. Gransden, 1964, 88–89.

15. Russell, 1959.

16. It is not clear, however, whether armed combat is any worse a way of settling disputes than hiring high-priced attorneys to wield the niceties of legal theory in courtroom battles.

battle and requiring the case be settled by a jury of twelve local knights. Since the defendant could elect to settle the dispute by battle or by jury, duels were still fought infrequently, when the party in possession of the land either knew the title was in some way defective or feared the views of those neighbors who would form the jury. Even though it formally persisted until 1819, the right to be tried by combat fell into disuse in the 1300s, replaced completely by the jury trial.[17] Without any formal reformation the system evolved to a more efficient state.

The evidence on whether institutions evolve toward efficiency is mixed. But institutions with high social costs tend to disappear. Indeed the forces of economic interest are so powerful that when an ideology conflicts with economic interest the solution has generally been to adapt the ideology to resolve the conflict.

An example is the payment of interest on loans. Under early Christianity, and to this day in Islam, the taking of such interest was regarded as usury, an immoral activity.[18] The idea behind this, at least in the case of Christianity, was that money by itself was sterile. If someone borrowed money, and repaid it after a year, why should they have to pay interest for the loan? The money itself was not capable of producing anything, so a bargain that required interest was unjust to the borrower.

But banning all lending at interest frustrates many possible mutually beneficial bargains in any economy. Thus under both Christianity and Islam religious scholars soon sought ways of reconciling the pure principles of faith with the profit opportunities of the market.

While the Catholic church formally adhered to the doctrine against usury throughout the Middle Ages, ingenious theologians showed that most types of interest payment were actually non-usurious. Since the church itself was a major lender, there was considerable pressure to find just such a reconciliation.

17. The 1819 repeal of "wager by battle" followed a celebrated case in 1817. The defendant, Abraham Thornton, a bricklayer, was accused of raping and murdering Mary Ashford. After a jury acquitted him her brother privately prosecuted Thornton for the murder. Under ingenious legal advice, Thornton, a strapping youth, demanded trial by combat. The plaintiff refused to fight, so the defendant won; Rayner and Crook, 1926, 167–71.

18. Modern Islam maintains the prohibition. The Koran prohibits "usury": "GOD permits commerce, and prohibits usury" [2.275]. Many Muslim countries have laws against the taking of interest on loans. But Islamic scholars differ in their interpretation of whether usury is any taking of interest or just the taking of excessive interest.

Thus by 1300 the following exceptions to the practice of collecting interest on loans were all well accepted in Christian Europe:

1. Profits of partnership. As long as each partner took the risks, returns were allowed on capital directly invested in an enterprise (i.e., equity finance was allowed).

2. Rent charges. Anyone could sell a proportion of rent on land or a house in return for a lump sum. Thus a perpetual loan secured by real estate was allowed. Indeed the church itself bought many rent charges as an investment for its substantial endowment.

3. Annuities. An annuity is a fixed annual payment made in return for a lump sum until the person named in the annuity dies. This was permissible since the amount of the payment was uncertain. The Prior of Winchester sold these, and they were also popular in many German cities.

4. Foregone profits. A lender could collect compensation for profits foregone in making a loan.

5. Exchange risk premium. A lender could collect a premium on a loan if it was made in one currency and repaid in another, to cover the exchange rate risk. To exploit this loophole lenders would draw up contracts in which they lent across foreign currencies twice in one transaction, so eliminating all currency risk but still collecting the premium.

The formal prohibition on usury had very little cost to preindustrial Christian society. It outlawed only certain types of bond finance. Since there was still a demand for such loans this was met in two ways. The first was by allowing Jews, as non-Christians, to engage in such lending. The second was by simply ignoring the church rules when it proved convenient. Large-scale finance—lending to princes and the Vatican—was largely untouched by such regulations. There was even an international financial crisis in 1341 when Edward III of England defaulted on his debts, causing the bankruptcy of two of the three largest banks in Europe (the Peruzzi in 1343 and the Bardi in 1346).

Islamic societies similarly found ingenious ways to circumvent the ban. The primary one was the *double sale*. In this transaction the borrower would get, for example, both 100 dinars cash and a small piece of cloth valued at the absurdly high price of 15 dinars. In a year he would have to pay back 100 dinars for the loan of the cash, and 15 for the cloth. These debts were upheld by

Sharia courts. A study of Islamic court records in the Ottoman Empire in the sixteenth century found, even more blatantly, thousands of debt contracts being enforced by the courts. Similarly the *waqfs,* the foundations set up by pious Muslims to maintain mosques, pay imams, support the poor, or provide public goods, frequently held cash assets that they lent at interest.[19] Even modern Muslim states that ban usury have banking arrangements under which depositors still collect interest on their money, though in a "partnership" instead of explicitly as "interest." Such banks currently operate in Egypt, Kuwait, the United Arab Emirates, and Malaysia.

In England usury itself became legal after the Catholic church was replaced by the Church of England, partly as a result of the marital problems of Henry III. But for three hundred years the law fixed a maximum interest rate. A loan violating the usury restriction was not legally enforceable. If the legal interest rate had been set very low, it might have seriously interfered with the capital market. But in practice the legal interest rate was normally set at or above the free market rate. Loans to the crown were exempted from usury restrictions. This was because the crown, an unreliable borrower, paid rates well above the market rate before about 1710. Furthermore, the interest rates specified in the usury laws were impossible to enforce, since the contracting parties could easily inflate the size of the loan in the written contract in order to circumvent the usury restrictions. Usury laws survived so long in England because they imposed very little restriction on the economy.

We can find even more startling examples of the power of economic interest to undermine ideology. In Western Samoa in the Pacific, for example, the traditional rule in choosing chiefs was that the person be a close relative of the previous chief. When interviewed by an anthropologist, people claimed they observed these rules. To confirm the legitimacy of the chief elaborate lineages were kept by each clan. But members have an economic interest in choosing as chief a rich person, since one of the duties of the chief is to provide feasts for the clan. The solution that was frequently used was that the lineages were distorted to make whoever was chosen seem more closely related to the previous chief. The interviewer would find that the new chief was described as more closely related to the previous chief than was in fact the case.[20]

19. Pamuk, 2006, 7–8.
20. The British colonial administrators upset this compromise system by keeping bureaucratic records that established once and for all the actual familial relationships of individuals; Pitt, 1970.

Multiple Equilibrium Theories

To encompass not only institutions that evolve in response to economic pressures but also the possibility that institutions can explain the Industrial Revolution, we need a theory of persistent bad institutions. The key idea here is that while "bad" institutions always cost output *as a whole,* they can and do benefit some *individuals.* If these individuals have the political or police power to preserve the institution, then they will seek to preserve it whatever the cost to society as a whole.

Thus medieval guilds, by keeping out new entrants, may have hurt output in the economy as a whole. But they helped the existing guild members, who therefore clung to the restrictions. The guilds in London in the years before 1688, for example, were politically powerful because they were able to raise money from their members to help the king in times of need. The consumers who might be hurt by the monopolistic guild regulations were less politically powerful because they were a more diffuse group with less ability to organize financial support for the king.

We can hence have a theory of institutions, a "political economy" of institutions, which explains their rise and fall in terms of the material interests of a ruling class. Acemoglu, Johnson, and Robinson, for example, propose the schema in figure 11.2 for any future theory of institutions. The basic driver of societies is no longer their economies, as in the "efficient institutions" view, but their political structure, as well as the distribution of resources among the various political actors. Those who end up with political power will arrange economic and political institutions to maximize their own economic benefits, not the efficiency of the economy as a whole. The system can still be shocked into changes by exogenous forces that change the income distribution and hence political power within the current political institutions. But now differences in initial political institutions or resource distributions can have long-lasting effects.[21]

If the "political economy" of institutions is to explain the pervasive slow growth before 1800, it must explain why early societies consistently had institutions that discouraged growth. For if institutions were chosen through the interplay of various interest groups, or even if they were randomly chosen,

21. This is the structure of the argument about the economic success of former colonies presented in Acemoglu et al., 2001, 2002, 2005a. Such a structure is also found in Engerman and Sokoloff, 2002.

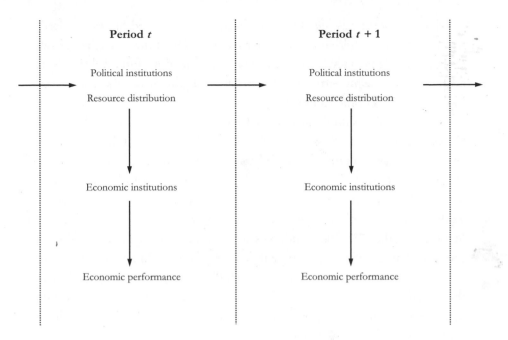

Figure 11.2   Politics as the economic driver. From Acemoglu et al., 2005b.

why would all societies in the thousands of years before 1800 end up with bad institutions? Wouldn't there be at least some that would by chance evolve good institutions? There must be something *systematic* that kept early societies from rewarding innovation. When the English arrived in Australia in 1788, to find a society that had experienced no technological advances for fifty thousand years, they also found that there were more than three hundred distinct Aboriginal languages, including five among the five thousand inhabitants of Tasmania alone. Thus there was not just one Aboriginal society that had failed to show any technological advance, but more than three hundred.[22]

The common feature to which Douglass North, Mancur Olson, and others point is that preindustrial societies were all "predatory states" ruled by "stationary bandits" who maximized their reward at the expense of economic efficiency. Only with the advent of democracy were economic institutions developed that made modern economic growth possible.[23] By the time England achieved its Industrial Revolution it was a constitutional democracy

22. Blainey, 1975, 37–38.
23. North and Weingast, 1989; Olson, 1993.

in which the king was merely a figurehead.[24] The United States, the leading nation in the world in economic terms since at least the 1870s, has also always been a democracy.[25] Where a small class ruled by force a disjuncture arose between the property rules that maximized growth and those that maximized the gains of the ruling elite.

Consider, for example, slave or serf societies: Haiti until 1793, the American South until 1860, Russia until 1861, Brazil until the 1880s. It is frequently argued that slavery and serfdom were inefficient.[26] Since the owner can seize all the output at any time, it is difficult to give slaves incentives to produce well. And the owner has to devote considerable resources to monitoring the work of the slave. Robert Fogel and Stanley Engerman cast doubt on these beliefs through their empirical work on slavery in the American South.[27] But for the sake of argument let us assume that slavery and serfdom were inefficient.

The statement that slavery is an inefficient institution is equivalent to the statement that if we freed a slave the total output of the society would increase. Suppose the output of a slave, the extra amount he or she produces for the owner, is y_s. The slave's marginal output as a free worker would then be higher than that under slavery. The measure of the marginal output of a free worker, the amount the worker adds to the output of society, is the worker's wage, w. Thus if slavery is inefficient

$$w > y_s.$$

Suppose that the owners have to spend the equivalent of a wage of w_s to feed, clothe, and house slaves. The annual profit from owing a slave, the surplus he or she produces, is thus

$$\pi_s = y_s - w_s.$$

The surplus the freed slave produces, $\pi_f = w - y_s$, is greater than this. That means that the slave could pay π_s to the former master and still have a surplus over his or her former subsistence consumption. The slave and the master can

24. The franchise was limited, however, being restricted to male property owners. Furthermore, since the vote was taken by a public ballot, vote buying was common.

25. Though, again, a limited democracy for much of that time.

26. Serfdom was a form of slavery, widespread across preindustrial Europe, under which the owner had property rights in the serf but custom limited the exactions.

27. Fogel and Engerman, 1974.

"If it made sense, that would be a very powerful idea."

Figure 11.3 Institutionalism?

reach an agreement giving each of them part of this surplus, and both would be better off.

Thus if slavery really is a socially inefficient institution it should end spontaneously, merely through market forces. There should be no need for abolition movements or antislavery crusades. The Civil War would have been unnecessary. Indeed in ancient Athens it was common for skilled slaves to live on their own in the cities and simply make an annual payment to their owners, who otherwise left them to their own devices. But suppose that the freed slaves, instead of using their freedom to happily make their annual payments to their former masters, organized and overthrew the unjust social order that had condemned them to labor for the ruling class. Or suppose they used their freedom to migrate to an adjacent society in which they would not have to pay the annual exaction.

Given these possibilities, even though emancipation increases the total amount of social product, it reduces the income to the ruling class. This situation is portrayed in figure 11.4. Stipulate, for example, that a society with slavery produces a total surplus of 1 unit, which all goes to the ruling class.

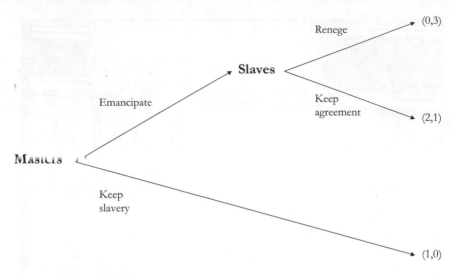

Figure 11.4 The emancipation decision analyzed.

The existing set of payoffs is shown as the number pair (1,0) in the bottom part of the diagram, where the first number denotes the masters' surplus, and the second number the slaves' surplus. Stipulate also that emancipation would increase the total surplus to 3 units. Then the conditions for slaves buying themselves out of slavery seem to exist.

In particular a deal by which after emancipation the masters get 2 units of the new surplus, while the ex-slaves get 1 unit, should be accepted by both parties. This outcome is shown as the path where the masters emancipate and the ex-slaves keep to the agreement. But once emancipation occurs, suppose that the ex-slaves get to control the distribution of income. Then they would take all the surplus for themselves, leaving the masters worse off. In this situation slaves cannot commit to uphold the initial deal, and thus masters will never agree to it. Without an outside arbiter of property rights, the agreement, even though it increases output, will be rejected by the ruling class.

The case of slavery is just a specific example of what "institutionalists" would argue is the general problem of preindustrial society: the unresolved struggle over the distribution of goods and power limited output. Note, however, that in many (but not all) preindustrial societies, slaves did buy their own freedom, or worked independently and paid a fixed sum per year to their owners. Thus, though there was a huge slave population in Roman Italy around AD 1 as a result of captures in Roman conquests, by AD 200, without any emancipation movement, most of these slaves had disappeared. In medieval England, although large numbers of slaves and serfs, making up the majority of the population, were recorded in the *Doomsday Book* of 1086, all slaves and serfs had been freed by 1500, without any emancipation movement.

So the general argument institutionalists would make is that preindustrial elites—typically a military ruling class—did not undertake policies to foster technological advance because economic growth would have seen the elites expropriated. Somehow, through chance, a social structure emerged prior to 1800 in countries like England under which the interests of a larger share of the population came to be represented in the government, which then was induced to pursue economic efficiency. Why, however, did this happen only once in the history of the preindustrial world? Why were there not many societies in which the rulers were secure enough that they were happy to reap the benefits of technological advance?

Human Capital

This argument that preindustrial society was stuck in a bad equilibrium has taken other forms. The one that has recently attracted the most attention from economic theorists is that in the Malthusian world parents were induced to have large numbers of children, to each of whom they provided little training or education. One of the great social changes in the advanced industrial economies since the Industrial Revolution is a decline in the number of children to whom the average woman gave birth, from five or six to two or fewer. Proponents of this interpretation, such as the Nobel laureates Gary Becker and Robert Lucas, argue that this switch, induced by changing economic circumstances, has been accompanied by a great increase in the time and attention invested in each child. People are not the same in all societies. With enough parental attention they can be transformed into much more effective actors. The continual efficiency growth of the modern world has thus been created by the production of higher-quality people.

Chapter 9 gives evidence that literacy and numeracy had increased greatly by the eve of the Industrial Revolution. We saw in chapter 10 that modern growth is seemingly the product of an expansion of the knowledge stock by investment in creating new production techniques. The institutional view explained above assumes that the demand for innovation was increased by better social institutions. But this alternative interpretation is that changes in

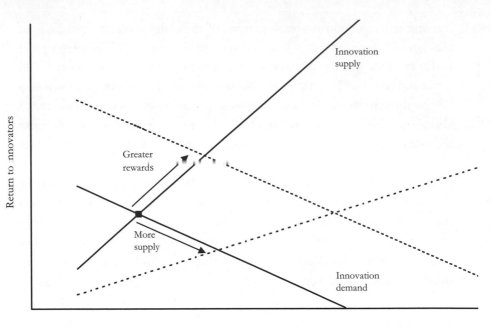

Figure 11.5 Demand and supply interpretations of the Industrial Revolution.

family size resulted in economic actors who were better educated and hence more effective at producing new techniques. The quality of a human agent depends on the time input of his or her parents, which in turn depends on family size. The contrast between these views is portrayed in figure 11.5. The proponents of institutional change as the cause see a change in the private reward to innovators as spurring the Industrial Revolution, while the proponents of human capital investments see an increasing supply of innovations at a given private reward as the key. We thus need not see any increase in the private returns to innovation in the Industrial Revolution under the human capital interpretation.

What would motivate families to have fewer but better-educated children? From the point of view of the individual family there must be some signal in the form of higher relative earnings for educated children. But why would such a change appear in the Malthusian economy? If education for children is in part a consumer good purchased by parents, then one obvious trigger for a change in behavior would be the higher incomes we have witnessed since the onset of the Industrial Revolution. But this would imply that higher-income families would have begun to reduce family size long before the Industrial Revolution. And we saw in chapter 6 that in fact in the preindustrial world the effective family size, measured by the numbers of children alive at the death of fathers, was significantly higher for higher-income parents, all the way up to very high income levels.

Another possible cause of a reduction in child numbers in favor of fewer, better-educated children would be an increase in the premium that the market offered for those children with better education. Here, however, we find absolutely no evidence as we approach 1800 of any market signal to parents that they need to invest more in the education or training of their children. Figure 9.4, for example, showed that the skill premium in the earnings of building craftsmen relative to unskilled building laborers and assistants was actually at its highest before the onset of the Black Death in 1348, when a craftsman earned nearly double the wage of a laborer. If there was ever an incentive to accumulate skills it was in the early economy. Thereafter the premium declines to a lower but relatively stable level from about 1370 until 1900, a period of over five hundred years, before declining further in the twentieth century. Thus the time of the greatest market reward for skills and training was long before the Industrial Revolution.

Proponents of a switch from a preindustrial low-human-capital equilibrium to a modern high-human-capital society are extraordinarily vague about what would trigger the switch between equilibria. Becker, Murphy, and Tamura, for example, argue that the transition was caused by "technological and other shocks. . . . improved methods to use coal, better rail and ocean transports, and decreased regulation of prices and foreign trade."[28] But the need here is for an explanation of these technological shocks.

A final empirical hurdle faced by human capital theories of the Industrial Revolution is that the timing of the demographic transition in Europe and the United States places it circa 1890, 120 years after the traditional dating of the Industrial Revolution. Figure 11.6, for example, shows the demographic transition in England and Sweden, two relatively well-documented countries. In both cases the decline in fertility does not start in any substantial way until well into the late nineteenth century, a hundred years after the traditional dating of the Industrial Revolution. We thus see a very poor timing match among the elements that would seem to be needed for a human capital–based interpretation of the Industrial Revolution—the revolution itself, the average size of families, and the premium paid in the labor market for skills.

28. Becker et al., 1990, S32–S33.

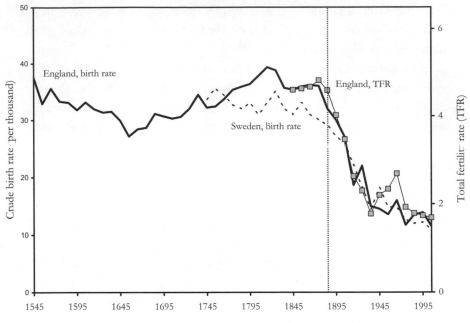

Figure 11.6   The demographic transition in Europe.

Furthermore, for England we have proxy measures for literacy that go back to 1580, such indicators as the percentage of grooms who signed the marriage register or the percentage of witnesses in court cases signing their depositions. These measures do show a long upward movement in implied literacy rates. But as we saw in figure 9.3 they show very little change, at least for men, during the years 1760–1860, the classic dates for the Industrial Revolution.

Endogenous Growth Theories

None of the above theories of institutional changes or of a switch between equilibria explains why the Industrial Revolution had to happen—or why it happened in 1760 as opposed to 1800 BC in ancient Babylonia or 500 BC in ancient Greece. Endogenous growth theories attempt to explain not just how the Industrial Revolution took place, but also why it occurred when it did. They argue that there was an internal evolution of the economic system that eventually led to modern growth.

A nice example of such an endogenous growth theory is that of Michael Kremer. Kremer assumes that the social institutions that provide the incen-

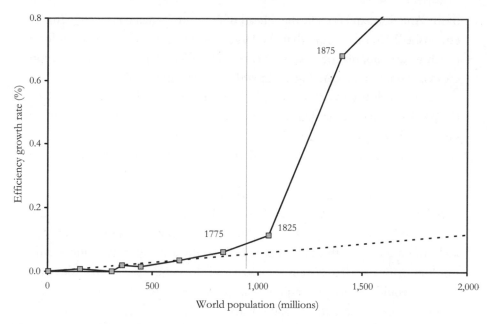

Figure 11.7 World population and growth rate of efficiency. World population is from the same sources as for table 7.1. The rate of efficiency advance is estimated from population until 1850, and thereafter from the fundamental equation of growth.

tives to individuals to create knowledge are the same in all societies. Each person thus has a given probability of producing a new idea. In this case the growth rate of knowledge will be a function of the size of the human community. The more people with whom you are in contact, the more you get to benefit from the ideas of others. There was substantial but slow productivity growth in the world economy in the years before 1800, and that was translated into a huge expansion of the world population. Modern economic growth is the result of sheer scale.

Kremer adduces two kinds of evidence for his position. The first is based on population growth rates for the world as a whole in the preindustrial era. In the years before 1850, when population growth rates effectively index the rate of efficiency advance, there is a strong positive correlation between the size of world population and the implied rate of efficiency advance, as shown in figure 11.7.

The second evidence Kremer brings forward is population densities circa 1500 across the major continents, which had been isolated from each other for millennia: Eurasia, the Americas, and Australia. Why was Eurasia so far ahead of the Americas, and even farther ahead of Australia, when contact was finally established? Kremer argues that the large land mass of Eurasia allowed for a much greater population at any level of technology. This greater population created more rapid technological growth rates in Eurasia.[29]

There is clearly a core of sense to the idea that increased population size, the product of past technological change in the preindustrial era, increased the rate of technological advance. But it is also clear that world population alone cannot explain the acceleration in efficiency growth rates after 1800 seen in figure 11.7.

Under Kremer's argument, the growth rate of ideas would be at best just proportionate to population size. This would occur where there is no rivalry in the production of ideas. That is, the more people there are, proportionately the more ideas there are. More realistically a larger population would produce many simultaneous introductions of the same ideas, so that idea production would expand less rapidly than population. To obtain a growth rate of ideas proportionate to population, idea production must also be proportional to the existing stock of ideas. Each idea opens the way for possible extensions: the more we know, the more easily we can add further to our stock of knowledge.[30]

With the two assumptions above we can take the world population observations from before 1800 and plot the relationship between the population size and efficiency growth rates. This is shown as the dotted line in figure 11.7. When we use this line to predict the expected rate of efficiency growth for fifty-year periods after 1800 we see that the actual efficiency growth rates increasingly deviate from the predicted rates.

The lack of fit seen here is going to be a problem with any endogenous growth theory of the Industrial Revolution: it is the Industrial Revolution's seemingly discontinuous nature. Oded Galor and Omer Moav, for example, propose a theoretical model that combines the Kremer population mechanism with endogenously changing household preferences for quality, as opposed to

---

29. Kremer, 1993b.

30. Formally we assume $\Delta A = hNA$, where A, the level of efficiency now, is also an index for the stock of ideas, ΔA is the addition to the stock of ideas in any year, N is the population level, and h is just a constant. This implies that the growth rate of ideas, which is also the growth rate of efficiency, is

$$g_A = \frac{\Delta A}{A} = hN.$$

quantity, of children. They do not, however, show that this model produces such a discontinuity.[31]

Challenges Ahead

There are many competing theories of the great break in human history that is the Industrial Revolution. Each is problematic for its own reasons, and none looks particularly plausible on its face. The next chapter considers the details of the Industrial Revolution, and whether they can be reconciled with any particular theory of the event.

31. Galor and Moav, 2002.

12 The Industrial Revolution in England

In the eighty years or so after 1780 the population of Britain nearly tripled, the towns of Liverpool and Manchester became gigantic cities, the average income of the population more than doubled, the share of farming fell from just under half to just under one-fifth of the nation's output, and the making of textiles and iron moved into the steam-driven factories. So strange were these events that before they happened they were not anticipated, and while they were happening they were not comprehended.   —Donald McCloskey (1981)[1]

The Industrial Revolution in England—the seemingly abrupt escape of this tiny island nation, within less than a generation, from millennia of pitifully slow economic progress—is one of history's great mysteries. Its apparent suddenness, in a society that was (and still is) noted for the evolutionary nature of all social change, poses a baffling challenge to those who would supply an economic explanation.

In one of the more delicious ironies of history the Industrial Revolution was precisely coupled with that other model of human liberation, the French Revolution. But the political revolutionaries who proclaimed their love for all humanity in 1789 were soon awash in the blood of an ever-expanding list of enemies. As the revolutionaries fed on each other, revolutionary equality soon yielded to a vainglorious military dictatorship that led hundreds of thousands to their starving, frozen end on the Russian steppes. Meanwhile a "nation of shopkeepers," incapable it seemed of vision beyond their next beef pudding, was transforming the possibilities for all humanity. And in the process, as we shall see, they ushered in more egalitarian societies than had been witnessed for thousands of years.

The events of the Industrial Revolution, thanks to two hundred years of historical inquiry, are widely known and reasonably well agreed upon. But their interpretation remains hotly contested, with no two scholars agreeing on what caused the Industrial Revolution and on what its wider significance is.

1. McCloskey, 1981, 103.

Here, after briefly detailing the major events of the Industrial Revolution, I argue that, contrary to appearances, the Industrial Revolution actually stretched back hundreds of years to its origin, and that it was a gradual and evolutionary development that affected other European economies almost as much as England. It was the product of the gradual progress of settled agrarian societies toward a more rational, economically oriented mindset, manifested in the many dimensions discussed in chapter 9.

While there is no doubt that a revolutionary change took place at some point, between preindustrial society with its 0 percent productivity growth rate and modern society with productivity growth rates exceeding 1 percent per year, the precise date of that transition is hard to identify, and it may remain forever indeterminate.

In particular, individual personalities and events, so beloved of narrative historians, do not matter. World history would have not changed in any significant respect had the future Sir Richard Arkwright—the sometime Bolton hairdresser, wigmaker, and pub owner who introduced mechanized factory spinning in 1768—instead opened a fish shop. We would not still be sitting in the Malthusian era had James Watt, inventor of separate condensers for steam engines in 1769, instead found God and trained for the ministry.

The appearance of a sudden shock to the economic system was created instead by accidents and contingencies. In particular the enormous population growth in England after 1760, Britain's military successes in the Revolutionary and Napoleonic wars, and the development of the United States all contributed to the appearance of an abrupt departure, as opposed to the continuation of more gradual changes.

The Details of the Industrial Revolution

The Industrial Revolution is unique in world history owing to the sudden appearance of a more rapid rate of efficiency advance than had been witnessed over sustained periods by any earlier economy.

The efficiency of any competitive economy, or indeed of any sector within the economy, can be estimated simply as the ratio of the average cost of the production inputs—capital, labor, and land—per unit to the average output price per unit. That is,

$$A = \frac{\text{Average cost of a unit of inputs}}{\text{Average price of a unit of output}}.$$

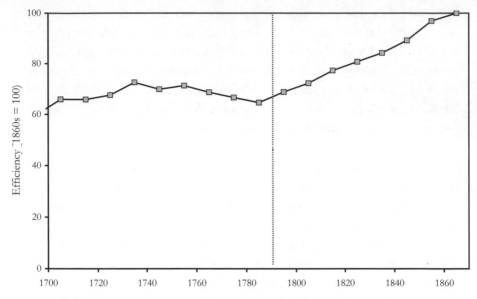

Figure 12.1 Production efficiency in England by decade, 1700–1869.

More efficient economies produce more output per unit of input. Since the value of payments to inputs has to equal the value of outputs, in more efficient economies output prices are low relative to input prices. The exact details of this computation are given in the technical appendix, but the concept itself is simple.

Thanks to the unique stability of England from at least 1200 onward, records of wages, prices, population, rents, and returns of capital can be constructed throughout these years, allowing us to estimate the efficiency of the English economy as far back as 1200.

Figure 12.1 shows production efficiency calculated in this way for the interval 1700–1869. In the immediate run-up to the Industrial Revolution in the eighteenth century there is no sign of any sustained efficiency growth. The English economy of the eighteenth century looks as Malthusian as any that came before. Then, around 1790, the steady, inexorable upward march of efficiency that characterizes the modern age first appears. From the 1780s to the 1860s the efficiency growth rate was still only 0.5 percent per year, less than half the typical modern rate. But this was nevertheless a period of unprecedented, sustained advance in efficiency.

The immediate sources of the productivity advance after 1790 are well understood. Table 12.1 shows the overall productivity growth rate from the

Table 12.1 Sources of the Industrial Revolution, 1760s–1860s

Sector	Efficiency growth rate (%)	Share of national income	Contribution to national efficiency growth rate (%)
All textiles	—	0.11	0.24
Cottons	2.4	0.06	0.18
Woolens	1.1	0.04	0.05
Iron and steel	1.4	0.01	0.02
Coal mining	0.2	0.02	0.00
Transport	1.2	0.08	0.09
Agriculture	0.3	0.30	0.07
Identified advance	—	0.51	0.42
Whole economy	—	1.00	0.40

1760s to the 1860s, as well as the contributions from the major sectors with known innovations. As noted, a nice property of the aggregate productivity growth rate is that it is just the sum of productivity growth rates in each sector weighted by the share of the value of output in that sector in the national value of output (see the technical appendix).

As the last column of the table shows, productivity advance in textiles accounted for more than half of all productivity advance for the hundred years of the Industrial Revolution. A small additional contribution came from coal and iron, but the other major contributing sectors were transport and agriculture. Transport because there was rapid productivity advance in that sector. Agriculture because, even though productivity advance was slow, the size of the sector allowed it to make a significant national contribution.

Textiles were the flagship industry of the Industrial Revolution. Efficiency in converting raw cotton into cloth increased fourteenfold from the 1760s to the 1860s, a growth rate of 2.4 percent per year, faster than productivity growth rates in most modern economies. In the 1860s the output of the economy was about 27 percent higher than it would otherwise have been, due solely to textile innovations—a gain in income equivalent to £169 million a year.

Figure 12.2 A water frame from Richard Arkwright's Cromford Mill, 1785.

While it took the equivalent of 18 man-hours to transform a pound of cotton into cloth in the 1760s, by the 1860s this was done in the equivalent of 1.5 man-hours. The cause of this gain is also clear. Beginning in the 1760s, a stream of technological innovations in textiles—some famous but most of them anonymous—transformed the industry. The machines that allowed this gain were still surprisingly simple in their construction, as figure 12.2 (showing the Arkwright water frame) demonstrates.

Institutionalists assert that an increased rate of innovation must stem from greater inducements offered by the economy to innovators. Yet the textile innovators of the Industrial Revolution, even those who were successful and are now famous, typically earned small returns.

Table 12.2 Gains from Innovation in the Textile Sector during the Industrial Revolution

Innovator	Device	Result
John Kay	Flying shuttle, 1733	Impoverished by litigation to enforce patent. House destroyed by machine breakers in 1753. Died in poverty in France.
James Hargreaves	Spinning jenny, 1769	Patent denied. Forced to flee by machine breakers in 1768. Died in workhouse in 1777.
Richard Arkwright	Water frame, 1769	Worth £0.5 million at death in 1792. Most of his fortune was made after 1781, when other manufacturers stopped honoring his patents.
Samuel Crompton	Mule, 1779	No attempt to patent invention. Granted £500 by manufacturers in the 1790s. Granted £5,000 by Parliament in 1811.
Reverend Edmund Cartwright	Power loom, 1785	Patent worthless. Factory burned by machine breakers in 1790. Granted £10,000 by Parliament in 1809.
Eli Whitney (United States)	Cotton gin, 1793	Patent worthless. Made money later as a government arms contractor.
Richard Roberts	Self-acting mule, 1830	Patent revenues barely covered development costs. Died in poverty in 1864.

Source: Usher, 1929, 249–69.

Table 12.2 lists the financial gains of the most famous innovators in the textile industries during the Industrial Revolution. These men—the few who succeeded where many others had tried and failed, who helped revolutionize textiles—typically benefited little from their endeavors. Even in Industrial Revolution England the market was just not very good at rewarding innovation.

The profit rates of major firms in the industry also provide evidence that most of the innovations quickly leaked from the innovators to other producers, with little reward to the originators. The cotton spinners Samuel Greg and

Partners earned average profits of 12 percent from 1796 to 1819. This was a normal return for a commercial venture of the time. Similarly William Grey and Partners made less than 2 percent per year from 1801 to 1810—a negative profit rate. If innovative firms could have guarded their discoveries, through secrecy or enforceable patents, they would have reaped large profits compared to their competitors. Instead innovations in cotton spinning mainly reduced prices, benefiting consumers. Thus Richard Hornby and Partners, operating in the weaving sector (which was not mechanized until the 1810s), posted an average profit of 11 percent during the interval 1777–1809. This was as high as the profit of Greg and Partners, operating in the innovating sector.[2]

Further evidence of the meager rewards to innovation in the textile industry during the Industrial Revolution comes from the wills of the rich in the nineteenth century. Only a handful of textile innovators, such as Richard Arkwright and Robert Peel, became wealthy. Of the 379 people who died in the 1860s in Britain leaving estates of more than £0.5 million, only 17 (4 percent) were in textiles.[3] Yet the industry produced 11 percent of Britain's national output and was responsible for the majority of the efficiency advance during the Industrial Revolution. The economy of the period was still spectacularly bad at rewarding innovation. Wage earners and foreign customers, not entrepreneurs, were the overwhelming beneficiaries of innovation. This is why Britain has few foundations to rival the great private philanthropies and universities of the United States. The Industrial Revolution did not make paupers into princes.

A similar tale can be told for the other great nexuses of innovation in Industrial Revolution England: coal mining, iron and steel, and railroads. English coal output, for example, exploded during the Industrial Revolution. Figure 12.3 shows that output by the 1860s was nearly twenty times as great as in the 1700s. This coal heated homes, made ore into iron, and powered railway locomotives. Yet there were no equivalents of the great fortunes made in oil, railways, and steel in America's late-nineteenth-century industrialization.

The new industrial priesthood, the engineers who developed the English coalfields, railways, and canals, made prosperous but typically moderate livings. Though their names survive to history—Richard Trevithick, George and Robert Stephenson, Humphry Davy—they too captured very few of the

2. Harley, 1998. The risk-free return on capital in these years was 5 percent or above.
3. Rubinstein, 1981, 60–67.

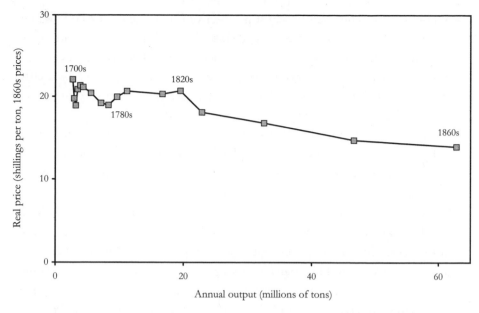

Figure 12.3　Coal output and real prices, 1700s–1860s. Data from Clark and Jacks, 2007.

social rewards their enterprise wrought. Richard Trevithick, the pioneer of locomotives, died a pauper in 1833. George Stephenson—whose famous locomotive *The Rocket* ran loaded at 15 miles an hour in a trial in 1829, an unprecedented speed for land travel in this era—did much better. Yet his country house in Chesterfield was but a small reward for his substantial contributions to railway engineering. Other locomotives competed in the famous trial, and soon a swarm of locomotive builders were supplying the expanding railway network.

As figure 12.3 illustrates, innovation in the Industrial Revolution era typically benefited mainly consumers in the form of lower prices. As coal output exploded, real prices to consumers steadily declined: the real price in the 1700s was 60 percent greater than that in the 1860s. Coal, iron and steel, and rail carriage all remained highly competitive in England during the Industrial Revolution. The patent system offered little protection to most of the innovations in these sectors, and they quickly leaked from one producer to another.

The increased rate of innovation in Industrial Revolution England was the result not of unusual rewards but of a greater supply of innovation, still modestly rewarded. Figure 11.5 illustrated two ways in which innovation rates might increase. The institutionalist perspective is that the rewards offered by the market shifted upward compared to those in all previous preindustrial economies. There is no evidence of any such change. The last significant reform of the patent system was in 1689, more than a hundred years before efficiency gains became common. And the patent system itself played little role for most innovation in Industrial Revolution England.

Instead the upsurge in innovation in the Industrial Revolution, in terms of figure 11.5, reflected a surge in supply. With the benefits to innovation no greater than in earlier economies, the supply of them nevertheless rose substantially. Facing the same challenges and incentives as in other economies, British producers were more likely to attempt novel methods of production.

The experience of agriculture supports the idea that the Industrial Revolution represented mainly a change in the supply of innovation rather than improved incentives. Historians have long written of an agricultural revolution accompanying the Industrial Revolution. Indeed generations of English schoolchildren have read, probably with bored bemusement, of the exploits of such supposedly heroic innovators as Jethro Tull (author in 1733 of *An Essay on Horse-Hoeing Husbandry*), "Turnip" Townsend, and Arthur Young. But this agricultural revolution is a myth, created by historians who vastly overestimated the gains in output from English agriculture in these years.[4] The productivity growth rate in agriculture was instead modest, at 0.27 percent per year, lower than for the economy as a whole. But even these modest gains represented considerably faster productivity growth than had been typical over the years 1200–1800. Figure 12.4, for example, shows wheat yields per seed sown in England from 1211 to 1453. Medieval agriculture seems to have been totally static over hundreds of years.

Yet the agricultural improvements of the Industrial Revolution had no discernible connection to events in industry. Mechanization remained minimal in English agriculture even by 1860, the only substantially mechanized task being grain threshing. Similarly, the insistence of the school curriculum notwithstanding, there were no heroic innovators, as in textiles and steam—no Hargreaves, Cromptons, Watts, or Stephensons—just an amorphous collec-

---

4. These output estimates were based on the food needs of a growing and also wealthier population. But they did not take into account the way coal and imported raw materials substituted for the former agricultural production of energy and raw materials, allowing English agriculture to feed more people with little additional total output.

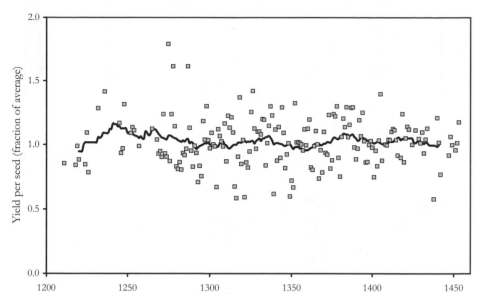

Figure 12.4 Wheat yields in England, 1211–1453. The boxes show annual yields, and the solid line a twenty-one-year moving average of these annual yields. Data from Clark, 2001a.

tion of anonymous sons of the soil, somehow bringing home more bacon. All subsequent accounts have been of incremental changes, carried out by a broad swath of farmers across a long sweep of time.[5]

Thousands of individual cultivators in Industrial Revolution England somehow learned incrementally better methods from their neighbors or from their own observations. They did this despite the fact that their medieval cousins, with the same incentives, were unable to progress.

When Was the Industrial Revolution?

The discussion above suggests that the transition between the static Mathusian economy, which lasted at least a hundred thousand years, and the modern economy can be dated to 1760–1800. But that appearance of a definitive break between the two regimes, in the blink of an eye in terms of human history, is mistaken. Instead a whole series of contingencies conspired to make the break seem much more definitive and sudden than it was.

5. See, for example, Overton, 1996, 4.

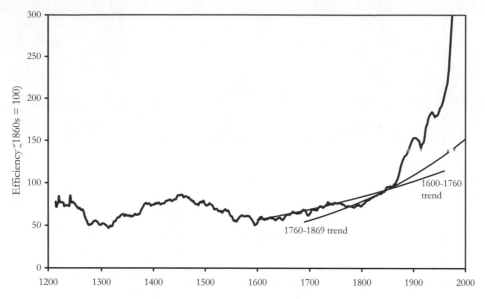

Figure 12.5 Long-run efficiency of the English economy, 1250–2000.

The first sign that the transition date is more ambiguous than the traditional histories suggest comes from an examination of the efficiency of the English economy all the way back to 1246. The efficiency measured here is the efficiency at producing income, whether the goods consumed came from England or abroad.[6] With the enormous rise in overseas trade in these years, and with that trade often involving territories ruled by British settlers and overlords, the boundary of the "English economy" becomes increasingly ill defined. Figure 12.5 shows the efficiency of the English economy on this basis from 1250 to 2000 as a ten-year moving average.

Overall the dramatic transition from the preindustrial to the modern world is clear. But the acceleration of efficiency growth during the Industrial Revolution, around 1800, is not so evident from this longer perspective. It is also clear that England experienced steady, but not spectacular, efficiency growth in the 160 years preceding 1760. The annual rate of 0.2 percent per year was slow by modern standards. But the slow growth of the interval 1600–1760 was still enough to increase the measured efficiency of the English economy 37 percent over these years, a much more rapid pace of advance than was

6. In contrast table 12.1 refers to the growth rates of efficiency of production of goods within England, which was faster since much of the textile output was exported.

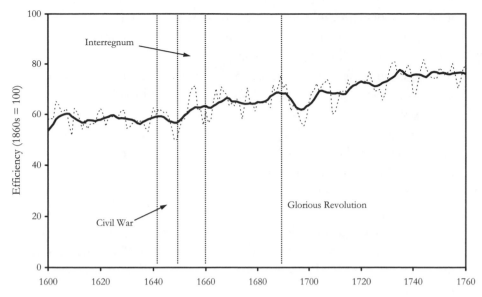

Figure 12.6 Efficiency of the English economy during the approach to the Industrial Revolution, 1600–1760.

generally seen in the Malthusian era. Indeed had this growth continued from 1760 without the hiatus witnessed in the last decades of the eighteenth century, the efficiency of the economy in the 1860s would have been at 95 percent of the level achieved after the Industrial Revolution.

The efficiency of production of income increased only 0.33 percent per year from 1760 to 1869, a rate fast by the standards of the Malthusian era but still slow by modern benchmarks. So one way the Industrial Revolution could be interpreted is as one phase within a general transition, from Malthusian stasis to modern growth, that the English economy began around 1600. It was not an abrupt start, but a continuation and acceleration of a process that, with ups and downs, has brought us to the present.

If growth really did begin in the early seventeenth century, then simple institutionalist explanations of the Industrial Revolution, which have focused on the arrival of modern democracy in England with the Glorious Revolution in 1688–89, look decidedly unpromising. Figure 12.6 shows the efficiency of the English economy in close-up view, by year from 1600 to 1760 and as a ten-year moving average. None of the political events—the Civil War of 1642–48, the reign of Parliament and Cromwell during the failed Interregnum, the restoration of the monarchy in 1660, or the Glorious Revolution of 1688–89—

makes any apparent difference to the slow upward movement of economic efficiency. Harvest successes and failures, which account for most of the short-term fluctuations, have much more impact than political events. And the rise of efficiency clearly started in the seventeenth century, before the great institutional change cited by Douglass North and his followers, the Glorious Revolution.

But figure 12.5 also reveals that before 1600 there were mysterious swings up and down in the measured efficiency of the English economy. Around 1450, at its late medieval maximum, the measured efficiency of the economy was within 88 percent of its level in the 1860s. Around 1300, at its minimum, it was only at 55 percent of the level in the 1860s. This suggests the possibility that the efficiency growth witnessed in the years 1600–1800 was really just a catch-up to the average medieval efficiency level, and that 1800 does represent the true beginnings of a break from the medieval regime. Without further information there is no way to tell.

Why Did the Industrial Revolution Appear so Dramatic?

The efficiency growth rates cited above suggest that a muted, gradual transition between the Malthusian and modern economies took place in England around 1800. Rapid productivity growth rates fully equal to those of modern economies did not appear until the late nineteenth century.

Why then did the Industrial Revolution appear so dramatic to contemporaries and to later observers? Why did nonfarm output increase almost ninefold between the 1730s and the 1860s? Why the new giant cities where before there had been only villages and fields, the transformation of the countryside through the enclosure of common lands, the building of a dense network of twenty thousand miles of new turnpike roads? Why the mining of vast quantities of coal—coal output was eighteen times greater in the 1860s than in the 1730s—with the scarring of the landscape by coal waste tips?

Why finally the ascendance of this minor country on the northwestern corner of Europe—which in 1700 had a population less than one-third that of France and about 4 percent that of both China and India—to the position of world dominance it achieved by 1850, if not for dramatic gains from the Industrial Revolution?

The answer proposed here is that the appearance of dramatic discontinuity in the Industrial Revolution comes from the coincidence of faster productivity growth in England with an unexpected and unrelated explosion in English population in the years 1750–1870. Britain's rise to world dominance was thus a product more of the bedroom labors of British workers than of their factory toil. English population rose from six million in the 1740s, no more than its medieval maximum in the 1300s, to twenty million in the 1860s, more than tripling. Other countries in Europe experienced far more restricted population gains. The French, for example, increased during the same interval only from twenty-one million to thirty-seven million. In addition the westward expansion of the United States was steadily adding more acres of farm output to the world economy. Thus England went from a country whose land area per person was similar to that of its trading partners in the 1760s to one that had significantly less land per person than all its trading partners by the 1860s (see table 12.6).

The population explosion seems completely unrelated to the productivity gains in textiles, steam, iron, and agriculture that characterized the Industrial Revolution. For a start, the growth in population was well under way before there were significant productivity gains in any sector. By the 1790s population was already 37 percent higher than in the 1740s. That was why Malthus, writing in the 1790s, saw only a problem of excess population, not one of population growth driven by economic changes. Since mortality declined little in the era of the Industrial Revolution, most of the increase in population came from fertility increases.

Chapter 4 showed how the birth rate was restrained in preindustrial England by women marrying late, by large numbers of women never marrying, and by women remaining celibate outside marriage. Even though fertility was unrestricted within marriage, this marriage pattern, at its extreme around 1650, avoided half of all possible conceptions.

In the early eighteenth century the age of first marriage for women began to decline. Figure 12.7 reveals that this drop began in the 1720s. This decline in age of first marriage was enough on its own to raise the birth rate by a fifth by 1800. At the same time as women married younger, more of them married. In 1650 a fifth of women never married. By the early eighteenth century the proportion of lifetime unmarried women had fallen to 10 percent, and the rate remained at this lower level through the Industrial Revolution. The greater frequency of marriage added another 12 percent to fertility. Finally, though fewer women were at risk for this outcome, illegitimate births increased, adding another 5 percent to overall fertility. Multiplying these factors we obtain an increase in fertility between 1650 and 1800 of 40 percent. Thus while in 1650

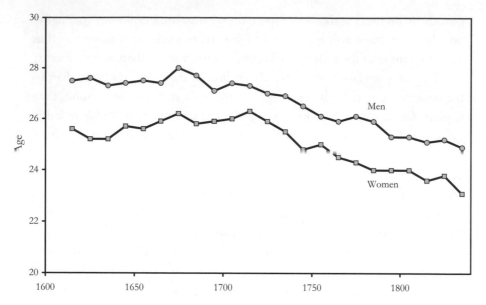

Figure 12.7   Age of first marriage by decade, bachelor-spinster marriages. Data from Wrigley et al., 1997, 134.

the net reproduction rate was only 1.93 children per woman and population was declining, by 1800 it was 2.68 and population was growing rapidly.

The sources of these changes in nuptiality do not seem to be economic. They occurred in both the north and the south of England even though the north was significantly transformed by the Industrial Revolution and the south was largely unaffected. They occurred in parishes where employment was predominantly in agriculture as well as in parishes mainly engaged in trade, handicrafts, and manufacturing, as table 12.3 shows. The only feature of this period that might explain earlier and more frequent marriage is the decline of maternal deaths from childbirth. Table 12.4 shows that in the seventeenth century 1.5 percent of pregnancies ended with the death of the mother.[7] A woman marrying at 25, who gave birth to the average of number of children for such a marriage, 5.6, would have a 9 percent chance of dying in pregnancy. The last column of the table shows the risk of death from pregnancy that a woman who married at age 20 would face in each half century. These were very high risks. By 1800 the mortality risk from pregnancy had dropped by two-thirds, even

7. The chance of dying as a result of the complications of pregnancy in England is now less than 0.006 percent per birth.

Table 12.3 Women's Average Age of First Marriage by Parish Type

Period	Agricultural parishes (8)	Retail and handicraft parishes (5)	Manufacturing parishes (3)	Mixed parishes (10)
1700–49	25.2	26.5	26.6	26.3
1750–99	24.3	24.8	24.6	24.7
1800–37	23.7	24.0	23.4	23.7

Source: Wrigley et al., 1997, 187.
Note: Numbers of parishes in parentheses.

Table 12.4 Deaths from Pregnancy

Period	Pregnancies resulting in death of mother (%)	Female mean age of marriage	Deaths from pregnancy of women marrying at age 20 (%)
Pre-1600	1.23	—	—
1600–49	1.34	25.4	9.7
1650–99	1.63	25.9	11.3
1700–49	1.28	25.7	9.0
1750–99	0.92	24.4	7.1
1800–37	0.55	23.5	4.3

Source: Wrigley et al., 1997, 134, 313, 399.
Note: The percentage of mothers dying from childbirth complications is calculated assuming that these were the only risks of mortality for married women. Deaths from other causes at ages 20–49 would reduce this percentage.

though there was little decline in overall mortality. Women would be well aware of the mortality risks of marriage. The high level of these risks in the seventeenth century might thus explain both delaying marriage, as a way of reducing these risks, and also the decision by many women to eschew marriage altogether.

The limited efficiency gains of the Industrial Revolution, detailed above, mean that population growth was more important than efficiency growth in driving up the output of the English economy. Figure 12.8 shows the rise of total income in England between 1700 and 1860 compared to the rise in population and the gain in income per person. While the total output of the

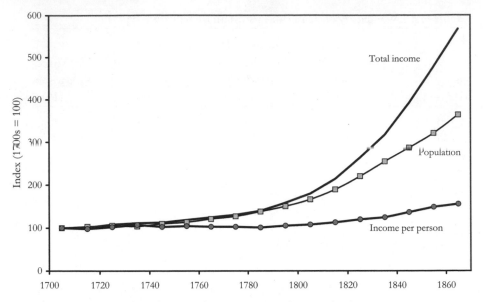

Figure 12.8 Population and economic growth in England, 1700s–1860s.

English economy was nearly six times as large by the 1860s, population growth alone explains most of this gain.

Furthermore, the gain in population was even more important to the relative size of the English economy than to its absolute size. The productivity gains during the Industrial Revolution had almost as much effect on the incomes of England's competitors in Europe as on England itself, for two reasons. The first was direct exports of cheaper textiles, iron, and coal by England to other countries. The second was the establishment in these countries of new manufacturing enterprises that exploited the innovative technologies of the Industrial Revolution.

Thus Ireland—a country which became more agricultural and indeed deindustrialized in response to the English Industrial Revolution—seems to have experienced as much income gain as its trading partner England. Real wages for Irish building workers rose as much as those in England in the years 1785–1869, as figure 12.9 shows. The figure reveals that these wage gains occurred before the Irish potato famine of 1845 led to substantial population losses and outmigration. Indeed between 1767 and 1845 it is estimated that the population of Ireland rose proportionately as much as that of England.

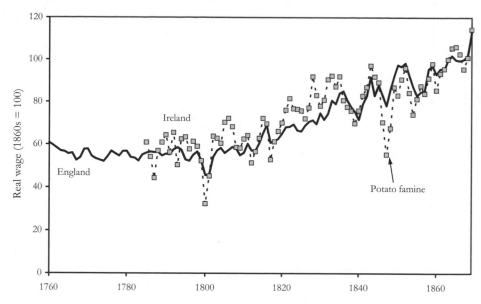

Figure 12.9 English and Irish real wages, 1785–1869. Data from Geary and Stark, 2004, and Clark, 2005.

Similarly there is little sign that England was gaining significant income per person relative to the Netherlands in the Industrial Revolution era. Figure 12.10 shows income per person in England by decade from the 1800s to 1910–13, taking Dutch income per person in 1910–13 as 82 percent of English income. Between the 1800s and the 1860s England, the white-hot center of the Industrial Revolution, saw income per person increase by 44 percent. In that same interval the Netherlands, a peripheral player making few or no independent contributions to industrial innovations during the period, saw income per person rise by 29 percent. England gained 11 percent on the Dutch in terms of income per person during the Industrial Revolution. This was trivial compared to the 64 percent gain in English total income relative to that of the Dutch from the 1760s to the 1860s as a result of faster English population growth.

The English population boom, the rise of real incomes during the Industrial Revolution, the limited land area of England, and the limited productivity gains in English farming all meant that domestic agriculture could not meet the food and raw material demands of the English economy. As table 12.5 shows, while population more than tripled in the course of the Industrial Revolution, domestic agricultural output did not even double. By the

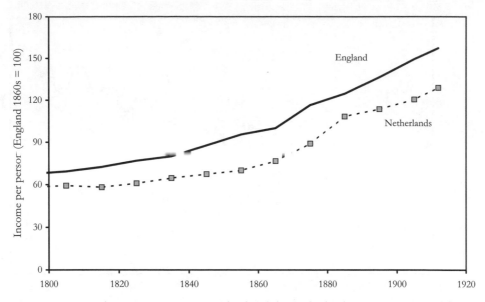

Figure 12.10   Real income per person, England and the Netherlands, 1800s to 1910–13. The estimate of English income per person until 1869 is continued to 1913 using an index of U.K. GDP per person from Feinstein, 1972, table T21. Dutch income per person from 1805 to 1913 is from Smits et al., 2000.

1860s England had gone from a country in which food and raw material imports were unimportant to one in which net food and raw material imports were equivalent to 22 percent of GDP.

This trade of manufactures for food and raw materials was made on relatively favorable terms because of the addition of substantial new territory to the north Atlantic trading area with the westward expansion of the United States. Table 12.6 shows the vast amount of farm acreage added to the United States by the 1860s.

The food and raw material imports of the Industrial Revolution had to be paid for by exports of manufactured goods. It was this, rather than technological advances, that made Britain "the workshop of the world." Had English population remained at six million into the 1860s, the country's domestic agricultural sector would have been able to feed and provide raw materials for the English population. The net exports of manufactures, which by the 1860s constituted nearly 20 percent of GDP, would have been close to zero. Thus without population growth nonfarm output in the 1860s, instead of being nearly ten times its level in the 1730s, would have been only double the earlier level.

Table 12.5 Population Growth and Food and Raw Material Supplies

	1700–09	1760–69	1860–69
Population (millions)	5.5	6.7	20.1
English farm net output (millions of £)	65	71	114
Net food imports (millions of £)	2	3	80
Net raw material imports (millions of £)	−2	−5	61
Domestic coal output (millions of £)	2	3	37
Nonfarm food and raw material supplies (millions of £)	2	2	178
All food and raw materials per person (£)	12	11	15

Sources: Farm output: Clark, 2002b. Imports: Parliamentary Papers, 1870; Schumpeter, 1960. Exports: Schumpeter, 1960; Mitchell, 1988, 221–22. Coal output: Clark and Jacks, 2007. *Note:* £ of 1860–69.

The unusual growth of population during the Industrial Revolution in England, and the simultaneous expansion of the cultivated area in the United States, were more important than the specific technological advances of these years for the transformation of the economy and the society.

How Gradual Was the Transition to Modern Growth Rates?

Figure 12.5 suggests that the date of the transition between the preindustrial world of almost no efficiency growth and the modern world of constant efficiency advance is impossible to determine from aggregate productivity levels. But the figure does reinforce the idea that the preindustrial world, at least as represented by England, was largely one of technological stasis.

The measured aggregate productivity level of the economy was as high in the thirteenth century as in the eighteenth century. This finding does not mesh with intellectual and social history, where we see in Europe, from the Middle Ages onward, a slow but steady diet of innovations in technology, science, architecture, and the arts. Table 12.7 offers a brief timeline of significant innovations in Europe between 1120 and 1670. Clearly this was not a world in which nothing was happening. The puzzle is that these developments had so little impact on production technologies.

Table 12.6 Farmland and Population in England Relative to
Europe and the United States

	1800–09	1860–69
England		
Population (millions)	9.2	21
Farm area (millions of acres)	26	26
Acres per person	2.8	1.2
Western Europe		
Population (millions)	103	152
Farm area (millions of acres)	317[a]	317[a]
Acres per person	3.1	2.1
Russia		
Population (millions)	53	74
Farm area (millions of acres)	702[a]	702[a]
Acres per person	13.2	9.5
United States		
Population (millions)	6.2	35
Farm area (millions of acres)	—	407
Acres per person	—	11.6

Sources: FAO, statistics database; Mitchell, 1998a. [a]Based on modern areas
from the Food and Agriculture Organization.
Note: Western Europe includes Austria, Belgium, Denmark, Finland,
France, Germany, Ireland, Italy, the Netherlands, Norway, Portugal,
Spain, Sweden, and Switzerland.

However, the aggregate productivity measure reported in figure 12.5 is
not the simple sum of productivity advances in the production of individual
goods. It is the sum weighted by the share of expenditures on each good. As
explained in chapter 7 economists use this weighting because it measures how
much technical changes mattered to the average consumer.

But if we are concerned with measuring the average rate of innovation in
a society this is not necessarily the best index to use. Significant innovations
may have an effect on the mass of people only long after they first appear.
At the time an innovation actually occurs, people may not, because of their
income or circumstances, employ it to any great extent. A classic example
of such a delayed effect is the introduction of the printing press in Europe in

Table 12.7 Innovations in Europe, 1120–1665

Date	Innovation	Location (person)
1120	Gothic architecture	France, England
ca. 1200	Windmill	Northern Europe
1275	Gunpowder	Germany
ca. 1285	Mechanical clock	Northern Europe
ca. 1315	*The Divine Comedy*	Italy (Dante)
ca. 1325	Cannon	Northern Europe
ca. 1330	Crown glass	France
ca. 1350	Spectacles	Venice
ca. 1350	*The Decameron*	Italy (Boccaccio)
ca. 1390	*Canterbury Tales*	England (Chaucer)
ca. 1400	Harpsichord	Flanders
1413	Perspective in painting	Italy (Brunelleschi)
ca. 1450	Printing press	Germany (Gutenberg)
ca. 1450	Quadrant (navigation)	—
ca. 1450	Arabic numerals	—
ca. 1475	Musket	Italy, Germany
1492	Discovery of the Americas	Spain (Columbus)
1498	Sea route to India	Portugal (da Gama)
1512	European postal service	Germany (Franz von Taxis)
1522	World circumnavigation	Spain (Magellan)
1532	Potato	Spain
1544	Tomato	Italy
ca. 1587	*Tamburlaine the Great*	England (Marlowe)
1589	Knitting frame	England (Lee)
1597	Opera (*Dafne*)	Italy (Peri)
1600	Electricity	England (Gilbert)
1602	*Hamlet*	England (Shakespeare)
1608	Telescope	The Netherlands (Lipperhey)
1614	Logarithms	Scotland (Napier)
c. 1650	Mechanized silk spinning	Italy
1654	Modern thermometer	Italy
1656	Pendulum clock	The Netherlands (Huygens)
1665	Microscope	England (Hooke)

1452 by Johannes Gutenberg. Prior to that innovation books had to be copied by hand, with copyists on works with just plain text still only able to copy 3,000 words per day. Producing one copy of the Bible at this rate would take 136 man-days. A 250-page book in modern octavo size would take about 37 man-days. In addition the imprecision of handwriting meant that the print had to be of larger size, demanding about twice the area per word on the page as in modern typeset books and thus driving up the cost of materials and binding.[8]

Figure 12.11 shows the estimated productivity level in book production by decade from the 1470s to the 1860s, calculated as the ratio between the wage of building craftsmen and the price of a book of standard characteristics.[9] The rate of productivity growth from the 1460s to the 1560s was 2.3 percent per year, as fast as that for cotton textiles in the Industrial Revolution. In the next hundred years productivity grew more slowly, at only 0.6 percent per year. But this was still faster than the rate seen in most of the economy during the Industrial Revolution. From the 1660s to the 1860s there were apparently few further productivity gains in printing. But all this increase in the efficiency of book production had no appreciable impact on the measured efficiency of the economy before the 1660s, since books were such a tiny share of expenditures for most of the preindustrial era. In the first decade of the sixteenth century the average annual output of books was about twenty thousand volumes, about 0.02 percent of English national income. By the 1550s this had risen to a hundred thousand volumes, but because of the falling prices of books that was still only 0.11 percent of national income.

Books were not the only goods that saw substantial efficiency advances in the years before 1800 yet had little or no impact on the overall efficiency of the economy because they represented such a small share of aggregate expenditure. Table 12.8 shows the price of nails by fifty-year periods, compared with wages, and the implied efficiency in nail production. A pound of nails in the early thirteenth century cost 3.3 pence, while a day's wage for a craftsman was 2.4 pence. Thus a pound of nails cost more than a day's wage. By the years 1850-69 the day wage had increased about seventeenfold, to 40 pence

8. Clark and Levin, 2001.
9. With both hand production and the printing press the main cost in book production was labor (paper and parchment production costs were mainly labor costs).

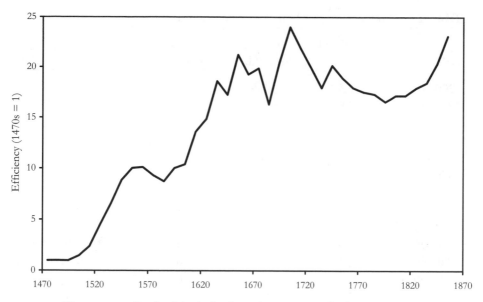

Figure 12.11   Productivity in book production in England, 1470s–1860s.

per day. But nail prices were only 3.2 pence per pound, so a craftsman could buy more than 12 pounds of nails with his day's wage.[10]

But most of the gain in efficiency in nail production was achieved before the Industrial Revolution, so that the efficiency of production was nearly seven times as great on the eve of the Industrial Revolution than it had been in 1200. This improvement had little economic impact, since nails were always a small share of construction costs for buildings and furnishings. Other goods whose prices relative to wages substantially improved before 1800 included paper, glass, spectacles, clocks, musical instruments, paints, spices such as pepper, sugar, fine textiles such as silks, tobacco, and gunpowder. And none of these improvements had much impact on living costs simply because most of these items were luxury goods consumed only by those with the highest incomes. The bulk of people's expenditures were for the basics: food, clothing, and shelter.

10. The near constancy of nail prices in nominal terms explains why in the United States nails are still designated as twopenny nails or threepenny nails. These were the prices of a hundred such nails in the fourteenth century in England. The terms became established as the names of the particular types of nails since their prices changed so slowly.

Table 12.8 Productivity Growth in Nail Production, 1200–1869

Period	Cost of nails (pence/lb)	Day wage (pence/day)	Efficiency of production	Efficiency growth (percent per year)
1200–49	3.3	2.4	100	0.31
1250–99	2.9	2.4	117	0.09
1300–49	2.9	2.5	122	−0.35
1350–99	5.3	4.0	102	0.72
1400–49	4.3	4.6	147	0.34
1450–99	3.8	4.8	174	0.38
1500–49	3.3	5.0	211	0.39
1550–99	4.6	8.6	256	0.63
1600–49	4.6	12	351	0.67
1650–99	4.6	16	492	0.40
1700–49	4.2	18	603	0.21
1750–99	4.2	21	670	1.05
1800–49	4.5	36	1,132	0.81
1850–69	3.2	40	1,693	—
1200–1799				0.38

Note: The efficiency growth rate for each period is calculated as average efficiency growth between the beginning of the half century and the end. This is why efficiency growth in the period 1300–49 is negative.

But let's say we were to measure the rate of technological advance in England from 1200 to 1869 by looking not at the consumption of the average person, but at the consumption of people like us. Then we would have a very different impression about the relative stasis of the economy before 1800. Figure 12.12 shows the real purchasing power of the average income in England from the 1270s to the 1860s based on the shares of goods that people actually bought. Though there was a doubling of real income between the medieval period and the 1860s, almost all that gain came after 1800. In contrast the figure also shows the hypothetical purchasing power of that income were it to be spent on goods in the manner of modern upper-class professionals—that is, were it to be spent on books, clothing, glass, home furnishings, travel, spices, sugar, and wine in the kind of proportions favored by this book's author. The purchasing power of income in terms of such a person rises much more, five-fold, between the medieval period and the 1860s. But now there is much less

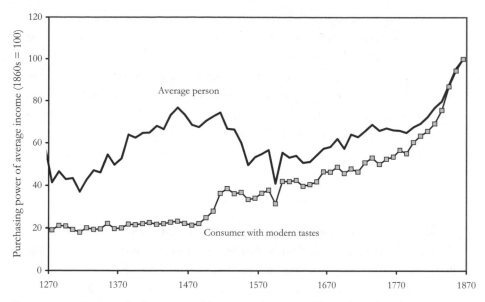

Figure 12.12 Real purchasing power of the average income and hypothetical modern consumers, 1270s–1860s.

discontinuity around 1800. Real purchasing power triples between the medieval period and 1800. While the growth rate of real purchasing power for such a consumer rose by 0.76 percent per year after 1800, from the 1480s to the 1800s real purchasing power rose at 0.33 percent per year, far beyond the average for the preindustrial world.

Thus the dynamism of the English economy in different periods seems to depend crucially on the consumption interests of the observer. From the perspective of the lowest-paid workers, farm laborers, even by the end of the Industrial Revolution they had not attained the living standards of the golden years of the late Middle Ages. From the perspective of a modern American with middle-class consumption habits, there was a world of change in consumption possibilities even before 1800. These changes made it possible to live in light-flooded houses, with painted or papered walls, and eat a wide range of tasty foods from fine china and glassware. They made reading a daily newspaper possible. They extended the length of the day by providing cheap artificial illumination.

If innovation were an activity that followed an economic logic, if the budget for innovative effort were devoted to producing the maximum value of productivity advance per research dollar, then the aggregate efficiency standard would be the most appropriate way of measuring the innovation rate of a society. But if instead innovative activities were guided mainly by noneconomic forces—curiosity, a love of novelty, a desire to impress others—then aggregate efficiency growth might provide a very poor guide to the rate of innovation in a society, or to the relative innovativeness of societies. The evidence from Industrial Revolution England suggests that, at least in early societies, the profit motive is a relatively weak stimulus to innovation. Thus measuring the rate of innovation using aggregate efficiency growth will not be appropriate

The Switch to Inorganic Technologies

As Anthony Wrigley has emphasized, the Industrial Revolution represented the beginnings of a switch from a largely *organic* system of production to the increasingly *inorganic* systems of the modern world. The bulk of the food, energy, and clothing and construction materials in the world before 1800 was produced in the farm sector using organic methods. The classic Industrial Revolution, with its reliance on coal and iron, was the first step toward an economy that relied less and less on current sustained production through plants and animals, and more on mining stores of energy and minerals.[11]

Organic production systems have three important features. The first is that all outputs drawn from the system in the long run have to be balanced by equivalent inputs. Every pound of nitrogen consumed off the farm in grain products in preindustrial England had to be balanced by a pound of nitrogen fixed from the air. This severely restrained potential output.[12]

The second feature is that, unlike inorganic systems in which the baseline rate of productivity advance is zero, in organic systems without any innovation efficiency growth is negative. Weeds and pathogens are constantly adapting, through the blind forces of natural selection, to reduce the productivity of crops and animals. Indeed some modern grain crops, such as rye, are believed to have evolved within crops of barley and oats as crop weeds. Under the harsher growing conditions of northern Europe rye proved to be more productive than the original grains, and it was eventually cultivated deliberately.[13]

11. Wrigley, 1990.
12. Clark, 1992.
13. Ghersa et al., 1994; Palumbi, 2001.

The inherent tendency of productivity to decline in farming systems is revealed most dramatically in such episodes as the Irish potato famine of 1845 and the Phylloxera attack on grape vines in Europe in the 1860s. Thus the absence of measurable productivity growth in the farm system in England before the Industrial Revolution need not imply an absence of innovation. The move from a 0 percent rate of productivity advance in the years before 1800 to a 0.3 percent rate of advance in 1800–60 may seem like an important phase change. But suppose this instead represents, for example, a change from a rate of innovation of 0.4 percent per year to one of 0.7 percent, being countered by a constant natural degradation of technique of 0.4 percent per year. Then the upward movement of innovation rates during the Industrial Revolution would be less dramatic and would seem to be less of a change in regime.

The third feature of organic systems of production is that experiments to devise better production methods are inherently difficult. In a cotton mill, for example, controlled experiments in changing manufacturing methods can be undertaken. Spindle speeds can be increased by 10 percent and the resulting changes in production costs observed immediately. But in agriculture observing the effect of any change is difficult. The production period is longer, and it may be years in the case of animals. Changes in the weather and in pathogens impart huge shocks to output each year. Soil conditions vary from field to field and even within fields, so a change that might be beneficial in one environment could prove ineffective or damaging in another. Thus the switch to more inorganic means of production may bias the seeming upturn in innovation rates in favor of the modern era.

The Transition to the Modern World

The Industrial Revolution in England in 1760–1860 saw dramatic changes in the English economy. But it is uncertain if we can identify the general switch from economies with little innovation in production techniques to modern economies, in which innovation is continuous, with the years 1760–1800. The upturn in productivity growth rates was a drawn-out process. Aggregate productivity growth rates are only one way of weighting the gains in efficiency across the many production techniques in any society, and based on other weightings the transition to modern growth rates would come sooner than 1800. Furthermore, the assumption that the rate of efficiency growth with no innovation in a society is zero is incorrect for preindustrial societies, in which innovation was needed just to maintain the productivity of organic production systems. Though the transition to the modern world was much more drawn out than is popularly supposed, it was definitely accomplished in Europe but not in Asia, despite Asia's long reign as the most technologically advanced area in the preindustrial world. In the next chapter we ask why this was so.

13 Why England? Why Not China, India, or Japan?

The people of this Island of Japan are good of nature, curteous above measure, and valiant in war: their justice is severely executed without any partiality upon transgressors of the law. They are governed in great civility. I mean, not a land better governed in the world by civil policy. —William Adams (1612)[1]

The previous chapter stresses that the suddenness of the Industrial Revolution in England was more appearance than reality. The coincidence of major population growth and improved trade prospects with raw material producers such as the United States made a modest acceleration of the rate of technological progress in England circa 1800 seem like an overnight transformation of the economy. In fact England by 1850 was, technologically speaking, little ahead of such competitors as the United States and the Netherlands.

Chapter 12 also emphasizes that the acceleration of advances in productivity came from the supply side. People responded differently to incentives that had been in place for generations. That difference in response was a dynamic inherent in the institutionally stable private property regime of preindustrial England. The characteristics of the population were changing through Darwinian selection. England found itself in the vanguard because of its long, peaceful history stretching back to at least 1200 and probably long before. Middle-class culture spread throughout the society through biological mechanisms.

But all of these observations still beg several questions: Why did the same conditions not lead to an Industrial Revolution at the same time, or even earlier, in Japan, in the Yangzi Delta, or in Bengal? What was special about Europe? Why did tiny England, with a population of around 6 million in 1760, achieve an Industrial Revolution, when Japan alone had about 31 million

1. Rundall, 1850, 32.

people living in a sophisticated market economy, and China had nearly 270 million? The million people in Edo (now Tokyo) in the eighteenth century, for example, made it the largest city in the world at the time.

This challenge has been sharpened in recent years by such books as Kenneth Pomeranz's *The Great Divergence.*[2] Pomeranz suggests that in most respects the densely settled core of China, areas such as the Yangzi Delta, was indistinguishable from northwestern Europe in 1800 in terms of "commercialization, commodification of goods, land, and labor, market-driven growth, and adjustment by households of both fertility and labor allocation to economic trends. He argues further that these patterns of market development and specialization were not in themselves paths to "an industrial breakthrough." Both sets of economies were still firmly in "the proto-industrial cul de sac," with incremental growth that could expand only population, not living standards.[3]

Pomeranz thus insists the Industrial Revolution was not the next step on a continuum, as argued here, but an abrupt and unexpected departure from the stagnant preindustrial equilibrium. He finds the source of this break in Europe in two accidents of geography—coal and colonies. For Pomeranz the crucial barrier to rapid growth in the long-settled core of the world's economies was an ecological one. All societies before 1800 had to produce resources—food, energy, raw materials—on a renewable basis from a fixed land area. The "advanced organic technology" of Europe and Asia was at its natural limits by 1800. The massive expansion in the output of energy-intensive goods, such as iron, that characterized the Industrial Revolution was possible only once new sources of energy and raw materials from outside the system had been found.

Europe made this leap because it had coal reserves readily accessible to its population centers.[4] In addition it had the massive, largely empty land area of the Americas relatively close at hand, to lift for a time the ecological constraint with a continent-sized flood of food and raw materials. These geographic advantages, rather than differences in innovative potential, explain English success and Asian failure.

2. Pomeranz, 2000.
3. Ibid., 107, 264.
4. Even Pomeranz has to allow that it was the technological breakthrough of the Newcomen engine in 1712, permitting the drainage of deep mines, that made this coal available on a large scale at the onset of the Industrial Revolution; Pomeranz, 2000, 66, 68.

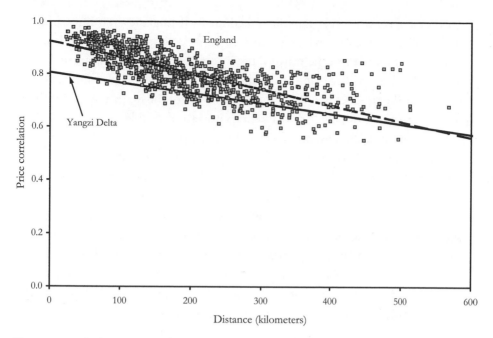

Figure 13.1 Grain price correlation and distance, England and the Yangzi Delta, 1770–94. Data from Shiue and Keller, 2006, figure 5.

Pomeranz is entirely correct that China, and indeed also Japan, differed little from England in 1800 in respect to land, labor, and capital markets. Recent research by Carol Shiue and Wolfgang Keller on grain markets in 1770–94, for example, supports the idea that grain markets were only modestly better integrated in Europe than in China.[5] Figure 13.1 shows the correlation of annual grain prices with distance in England and the Yangzi Delta in 1770–94. England was better integrated. Grain prices in any two locations correlated better, suggesting that grain flowed more freely between local markets in England. But the difference was modest. At a distance of 50 miles the correlation of prices, which could be at maximum 1, was 0.88 in England compared to 0.77 in China. These were both markets in which grain was being actively traded over considerable distances.[6]

But Pomeranz is caught in the Smithian straitjacket criticized above. He assumes that markets and incentives are sufficient for rapid economic growth,

5. Shiue and Keller, 2006.
6. It should be noted that Shiue and Keller ascribe more significance to these differences.

unless there is some other external impediment. If England grew but China, with similarly extensive markets and well-defined property rights, did not, then the problem must, he reasons, lie in some external constraint, such as geography. But in discussing the Industrial Revolution I have emphasized that it was the product not of Smithian perfection of the market, but of a differential response of people to market incentives that had long been present.

And on these dimensions, if we look at the visible correlates of the arrival of the dynamic middle class society—in particular levels of education and interest rates—England was certainly ahead of its Asian competitors by 1800.[7]

Recent studies of Qing China (1644–1911) and Tokugawa Japan (1603–1868) have emphasized that these were not static, technologically ossified societies, as has traditionally been assumed. Remarkably, given their isolation from developments in Europe before 1800—the result of both distance and government policy—they appear to have been changing in the same ways as northwestern Europe. Education levels rose markedly in both Japan and China between 1600 and 1800. In time, these countries would have had their own Industrial Revolutions. Cotton was only introduced to Japan in the later Middle Ages, and it was little grown before the Tokugawa era.[8] Yet by the late seventeenth century, despite Japan's isolation by then from the rest of the world, an extensive domestic cotton textile industry, centered in Osaka, had emerged.[9] Though this was a handicraft industry, plenty of water power was available, had the Japanese eventually chanced upon the innovations of Industrial Revolution England.

But though these societies were on the path to an eventual Industrial Revolution, they were progressing more slowly than England, and they had not progressed as far as England by the late nineteenth century, when they ended their self-imposed isolation from the West.

How Bourgeois Was Asia in 1800?

By 1800 Japan was the closest of the Asian economies to England in terms of social characteristics. While Japan could eventually have developed an Indus-

---

7. Jack Goldstone has also emphasized that the advantage of England in 1800 was in its greater propensity to innovate, though he grounds this English propensity in a complex mixture of political crises and institutions within each society; Goldstone, 1987.

8. The first definitive reference to cotton cultivation in Japan is in 1429; Farris, 2006, 160.

9. Hauser, 1974.

trial Revolution in isolation, at the start of the Tokugawa era in 1603 it had the look more of medieval England than of England in 1760. Interest rates, for example, were still high. In the mid-seventeenth century interest rates for loans made to local governors (*daimyo*) in anticipation of receipts from the land tax were 12–15 percent, even though these were secured loans. The banking system which developed in the late seventeenth century made loans on real security such as buildings at rates averaging 15 percent, though more creditworthy borrowers could get lower rates.[10]

Literacy levels also seem to have been low at the beginning of the Tokugawa era. Literacy then was confined mainly to temple priests, and written records were used only to document important matters like landholdings.[11] The similarity of this society to the innumeracy of the medieval or Roman world is revealed in the account of Japan in the years 1577–1610 by the Portuguese Jesuit Joao Rodrigues. Commenting on the absence of diseases such as the plague, and the long lives of even ordinary Japanese, Rodrigues reports his informants had assured him that "there was a man in the Hokkoku region who lived seven hundred years, and we saw a reliable Christian who had seen and met him, as well as many other pagans who knew him. . . . Also in our time there lived a robust man in the town of Chiriku, in the kingdom of Hizen, who was one hundred and thirty years old and still played chess."[12] In the Tokugawa period there was, however, a steady spread of literacy through the ranks of society, as in England. By 1700 books were being printed in editions as large as ten thousand copies. Commercial lending libraries had even emerged to meet popular demand.[13] In the eighteenth and nineteenth centuries village schools (*terakoya*) were established with increasing frequency. Before 1804, 558 such schools had been established; between 1804 and 1843 a further 3,050 were founded; and from 1844 to 1867 6,691 were added.[14] The result was a literacy rate for men estimated at 40–50 percent by the time of the Meiji Restoration of 1868, and a rate for women of 13–17 percent.[15] These rates were, however, still significantly lower than those achieved in northwestern Europe by the advent of the Industrial Revolution.

10. Crawcour, 1961, 350, 356. In this same period loans on good credit in England were made at 5–6 percent, and at even lower rates in the Netherlands.

11. Dore, 1965, 1–2.

12. Rodrigues, 1973, 50–51.

13. Passin, 1965, 12.

14. Nakamura, 1981, 276.

15. Passin, 1965, 44–47.

India, China, and Korea also retained characteristics into the nineteenth and early twentieth centuries that made them resemble medieval Europe or the ancient world more than England on the eve of the Industrial Revolution.

There has been recent debate, for example, as to the relative living standards in India versus England around 1800.[16] This—as should be evident from the discussion of the Malthusian economy in the first part of the book—tells us nothing about the relative technological sophistication or growth potential of these two economies. However, the paucity of wage quotes in India from any time before 1856 speaks volumes about the relative sophistication of Indian relative to English society before that time.

In England we have evidence on real wages from 1209 onward, and by 1275 such evidence comes from an abundance of sources. By the eighteenth century there are wage data for hundreds of different towns throughout England. There are wage quotes from churchwardens; town corporations; the county magistrates who maintained bridges, jails, and prisons; London guilds that paid for repairs to their properties; the royal household; larger religious institutions such as Westminster Abbey; charitable institutions; Oxford and Cambridge colleges; and the households and estate accounts of private magnates. Thus we can calculate not just wages, but wages by type of worker, the typical length of the workweek, wages by location, and even, for the years after 1800, implied daily hours of work.

In contrast, India, a continent-size society with a population at least ten times that of England in 1800, has a startling poverty of wage, price, and population records before the nineteenth century. If we exclude the reports of the Dutch and English East India Companies and of British travelers, then for the entire period 1200–1856 the only quotes on real wages that are available are from the Ain-I-Akbari, an account book of the Mogul emperor Akbar in 1595, a handful of quotes from the Tamil Nadu archives from 1768 and 1800–02 utilized by Parthasarathi, and then from Maratha sources for Pune circa 1820.[17] The documentary record of medieval England by 1209 is incomparably superior to that of eighteenth-century India.

This paucity of documentation reflected a society with levels of nineteenth-century literacy little greater than those for medieval England. The Indian

16. Parthasarathi, 1998; Broadberry and Gupta, 2006.
17. Divekar, 1989; Parthasarathi, 1998, 84.

Figure 13.2 The bazaar at Vijaynagara (now Hampi), with a modern village school operating in the ruins.

census as late as 1901, for example, reveals a literacy rate for men of 9.8 percent, and for women of 0.6 percent.

Further evidence of the technological backwardness of at least southern India in the preindustrial era comes from the area's architecture. Vijaynagara, the capital of the Vijaynagara Empire, which comprised all of southern India from AD 1336 to 1660, was sacked in 1565 and then abandoned. The ruins now cover an impressive nine square miles, where modern Indian villagers in what is now called Hampi squat in crude shelters among imposing stone arcades and temples (figure 13.2). Yet impressive as the scale of the monuments is, and as elaborate as the decorative carvings are, the engineering of the building is much less sophisticated than that achieved in Europe even before the end of the Middle Ages. The Pantheon in Rome, completed about AD 125, has a dome spanning 43 meters. The dome of the Duomo in Florence, completed in 1436, spans 42 meters. These buildings required design and construction skills an order of magnitude ahead of those evident at Vijaynagara.

China in 1800 seems to have occupied a place intermediate in social sophistication between Japan and India. John Lossing Buck's survey of 1929–33 suggests that 30 percent of men in China were literate. Between 1882 and 1930 there was seemingly no change in exposure to schooling, so this was likely also the male literacy rate back in 1882. This observation led Evelyn Rawski to conclude that late Qing China was "an advanced, complex society . . . remarkably modern in many respects."[18] But this still places nineteenth-century China only at the level of England in the seventeenth century.

The main vehicle of mass education in the Qing era was village-level charitable schools. Since the number of such schools found by Rawski nearly doubled between 1750–1800 and 1850–1900, educational exposure was most likely only half as great in the late eighteenth century, suggesting that male literacy might have been as low as 15 percent in 1800.[19] This would imply that, while China had high levels of education for a preindustrial society, they were still significantly lower than for northwestern Europe at the commencement of the Industrial Revolution.

Buck's finding that the average return on land ownership over a variety of locations in 1921–25 averaged 8.5 percent also makes China seem more similar to earlier societies than to England or the Netherlands in 1800.[20] A study of the return on land ownership in Korea over the years 1740–1900 similarly found rates of return that exceeded 10 percent in most periods.[21]

Thus it seems that England's Asian competitors in 1800, Japan, China, and India, lagged behind it in establishing bourgeois society through all ranks of the population. These societies, or at least Japan and China, were not static, as Smith and Malthus assumed. They were evolving along the same path as northwestern Europe, at least in terms of the spread of education. But they had not evolved as far.

Why Was Asia behind Europe?

I have emphasized that social evolution in England had a biological basis, that it was driven by the selective survival of types in an institutionally stable society of private property rights. That raises the issue of why, given the even longer history of stable property rights in China and Japan at least, the same

18. Rawski, 1979, 17–18, 140; quotation on page 140.
19. Ibid., 90.
20. Buck, 1930, 158.
21. Jun and Lewis, 2006, figure 7.

Table 13.1 Population Growth in England, Japan, China, 1300–1750

Period	England	Japan	China
ca. 1300	5.9	6	72
ca. 1750	6.2	31	270

Sources: England, Clark, 2007a. Japan, Farris, 2006, 26, 165; estimated population in 1280 5.7–6.2 million. China, Perkins, 1969, 16; value for 1300 is estimated population in 1393.

process had not operated there to generate the same conclusion at an earlier date.

Here the limitations of Chinese and Japanese demographic data before 1800, and their almost complete absence in India, push us into the realm of speculation. But we can point to two possible explanations.

The first is that, surprisingly, the Malthusian constraints seem to have operated much more tightly on England than on either Japan or China in the years 1300–1750. Table 13.1 shows the populations of all three countries estimated for years close to 1300 and then for 1750. In England the population barely grew over these 450 years. In Japan, however, it is estimated to have increased fivefold, while in China the increase was more than threefold. The bite of the Malthusian constraints was tighter in England than in Asia. The processes of selective survival were actually more severe in preindustrial England.

China's rapid population growth is due in part to its having been a frontier society, in which there was constant migration of Han Chinese from the core of the country to underpopulated regions in the south and west. Thus the cultivated area in China was estimated to have grown from 62 million acres in 1393 to 158 million acres by 1770, explaining most of the population growth.[22] In England, in contrast, the cultivated area in 1300 seems to have been almost as great as that in 1750. There was no new land to expand to. Japan was able to expand its population so greatly because of remarkable increases in the yields of rice cultivation.

The second difference between England on the one hand and Japan and China on the other is that income-based differences in fertility seem to have

22. Perkins, 1969.

been much less pronounced in both Japan and China. The rich do not seem to have been spreading constantly downward through the ranks of Japanese and Chinese society, bringing with them middle-class attitudes and culture, as they did in England. Unfortunately, the richer groups we observe are both from the hereditary nobility: samurai in Japan and the Qing nobility in China. It would be helpful to be able to study richer commoners as well, but these records are not available.

In Japan we have evidence on the reproductive success of the samurai class through records of adoption frequency. To maintain the line adoption was used whenever the head of the lineage had no surviving son at death or retirement from office. The samurai studied were local officials who had the hereditary rights to offices with attached stipends that in most cases ranged from 50 to 15,000 *koku* of rice. Since 10 *koku* of rice was the equivalent of the annual wage of a laborer in seventeenth-century England these samurai were very wealthy even by English standards.

Yet these families had to resort to high rates of adoption. In the seventeenth century, a time of rapid population growth for the population as a whole in Japan, the adoption rate was 26.1 percent, implying fertility rates among samurai similar to those of the rich in England. However, the adoption rate rose to 36.6 percent in the eighteenth century, implying that samurai net fertility was then equivalent to that of someone owning only 4 acres of land or a cottage in England. The adoption rate was even higher, at 39.3 percent, by the nineteenth century. Figure 13.3 shows the frequency of samurai with a surviving son by century compared to that frequency in England in 1620–38 as a function of wealth. The average wealth of the samurai would place them in the highest English wealth classes. Thus after 1700 their implied fertility was much lower than that for the English rich.

Since in England about 55 percent of men with a net replacement rate of 1 had surviving sons, this implies that after 1700 the samurai, despite their considerable wealth, had a net replacement rate only modestly above that of the general population in Japan in a time of population stasis. Since the adoptees were overwhelmingly younger sons from samurai families with multiple sons, there was no flood of position-less samurai into the ranks of the commoners in preindustrial Japan.[23]

23. Moore, 1969, 619. Yanamura, 1974, 104, gives evidence for bannermen, an even richer class of Edo samurai, that implies an even higher adoption rate in the eighteenth century of 52 percent.

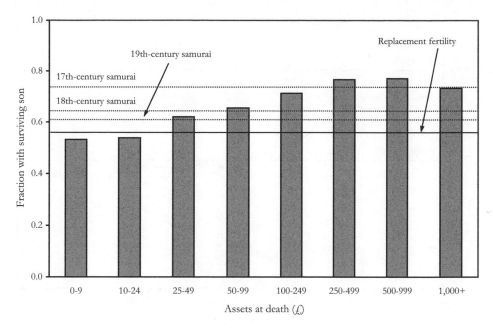

Figure 13.3 Samurai net fertility by century compared to English net fertility 1620–38 by size of bequest.

In China the evidence for the fertility of the elite comes from the genealogical archives of the Qing imperial lineage. The group studied were members of the royal family resident in Beijing in the period 1644–1840. For this group Wang Feng, James Lee, and Cameron Campbell have calculated, by decade of the birth of the first child, the total number of births per married man living to age 45 or greater for monogamous and polygamous men.[24] Using their data figure 13.4 displays a roughly calculated measure of the "total fertility rate" of all men of the imperial lineage.[25] This declines from about 7 in the early eighteenth century to an average of 4.8 for the period 1750–1849.

This rate is above the overall estimated total fertility rate for men in preindustrial China, which is only about 4.2.[26] But the difference in favor of

24. Feng et al., 1995, 387.

25. It is only a rough calculation since Feng et al. do not report the percentage of men unmarried by decade, nor the fraction of monogamous and polygamous marriages.

26. In chapter 4 we saw that the total fertility rate for married women was about 5, but that about a fifth of men would never marry because of infanticide.

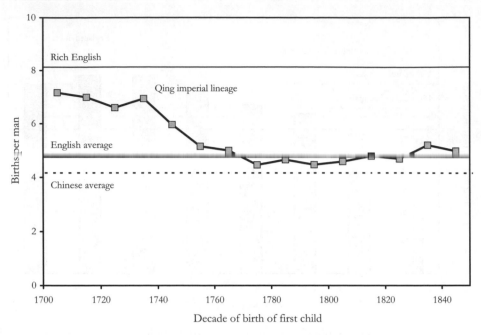

Figure 13.4 Male total fertility rate for the Qing imperial lineage.

the imperial lineage is relatively modest. The same diagram shows the total overall fertility rate for men in England before 1790, about 4.75, compared to the total fertility rate of rich men from the sample of wills in the seventeenth century, about 8.1. There the differences in favor of the rich are much more dramatic.

We see from both these examples of the rich in preindustrial Japan and China, admittedly for somewhat specialized groups, that rich men seem to have a reproductive advantage over poor men. However, it is also evident that their advantage is much less pronounced than in preindustrial England. An explanation of this difference is beyond the reach of the sources at hand. But the wave of downward mobility that washed over preindustrial England would have been a mere ripple in the case of China and Japan.

Thus to the questions "Why England? Why not China, India, or Japan?" the answer seems to be as follows. China and Japan, with their longer history of settled stable agrarian systems, were independently headed on a trajectory similar to that of northwestern Europe during the period 1600–1800. They were not static societies. However, this process occurred more slowly than in England. Two important factors may help explain this. Population growth was faster in both China and Japan than in England in the period 1300–1750. And the demographic system in both these societies gave less reproductive advantage to the wealthy than in England. Thus we may speculate that England's advantage lay in the rapid cultural, and potentially also genetic, diffusion of the values of the economically successful throughout society in the years 1200–1800.

14   Social Consequences

In proportion, therefore, as the repulsiveness of the work increases, the wage decreases.   —Karl Marx and Friedrich Engels (1848)[1]

The Industrial Revolution was driven by the expansion of knowledge. Yet, stunningly, unskilled labor has reaped more gains than any other group. Marx and Engels, trumpeting their gloomy prognostications in *The Communist Manifesto* in 1848, could not have been more wrong about the fate of unskilled workers. Figure 14.1 shows a typical image of Industrial Revolution misery that somehow has worked its way into modern popular consciousness.[2] The reality is very different. By 1815 real wages in England for both farm laborers and the urban unskilled had begun the inexorable rise that has created affluence for all.[3]

Nor was it even the case that the gains to land and capital initially exceeded those of labor. From 1760 to 1860 real wages in England rose faster than real output per person.[4] The innovators, the owners of capital, the owners of land, and the owners of human capital all experienced modest rewards, or no rewards, from advances in knowledge. Thus modern growth, right from its

1. Marx and Engels, 1967, 87.
2. A Google search under the terms "Industrial Revolution" and "misery" returned 217,000 pages.
3. Clark, 2001b, 2005.
4. See figure 14.4, which shows that wages rose as a share of national income between 1750 and 1860. Allen, 2005, 1, states, to the contrary, that "Between 1800 and 1840, GDP per worker rose 37 percent, real wages stagnated and the profit rate doubled." This result, however, is grounded on the real wage series of Feinstein, 1998, which Clark, 2001b, 2005, shows to be too pessimistic. The earlier, more optimistic, real wage series of Lindert and Williamson, 1983, 1985, turns out to be accurate.

Figure 14.1 Able-bodied poor breaking stones for roads in Bethnal Green, London, 1868.

start, by benefiting the most disadvantaged groups in preindustrial society, particularly unskilled workers, has reduced inequality within societies.

But while growth so far has been benign, there is no guarantee that it will continue to promote equality within societies. We may soon face the gloomy dystopia feared by so many writers, in which the wages of unskilled labor drop below the socially determined "subsistence wage" and societies are forced to support a large fraction of the population permanently through the public purse.

Sharing the Spoils

To see why unskilled labor enjoyed the bulk of the gains from efficiency advance in the modern economy, note that, when more output is produced per unit of capital, labor, and land engaged in production, the average payments to these three factors of production must increase. But there is nothing in the fundamental equation of growth that describes exactly how the factors share the gains. All that must happen formally is that

$$g_A = a g_r + b g_w + c g_s,$$

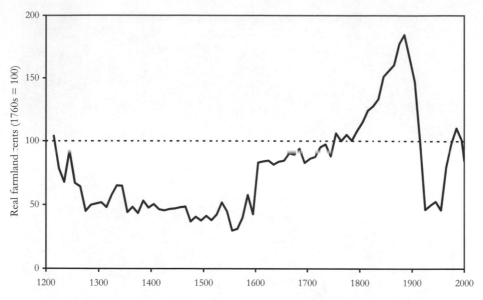

Figure 14.2   Real farmland rents per acre in England, 1210–2000.

where g_r, g_w, and g_s are the growth rates of the real payments to capital, labor, and land. A 1 percent gain in efficiency must average a 1 percent increase in payments to the factors of production. But the equation alone allows an infinity of patterns of gains, and even of losses.

Land, in the long run, received none of the gains from the Industrial Revolution. David Ricardo, the first economist to focus explicitly on the distribution of income, writing in the England of 1817 during the early years of the Industrial Revolution, foresaw a future in which wages would stay at subsistence, land rents would increase, and the return on capital would decline as population increased, because land was the fixed factor in production.[5] The actual future in England could hardly have been more different.

Figure 14.2 shows the real rents of farmland, the nominal rent per acre divided by the average price of goods, in England from 1210 to 2000. Real farmland rents peaked in the late nineteenth century, but they have declined since. The rent of an acre of farmland in England currently buys only as many goods as it did in the 1760s. Indeed the real earnings of an acre of land are little

5. Ricardo, 1821.

higher than in the early thirteenth century.[6] Without the Common Agricultural Policy subsidies to farmers, the real earnings from land would undoubtedly be less than in the High Middle Ages.

As farmland rents declined, urban rents increased. Indeed in 2000 in England, while an acre of farmland sold for an average of £2,900, an acre of potential building land cost £263,000, and an acre of building land for which permission to build had already been secured was worth £613,000.[7] But as figure 10.3 shows, even in densely populated England, where rents for urban sites may be two or three times the level in most countries at this income level, they are still only about 4 percent of national income.[8]

Because there is a fixed stock of land, the failure of real rents per acre to increase significantly has meant that, as economic output marched upward, the share of land rents in national income has correspondingly declined to insignificance (as is shown in figure 10.3). Precisely because land is in fixed supply, this result, so contrary to the Ricardian expectation, is surprising. It is considered further below.

Physical capital owners also received none of the gains from growth. The real rental of capital (net depreciation) is just the real interest rate. But consider figure 9.1. It shows that the real interest rate, if anything, declined since the Industrial Revolution.

Total payments to capital have expanded enormously since the Industrial Revolution, but only because the stock of capital grew rapidly. The stock of capital has been indefinitely expandable. It has grown as fast as output, and its abundance has kept real returns per unit of capital low. The product ag_r has been 0. Thus all the efficiency gains have shown up as wage increases. That is

$$g_A \approx bg_w.$$

6. These statements do not take into account changes in the value of urban land, for which it is difficult to get long-term measures, and for which the implicit rental value rose by greater amounts. But even taking this into account, landowners have profited little from the productivity growth since the Industrial Revolution.

7. Farmland prices from United Kingdom, Department of Environment, Food, and Rural Affairs, 2005, table 4.3. Building land prices from United Kingdom, Department of Communities and Local Government, 2007, tables 561, 563.

8. The U.S. Department of Defense overseas housing allowances imply that the cost of rental housing in England is nearly double that of other European countries at the same income level. Thus urban site rents would be no more than 2 percent of all income in these countries.

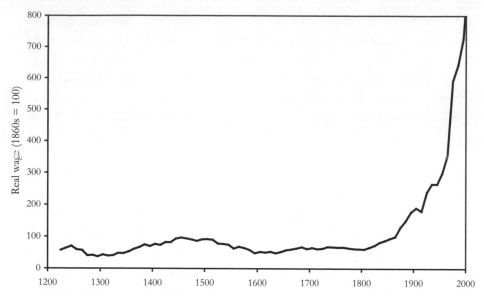

Figure 14.3 Real hourly wages for building laborers in England, 1220–2000. Data from Clark, 2005.

Since $b \approx 0.75$, every 1 percent efficiency advance since the Industrial Revolution has thus tended to increase wages on average by 1.3 percent.

We might have expected wage gains to have gone disproportionately to skilled workers with much human capital, especially since innovation and new technology were the basis of growth. But as figure 9.4 showed unskilled male wages in England have risen more since the Industrial Revolution than skilled wages, and this result holds for all advanced economies.[9] The wage premium for skilled building workers has declined from about 100 percent in the thirteenth century to 25 percent today. Figure 14.3 shows the real wages per hour for building laborers, the unskilled, in England from 1220 to 2000. The enormous gains even for these unskilled workers are evident.

A simple interpretation of the shrunken skill premium is that it is at least partly the result of the declining rate of return on capital. The wage pattern over a lifetime for skilled workers is typically that in the earliest years they earn less than the unskilled, since they have to spend time training or working as an apprentice to acquire their skills. In the preindustrial period parents

9. Van Zanden, 2004.

would often have to pay a significant lump sum for a child to secure an apprenticeship. The relative supply of skilled workers will thus be influenced by the interest rate on capital. At high interest rates, such as prevailed in the medieval era, financing training through borrowing is expensive, and funds spent on training have a high return if invested elsewhere. Hence we would expect the skill premium to be higher in high-interest-rate societies.

Another trend is the narrowing gap between men's and women's wages. In the preindustrial era women's wages averaged less than half of men's. Even in unskilled occupations the gap was great. Women's wages as field laborers in England over the years 1770–1860 were only 43 percent those of male farm laborers.[10] Now unskilled female workers in the United Kingdom earn 80 percent of the male unskilled hourly wage.[11]

The low wages of unskilled women laborers in the preindustrial era seemingly did not reflect discrimination against women once they entered the labor market (though there was undoubtedly a prejudice against training women for skilled occupations). Preindustrial societies typically had little objection to hiring women as brute laborers. In England, for example, women show up as basic agricultural laborers, weeding grains and reaping, in the very earliest records from the thirteenth century. Where women had a comparative advantage in tasks that required more dexterity than strength, such as in reaping or winnowing grain, they were widely employed. In building in the medieval period, thatchers' assistants were often female, since the preparation of the straw was not a task requiring great strength. The low relative pay for women seems instead to have reflected the premium attached to physical strength in a world where humans still supplied brute strength.[12] In an era in which men and donkeys were relatively close equivalents, women competed at a disadvantage.

The Industrial Revolution improved woman's economic position in two ways. Rising incomes switched the emphasis of production away from sectors such as agriculture (which demanded strength) toward such sectors as manufacturing and service (in which dexterity was more important) through the operation of Engel's law (see chapter 3). And the Industrial Revolution's innovations in power delivery eventually reduced the demand for humans as

10. Burnette, 1997; Clark, 2003.
11. United Kingdom, Office of National Statistics, 2006a.
12. Burnette, 1997.

suppliers of brute strength. Instead skills such as dexterity or social interaction, in which women had no disadvantage, became more important.

For England in the late nineteenth century we have measures of men's and women's comparative productivity on such textile factory tasks as weaving. In 1886 women cotton weavers in Lancashire averaged 82 percent of male weavers' production. Nevertheless the average woman in cotton textiles earned just 68 percent of the average man's wages because only men filled such skilled occupations as foreman, mechanic, or mule spinner.[13] But despite these barriers to promotion, their relative wage was already an improvement over the situation in preindustrial agriculture.

By reducing the gap in earnings between men and women the Industrial Revolution again narrowed overall inequality in modern societies. Thus the payment per unit of unskilled labor rose farther as a result of the Industrial Revolution than the payment for land, the payment for capital, or even the payment per unit of skilled labor.

Income Inequality

While the rewards for the different types of factors cooperating in production are unambiguous, the distribution of income across individuals or families makes for a more complex story. For each family possesses a portfolio of unskilled labor, skilled labor, land, and capital. And the amounts of some of the elements in this portfolio, particularly skilled labor and capital, have expanded greatly with modern growth. In addition income inequality is not something that can be measured by one number: how best to measure it depends on how important to the inquirer are income differences at different points in the distribution.

Did the Industrial Revolution on average increase or reduce income inequality, even before taxing and redistributing measures, in modern industrial societies? There is an enormous literature that debates whether there was an initial association between faster growth and inequality, the so-called Kuznets curve, in the transition out of the Malthusian state.[14] There is not enough room here to address that issue in any detail, though the faster growth of real

13. Wood, 1910, 620–24.
14. See van Zanden, 1995, on this in Europe on the eve of the Industrial Revolution.

Table 14.1 Distribution of Wages and Wealth, United Kingdom, 2003–04

Decile	Share of wages	Share of wealth
90–100	26	45
80–90	14	16
70–80	12	10
60–70	10	10
50–60	9	8
40–50	8	5
30–40	7	4
20–30	6	2
10–20	5	0
0–10	4	0

Sources: United Kingdom, Office of National Statistics, 2006a; United Kingdom, H.M. Revenue and Customs, 2007, table 13.1. *Note:* The wage distribution is for full-time adult workers. Wealth ownership is the assets of those dying in 2003.

wages versus real income, and the stability of the skill premium over these years, suggest that rising inequality was unlikely.[15]

Instead the question addressed is whether in the long run Malthusian economies were likely to have had greater inequality than modern industrialized economies. On balance it would seem that even pretax income is more equally distributed than in the preindustrial world.

We saw that the payments per unit rose only for labor and increased most for unskilled labor. But there has also been an enormous increase in the stock of physical capital per person. In all societies the ownership of capital and land tends to be highly unequal, with a large share of the population possessing no marketable wealth. Table 14.1, for example, shows the distribution of wage income in the United Kingdom in 2003–04 (for full-time workers) compared to the distribution of marketable wealth. Despite the much greater importance of human capital in modern societies than in earlier economies, the distribution of wages is still much more equal than the distribution of the

15. Partly driving the idea that inequality must have increased have been indicators of living standards, such as food consumption and heights, which in the Industrial Revolution did not rise as much as the real wage series would imply; Mokyr, 1988; Komlos, 1998.

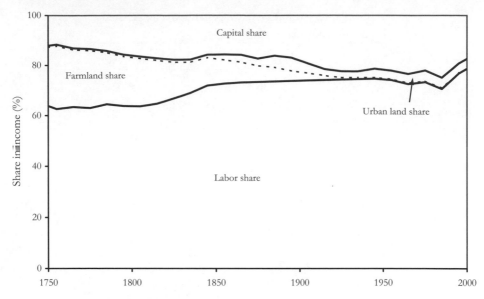

Figure 14.4 Shares of labor, capital, and land in net national income in England, 1750–2000. The urban and farmland shares were derived as in figure 10.3.

ownership of capital. The lowest-paid decile still gets about 40 percent of the average wage, and the highest-paid decile gets less than three times the average wage. With increased wealth the poorest decile has none, while the richest decile has five times the average wealth per person.

Thus one crucial determinant of inequality in any society is the share of labor income in all income. The larger this is, ceteris paribus, the lower inequality will tend to be. Figure 14.4 shows this share for England from 1750 to 2004. The share of labor in net national income seems to have risen from about 0.63 in the early eighteenth century to closer to 0.75 today. There is reason to believe that this trend must be a general one in the transition between the Malthusian era and the modern world. Land rents were typically 20–30 percent of income in settled agrarian societies, so that, once we also allow for returns to capital, the share of labor in all incomes was lower in the preindustrial world.

Earlier, in foraging societies that had no individual ownership of land and almost no capital goods, labor income accounted for essentially all income. Thus over the long stretch of human history there may well have been a type of Kuznets curve. The Neolithic Revolution, which brought settled agriculture, greatly increased the share of assets in all income, raising inequality. But the

Table 14.2   Preindustrial Wealth Distributions

Location	Source	Year	Top 1%	Top 5%	Gini coefficient
Perugia[a]	Taxes	1285	18	29	0.72
Paris[b]	Taxes	1292	26	52	0.75
London[b]	Taxes	1319	34	57	0.76
Florence[c]	Taxes	1427	27	67	0.79
England (Suffolk)[d]	Estates	1630	19	50	0.83
England[e]	Estates	1670	49	73	—
	Estates	1740	44	74	—
	Estates	1875	61	74	—
United Kingdom[f]	Estates	2003	17	32	0.60

Sources: [a]Blanshie, 1979, 603. [b]Sussman, 2005, table 9. [c]Van Zanden, 1995, table 1. [d]Calculated from the sample described in Clark and Hamilton, 2006, assuming those without wills had zero wealth. [e]Lindert, 1986, 1145. [f]Source as for table 12.2.

Industrial Revolution, by wiping out the value of land as an asset, has again raised the importance of labor in income determination. Since labor—the one income source of which every citizen has an equal allocation and the one income source that people cannot alienate—has become more important in the modern world, this trend promotes income equality.

Furthermore, the existing evidence suggests that in the Malthusian world, at least in Europe, wealth inequality was greater than that after the Industrial Revolution. Table 14.2 shows different measures of wealth inequality going back to 1285 for various places in Europe. These are the share of assets held by the top 1 percent and 5 percent of households or persons, and the Gini coefficient of the wealth distribution.[16]

All these samples suggest great wealth inequality in the preindustrial world compared to the typical industrialized country today. The earliest of these samples are household tax assessments based on assets in large cities such as London and Paris. They may show greater inequality than for countries as a whole because of the special conditions of large cities.[17] But the sample of

16. A Gini coefficient of 0 implies complete equality; a Gini of 1, that one person owns everything.

17. Van Zanden, 1995, notes that the degree of wealth inequality was less in the Tuscan countryside than in Florence in 1427.

Table 14.3 Unskilled Incomes Relative to Average Incomes, England

	1770s	1850s	2004
Annual wage, unskilled men	£15.4	£27.2	£16,898
Annual wage, unskilled women	£6.9	£12.3	£12,516
Ratio of female to male workers	0.38*	0.38	0.79
Annual wage, unskilled couple, per person	£10.4	£18.5	£13,393
Average adult (16+) income	£22.0	£40.0	£23,452
Unskilled worker, average income relative to all adults	47%	46%	57%

Sources: Earnings in 2004 from the United Kingdom, Office of National Statistics, 2006a.
Notes: * denotes value assumed to be the same as in the 1850s. Agricultural laborers are taken as the unskilled laboring class in the 1770s and 1850s.

English wills circa 1630 is for a representative subgroup of the population. Since it is based on bequests it is very similar to the modern wealth inequality data for England derived by the Department of Revenue and Customs. Asset inequality was greater in 1630 than in 2000, whether we measure the share of the top 1 or 5 percent or the Gini coefficient. The estimates by Peter Lindert for the entire population of households in England in 1670, 1740, and 1875 find even greater inequality compared to modern data.

Thus assets were a greater share of total income in the preindustrial world, and assets were held more unequally than in recent years.

Table 14.2 focused on the position of the upper-income groups; it says little about the position of the unskilled wage laborer over time relative to the rest of society. Table 14.3 attempts in a crude way to measure that parameter for England. It shows the annual pretax earnings of an unskilled laboring couple, per adult, relative to average income per adult in the society as a whole. In 1770 and 1851 agricultural laborers were taken as representing unskilled workers. In 1770 the family of a male agricultural laborer would earn an average of £10.4 per person, assuming women were employed in the same proportion as at the 1851 census. These earnings would represent 47 percent of the average income per adult in the society. This ratio was unchanged by 1851, even though farm wages declined relative to urban wages with the great growth of English cities and the migration out of the countryside. But by 2004 a typical couple in which both members were unskilled laborers would earn 57 percent of the average income per adult in the United Kingdom. Thus the

Table 14.4 Life Prospects of Rich and Poor in England

Period, group	Stature (males, centimeters)	Life expectancy	Surviving children	Literacy (%)
Preindustrial				
Rich	174.0	39	3.85	85
Poor	168.5	33	1.93	30
Difference	3%	18%	99%	183%
Modern				
Rich	178.2	80.8	1.33	100
Poor	176.0	74.3	1.64	88
Difference	1%	9%	−19%	14%

Sources: Preindustrial: Statures, 1790s, 1800s: Poor, 20- to 23-year-old English soldiers; Komlos, 1998, 781. Rich, Sandhurst cadets, adjusting heights of 15-year-olds to 19-year-olds by adding 11.5 cm; Komlos, 2004, figure 7.14. Life expectancy, surviving children, and literacy: Based on testators circa 1630 leaving less than £25 in assets versus those leaving £1,000 or more; *Modern:* Stature, 1991: parent social class I (professional) and II (intermediate) versus social class IV (skilled manual) and V (unskilled manual); Power et al., 2002, 132; Life expectancy, 1997–2001, social class I versus social class V. United Kingdom, Office of National Statistics, 2006b, tables 1, 3. Surviving children, 1999: children in household by income; Dickmann, 2003, 17. Literacy, 2003: percentage not achieving entry-level literacy, social class V, United Kingdom, Department of Education and Skills, 2003, 3.

poorest families seem to have improved their relative position in England as a result of the Industrial Revolution.

Inequality in Life Prospects

This far we have discussed only material incomes. But other aspects of the quality of life include life expectancy, health, numbers of surviving children, and literacy.[18] On all these other dimensions the differences between rich and poor have probably narrowed since the Industrial Revolution. Table 14.4 shows the differences in stature, life expectancy, surviving children, and literacy for the rich and the poor circa 1630 (except for stature) and 2000 in England.

18. Thus the United Nations *World Development Report* ranks countries through a Human Development Index, which includes measures of life expectancy and education.

In the preindustrial world the rich were significantly taller than the poor. Sandhurst cadets circa 1800 were nearly 6 centimeters taller than regular army soldiers. Based on the numbers of surviving children, and on adult life expectancy for testators of different asset classes, the life expectancy of the poorest testators was only 33 at birth, compared to 39 for the richest, a difference of 18 percent. Furthermore, rich testators had twice as many surviving children, and nearly triple the chance of being literate. Thus the life prospects for the rich were markedly better than those for the poor in the preindustrial era.

By 2000 these differences in life prospects still existed, but they were much more muted, and in some respect the poor had an advantage. The rich are still taller, but by very modest amounts. By 1991 men whose origins were in professional families were only 1 percent taller than those from laboring backgrounds. They still have greater life expectancy, but the difference is relatively small. And now the rich in England have fewer children than the poor, so if children are to be counted a blessing and not a burden the advantage now lies with the poor (though in some other advanced economies there is no difference between rich and poor in this respect).[19] The gap in literacy rates between rich and poor has also narrowed sharply.

Thus, in terms of the general life prospects of the rich and the poor, the Industrial Revolution seems to have narrowed the differences even more than would be suggested by measures of income distribution or asset distribution alone.

Why Did Landowners Not Receive the Gains?

Given that we had an Industrial Revolution that first improved the productivity of the industrial sector relative to the agricultural, why did landowners not benefit hugely from an increased scarcity of land as population and incomes rose rapidly after 1800, as Ricardo imagined would happen? The reasons that land saw declines in real returns, after some initial gains early in the Industrial Revolution, are threefold.

First, the income elasticity of the demand for many land-intensive products has been low. Thus the number of calories consumed per day by modern high-income consumers is *lower* than that for workers before the Industrial Revolution, because a major determinant of calorie consumption is the amount of physical labor people undertake.

19. Dickmann, 2003.

In the preindustrial era people supplied a lot of the power in production, whether as farm laborers digging, hauling, and threshing, or as wood hewers, brick makers, metal formers, or porters. In our society not only do we have machines to perform all these tasks, we also have machines to move us from house to coffee shop to workplace. Within these workplaces machines haul us up and down between floors. Thus, despite our very high incomes and relatively large stature, the average male in the modern United States consumes only about 2,700 kilocalories per day, and many have nevertheless gained substantial amounts of weight. In the 1860s male farm workers in some areas of Britain, generally smaller and lighter than modern U.S. males, took in some 4,500 kilocalories per day.[20] They consumed this much because they engaged in physical labor ten hours a day for three hundred days per year. Thus, as incomes expanded, the demand for land for production did not expand proportionately.

Second, there has been enormous growth in the productivity of agriculture, specifically in land-saving technologies, so that, despite being restricted by a largely fixed supply of land, farm output has risen faster than population.

Third, the mining of fossil fuels, principally coal and oil, has provided for modern societies the energy of which agriculture used to be a major provider. By mining the energy produced by the land over eons, and stored in the ground for the ages, our society has at least temporarily expanded the land supply by enormous amounts. By the 1860s in England, for example, farm outputs were worth £114 million per year. Coal outputs by that date, valued as deliveries to consumers, were £66 million per year, so that energy from coal already added a huge supplement to the output of the agricultural sector.[21]

Technological Advance and Unskilled Wages

We think of the Industrial Revolution as practically synonymous with mechanization, with the replacement of human labor by machine labor. Why in high-income economies is there still a robust demand for unskilled labor? Why do unskilled immigrants with little command of English still walk across the deserts of the U.S. Southwest to get to the major urban labor markets to reap enormous rewards for their labor, even as undocumented workers? Why

20. Clark et al., 1995.
21. Clark, 2002b; Clark and Jacks, 2007.

were there people camped out for months and even years at the Channel Tunnel freight depot in northern France, waiting for a chance to break through the security fence and hop onto a train for Britain?

Soon after the arrival of the Industrial Revolution the *machinery question* became a matter of debate among political economists. Would new labor-saving machines reduce the demand for labor? Famously Ricardo, who had initially defended the introduction of machinery as benefiting all, by 1821 constructed a model according to which some types of labor-saving machinery produce technological unemployment.[22] His demonstration, however, relied on workers receiving a fixed subsistence wage, and it was later appreciated that, as long as there are sufficient substitution possibilities between capital and labor, there will always be a positive marginal product for each type of labor (see chapter 2), and hence the possibility of full employment.

This general reassurance from economic reasoning is of little practical value, however, since it offers no assurance on what the actual level of wages will be. Why was it that there was not only a job for all unskilled workers, but a well-paying one? After all, there was a type of employee at the beginning of the Industrial Revolution whose job and livelihood largely vanished in the early twentieth century. This was the horse. The population of working horses actually peaked in England long after the Industrial Revolution, in 1901, when 3.25 million were at work. Though they had been replaced by rail for long-distance haulage and by steam engines for driving machinery, they still plowed fields, hauled wagons and carriages short distances, pulled boats on the canals, toiled in the pits, and carried armies into battle. But the arrival of the internal combustion engine in the late nineteenth century rapidly displaced these workers, so that by 1924 there were fewer than two million.[23] There was always a wage at which all these horses could have remained employed. But that wage was so low that it did not pay for their feed, and it certainly did not pay enough to breed fresh generations of horses to replace them. Horses were thus an early casualty of industrialization.

Many tasks performed by people seemed as replaceable as those of horses. And indeed a number of human tasks were quickly mechanized. Threshing grains, the staple winter occupation, which absorbed as much as a quarter of agricultural labor input, was mechanized by the 1860s. Reaping and mowing

22. Ricardo, 1821
23. Thompson, 1976, 80.

Figure 14.5   McDonald's—the foundation of an egalitarian society?

followed later in the nineteenth century. But the grim future of a largely un-skilled and unemployable labor force has not come to pass. Instead the earn-ings of these unskilled workers, as shown in figure 14.3, have risen relative to those of the skilled.

There seem to be two explanations for the relatively high value to the mod-ern economy of even unskilled labor. The first is that, unlike horses, people have attributes that machines so far cannot replace, or can only replace at too high a cost. People supply not just power but also dexterity. We are very good at identifying objects and manipulating them in space, and machines are still surprisingly poor at these tasks. Thus the fast-food industry that feeds a highly standardized product to legions of Americans every day still does so using human labor to bring meat to heat and seared flesh to bun (figure 14.5). Houses and hotel rooms are still cleaned by maids, gardens are still weeded by garden-ers. People guide trucks and cars on highways, and they guide powered tools in farming, mining, and construction. Supermarkets contain thousands of stan-dardized packages of product, but they are still placed on the shelves by people, and priced and bundled at checkout by people. Recently there have been attempts to develop services through which customers order groceries on the web and have them delivered to their homes. Some purveyors invested in large custom-designed automated warehouses where machines assembled the order from the previously encoded instructions of the customer and packed them into containers. These attempts were unsuccessful, however, and the surviving online grocery purveyors now combine high-tech ordering with unskilled workers who pick the goods from the shelves and pack them into containers.

Ironically computers have found it much easier to replace what we think of as the higher cognitive functions of humans—determining amounts due, calculating engineering stresses, taking integrals—than to replace the simple skills we think of even the most unlearned as possessing.

Another difficult-to-replace ability of humans is our ability to interact with other people. We have a social intelligence that alerts us, at least in part, to the thoughts and moods of others, and that ability can be very valuable in modern commerce. The increasing returns to scale inherent in most modern production processes imply that for the typical transaction the price, p, is much greater than the marginal cost, mc, the cost of producing the last unit of the good sold. That means that modern markets for industrial products—unlike the markets for farm produce in the preindustrial era, when for all goods $p = mc$—are imperfectly competitive.

The difference between price and marginal cost means that producers have an incentive to spend resources in trying to sell more product at the current price, through trying to get customers to choose their products rather than the nearly identical products of their competitors. Selling is a huge part of modern economies, and on the front lines in that war of commerce people are still very useful foot soldiers. A pleasant interaction with the seller can make customers choose to eat in this restaurant as opposed to that one, to shop here as opposed to there. Customer service agents in call centers are thus now guided by computers through decision trees that instruct them how to interact with customers. They are not called upon to exercise much judgment or discretion; they are simply the human face of a planned strategy of interaction—but a face that is still necessary.

The past in this respect, however, is no guide to the future. As long as computer processing power continues to become cheaper, the threat will always be present that these last scarce attributes of even unskilled human labor will lose their value. Then there truly will be a class of displaced workers forced to look to the charity of their fellow citizens for their subsistence.

We have considered two attributes of the human machine that are hard to replace. The other factor that has kept unskilled wages high since the Industrial Revolution has been the unexpected curtailment in the supply of people in the most rapidly growing economies. We saw for the Malthusian era in England that the more income and assets people had at the time of their deaths the more surviving children they had. Economic success and reproductive success went hand in hand. If this pattern had continued to the present, the population would have grown enormously, and the Ricardian dystopia in which growth is eventually curtailed by the fixed amount of land would have been closer to realization. I now consider these demographic changes in detail.

The Demographic Transition

Demography mattered crucially to living standards in the Malthusian era because the fixed factor, land, was an important share of national income. Any increase in population substantially reduced living standards.

After the Industrial Revolution the share of land and natural resources in national income has dropped to insignificance in the industrialized world. Demography would thus seemingly be a minor cause of the surprising shift of income to unskilled labor. Only in the poorest countries, as in sub-Saharan Africa, and in those with large endowments of natural resources, such as Saudi Arabia, do population levels remain important determinants of income per person.

But the small share of land in national income is plausibly the result of the fact that the income gains of the Industrial Revolution ceased to be translated into more surviving children and instead went into material consumption. Demography is now unimportant in such societies as England or the United States because of reductions in fertility. Following the Industrial Revolution events could have led to another possible world—one in which technological advances resulted in larger and larger populations, depleting the world's resource base and eventually choking off the growth in income per person.

Figure 14.6 shows the course of the so-called *demographic transition* in England. The figure shows two measures of fertility. The first is the gross reproduction rate (GRR), the average number of daughters born to a woman who lived through the full reproductive span, by decade. Since there were roughly as many sons as daughters born, such a woman would have given birth to nearly five children all the way from the 1540s to the 1890s. Since in England 10–20 percent of each female cohort remained celibate, for married women the

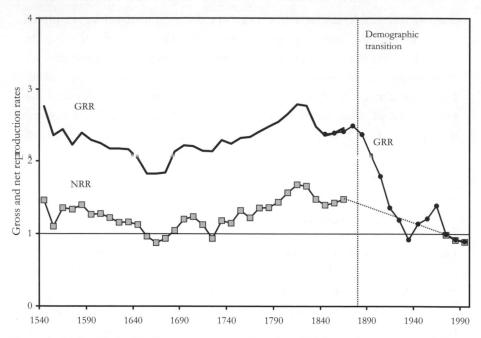

Figure 14.6   English fertility history, 1540–2000. Data from Wrigley et al., 1997, 614, and United Kingdom Office of National Statistics.

average number of births was close to six. The *demographic transition* to modern fertility rates began only in the 1890s and then progressed rapidly. By 2000 English women gave birth on average to less than two children. This transition in England was similar in timing to that across a whole range of European countries at the end of the nineteenth century.

The second measure of fertility is the net reproduction rate (NRR), the average number of daughters that would be born though her lifetime by the average female born in each decade. If the NRR is 1, then each female born merely replaces herself over the course of a lifetime (having two children on average). Net reproduction rates fell much less. Indeed for the average pre-industrial society the NRR would be much closer to 1 than in prosperous preindustrial England in the years 1540–1800. So the decline in NRR with the arrival of the modern world has been minimal. As we saw in the previous chapter the GRR and NRR both rose in the era of the classic Industrial Revolution in England.

What triggered the switch to the modern demographic regime with few children despite high incomes? In particular, was this another independent innovation, as significant for human history as the Industrial Revolution? Or was it just a delayed echo of the earlier Industrial Revolution?

The first possibility is that the general rise of incomes reduced fertility. The decline in gross fertility, the number of children born to women, is clearly correlated with income, both across societies and within particular societies over time. This fact has led some economists, such as Gary Becker, to posit that the driving force in declining fertility was just the great gain in incomes since the Industrial Revolution.[24] That would make the demographic transition a mere echo of the Industrial Revolution, another consequence of the technological break from the Malthusian regime.

But if people have fewer children as incomes rise, it implies that children, in economic terms, are "inferior" goods, in the same category as potatoes. Why do people want more housing space, more cars, and more clothes as they get richer, but not more children? Becker argued that the demand for children can be analyzed as one would the demand for any commodity, as long as we are careful to note that there are two constraints on consumption. The first is the budget constraint: how much a person has to spend. The second is the time constraint: there are only 24 hours in each day within which to consume things. As incomes have risen and the budget constraint has relaxed, the time constraint on consumption has become ever more important. Richer consumers switched their consumption patterns away from time-intensive activities toward goods that require less time to consume. As people get richer they tend to buy many time-saving products and services, such as prepared foods and restaurant meals.

Children as a consumption item are time intensive in the extreme. Thus higher-income consumers have switched their consumption away from children to less time-intensive goods: expensive homes, fancy cars, nice clothes. But since time constrains rich people to have few children, there has also been a switch toward having children of higher "quality." Time constraints mean that millionaires do not get to drive any more than fast-food workers. But the rich consume more car services by riding in expensive new Porsches and BMWs, while the poor make do with Hyundais. Parents whom time constrains to only a few children want the best possible children that money can buy, so they invest in enrichment programs, orthodontists, private schools, athletic camps, ceramics classes. The rich are having fewer children than the

24. Becker, 1981.

Table 14.5   Children Born per Married Man in England,
1891–1911

Occupation	1891	1901	1911
Professional	4.9	4.7	3.8
Miner	6.7	6.5	5.9
Construction laborer	6.4	5.6	5.4
General laborer	6.4	6.4	5.2
Agricultural laborer	6.6	5.9	4.9

Source: Garrett et al., 2001, 291, 297.

poor only if we count children by heads. If we count by expenditures richer parents still spend much more on their children than the poor. Figure 14.3, for example, which showed the hourly real wage of English building workers from 1200 to 2000, reveals that real income gains were actually modest until after the 1860s. Thus the delay in the decline in fertility until long after the onset of the Industrial Revolution would be explicable if income drives fertility. Similarly in the modern world there is a strong negative relationship between gross fertility and income across countries.

We also see in late-nineteenth-century England during the demographic transition a negative association between income and numbers of children born. Table 14.5 shows for 1891, 1901, and 1911 the estimated numbers of children present in households by the occupation of the male household head. The numbers of children born in 1891 were unchanged from the preindustrial era for low-income groups, but they had already fallen for the professional classes. In all the cross sections the high-income group had lower gross fertility, even as by 1911 the gross numbers of children begin to fall for the poorest groups.

Income, however, certainly cannot by itself explain the modern decline in fertility. For we have already seen for the preindustrial period that net reproduction rates were *positively* associated with income. The male testators in England in 1585–1638, with wealth that would make them rich even by the standards of 1891, left nearly four children each. Their gross fertilities would be as high as those for the working classes in England in the 1890s. Figure 14.7 shows surviving children as a function of wealth even up to those with assets of £1,500 or more (averaging £2,600). These assets would produce an income

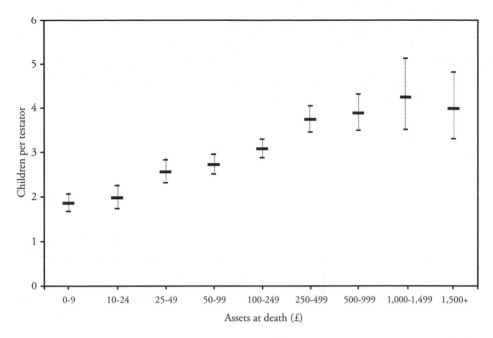

Figure 14.7 Surviving children as a function of wealth in England, circa 1620. The bands for each wealth class show the range of values within which we can be 95 percent confident that the true numbers of surviving children per testator lay.

equivalent to about £260 a year in 1891, well above the annual earnings of about £80 per year for building craftsmen or £50 for laborers in this period. Had income alone been determining fertility, the rich in the preindustrial world would already have been restricting their fertility.

Could the rich of the preindustrial world actually have wanted fewer children, but been unable to achieve that desire because of a lack of effective contraception? No. Figure 14.6 shows that most of the decline toward levels of gross fertility characteristic of modern developed economies had been accomplished in England (and indeed elsewhere in Europe) by the 1920s, long before modern condoms, hormonal contraceptive pills, legalized abortion, or vasectomies.

Using only abstinence, withdrawal, and more primitive barrier methods, technologies available in England at least as early as the seventeenth century, birth rates for married women by the 1920s were reduced to less than half their previous levels. And this happened in a social environment in which birth control was rarely discussed in public forums. Even more persuasively, in the late eighteenth century the French began to reduce their fertility rates within marriage. By the 1850s they already had fertility levels equivalent to those of England in 1901. Thus the possibility of controlling fertility existed long before the demographic transition of the late nineteenth century. The lack of fertility control before then was an issue more of motivation than of means.

Another indication that income alone cannot explain fertility declines is the lack of any association in modern high income economies between income and fertility. For example, for both 1980 and 2000 there was no link between household income and fertility, measured as the numbers of children present in the households of married women aged 30–42, for Canada, Finland, Germany, Sweden, the United Kingdom, and the United States.[25] It is only in the course of the demographic transition that we observe a negative relationship between income and fertility across income groups in a society.

An alternative possibility is that the desired number of children per married couple is actually independent of income, and that the preference was always for only two or three surviving children. But to achieve a completed family size of even two children in the high-mortality environment of the Malthusian era required five or more births.

Furthermore, the random nature of child deaths meant that, in order to ensure a reasonably good chance of a surviving son, average family sizes had to be large. Figure 14.8 shows the distribution of the numbers of surviving sons for men leaving wills in England between 1585 and 1638. Nearly 40 percent of the poorest married men leaving wills had no surviving son. Even among the richest married men nearly one-fifth left no son. The average rich man left four children because some families had large numbers of surviving children. Hence the absence of any sign of fertility control by richer families in preindustrial England may stem more from the uncertainties of child survival in the Malthusian era. With a greater fraction of child deaths the variance of resulting family sizes at an average completed family size of two children would necessarily be greater. As the fraction of children surviving increased, risk-averse families could afford to begin limiting births.

In the late nineteenth century child mortality in England had fallen substantially from the levels of the eighteenth century, and the rate of that decline was strongly correlated with income. For families living in homes with ten or

25. Dickmann, 2003, table 2.

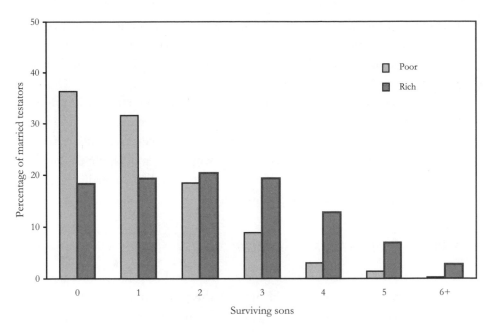

Figure 14.8 Percentage of men with particular numbers of sons, England, 1585–1638.

more rooms only 13 percent of children failed to reach age 15, while for those living in one room 47 percent of children failed to reach that age.[26] Thus the lower gross fertility of high-income groups at the end of the nineteenth century portrayed in table 14.5 translates into a more muted decline in net fertility among higher-income groups. And these groups faced a substantially reduced variance in family size outcomes compared to low-income groups.

Another possible element in the decline of fertility since the Industrial Revolution is the increased social status of women. Men may well have had greater desire for children in preindustrial society than women. Women, not men, bore the very real health risks of pregnancy, and they did most of the child rearing. But typically men had a much more powerful position within the family. Thus women may always have desired smaller numbers of surviving children than men but only been able to act on those desires as of the late nineteenth century.

Women's relative status and voice were clearly increasing in the late nineteenth century in England. Literacy rates for women had by then advanced to

26. Haines, 1995, 303.

near equality with those of men. Women had gained access to universities by 1869, enhanced property rights within marriage by 1882, the right to vote in local elections by 1894, and finally a vote in national elections by 1918. These gains proceeded most rapidly among higher-income groups.

These assumptions could explain why net fertility falls after the late nineteenth century even though in cross section in the sixteenth century and in 2000 there is either a positive connection between income and net fertility or no connection. They could also explain why the demographic transition appeared first in the higher socioeconomic groups, so that net fertility is negatively related to income during the transition period.

Why Did Owners of Capital Not Gain More?

Chapters 10 and 11 showed why from the Industrial Revolution onward innovators have generally collected little of the productivity advances their innovations produced. The returns to capital employed in industrial production have often exceeded the competitive market return on capital. But the presence of these higher returns seems to owe more to the ability of some firms to create barriers to entry to their sectors than to rapid productivity growth in the sectors. These entry barriers generally have little to do with technological advances. They owe more to factors such as increasing returns to scale or the ability to create brand images through advertising.

Productivity growth in cotton textiles in England from 1770 to 1870, for example, far exceeded that in any other industry. But the competitive nature of the industry, and the inability of the patent system to protect most technological advances, kept profits low. Cotton goods were homogenous. Yarn and cloth were sold in wholesale markets where quality differences were readily evident to buyers. The efficient scale of cotton spinning and weaving mills was always small relative to the market. New entrants abounded. By 1900 Britain had about two thousand firms in the industry. Firms learned improved techniques from innovative competitors by hiring away their skilled workers. Machine designers learned improved techniques from operating firms. The entire industry—the capital goods makers and the product producers— over time clustered more and more tightly in the Manchester area. By 1900 40 percent of the entire world output of cotton goods was produced within 30 miles of Manchester. The main beneficiaries of this technological advance thus ended up being consumers of textiles across the world and landowners in the cluster of textile towns, whose largely worthless agricultural land became valuable building sites.

The greatest of the Industrial Revolution cotton magnates, Richard Arkwright, is estimated to have left £0.5 million when he died in 1792.[27] His son, also named Richard, inherited his father's spinning mills. But though Richard the son had managed his own mills and had much experience in the business, and though the industry itself was still showing rapid productivity growth, he soon sold most of his father's mills, preferring to invest in land and government bonds. By 1814 he owned £0.5 million in government bonds alone. He prospered mainly from those bonds and from real estate, leaving £3.25 million when he died in 1843, despite having sunk a substantial sum into a palatial country house for his family.[28] But Arkwright Senior accumulated less wealth than Josiah Wedgwood, who left £0.6 million in 1795, even though Wedgwood operated in a sector, pottery, which had seen far less technological progress and was still largely dependent on manual labor even in the late nineteenth century.

Though the first wave of great innovations of the Industrial Revolution, in textiles, did not offer above-average profits because of the competitive nature of the industry, the second wave, in railroads, seemed to offer more possibilities. Railways are a technology with inherent economies of scale. To begin with, one line has to be built between two cities, and once it has been built a competitor wishing to enter the market can do so only by building, at a minimum, a complete line of its own. Since most city pairs could not profitably support multiple links, exclusion, hence profits, seemed possible.

The success of the Liverpool-Manchester line in 1830—by the 1840s equity shares in this line were selling for twice their par value—inspired a long period of investment in railways. Figure 14.9 shows the rapid growth of the railway network in England from 1825 to 1869, by which time more than 12,000 miles of track had been laid across the relatively small country. The pace of investment and construction was so frenetic that economic historians speak of "railway manias" in 1839 and 1846. Railways absorbed a large fraction of all fixed capital investment in England in the mid-nineteenth century.

27. Fitton, 1989, 219.
28. Ibid., 296.

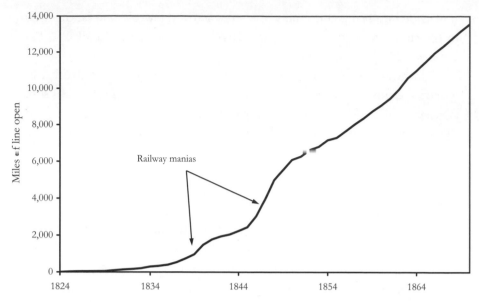

Figure 14.9   British railroad construction, 1825–67. Data from Mitchell and Deane, 1971, 225.

But again the rush to enter quickly drove down profits to very modest levels, as table 14.6 shows. Even in the first decade of railway construction the profit rate on the capital invested was modest. By the 1860s real returns, the return on the capital actually invested, were no greater than for very safe investments in government bonds or agricultural land. While railway lines had local monopolies, they ended up in constant competition with each other through roundabout routes.

Thus while, for example, the Great Western line may have controlled the route from London to Manchester, freight and passengers could cross over through other companies to link up with the East Coast route to London. Once more profits inspired imitation and the high returns were squeezed out of the system. Consumers were again the main beneficiaries.

It is for this reason that in Britain, unlike in the United States, there are very few universities and major charities funded by private donors. The Industrial Revolution did not result in great personal or family fortunes in England. By the 1860s the rich were still by and large the descendants of the landed aristocracy. Of 379 men dying between 1860 and 1879 in Britain who left at least £0.5 million, 256 (68 percent) owed their wealth to inherited land. As we saw in chapter 11, only 17 (4 percent) were textile magnates, even though

Table 14.6   Profit Rates on the Capital Invested in British-Owned Railways, 1830–1912

Period	Rate of return, United Kingdom (%)	Rate of return, British Empire (%)	Rate of return, foreign (%)
1830–39	3.9	—	—
1840–49	4.8	—	—
1850–59	3.8	—	—
1860–69	3.8	—	4.7
1870–79	3.2	—	8.0
1880–89	3.3	1.4	7.7
1890–99	3.0	2.5	4.9
1900–09	2.6	1.6	4.4
1910–12	2.6	3.1	6.6

Sources: Before 1860: Arnold and McCartney, 2005, table 2. After 1860: Davis and Huttenback, 1986, table 3.8.

the textile industry had driven the productivity advance of the Industrial Revolution.[29]

Thus the lack of any inherent connection between more rapid technological advance and the generation of above-average profits by firms, with consumers instead reaping most of the benefits of technological advance, further explains the equalizing tendencies of growth since the Industrial Revolution.

Within societies the forces set in motion by the Industrial Revolution have moved toward equality and social harmony. But across societies, as we shall see in the next part of the book, the Industrial Revolution led to a marked increase in income differences. Before the Industrial Revolution the rich and the poor were close neighbors. Now they are but distant cousins, gazing at each other across national borders and widening income gaps.

29. Rubinstein, 1981, 60–67.

PART III

The Great Divergence

15   World Growth since 1800

The bourgeoisie, by the rapid improvement of all instruments of production, by the immensely facilitated means of communication, draws all, even the most barbarian, nations into civilization. The cheap prices of commodities are the heavy artillery with which it batters down all Chinese walls, with which it forces the barbarians' intensely obstinate hatred of foreigners to capitulate. It compels all nations, on pain of extinction, to adopt the bourgeois mode of production; it compels them to introduce what it calls civilization into their midst, i.e., to become bourgeois themselves. In one word, it creates a world after its own image.
—Karl Marx and Friedrich Engels (1848)[1]

By the mid-nineteenth century the efficiency of the English economy was clearly growing at an unprecedented pace. That this improvement in efficiency was based on knowledge creation, rather than the accumulation of physical capital or the exploitation of natural resources, seemed to imply the rapid worldwide spread of the techniques and industries of the Industrial Revolution. For while developing knowledge is an arduous task, copying the inventions of others can be easy.

The increasing prosperity and economic power of Britain impressed both foreign governments and individuals, especially since it was accompanied by growing military and political power. Thus there were soon both private and governmental attempts to import the new British technologies. A series of eighteenth-century Parliamentary Acts restricted the emigration of artisans and the export of machinery, plans, or models in the textile and other industries. Only after 1825 were artisans free to work abroad, and only after 1842 were machinery exports deregulated.[2] But England still swarmed with foreign dignitaries, industrial spies, adventurers, and prospective manufacturers doing the rounds of its mills, foundries, factories, mines, and railways. Skilled workers were regularly propositioned with the promise of riches abroad. Despite the difficulties of travel and the language and cultural barriers, thousands

1. Marx and Engels, 1967, 84.
2. Henderson, 1965, 4, 139–41.

Table 15.1   Time Lags in the International Diffusion of Innovations

Country	Cotton mill (1771)	Watt-type steam engine (1775)	Steam railway (1825)
Austria	30	42	13
Belgium	28	16	10
Brazil	75	35	29
Canada	—	36	11
Denmark	—	29	19
France	7	3	7
Germany	13	8	12
Hungary	—	28	21
India	46	30	28
Ireland	19	15	9
Italy	—	12	14
Mexico	64	43	48
Netherlands	24	10	14
Portugal	—	28	31
Russia	22	23	11
Spain	—	7	23
Switzerland	23	49	22
Sweden	—	23	30
United States	20	28	5

Sources: Cotton mill: Clark, 1987a. Watt engine: Robinson, 1974; Tann and Breckin, 1978. Steam railway: Mitchell, 1995, 1998a, 1998b.
Note: The table gives the time to the first use found by a survey of the literature. More rapid adoption is possible.

responded.[3] King Canute probably had as much success in holding back the tide as did British governments in protecting trade secrets during the Industrial Revolution.

Table 15.1 quantifies the rapidity of the spread of cotton mills, Watt-type steam engines, and steam railways to other countries. The table shows the time in years between the introduction of the new technique in England and its first known use in other countries. Clearly there was a diffusion lag. For western European countries it was on the order of thirteen years; for eastern

3. It was estimated that by 1824 there were 1,400 British artisans in France alone; Henderson, 1965, 141f.

and southern Europe, more like twenty-two years; India, thirty-five years; Latin America, fifty-two years. Such lags would translate into moderate differences in the efficiency levels of economies. But at the rates of efficiency advance for England during the Industrial Revolution, even a county such as India would have an income per person only 17 percent less than that in England as a result of the delay in acquiring the most up-to-date techniques.

But in the nineteenth century technological advance was particularly strong in techniques that determined the speed of travel of information and the cost of shipment for goods. Thus there was every hope that by the late nineteenth century the world would be sufficiently globalized that diffusion lags would drop rapidly, and industrialization would proceed in even the poorest countries.

The Instruments of Globalization

In the late eighteenth and early nineteenth centuries a series of technological, organizational, and political developments seemed to imply the coming integration of all countries into a new industrialized world.

The technological changes were the development of railways, steamships, the telegraph, and the mechanized factory. The organizational change was the development of specialized machine-building firms in Britain, and later the United States, whose business was the export of technology. The political changes were the extension of European colonial empires to large parts of Africa and Asia, and internal political developments within Europe.

The world before 1800 was one in which information and people traveled at astonishingly slow speeds. We have a nice example of the speed of information flow for the later Roman Empire from the work of Richard Duncan-Jones. Legal documents in Roman Egypt under the empire listed both the calendar date and the name of the reigning emperor. When a new emperor came to power in Rome there was thus a period when legal documents in Egypt carried the name of the previous emperor. The length of this period indicates how long it took information to get to Egypt.[4] The estimated average transmittal time, shown in table 15.2, was 56 days. Thus along the major trade

4. Since few documents survive for each transition between emperors, the first document with the correct name of an emperor provides just an upper bound on the transmittal time. Similarly the last document with the wrong name gives a lower bound. The mean of these two estimates gives an unbiased estimate of the true transmittal time.

Table 15.2 Speed of Information Travel in the Mediterranean

Period	Journey	Distance (miles)	Days	Journeys	Speed (mph)
54–222	Italy-Egypt	1,323	56	23	1.0
1500	Damascus-Venice	1,514	80	56	0.8
	Alexandria-Venice	1,366	65	266	0.9
	Lisbon-Venice	1,180	46	35	1.1
	Palermo-Venice	507	22	118	1.0

Source: Duncan-Jones, 1990, 7–29.
Note: Distances are calculated along the great circle.

routes of the Roman Empire information flowed at an average speed of 1 mile per hour.

We also have estimates of travel speeds in the Mediterranean circa 1500 from the diaries of Venetians. These show the days between events occurring elsewhere and a report of them appearing in a Venetian diary. The speed of information travel is very similar to that in Imperial Roman times.

Thus in the Malthusian era people lived in a world where information spread so slowly that many died fighting over issues that had already been decided. The Battle of New Orleans, fought on January 8, 1815, between the British and the Americans, which resulted in a thousand deaths, occurred because neither commander knew that the Treaty of Ghent had concluded a peace between the countries on December 24. The British commander, who then moved on to take Biloxi, heard the news only on February 14.

Information flows were not much faster in 1800 than in the classical world. The *Times* of London reported Nelson's triumph at the Battle of the Nile on August 1, 1798, only on October 2, 62 days later: the news traveled at 1.4 miles per hour. Nelson's victory over the French and his glorious death at Trafalgar, off the Portuguese coast, on October 21, 1805, was first reported in the *Times* 17 days later: a transmission speed of 2.7 miles per hour. Table 15.3 gives a sampling of how long it took news of events elsewhere in the world in the nineteenth century to reach the *Times* of London. By the early nineteenth century information flowed at somewhat faster rates than in the classical and medieval worlds. Nevertheless news could still take six months to reach Britain from India.

Table 15.3 Speed of Information Travel to London, 1798–1914

Event	Year	Distance (miles)	Days until report	Speed (mph)
Battle of the Nile	1798	2,073	62	1.4
Battle of Trafalgar	1805	1,100	17	2.7
Earthquake, Kutch, India	1819	4,118	153	1.1
Treaty of Nanking	1842	5,597	84	2.8
Charge of the Light Brigade, Crimea	1854	1,646	17	4.0
Indian Mutiny, Delhi Massacre	1857	4,176	46	3.8
Treaty of Tien-Sin (China)	1858	5,140	82	2.6
Assassination of Lincoln	1865	3,674	13	12
Assassination of Archduke Maximilian, Mexico	1867	5,545	12	19
Assassination of Alexander II, St. Petersburg	1881	1,309	0.46	119
Nobi Earthquake, Japan	1891	5,916	1	246

Note: Distances are calculated along the great circle.

In the mid-nineteenth century the introduction of the telegraph in 1844, and particularly the laying of the first undersea telegraph cable between France and England in 1851, changed by a factor of nearly 100 the speed of travel of information. In 1866 transatlantic telegraph service was established.[5] By 1870 India was linked to Britain by a telegraph system, partly over land and partly undersea, which could transmit messages in twenty-four hours. This explains the explosion in the speed of information transmission in table 15.3 between 1858 and 1891.

The cost of carriage for goods also declined dramatically in the nineteenth century, both on land and across the sea. Table 15.4 shows the miles of railroad completed in selected countries by 1850, 1890, and 1910. The great expansion of the rail network in the late nineteenth century, even in countries otherwise little affected by the Industrial Revolution, such as Russia and India, improved communication immensely.

Ocean transport was similarly revolutionized in this period by the development of faster and more cost-effective steamships. By the 1830s steamships

5. A cable laid in 1858 had failed.

Table 15.4 Railway Mileage Completed (thousands of miles)

	1850	1890	1910
Britain	6.1	17	20
United States	9.0	208	352
Germany	3.6	27	38
France	1.8	21	25
Russia	0.3	19	41
India	0.0	17	33

Sources: Mitchell, 1995, 1998a, 1998b.

were already speedier and more reliable than sailing ships, but they were used only for the most valuable and urgent freight, such as mail. Their high coal consumption limited the amount of cargo they could carry. To sail from Bombay to Aden in 1830 the *Hugh Lindsay* "had to fill its hold and cabins and pile its decks with coal, barely leaving enough room for the crew and the mail." In the 1840s the liner *Britannia* required 640 tons of coal to cross the Atlantic with 225 tons of cargo. Thus even in the 1850s steam power was used only for perishable cargos, and even then only on certain routes.[6]

But in the 1850s and 1860s four innovations lowered the cost of steam-powered ocean transport: the screw propeller, iron hulls, compound engines, and surface condensers. Screw propellers translated power into motion through the water more effectively. Iron-hulled ships were 30–40 percent lighter and offered 15 percent more cargo capacity for a given amount of steam power. Compound engines converted coal into mechanical power more efficiently. Surface condensers conserved water (ocean steamships had previously had to make steam from seawater, which led to corrosion and fouling of their engines).

These last two innovations greatly reduced the coal consumption of engines per horsepower-hour. In the 1830s it took 10 pounds of coal to produce one horsepower-hour, but by 1881 the amount was down to 2 pounds. This advance not only reduced costs directly but also allowed ships to carry less coal and more cargo, thus further reducing them.[7]

6. Headrick, 1988, 24.
7. Headrick, 1988, 24–31.

Steamship speeds also increased. On the Atlantic the *Great Western* in 1838 had a maximum speed of 10 miles per hour. By 1907 the *Mauretania* could make 29 miles per hour.[8]

Finally the completion of the Suez Canal in 1869 and the Panama Canal in 1914 greatly reduced distances on some of the major ocean routes. The Suez Canal reduced the length of the journey from London to Bombay by 41 percent, and that from London to Shanghai by 32 percent, thus bringing the markets of Europe and Asia substantially closer.

The result of these technological changes was a significant decline in real ocean transport costs by 1900. In 1907, for example, it cost £0.40 to carry a volume ton of cotton goods by rail the 30 miles from Manchester to Liverpool, but only £0.90–1.50 more to ship those goods the 7,250 miles from Liverpool to Bombay.[9] Since a volume ton of cotton textiles at that time would have a value of about £80, these costs represented a mere 2 percent of the value of the product.[10] In comparison the rate for cotton goods carried from Bombay to London by the East India Company in 1793 was £31 per ton.[11] In terms of day wages shipping costs to the East by 1906 were only 2 percent of the level of 1793. Much of this decline in cost, however, had been achieved by the 1840s, with sailing vessels and well before the Suez Canal opened. In the 1840s it cost £3.60 to ship a volume ton of goods from Calcutta to England.[12]

By the late nineteenth century industrial locations with good water access that were on well-established shipping routes—Bombay, Calcutta, Madras, Shanghai, Hong Kong—could gain access to all the industrial inputs of Britain at costs not too much higher than those of many firms in Britain. Table 15.5 shows shipping costs per ton for cotton goods from English ports to various destinations in 1907. By 1907 production of goods like cotton textiles was feasible anywhere in the world close to an ocean port.

Figure 15.1 shows the costs of another important industrial input, energy, measured as coal costs at various ports around the world, standardized to the price of Welsh steaming coal. The low shipping costs meant that British coal

8. Kirkaldy, 1914, appendix XVIII.

9. A volume ton is equal to 50 cubic feet. For cotton textiles a volume ton weighed 1,344 pounds.

10. Deane and Cole, 1967, 187.

11. MacGregor, 1850, 389. It is not clear if this was a weight or volume ton.

12. McGregor, 1850, 917. O'Rourke and Williamson, 2002a, 2002b, argue that from 1500 to 1800 declines in transport costs between Asia and Europe were minimal, the gains in trade volume being largely a function of increased European demand.

Table 15.5   Transport Costs for Cotton Goods from England, 1907

Origin	Destination	Ocean distance (miles)	Cost per 40 cubic feet (£)
Manchester	Bombay	6,851	0.93
Manchester	Calcutta	8,751	1.50
Birkenhead	Shanghai	11,676	1.66
Birkenhead	Japan	12,461	1.66
Manchester	Buenos Ares	6,844	1.75
Liverpool	Sydney	12,366	1.78
Liverpool	Java	9,441	1.88
Birkenhead	Manila	10,667	2.08
Liverpool	Cape Town	6,663	2.12
England	Lagos	4,199	2.25
Manchester	Limon (Costa Rica)	5,337	2.38
England	Valparaiso	8,060	2.50
Manchester	Rio de Janeiro	5,577	3.25

Sources: Transport costs: Parliamentary Papers, 1909a. Distances between ports: United States, Naval Oceanographic Office, 1965.

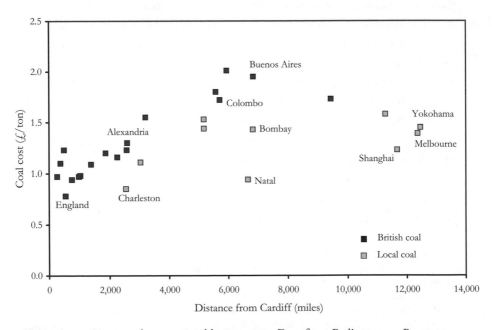

Figure 15.1   Steam coal costs at world ports, 1907. Data from Parliamentary Papers, 1909a.

was available in a surprising range of ports across the world. The dark squares in the figure show places where British coal was available. In 1907 steamers at such distant locations as Singapore, Colombo, Alexandria, Buenos Aires, and Istanbul could fuel using English coal. Coal costs were higher in many countries than in northern Europe and the United States, but the range of costs for such a heavy material, found in such uneven distribution across the world, was remarkably small: little more than 2:1.

The last of the great technological changes of the nineteenth century was the introduction of the mechanized factory. Industrial production before the Industrial Revolution was generally directed by many skilled artisans who learned their crafts through personal apprenticeships. In the preindustrial period when countries wanted to develop new industries they generally had to recruit whole communities of foreign artisans. The French in the 1660s even went so far as to abduct a group of Swedish iron workers in hopes of having them establish an iron industry.[13]

The textile industry during the Industrial Revolution was revolutionary in its rate of productivity advance. But it was also revolutionary in its ability to employ, with minimal skilled supervision, large numbers of unskilled, untrained, short-term workers. The replacement of skilled lifetime workers by cheaper forms of labor did not occur all at once, and it was not completely possible until the development of the ring spindle in the late nineteenth century. But all through the nineteenth century adult males, traditionally the most expensive and intractable form of labor, accounted for less than 30 percent of cotton textile operators, even in Britain, where skill-intensive mule spinning predominated.[14] By the late 1930s, for example, when the Japanese cotton spinning industry had labor productivity levels not much below those of Britain, the labor force in Japan was 88.5 percent female, and the average female cotton operator was 17 years old with 2.3 years experience in the industry.[15]

The ability of the textile industry to keep operator skills, education, and supervision requirements to a minimum is well illustrated by ring spinning. This was a spinning technique, developed in the nineteenth century, which

13. Cipolla, 1972, 50–51.
14. Deane and Cole, 1967, 190.
15. Shindo, 1961, 233–36.

succeeded in part because it minimized necessary worker skills. Ring spinning operators needed to perform only the following five tasks:

1. *Piecing.* Twisting together the broken pieces of thread when a break occurs.
2. *Creeling.* Replacing the bobbins that supply the unspun cotton to the ring spindle.
3. *Cleaning.* Wiping away tufts of loose cotton fibers which accumulate on the spinning frames.
4. *Doffing.* Removing the full bobbins of spun yarn and replacing them with empty bobbins. This is normally done at regular planned intervals by specialized squads of doffers.
5. *Patrolling.* Walking around the machines inspecting for spindles in need of tasks 1–3.

Work organization was extremely simple. Each spinner (*piecer* in India) was assigned a set of spindles. During a shift the spinner walked around the set of spindles on the same path. Each spindle was inspected to see if it needed piecing, creeling, or cleaning. If so the task was performed. Spinners needed no literacy, nor even particular strength or dexterity. Nor did they need to plan ahead. They merely proceeded from spindle to spindle doing whichever of the three tasks was necessary.

The foreman could check if operators had been diligent simply by periodically counting how many of the spindles under their care were stopped (in the terminology of the industry, how many *ends were down*) and comparing that with the rate for other operators.

Most of the tasks in other parts of the spinning industry had exactly the same character. It was for these reasons that the textile industry was hailed by some, and reviled by others, as the precursor of a new industrial order in which work would be machine regulated and machine paced.

Thus while the sophistication of technology was increasing after the Industrial Revolution, for many production processes the tasks, by design, were simplified and routinized. Technology might be designed by those countries with high levels of education, but much of its operation was well suited to poor economies such as India and China.

Added to the various technological ways in which world industrialization was hastened were organizational changes that facilitated the diffusion of technologies.

In the early nineteenth century the heroic age of innovation by the lone inventor ended, and a specialized machine-building sector developed within the Lancashire cotton industry. These firms played an important role in exporting textile technology. As the rate of growth of the English industry slowed in the late nineteenth century, British manufacturers looked abroad for markets. The textile machinery maker Platt Brothers, for example, was exporting at least 50 percent of its production as early as 1845–70. Such capital goods firms were able to provide a complete package of services to prospective foreign entrants into the textile industry, including technical information, machinery, construction expertise, and managers and skilled operators. By 1913 the six largest textile machine producers employed over thirty thousand workers mainly producing for the world market.[16] These firms reduced the risks to foreign entrepreneurs by selling machines on a trial basis and supplying skilled workers to direct operations and train local labor forces.

Table 15.6 shows a sample of the number of orders Platt took for ring-spinning frames, where each order typically involved multiple machines, in the periods 1890–1914 and 1915–1936. England was a small share of Platt's market for ring frames throughout these years.

Similar capital goods exporters developed in the railway sector, and later in the United States in the boot and shoe industry. British construction crews completed railways in many foreign countries under the captainship of such flamboyant entrepreneurs as Lord Thomas Brassey.[17] The overseas exodus was due in part to the saturation of the rail market within Britain by the 1870s. By 1875, in a railway construction boom lasting just forty-five years, 71 percent of all the railway lines ever constructed in Britain had been completed. As table 15.4 suggests, thereafter the major markets for British rail contractors and engine constructors were overseas. India, for example, got most of its railway equipment from Britain, and Indian railway mileage by 1910 was significantly greater than that of Britain.

The final set of developments in the nineteenth century that should have speeded world industrialization was political. The most important of these was the expansion of European colonial territories. By 1900 the European states controlled as colonies 35 percent of the land surface of the world, even

16. Bruland, 1989, 5, 6, 34.

17. Brassey built railways in Argentina, Australia, Austria, Britain, Canada, Denmark, France, India, Italy, Mauritius, the Netherlands, Poland, Prussia, Russia, and Spain; Helps, 1874, 161–66.

Table 15.6 Platt Ring Frame Orders by Country, 1890–1936

Country	Sales, 1890–1914	Sales, 1915–1936
Austria/Hungary	4	4
Belgium/Netherlands	24	17
Brazil	95	43
Canada	15	17
Central America	3	1
China	5	64
Czechoslovakia	14	10
Egypt	0	5
England	110	74
France	41	31
Germany	47	6
India	66	132
Italy	69	29
Japan	66	117
Mexico	75	7
Peru	7	0
Poland	41	8
Portugal/Spain	103	35
Russia	131	23
Scandinavia	4	0
Switzerland	3	0
Turkey	0	6
United States	2	0
West Africa	0	2

Source: Lancashire Record Office, Platt Ring Frame Order Books. Data from nine years in each period.

excluding Asiatic Russia. Of a world area of 58 million square miles Europe itself constitutes only 4 million square miles, but by 1900 its dependencies covered 20 million square miles. The British Empire was the largest, covering 9 million square miles. The French had nearly 5 million square miles; the Netherlands, 2 million square miles; and Germany, 1 million square miles.

Even many countries that formally remained independent were forced to cede trading privileges and special rights to European powers. Thus at the conclusion of the First Opium War in 1842 China, by the Treaty of Nanjing, was forced to allow European imports, including opium, at low tariff rates, to allow foreign residence in treaty ports such as Shanghai, and to concede Hong Kong to the British. Further conflicts resulted in more Chinese defeats, and the creation of what was essentially an international city in Shanghai.

Despite its many unpleasant aspects, imperialism would seem to have been a potent driving force for world industrialization. Foreign entrepreneurs investing in independent countries always faced the danger of expropriation if local political conditions changed. By the late nineteenth century the political control by countries such as Britain of so much of the world allowed European entrepreneurs to export machinery and techniques to low-wage areas with little risk of expropriation.

The most important colonial empire was that of the British, whose major possessions by the end of the nineteenth century included most of India, Pakistan, Burma, Sri Lanka, South Africa, and Egypt. The nature of British imperialism also ensured that, up until 1918, no country was restrained from the development of industry by the absence of a local market of sufficient size. Because of the British policy of free trade Britain itself and most British dependencies were open to imports, either with no tariffs or else with low tariffs intended solely to raise revenue.

In cotton textiles, the major manufacturing industry of the world before 1918, table 15.7 shows the major net exporters and importers of cotton yarn and cloth in the international market of 1910. India, the largest market, was served almost exclusively by English mills, but was in fact open to all countries, the only barrier being a 3.5 percent revenue tariff on imports. Even this impediment had been balanced by a countervailing tax applied to local Indian mills, at the insistence of Manchester manufacturers. The Chinese market, the next largest, by fiat of the imperial powers was similarly protected by only a 5 percent ad valorem revenue tariff. Australia also maintained an ad valorem tariff of only 5 percent, having no domestic industry to protect.

Thus in 1910 the total size of the open cotton textile market was on the order of $400 million, a quarter of world production. This market would be enough to sustain 35 million spindles and 400,000 looms. In 1910 the British textile industry, the largest in the world, had 55 million spindles and 650,000 looms in operation, since the British also sold in protected foreign markets. Thus by the early twentieth century 40 percent of the world cotton textile market was available to any entrant on the same terms as for British mills.

The pre–World War I Pax Britannica was also a major element in reducing transport costs on the oceans. Prior to the nineteenth century shipping

Table 15.7 Net Exports of Cotton Yarn and Cloth, 1910 (millions of dollars)

Country	All	Yarn, thread	Gray woven cloth	Colored cloth
Major exporters				
United Kingdom	453	83	100	270
Japan	26	22	5	−1
Italy	24	4	3	17
France	23	−3	4	22
Germany	15	−11	−3	29
Major importers				
British India	−100	18	−53	−65
China	−81	−41	−11	−30
Argentina	−29	−3	−1	−25
Australia	−25	−2	−1	−22
Ottoman Empire	−20	−1	−7	−11
Egypt	−18	−1	−17	
Canada	−12	−2	−1	−9
Brazil	−11	−2	0	−9

Source: United States, House of Representatives, 1912, volume 1, appendix A, 212–18.

rates were often driven up by armed conflicts and by piracy. The supremacy of the British Navy, and its mandate to keep sea lanes open for trade, ensured that military conflicts were rarely a barrier to commerce and banished piracy from the seas.

British imperialism thus seemed to contain the seeds of its own downfall. It had created across Asia and the Middle East giant new coastal cities such as Alexandria, Bombay, Calcutta, Madras, and Shanghai that enjoyed the cheapest labor in the world; security of property; complete freedom to import technicians, machinery, capital, and even the entrepreneurs themselves; easy access to major sea routes; and access to the largest market in the world. Any manufacturer from anywhere in the world could set up a cotton mill in these cities and be assured that he or she would have access to an extensive market in the British Empire on the same terms as British producers.

An outstanding example of the entrepreneurial freedom within the British Empire is the history of the Sassoon family. The founding member of this family was David Sassoon, a Sephardic Jew born to the richest merchant family in Baghdad in 1792. Arrested in 1828 by order of the Ottoman governor for

Figure 15.2 David Sassoon with three of his eight sons in Bombay in 1858. His son Sassoon David Sassoon was the first in the family to adopt Western dress. From Jackson, 1968, facing page 32.

defending the Jewish community's rights, he was ransomed by his father and fled first to Bushire in Persia. From there he relocated to Bombay in 1832.[18] He and his large family prospered as traders in the rapidly growing city. Though he spoke not a word of English, in 1853 he became a British citizen and proudly flew the Union Jack. Figure 15.2 shows David Sassoon with three of his sons in Bombay in 1858.

By 1844 his son Elias had emigrated to China to pursue the opium trade with India, moving to Shanghai in 1850. Elias soon also invested in the China Steam Navigation Company and in undeveloped urban land. Another son,

18. To add to the exoticism he brought with him a number of slaves bought from Arabic tribes, and they continued to serve the family in Bombay; Jackson, 1968, 32.

Figure 15.3 Sir Phillip Sassoon (left) with the Prince of Wales and Winston Churchill in 1921. From Jackson, 1968, facing page 209. Original photograph from *The Tatler*, 1921.

Sassoon David, was sent to London in 1858 to facilitate the growing trade in cotton and cotton goods. By the 1880s the family constituted several global enterprises, investing not only in trading enterprises but also in docks and cotton factories in Bombay and housing developments in Shanghai. By the 1920s they owned more than one-tenth of the Bombay cotton mills, and they were the most innovative of the mill owners there.

Many members of the family moved to England and were quickly absorbed into the English aristocracy. David Sassoon's great-grandchildren thus included Siegfried Sassoon, the World War I poet; Sir Phillip Sassoon, friend of Churchill and the Prince of Wales; Sybil, Marquess of Cholmondeley; and Rabbi Solomon Sassoon, president of the largest Sephardic seminary in Israel. Figure 15.3 shows Sir Phillip playing polo.

The world thus seemed poised by the 1850s for rapid economic growth and for the eventual elimination of international income disparities.

The golden age of the first globalization, 1870–1913, came to an end with World War I. The disruptions of the war itself were followed by six decades of relatively turbulent times in the world economy. In the 1920s monetary problems led to the imposition of tariff controls and limits on capital movements. The Communist takeover isolated the Russian Empire from the world economy. The global Depression of the 1930s led to further disintegration of the world economy as nations lost faith in free markets and strove to solve their problems through protection, capital controls, and currency devaluations. The disruptions of World War II led to further fragmentation of the world economy with the creation of a raft of new Communist regimes and the breakup of much of the British Empire into independent states.

Inspired by economic models that rejected the classical liberal economics of the British and emphasized instead autarky and centralized government planning, countries such as India imposed controls on imports of technology, managerial expertise, and capital. The international currency stability of the gold standard in the years 1870–1913 was impossible to re-create over the long run under the Bretton Woods system, leading by the 1970s to floating currencies that fluctuated wildly in value. By then inflation and unemployment had also become persistent problems in many industrialized countries to an extent not witnessed in the nineteenth century. Only in the 1980s did a new era of globalization emerge, with worldwide movement toward freer trade in goods and capital among democracies, combined with the end of Communist rule (or else its transformation into a Communism in name only, as in China).[19]

World Growth since 1800

What actually happened? The answer, of course, is that, instead of following England and the other European countries on the path to rapid growth, much of the rest of the world languished in poverty. In India, after more than a hundred years of British rule, there were still fifty million hand spindles and two million hand looms in the 1920s. Figure 15.4 shows just how primitive this technology was.

The divergence of national incomes and living standards that began with the Industrial Revolution continues to widen to the present day. In a world of ever more rapid communication and ever-falling transport costs, the gaps between countries based on material living standards have become enormous. The gap between material living standards in the richest and poorest

19. O'Rourke and Williamson, 2001; Obstfeld and Taylor, 2004.

Figure 15.4 Hand spinning and weaving in India, 1920s. From Pearse, 1930, 25.

economies of the world is now more than 50:1, while in 1800 it was probably at most 4:1. Material living standards have increased only tenfold in successful economies such as England and the United States since the Industrial Revolution. So the poorest economies now, places like Tanzania and Ethiopia, are poorer than the average society before the Industrial Revolution. Just as income inequalities have been compressed within countries since the Industrial Revolution, so have they widened across countries.

Figure 15.5 shows per capita income for a sample of countries—the United States, England, Argentina, Bolivia, India, and Uganda—from 1800 to 2000, all measured in U.S. dollars at the prices of 2000. The divergence in fortunes since 1800 is very clear. What is also clear is that the divergence was already well under way during the first period of globalization, 1870–1913; continued through the period of international economic disintegration, 1913–80; and

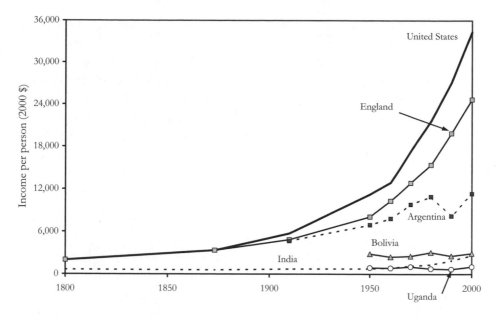

Figure 15.5 Incomes per capita (2000 $). Data from Prados de la Escosura, 2000 (1910) and Heston et al., 2006 (1950–2000).

persisted as we returned to a more globalized international economy over the past twenty-five years.

The most notable success has been the United States, which may even have surpassed Britain in per capita income before 1870.[20] Certainly by 1913 the United States was the richest economy in the world. It was also the biggest, accounting for 17 percent of the entire material output of the world economy. By 2000 the United States' share of world output had risen to 22 percent.

Within Europe the countries of northwestern Europe—Belgium, Denmark, France, Germany, the Netherlands, Norway, Sweden, and Switzerland—all behaved as expected and maintained a per capita income relative to Britain similar to the levels of 1800. In 1913 their incomes all lay within about 80 percent of the per capita income of England.[21] A number of countries mainly

20. Relative incomes per person in the United States and the United Kingdom in the nineteenth century are a matter of continuing controversy. Ward and Devereux, 2003, argue for high U.S. incomes from early on. Broadberry and Irwin, 2004, argue for the traditional interpretation that the United States overtook Britain only late in the nineteenth century.

21. Prados de la Escosura, 2000.

settled by Europeans also had incomes close to Britain's: Argentina, Australia, Canada, and New Zealand. But outside this small club, the technologies of the Industrial Revolution had surprisingly little effect on incomes per person, even within Europe. Ireland, only fifty miles across the sea from Britain, still maintained a per capita income only 60 percent of British levels, and it saw steady depopulation after 1845 as its workers emigrated to better opportunities in Britain and the United States. All of southern and eastern Europe remained poor, with incomes per person at only 30–60 percent of British levels. By 1913 these countries also remained largely devoted to peasant agriculture, just as they had been in the eighteenth century. In 1913 the share of the population employed in agriculture in Britain was a mere 8 percent. In Romania it was 80 percent and in Bulgaria, 82 percent.

Outside Europe the effects of the Industrial Revolution more than a hundred years after its onset in England were even more slight. Estimated per capita industrial output actually declined in both India and China up to 1913, as these countries began exporting raw materials (wheat, jute, indigo, and opium, in the case of India) to pay for manufactured imports from Britain. Table 15.8 shows the composition of British India's imports and exports in 1912–13. As a result of the Industrial Revolution and the British policy of free trade, low-wage India found its comparative trade advantage in exporting food and raw materials and importing manufactured products.

In the most dramatic example, Indian raw cotton was exported through Bombay over 6,800 miles to Lancashire mills, where workers paid four to five times the daily wages of mill operators in Bombay manufactured it into cloth, which was then shipped back over 6,800 miles through Bombay to be sold back to the cultivators of the raw cotton. The net raw material exports of India in 1912 were about 4 percent of the country's GDP. Since the agricultural sector experienced little measurable productivity growth in the years from 1870 to 1949, India benefited from the Industrial Revolution largely through improving terms of trade for its manufactured imports.

Because we have relatively accurate GDP figures for India dating back to 1873, we can measure its economic decline relative to Britain and the United States from 1873 to 2003. Figure 15.6 shows calculated GDP per capita for India from 1873 to 2000 measured relative to that of the United States and Britain. India did show a substantial increase in absolute GDP per capita over these years. Real incomes per capita in 1998 were 3.6 times those estimated for 1873. But relative to both Britain and the United States Indian income per

Table 15.8 The Commodity Trade of British India, 1912–13

Commodity	Imports (millions of dollars)	Exports (millions of dollars)	Net exports (millions of dollars)
Grain, pulse, and flour	0	196	195
Jute, raw	0	88	88
Cotton, raw	7	91	84
Seeds	0	74	74
Hides and skins	1	53	52
Tea	0	43	43
Opium	0	36	36
Oils	17	3	–14
Sugar	46	0	–46
Other raw materials	34	65	31
All raw materials	106	648	542
Cotton goods	196	40	–156
Jute goods	0	74	74
Metals	50	4	–47
Railway equipment	21	0	–21
Other manufactures	127	6	–121
All manufactures	393	123	–270

Source: United States, Department of Commerce, 1915.

person fell from 1873 to the mid-1980s, before rising from 1987 to the present. As late as 1931, 150 years after the factory was introduced in Britain, fewer than 1 percent of Indian workers were employed in modern factory industries.

Many other countries have witnessed a declining relative income level as the result of the breakdown of political and social institutions. Thus many of the countries of Africa, which are now among the world's poorest, have suffered from ethnic strife and the collapse of political institutions since their independence. But the Indian economy experienced its decline during a long period of relative political and social stability, under British colonial rule until 1947 and even after independence.

The result of the Industrial Revolution was thus an increased concentration of global economic output in a very small portion of the world. Table 15.9

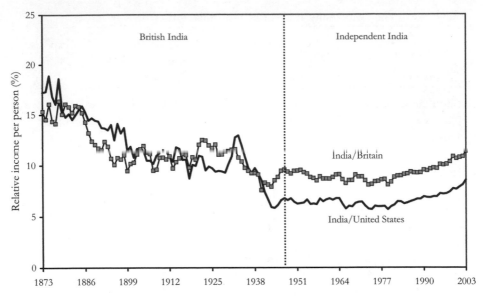

Figure 15.6 Indian GDP per capita relative to Britain and the United States, 1873–2003. Data for India from Heston, 1983 (pre-1947); Heston et al., 2006 (1950–2003). Data for United States from Balke and Gordon, 1989 (1873–1929); United States, Economic Report of the President, 2004 (1930–2003). Data for Britain from Feinstein, 1972 (1873–1965); United Kingdom, National Statistical Office (1965–2003).

shows estimates of the world distribution of population and income for 1800, 1870, 1913, and 2000. For most countries outside western Europe, North America, and Oceania, income per person in the years before 1913 is taken as just the same as in 1913, on the grounds that these were still Malthusian economies then. (North America and Oceania includes Canada, the United States, Australia, and New Zealand.)

In 1800 western Europe, North America, and Oceania had 12 percent of world population but 27 percent of world income. Thus even before the Industrial Revolution western Europe and its settlements were a relatively rich area of the world, producing more than a quarter of its output. By 1913, as a result of the Industrial Revolution and its delayed diffusion, these two regions saw their population grow to 20 percent of the world total, and they were producing 51 percent of all economic output. Output per person in these regions averaged more than four times that in the rest of the world.

By 2000 the share of world output from these regions had fallen to 45 percent. But that was mainly because their population share had fallen to

Table 15.9 World Population and Income Shares, 1800–2000 (percent)

Region	Measure	1800	1870	1913	2000
Western Europe	Population	11	15	14	6
	Income	24	37	31	20
North America, Oceania	Population	1	4	6	6
	Income	3	10	20	25
East and South Asia	Population	64	56	56	53
	Income	47	31	24	32
Latin America	Population	2	3	4	8
	Income	4	4	4	8
Africa	Population	7	7	5	13
	Income	9	7	4	4

Sources: Heston et al., 2006, for 2000; Prados de la Escosura, 2000, and Maddison, 2001, for 1913; Maddison, 2001, for incomes and populations in 1870 and populations in 1800. For 1800, incomes in western Europe relative to England were estimated from van Zanden, 1999, and Allen, 2001. For other countries income in 1800 was taken to be the same as in 1870. *Note:* Shares are percentages. Western Europe includes Austria, Germany, Italy, Sweden, and all countries to the west.

12 percent of the world total. Output per person in western Europe, North America, and Oceania had now actually risen to six times that in the rest of the world.

South and East Asia have always held the majority of the world's population, though that preponderance has been declining. But by 1870 the regions' share of world output had fallen to less than a third, and it was still at that level in 2000. By 2000 output per person in Asia was rising relative to the rest of the world, but this gain has been balanced by a steady decline in Africa. While Africa's share of world population has increased, output per person in Africa is now just 30 percent of the world average. Output per person in North America and Oceania in 2000 was fourteen times that of Africa.

There is now almost instant communication between different countries of the world; a vigorous exchange of foods, styles, and music; and an ever-rising flow of goods internationally. But the divergence of incomes ensures that the poor countries of the world remain as exotic to the rich as they were in the seventeenth or eighteenth century. Even in as relatively prosperous a part of the underdeveloped world as India, workers new to cities such as Bombay (Mumbai) or Madras (Chennai) sometimes still sleep on the streets.

Figure 15.7 Slum dwellings occupied by squatters at Bandra Station in Mumbai, India.

Figure 15.8 Middle-class living in the United States: 4,000 square feet inhabited by two people and one small dog.

Thousands live in improvised shacks without water or toilet facilities on public lands, on pavements, or along the edges of the commuter rail lines. In India as a whole in 2002 the average dwelling area per person was 84 square feet (figure 15.7).[22]

In contrast, in the richest major country in the world, the average American in 2001 lived in a dwelling with 750 square feet per person, and even the poorest fifth of the population enjoyed 560 square feet per person. Some 8 percent of American houses now have 4,000 square feet or more, for an average family size of 2.6 people.[23] These new McMansions (figure 15.8) are now a standard feature of middle-class American life. How did such a world arise? We seek the answer in the next chapter.

22. Government of India, Ministry of Statistics and Programme Implementation, 2004.
23. United States, Department of Energy, Energy Information Administration, 2004, tables HC1-1a and HC1-3a.

16 The Proximate Sources of Divergence

True Philosophy invents nothing, it describes and establishes what is.
—Victor Cousin (1854)[1]

Why has world development since the Industrial Revolution demonstrated the surprising divergence described in the previous chapter? This question has occasioned a mountain of printed pages, and a storm of debate, ever since the increasing gap between rich and poor nations became apparent in the late nineteenth century.

Commentators, having visited climate, race, nutrition, education, and culture, have persistently returned to one theme: the failure of political and social institutions in poor countries. Yet, as we shall see, this theme can be shown to manifestly fail in two ways. It does not describe the anatomy of the divergence we observe: the details of why poor countries remain poor. And the medicine of institutional and political reform has failed repeatedly to cure the patient.[2]

Yet, like the physicians of the prescientific era who prescribed bloodletting as the cure for ailments they did not understand, the modern economic doctors continue to prescribe the same treatment year after year through such cult centers as the World Bank and the International Monetary Fund. If the medicine fails to cure, then the only possible conclusion is that more is needed.

Like growth itself, described in chapter 10, differences in income per person across economies can have only three basic sources: differences in capital per person, differences in land per person, and differences in efficiency.

---

1. Cousin (1854), 216.
2. See, for example, Easterly, 2001.

This chapter shows that, at the most general level, differences in efficiency are the ultimate explanation for most of the gap in incomes between rich and poor countries in the modern economy. Just as with growth over time, discussed in chapter 10, the proximate cause of differences in income per person across countries is about one-quarter the stocks of physical capital per person and three-quarters the efficiency of utilization of all inputs.[3] But, to an approximation, we can take the world capital market as having been integrated since the nineteenth-century improvements in communication and trade. In a world where capital flowed easily between economies, capital itself *responded to* differences in country efficiency levels. Inefficient countries ended up with small capital stocks and efficient ones large amounts of capital. And efficiency differences explain almost all variations between countries in income levels.

Differences in efficiency could stem from discrepancies in access to the latest technologies, from economies of scale, or from failures to utilize imported technologies appropriately. The argument below is that the major source of these efficiency differences was a failure to utilize technologies effectively. But this failure took a peculiar form. It was rooted in an inability to effectively employ labor in production, so that output per worker, even using the latest technology, was peculiarly low in the poorest countries.

Capital and Divergence

There is ample evidence that capital returns (the interest rate earned on capital), though not fully equalized, were similar enough that we can regard capital as flowing freely around the world by 1900.[4] Figure 16.1, for example, shows rates of return on government bonds in nineteen countries in 1900–14 at a variety of income levels as a function of the relative level of output per capita in 1910. There was variation in the rates of return on these bonds in the range of 2:1. So the market is clearly not functioning perfectly. But whatever variation there was had little correlation with the income level of the country. Indeed there is no statistically significant decline in bond returns with income. As far as we know capital returns were not correlated with the income level,

3. See, for example, Easterly and Levine, 2001.
4. International capital markets did disintegrate during the economic and political troubles of the 1920s and 1930s, and they have only recently returned to the level of integration of 1870–1914. See Obstfeld and Taylor, 2004.

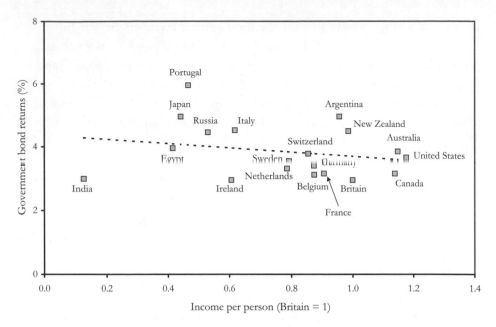

Figure 16.1   Government bond returns, 1900–14. In the absence of national bonds for the United States municipal bonds were used. Egyptian income per person was assumed the same as in the Ottoman Empire. Irish returns were assumed the same as British. Data from table 14.1. Realized returns for India and New Zealand (1870–1913): Edelstein, 1982, 125. Belgium, Britain, Canada, France, Germany, Ireland, Italy, Netherlands, Switzerland, United States: Homer and Sylla, 1996. Argentina, Australia (sterling bonds in London), Egypt, Japan, Portugal, Russia, Sweden: Mauro et al., 2006.

hence the efficiency, of countries, and so they cannot explain why richer countries had more capital.

We can also get rates of return on private borrowing by looking at returns on railway debentures. Railways were the biggest private borrowers in the international capital markets of the late nineteenth century. And their capital needs were so great that, if they were able to borrow at international rates of return, such borrowing would help equalize rates of return across all assets in domestic capital markets. Table 16.1 shows the *realized* rates of return (the returns after taking into account defaults) earned by investors in railway debentures in the London capital market between 1870 and 1913. Again there are variations across countries. But importantly for our purposes this variation does not correlate with output per person. Indeed India, one of the poorest economies in the world, had among the lowest railway interest costs because

Table 16.1 Realized Rates of Return on Railway Debentures, 1870–1913

Country or region	Output per person (2000 $)	Rate of return (%)
United States	5,116	6.03
Canada	4,953	4.99
United Kingdom	4,300	3.74
Argentina	4,136	5.13
Brazil	—	5.10
Western Europe	3,320	5.28
Eastern Europe	2,231	5.33
British India	544	3.65

Source: Edelstein, 1982, 125.

the Indian government guaranteed the bonds of the railways as a way of promoting investment in infrastructure.

World capital markets were well integrated by 1913 for three reasons: the huge overseas investments of the British, the secure investment environment of the British Empire, and the popularity of the gold standard. The British by 1910 had overseas investments that amounted to about twice their GDP. This implied that about a third of the capital owned by British investors was invested abroad. The existence of this huge pool of investment seeking a home overseas helped make London the preeminent world financial center before 1914. But it also helped lubricate the market by creating a center where investors and borrowers could gather, and where information about opportunities could be aggregated. The British Empire aided the export of capital from all the advanced economies to the poorer ones by giving investors security through the guarantee offered by imperial laws and protections. Finally the pegging of many currencies to gold in the late nineteenth century removed much of the currency risk from investing abroad, since the relative value of many currencies remained unchanged for thirty or forty years prior to 1914.

This rich capital market allowed poor countries to borrow large sums, and the significant capital flows into these countries helped achieve a rough equalization of returns to poor and rich countries. By 1913 Argentina, Brazil, Egypt, Mexico, the Ottoman Empire, and Peru had all attracted at least $50 of foreign investment per capita. This implies that nations such as the Ottoman Empire, with an estimated income per person of $125 in U.S. prices of 1913, had significantly augmented their capital stock through foreign borrowing.[5]

The numbers in table 16.1 show how the London market valued railroad investments, not the actual rate of return on the money spent on railway infrastructure in these countries. If the developers of railroads in poorer countries, for example, had access to monopoly opportunities or franchises, then the rate of return on the investments could exceed the rate of return available to financial investors on the London market. Yet the financial rate of return in London would still indicate the cost of borrowing for railway enterprises in these countries.

Lance Davis and Robert Huttenback calculated the actual profit rate of firms in various parts of the world by comparing earnings to the book value of their capital (the cost of their initial investment). In 1860–1912 the returns on all capital were as follows: British companies investing at home, 5.6 percent; British companies investing in the British Empire, 6.5 percent; and British companies investing in other foreign countries, 5.5 percent.[6] The similarity in rates of return suggests that, whatever was slowing down the rate of industrialization in poor countries, it was not a lack of capital, for capital invested abroad seems to have earned little or no more than capital invested at home, at least in the case of British investors. This is what we would expect if capital markets functioned reasonably well.

The one case we can find in which capital markets seem to have functioned badly is, ironically, within the United States, the world's richest economy. Here rates of return throughout the nineteenth century were much higher in the West than in the older, settled East. In the 1860s, for example, as the central valley of California was being settled, mortgage loans were made at the rate of 26 percent per year at a time when mortgages in Boston were offered at 6 percent. Rates fell rapidly in California, but in 1889 West Coast interest rates were still 4–6 percent above those in the Northeast.[7] These disparities

5. Pamuk, 1987. Relative incomes from Prados de la Escosura, 2000.
6. Davis and Huttenback, 1988, 107.
7. Rhode, 1995, 789. Rates in California were 9.0 percent, as opposed to 5.6 percent in Massachusetts; Eichengreen, 1984, 1010.

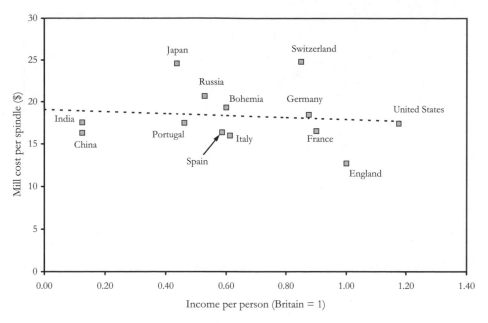

Figure 16.2 Estimated purchase price of capital goods, textile mills, 1910. Data from table 14.1 and Clark, 1987a.

were the result of legal limitations on the development of interstate banking in the United States, which made it difficult for capital to flow from Europe or the eastern United States to the West. Yet, despite the persistently high cost of capital, the American West developed rapidly in the late nineteenth century. Thus in the late nineteenth century capital was scarce in the richest economy in the world, the United States, and cheap in perhaps the poorest, India.

The second important element in the cost of capital, along with the rate of return, is the cost of capital goods. If these were very expensive in poor economies this would also drive up the overall cost of capital.

We can measure this cost for textile mills around 1910 across the richest and poorest countries. Figure 16.2 shows the cost per spindle for a fully equipped new textile mill in 1910 in various countries around the world, as a function of levels of income per person. There is no correlation between the cost of these capital goods, in textiles generally imported from Britain, and the level of income per person. On average, at least by 1910, poor countries had access to capital goods in a major industry like textiles on the same terms as rich ones.

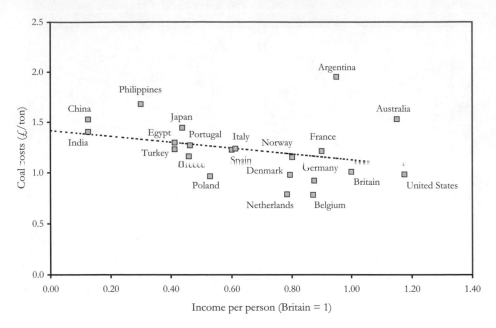

Figure 16.3 Coal costs versus GDP per person, circa 1910. Coal costs from table 16.2 and Clark, 1987a. Incomes from Prados de la Escosura, 2000.

Resources and Divergence

The improvements in transportation discussed in chapter 15 also ensured that access to the resources needed for industrialization was not a big obstacle for most economies by 1900. Figure 16.3 shows, for example, the cost of a ton of coal of constant quality relative to the GDP per person in various economies in 1907. Coal, the main source of energy for industry in 1907, was slightly cheaper in the high-income economies, but the difference was modest. Geography and access to resources explain little of the divergence in incomes. The world created by the Industrial Revolution is one in which lack of native resources became unimportant as a barrier to industrialization, except for a few landlocked or topographically disadvantaged countries.

Efficiency and Divergence

The unimportance of resources and the relatively uniform cost of capital, at least in 1870–1913, imply that differences in efficiency must be the overwhelm-

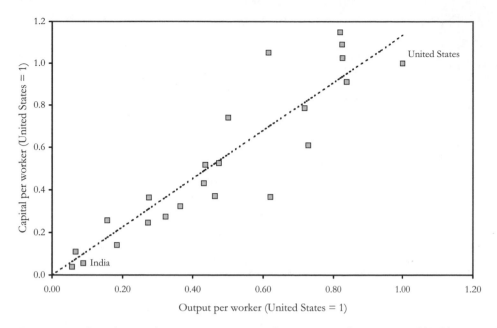

Figure 16.4   Capital per worker versus output per worker, 1990. Data from Penn World Tables, 5.6.

ing cause of differences in income per capita across countries in the modern world.

There is always a strong correlation between physical capital per person and income per person across countries in the modern world. Figure 16.4 shows this association for a sample of countries in 1990. At a proximate level capital per person explains perhaps a quarter of income differences across countries in the modern world. But with capital free to flow across countries, and earning a rental that differs little across income levels, efficiency differences explain most of the variation in capital stocks. So at a deeper level efficiency differences are the core of the variation in income per capita across economies since the Industrial Revolution. The same formula that explained how income grew over time,

$$g_y \approx g_k \approx \frac{g_A}{(1-a)},$$

explains why income varies across countries in the modern world. Indeed taking the income levels of a group of countries across the world in 1913, and making corrections for the amount of land per person and the effect of the

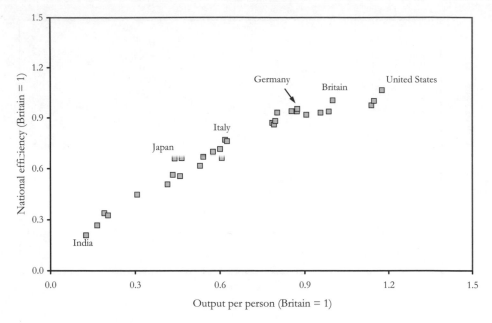

Figure 16.5 Efficiency versus output per worker, 1913.

return on capital on capital stocks, we still see that income per person variation is overwhelmingly associated with efficiency differences.

Figure 16.5 shows this connection. By 1913 the efficiency of economies around the world, the amount of output per unit of all inputs, varied by a factor of at least 5:1. In a world of free-flowing capital, differences in the efficiencies of economies are translated into much bigger differences in income through the concentration of capital in the high-efficiency areas. Thus Britain is estimated to have five times the efficiency of the Indian economy in 1913, but nearly eight times the income per person.

Thus there is a surprising correspondence between the sources of income growth over time since the Industrial Revolution and the causes of the divergence in incomes between economies in the modern world. But the cause of the differences in efficiency across countries is very different from the cause of the differences in efficiency over time

Why Were Poor Countries Inefficient?

Poor economies since the Industrial Revolution have been characterized mainly by inefficiency in production. Their problem, however, was typically not in gaining access to new technologies. The problem, it turns out, was in using these new technologies effectively. We can see this most clearly by looking at the two major industries found in almost all economies by 1910: factory production of cotton textiles and railways.

Cotton textiles seemed the path to industrialization for the poor countries of the world before World War I. There was a ready local market for textile products everywhere and also a huge, open international market. Textile mills were not capital intensive. And the optimal mill size was small compared even to market sizes in the smallest countries. In practice, as table 15.7 shows, England dominated the world market, with only modest competition from Japan, Italy, France, and Germany.

The technology was readily available internationally, at moderate prices, through exports of machinery by British engineering firms. Unskilled labor accounted for the majority of production costs in such countries as England. And the poor countries had abundant quantities of cheap, unskilled labor. A contemporary writer on the cotton industry thus noted that

> India enjoys a great advantage over England, for the advantage which England possessed in regard to skilled labor most certainly does not apply as in former years . . . with the marvelously perfect and self-acting machinery of today no special skill is required on the part of the attendant. The machinery itself supplies the intelligence; all that is required from the workman is attention in "following up" the machinery, such as piecing up broken ends, doffing, and other simple details, which are performed by the native Indian cotton factory operative almost as well as by his European brethren, and at far less cost to the spinner.[8]

From at least the 1850s onward poor countries, with their huge advantages in labor cost, should have taken over the cotton textile industry, driving out the British from the unprotected markets.

Table 16.2 shows the comparative costs of England and some low-wage competitors in 1910. Wages in the textile industry varied widely. Those in England were ten times those in China. Indeed wages were so low in China that some mills searched workers leaving the mills to ensure they had not stuffed any cotton into their pockets, since even small amounts of cotton would have added significantly to their wages (a pound of raw cotton was

8. Walmsley, 1893, 50.

Table 16.2 Cotton Textile Costs, 1910

County or region	Weekly wage ($/55 hours)	Plant and machinery ($/spindle)	Coal ($/ton)	Total cost (England = 100)	Implied profit rate (%)
U.S. South	6.5	17	3.8	130	−1
England	5.0	13	2.5	100	8
Spain	2.7	19	6.5	91	10
Mexico	2.6	19	10.0	94	10
Russia	2.4	21	7.2	91	10
Italy	2.4	16	7.2	81	14
Japan	0.8	25	2.6	73	14
India	0.8	18	5.0	61	19
China	0.5	16	3.2	53	22

Source: Clark, 1987a.

worth about $0.25). In most countries wages were the most important element in producing cloth, after the cost of the raw cotton. In England in 1911 the costs (excluding that of raw cotton) broke down as follows: wages, 62 percent; machinery depreciation plus supplies, 12 percent; power, 3 percent; interest costs on capital, 22 percent.

Machinery was less expensive in England than in most other countries. England was the center of the textile machine–building industry, and most other countries bought their machinery from England. Their costs were thus inflated by the expenses of transporting the machinery to their mills, and the additional costs of setting it up when mechanics had to be brought out from England. It is estimated that the cost of shipping English machinery to U.S. mills was about 25 percent of the value of the machinery. The countries with high machine costs, such as Russia, often had a tariff on machine imports.[9]

England also had low power costs, because its cotton industry was centered in the same region as its coal fields. Some other countries, such as Mexico, had high power costs because coal had to be imported first by sea and then by rail from the port. But as figure 16.2 shows the costs were only slightly higher on average for low-wage countries.

9. Japanese mills were so expensive per spindle because the costs included dormitories built to accommodate the workers, who were mostly teenage girls.

The fifth column of table 16.2 shows what total manufacturing costs should have been in each country if each country operated under exactly the same conditions as in England: kept its mills open for the same number of hours, used steam engine boilers requiring as much fuel per hour as those in England, and ran the machines at English speeds. The last column shows the implied profit rate in each country if it were to sell its output in the English market, assuming English mills made an 8 percent return. Most of the low-wage competitors should have been able to sell profitably in English markets in 1910. Some of them, such as India and China, should have made enormous profits selling in the open international market.

The low-wage countries actually had a further major advantage over British producers. The struggles of social reformers and labor unions in England in the nineteenth century had led to a series of Factory Acts that sought to tame what was perceived as the savage mastery of machine over worker. These laws limited adult workers to fifty-five-hour weeks and children to half these hours. Women and children were prohibited from doing night work. Since women represented over 60 percent of the labor force in English mills, and an even higher proportion in some occupations such as weaving, the mills chose not to run at night. English mills ran only 2,775 hours per year.

Low-wage countries either had no such restrictions or else did not enforce the ones they did have. Most chose to run long hours using night workers. Mexican mills, for example, ran 6,750 hours out of a possible 8,760 in the year, an average of 18.5 hours per day. The work day was longer, double shifts were assigned, and fewer holidays were taken.

Longer hours substantially lowered the cost of production by reducing the capital costs per spindle-hour. Table 16.3 shows the hours of operation for mills in the various countries and their revised capital costs, total manufacturing costs, and implied profit rates. All the low-wage countries look as though they ought to have been able to undersell the English. Some, like the Chinese, ought to have made enormous profits. The puzzle is all the stranger since many of the lowest-wage producers had both native raw cotton and access to major ocean trade routes. Brazil, China, Egypt, India, Mexico, Peru, Russia, and Uganda all produced cotton, and Brazil, China, Egypt, and India all had excellent ocean transport facilities.

Yet up until 1913 England remained the low-cost producer for both yarn and cloth, as witnessed by table 16.2. Its only competitors were Japan, Italy, France, and Germany. High-wage England led the world market because the

Table 16.3 Cotton Textile Costs Adjusted for Hours, 1910

County or region	Hours per year	Plant and machinery ($/spindle)	Total cost (England = 100)	Implied profit rate (%)
U.S. South	3,450	16	126	−1
England	2,775	13	100	8
Spain	4,455	15	84	14
Mexico	6,730	12	82	14
Russia	4,061	16	84	17
Italy	3,150	16	79	14
Japan	6,526	13	62	25
India	3,744	15	58	23
China	5,302	12	48	33

Source: Clark, 1987a.

mills in these other countries could never attain English efficiency levels. But their inefficiency had a peculiar form. They were inefficient in the use of labor, not in the use of capital. Even though they were using the same machines as the high-wage economies, they employed many more workers per machine, without obtaining any additional output from the machines. Thus in ring spinning one worker in the northern United States tended 900 spindles, while one worker in China tended only 170. On plain looms a worker in the northern United States managed eight looms at a time, in China only one or two. The numbers of workers per machine varied by about 6:1 across countries (figures 16.6 and 16.7).

Figure 16.8 shows actual labor costs per unit of output versus the wage rate per fifty-five hours in the international cotton textile industry around 1910. Wage costs were on average lower in the lowest-wage countries, but by very modest amounts compared to the huge differences in wage rates. Labor costs per hour varied by 16:1, while labor costs per unit of output varied by only 3:1.

This extra labor employed in the low-wage countries was not an attempt by management to utilize expensive machines more intensively. There is no sign that mills in low-wage countries gained more output per machine by employing these supernumerary workers. Output on ring spinning machines, for example, was almost entirely a function of the speeds at which the machines

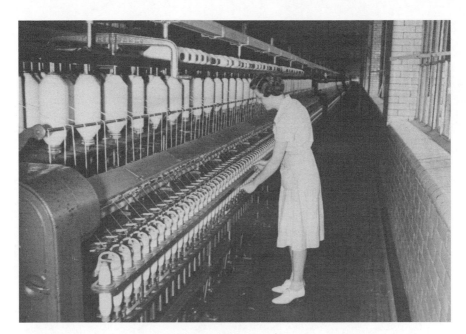

Figure 16.6　Ring spinning in the United States, 1939.

Figure 16.7　Indian ring spinners and supervisor, 1920s.

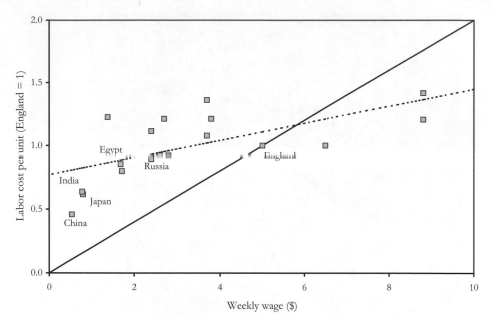

Figure 16.8 Labor costs per unit compared to wage rates, 1910. Data from Clark, 1987a, 152.

ran. It was possible to vary the speed, with faster running requiring more tenders per machine, since the threads would break more frequently. Figure 16.9 shows the speeds specified for ring spinning machines ordered by different countries from Platt as a function of the wages of operators in those countries. The poorest countries specified slightly faster operating speeds, but this was an insignificant difference compared to the extra labor they employed.

Another modern industry found in both the richest and poorest countries before 1914 was the railway. As with cotton textiles, there seems to have been little variation in the technology between rich and poor countries. Many railways across the world were built by British engineers, who employed the latest British technology. British locomotive constructors in the late nineteenth century produced the bulk of their locomotives for foreign markets, particularly those in the British Empire. Figure 16.10 shows a mainstay of the Indian railways, the 0-6-0 locomotive, and its English counterpart from the same period. Even to the untrained eye the technology looks the same.

The major complaint about railways in India in the British period was indeed not inferior technology, but railways that were built to an uneconomically high standard. Encouraged by the guarantee system, which promised

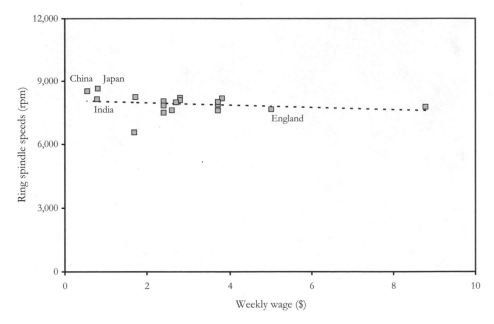

Figure 16.9   Machine outputs and operative wages, 1910.

bondholders a generous minimum return, railroad builders in India were happy to indulge their British engineers' taste for high-quality rails, locomotives, and rolling stock. A manager of the Eastern Bengal State Railway, touring the United States in 1901, remarked that most American railways were not up to "European or Indian standards."[10]

But if the equipment was often British, the staffing practices of railways in poorer countries were decidedly un-British. Figure 16.11 shows the revenue generated per worker-hour in twenty-two countries around 1913. The range in output per worker-hour is about 6:1, and again the United States is the highest and India the lowest.

The Indian rail system took advantage of extensive English operating expertise. In 1910 the Indian railroads employed 7,207 "Europeans" (mainly British) and 8,862 "Eurasians" (principally Anglo-Indians), who occupied almost all the supervisory and skilled positions. Indian locomotive drivers were employed only after 1900, and even as late as 1910 many of the locomotive drivers were still British.[11]

10. Headrick, 1988, 75.
11. Morris and Dudley, 1975; Headrick, 1988, 322.

Figure 16.10 Indian and English locomotives of the same class, built in 1905 and 1908. Which is which?

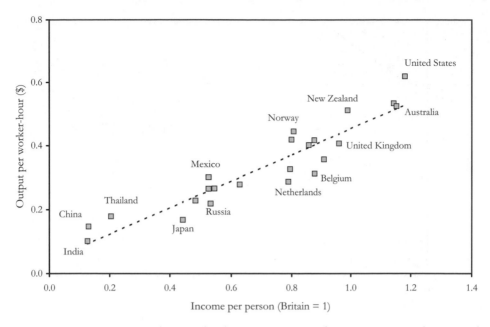

Figure 16.11 Output per railway worker-hour, 1913–14. Data from Boag, 1912, and Bureau of Railway Economics, 1915.

Yet again the extra workers in India, and in other poor countries, do not seem to have procured for their employers any increase in output per unit of capital. Because of the very different operating conditions of railways in different countries, capital utilization is hard to compare. But there are partial indicators that suggest no gains for countries that employed huge excesses of labor.

One that is available for most countries, and that is shown in figure 16.12, is miles run per locomotive per year. Locomotive utilization was no higher in low-income, low-output-per-worker countries. As in cotton textiles, managers of railways in these countries seemingly gained nothing from their extra labor inputs.

Thus in both cotton textiles and railways around 1910 we observe the same picture. Poor countries used the same technology as rich ones. They achieved the same levels of output per unit of capital. But in doing so they employed so much more labor per machine that they lost most of the labor cost advantages with which they began.

The problem of persistent inefficiency in labor use in poor countries like India was the main barrier to the spread of the technologies of the Industrial

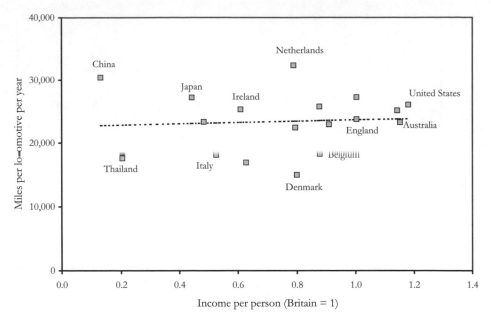

Figure 16.12   Miles run per locomotive per year (an indicator of capital utilization on railways) across countries, 1913–14. Data from Boag, 1912, and Bureau of Railway Economics, 1915.

Revolution. Table 16.4, for example, shows the gross profit rates of Bombay cotton mills from 1907–09 to 1935–38, as well as the size of the Bombay industry and output per worker as an index, with 1905–09 set at 100. Since the mills operated in a competitive market profits were never high. The best years for the industry, during World War I and its immediate aftermath, saw profit rates of only 7–8 percent. Despite profit rates that averaged only 6.5 percent between 1907 and 1924, the industry in Bombay grew by 45 percent, once again testifying to the smooth functioning of international capital markets in these years.

However, from 1907 to 1924 there was no increase, and perhaps a slight decline, in output per worker in Bombay. At the same time the Japanese cotton industry increased output per worker by 80 percent. By the late 1920s Japanese competition had eliminated all profits from the Bombay industry. As output per worker in Japanese mills marched ever upward through the 1920s and 1930s, Bombay mills were hardly able to cover their operating costs. By 1938 nearly 15 percent of the capacity in the Bombay mills had been scrapped.

Table 16.4   The Bombay Cotton Textile Industry, 1907–1938

Year	Gross profit rate on fixed capital (%)	Industry size (million spindle-equivalents)	Output per worker (1905–09 = 100)	Output per worker in Japan (1905–09 = 100)
1907–09	6	3.1	100	100
1910–14	5	3.4	103	115
1915–19	7	3.7	99	135
1920–24	8	4.0	94	132
1925–29	0	4.5	91	180
1930–34	0	4.4	104	249
1935–38	2	3.9	106	281

Sources: Profits and output per worker were calculable only for the mills listed in the *Investor's India Yearbook;* Wolcott and Clark, 1999.

The situation in 1910, in which excess labor without apparent benefits in the form of capital utilization was found in low-income countries, persisted throughout the twentieth century in the cotton textile industry. A 1969 study by the English Textile Council looked at output per machine-hour and per worker-hour in the best-performing quartile of cotton spinning and weaving firms across eleven major producer nations in 1967. Howard Pack added to this comparison the performance of the best quartile of Kenyan and Philippines firms in 1980 (on the same vintage of equipment as the earlier study). Figures 16.13 and 16.14 show the estimated output per machine-hour, averaged over spinning and weaving, and output per worker-hour.

The strong correlation between wages and output per worker continues until the present day, as do surprisingly high labor costs in low-wage countries. The increased divergence in incomes between regions, even since 1910, created an even greater divergence in the wages manufacturers faced in different countries of the world by 2000. Figure 16.15 shows the full hourly labor cost of production workers in garment manufacturing, a simple industry using small amounts of capital, across various countries in 2002. Even discounting the outliers, labor costs varied from $0.40 per hour to $12 per hour, a range of about 30:1.

The technology in industries such as garment making and textiles is relatively standard. In making a pair of jeans, labor costs even in such low-wage

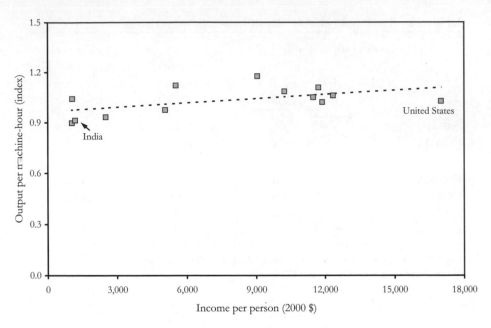

Figure 16.13 Output per cotton textile machine-hour, 1967. Data from Pack, 1987, 140–45.

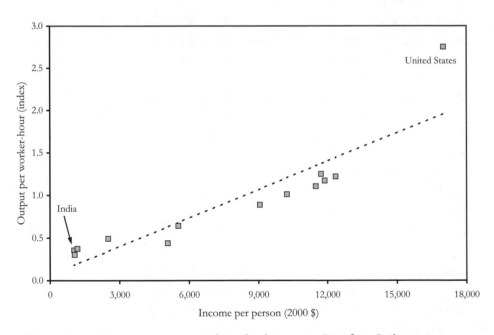

Figure 16.14 Output per cotton textile worker-hour, 1967. Data from Pack, 1987, 140–45.

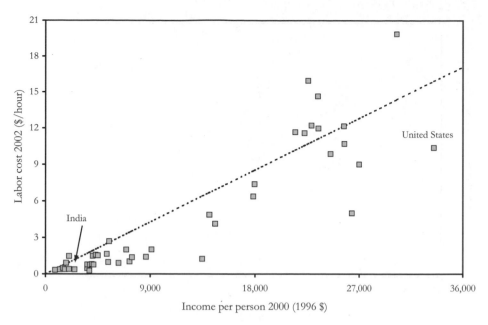

Figure 16.15 Wages in garment manufacturing, 2002, versus income per person, 2000. Wages from Abernathy et al., 2005, table 1, and United States, Department of Labor, Bureau of Labor Statistics, 2006.

economies as China, Mexico, and Nicaragua, account for about 75 percent of all costs, including transport to the U.S. market. The cost of shipping a pair of jeans from a clothing workshop almost anywhere in the world to the high-wage markets of the United States is no more than $0.09 per pair (1 percent of the wholesale cost of about $8).[12] With the ending of quotas in the U.S. market, and the agreement of the European Union countries to allow manu-factures from the fifty poorest countries, as well as twelve Mediterranean coun-tries, to be imported free of tariffs, we would expect to see apparel manufac-turing booming across Africa, and apparel industries disappearing in any high-wage country.

While there have been major increases in imports into countries like the United States, a number of surprising features appear. The first is that, despite its extraordinarily high labor cost, U.S. production of apparel in 2004 was still 42 percent of its consumption.[13] The second is that the major exporters to

12. Abernathy et al., 2005, table 2.
13. Ibid., figure 1.

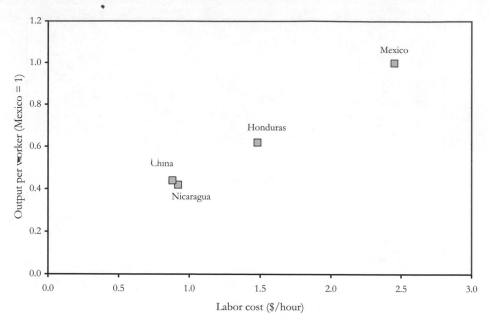

Figure 16.16 Wage rates and output per worker in clothing production, 2002. Data from Abernathy et al., 2005, table 2.

the United States and the European Union were often countries with high wages compared to sub-Saharan Africa. Thus Mexico and Costa Rica continue as major suppliers to the U.S. market, even though they have wages more than six times those of most sub-Saharan countries and of the Indian subcontinent. Turkey, with wages similar to Mexico, continues as a major supplier to the European Union, in free competition for some time with sub-Saharan countries and the Indian subcontinent.[14] Indeed the level of African exports of apparel remains extremely small.

It is clear once again that this situation is sustained by differences in output per worker across exporters that correlate with the countries' wage levels. Figure 16.16 shows, for China, Honduras, Mexico, and Nicaragua, labor productivity in 2002 versus the industry wage rate.

There has been a suggestion that Africa's soils and climate have been the major impediment to agricultural advance, explaining its recent extreme

14. Abernathy et al., 2005, table 5-6, figure 2.

poverty.[15] The majority of the populations in tropical Africa still depend on agriculture for their livelihoods. But any such considerations would quickly become irrelevant had African countries been able to exploit their expected cost advantage in such basic manufacturing industries as apparel and textiles. Yet we know that as far back as the 1950s textile manufacturers from India and England were finding that mills established in Uganda and Kenya offered little or no profit despite protective tariffs.[16]

Thus the crucial variable in explaining the success or failure of economies in the years 1800–2000 is the efficiency of the production process within the economy. Inefficiencies in poor countries took a very specific form: the employment of extra production workers per machine without any corresponding gain in output per unit of capital. The next chapter investigates the source of these puzzling efficiency differences.

15. Gallup and Sachs, 2000; Sachs, 2001.
16. Clarence-Smith, 2005, 35–36.

17 Why Isn't the Whole World Developed?

It is difficult to conjecture, from the conduct of him whom we see in a low condition, how he would act if wealth and power were put into his hands.
—Samuel Johnson, *Rambler* No. 172 (November 9, 1751)

In the previous chapters we saw that one of the surprising root causes of the increasing differences in income across the world was low output per worker, with no compensating gain in output per unit of capital, even when the most modern technologies were in use. This finding makes institutional explanations for the Great Divergence hard to sustain. Why would institutions influence the internal efficiency of production enterprises once they have been established?

These international differences in output per worker had appeared in the cotton textile industry by the 1840s, and they are even more pronounced in many sectors now. This chapter seeks explanations for these output differences, and for the pattern of increasing divergence in incomes seen since the Industrial Revolution.

The first argument is that these differences in labor productivity must stem from differences in the quality of labor in production across societies, differences that stem largely from the local social environment. That much can be firmly established.

Regarding the deeper issue of why these differences have had such a profound influence on income per capita in the modern world compared with earlier periods, we can pose a number of hypotheses. The first is that the ending of the Malthusian era allowed existing differences in social energy across societies to translate into much larger differences in income. The second is that modern medicine has lowered the floor established through the subsistence wage. The third is that the technology developed since the Industrial Revolution has been of a kind much less forgiving of deficiencies in the quality of labor input.

Finally at the even deeper level, of what might be the ultimate source of these socially determined differences in labor quality, we can offer only the most tentative of ideas. The strange thing about world history is that, while the world before 1800 is fairly knowable, the world since then has become increasingly difficult to understand.

Is Labor the Problem in Poor Countries?

Despite the fact that in low-wage economies we observe empirically many more workers per machine than we would expect, with no greater output per machine, it is not obvious that deficiencies in the labor input are the problem. Perhaps the problem is one of management.

The idea that there were great variations in the quality of labor forces between rich and poor countries was certainly a staple of writing on trade and industry in the era of the Pax Britannica.

When Britain was at its economic apogee in the middle and late nineteenth century, a number of writers argued that its ability to pay high wages and still prosper in international competition derived mainly from the much greater intensity of labor in Britain compared to its low-wage competitors. These writers maintained that British workers were able to operate more machinery per worker, mitigating or even eliminating the wage cost advantage of the low-wage countries.

Karl Marx himself endorsed this view. The first volume of *Capital*, published in 1867, contains a short chapter, "National Differences in Wages," which attributes high output per worker in British textile mills to high labor intensity.[1] For Marx it was further proof of the poor treatment of workers under capitalism that the higher wages of workers in the advanced capitalist economies were in large part the result of their own greater efforts. Per unit of effective labor, he argued, workers in Britain were still paid the subsistence wage.

This view of higher British labor intensity was not original to Marx. He was merely quoting what seems to have been, for British and American econ-

1. Marx, 1990, 701–06.

omists of the late nineteenth century, a kind of orthodoxy. By that time British managers had had plenty of experience working with foreign labor in railway construction and in the international textile industry. Under British management production in different countries required different amounts of labor. Indeed there were overtly racist discussions at the time, focused on such questions as how many Chinese, Indian, or African workers were the equivalent of one British worker.[2] There were also arguments about whether differences in labor efficiency did or did not completely offset differences in day wages, making the real cost of labor constant internationally.[3]

This was probably the dominant view of the cause of variations in output per worker in modern industry across countries up until World War II. A 1922 report by an agent of the U.S. Department of Commerce informed potential purchasers of machinery for use in Southeast Asia that "One of the most common errors made in selecting machinery for Asia is in connection with labor-saving devices. It is felt that labor is so cheap that it need not be saved. . . . Because of the extreme inefficiency of Asiatic labor, well-informed buyers will invest heavily in labor-saving devices."[4] A 1929 report on the Indian industry in the *Journal of the Textile Institute* states baldly that "India is obliged to engage three persons in place of one employed in the Lancashire mills."[5] In 1930 Arno Pearse, the international textile expert, offered the opinion that "Labour in India is undoubtedly on a very low par, probably it comes next to Chinese labour in inefficiency, wastefulness, and lack of discipline."[6]

Although the disparities in performance across countries remained unchanged, the "labor quality" explanation disappeared from the economics literature after World War II. Most economists now attribute the poor performance of industry in underdeveloped economies not to labor problems but to a generalized failure by management to productively employ all the inputs in production—capital and raw materials as well as labor. Unskilled

2. Stuart, 1902.

3. See, for example, Brassey, 1879, 157–96; Jeans, 1884, 623–24; Schulze-Gaevernitz, 1895, 85–130.

4. Rastall, 1922, 71.

5. Cotton Yarn Association, 1929, T11.

6. Pearse, 1930, 188.

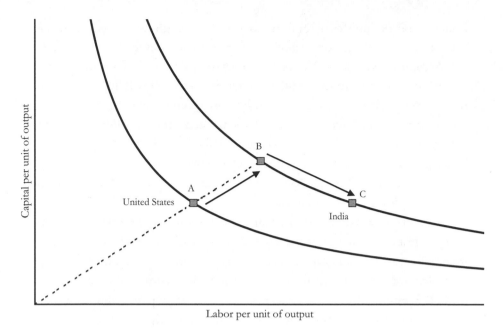

Figure 17.1 Production choices in the United States and India.

labor is assumed to be of the same quality everywhere.[7] Managers, however, differ from country to country, with the poorest countries having the least effective management.

Why then is output per machine-hour the same across economies while output per worker is much lower in low-wage countries? According to the modern view two circumstances coincide in poor economies. The first is that, because managers were, and are, deficient in low-wage economies they employ both more capital and more labor per unit of output than are required in the advanced economies. This is shown in figure 17.1. The vertical axis shows the capital used per unit of output, the horizontal axis, the labor employed. To produce a unit of output there will typically be many possible choices of capital and labor inputs per unit, a range of choices shown in the figure as the curve running through point A. By using more capital, some labor can be saved, and vice versa. For example, in ring spinning, if the speed of the machines is reduced, the

7. See, for example, Pack, 1987.

capital input per unit of output increases. But since at lower speeds there are fewer thread breakages, some labor in repairing these is saved.

A country with less-effective management will also face a trade-off between capital and labor in production. But this trade-off will lie farther from the origin in figure 17.1, as at point B. For any given ratio of capital to labor, the country with less-effective management needs more of both inputs. In cotton spinning, for example, if the raw cotton is not blended correctly the breakage rates in spinning will be higher, reducing output both per worker and per unit of capital. With ineffective management machines will break down more often, idling both capital and labor.

There is, however, a second circumstance in low-wage economies. Managers there are encouraged by the low wages to substitute labor for capital. For them labor is cheap and capital relatively expensive. So, in the ring spinning case, they will be encouraged to speed up machines and employ more labor to fix the resultant breaks. Thus managers in low-wage economies like India, faced with very cheap labor, rationally choose to use the combination of capital and labor represented by point C.

To see how this process operates in practice consider weavers assigned to looms. If there were one weaver per loom, as in India in 1910, then, whenever the loom ran out of weft thread or a warp thread broke, the worker could immediately fix the problem. Thus there should have been a high level of output per unit of capital. If, as in the United States, each worker tended eight looms, then it would typically take some time for the loom to be put back into service after the weft ran out or the warp broke. For the weaver was not constantly watching each loom but was instead often busy repairing one of the other looms. Here output per worker should have been high, but output per machine would have been low.

The modern view of the cotton textile industry is that the low wage costs in poor countries led managers to add so much more labor per machine that they were able to raise output per machine back up to the level of the advanced economies despite their general inefficiency. But they did so at the expense of further reducing output per worker.

Capital required per unit of output is driven up by managerial inefficiencies, but then driven down again by substituting cheap labor for capital. On balance the effects cancel out. In contrast labor required per unit of output is driven up by managerial inefficiencies, but then driven up again by substituting cheap labor for capital.

For this explanation of the observed international patterns of capital and labor productivities to work, there has to be plenty of room for substitution of capital and labor in production.[8]

We thus have two competing visions of the economic problems inherent in production in poor countries. The nineteenth-century view blamed these on the quality of workers, whereas according to the twentieth-century view the problem lay in managerial failings. If all we have are records of output, labor and capital from each industry then we cannot argue for one view over the other, since they are at this level observationally equivalent.

But in the case of the international textile industry, for which we have much more evidence on management, equipment, and labor assignments, it becomes apparent that the nature of the labor force was the key issue limiting efficiency in low-wage economies.

Management in Low-Wage Economies

Did poor countries suffer from poor management? Managers, like machines, can be imported into low-wage economies if the local supply is deficient. This was particularly easy in the cotton textile industry since cotton mills had a relatively flat managerial structure. The managers oversaw the purchase of the cotton, set the machines for the type of output to be produced, and supervised the workers. But since the workers had, as noted above, well-defined tasks whose completion was easy to check, supervision should have required only modest amounts of time.

In the cotton textile industry around 1910, when the international differences in staffing levels were already very clear, Britain not only exported machines, it also exported large numbers of managers and skilled workmen to foreign mills. Brazil, China, India, Mexico, and Russia all had significant numbers of British managers around 1910.[9] In 1895 there were fifty-five mills in Bombay, twenty-seven with British managers. In these mills there were 190 deputy managers who supervised the loom sheds, the spinning and carding rooms, and the steam machinery, of whom 77 were British.[10]

---

8. For the process to produce the observed effects production processes must follow the Cobb-Douglass production function (see chapter 7).

9. Clark, 1987a.

10. Rutnagur, 1927.

Similarly at least a third of the Chinese industry was under British management in 1915, and some of the mills owned by Chinese entrepreneurs were operated by British mill managers. Most Brazilian mills had British managers, room bosses, and engineers. Unless there was a selection process (for which there would have been no economic rationale), according to which only the least competent British managers went to the lowest-wage economies, those with the intermediate competence went to middle-wage societies, and the best stayed in the high-income economies, management cannot have been the issue

In places like Bombay the industry was highly competitive. Table 16.4 showed that profit rates in the industry, even in the growth years 1907–24, were modest. Managers were thus under constant pressure to improve the efficiency of their mills. Thus in 1925, of eighty-five cotton mills in Bombay, forty-five had failed and been reconstituted under new management at some point in their history, while sixteen others had transferred managerial control voluntarily.[11] There is no sign of any obvious managerial failings persisting in the industry, such as choosing the wrong types of machinery, the wrong scale of production, or the wrong level of vertical integration.[12]

Substitution Possibilities

The modern view of excess labor in factories, mills, and railways in poor countries depends on management choosing to substitute labor for capital. But there are some tasks in cotton mills for which such substitution is not possible, and so the staffing levels should be much closer to, or even be the same as, those in high-wage economies.

One such task is doffing. Doffers remove the full spindles of yarn at set intervals from the spinning machines. The machines must be stopped while the doffing is in progress, so all four hundred or so spindles on a frame are doffed at the same time. In India in the 1930s and 1940s machines spinning standard yarn would be doffed once every three hours. Since it took about 3.3 seconds to doff each spindle, if only one person were to doff the entire frame, the spindles would be stopped for doffing for 20 minutes out of each 200, or 10 percent of the total running time. To avoid this down time doffing was per-

11. The first mill was built in 1856, but the industry began to grow strongly only in the 1880s; Rutnagur, 1927.
12. Wolcott and Clark, 1999.

Table 17.1 Doffs per Hour, United States, Britain, and India

Year	United States	Britain	India
1907	—	—	*102*
1921	*728*	—	*118*
1944–49	770	462	*124*
1959	1,000	—	—
1969	—	600	—
1978	—	—	*160*
1996	—	—	319

Sources: Clark, 1907; Shirras, 1923; Cotton Spinning Productivity Team, 1951; Textile Council, 1969; Ratnam and Rajamanickam, 1980; Doraiswamy, 1983; Rajamanickam and Ranganathan, 1997, 2.
Note: Figures in italics are doffing rates inferred from the number of spindles per doffer or the number of pounds doffed per hour per doffer.

formed by specialized teams of doffers, and this practice reduced the doffing time per frame to 2–4 minutes, only 1–2 percent of the running time.[13]

Table 17.1 shows doffers' work rates per hour in the United States, Britain, and India over the years 1907–96. The Indian doffing rates are extraordinarily low all the way from 1907 to 1978, and they show very limited improvement by 1996. In the 1940s Indian doffing rates were 16 percent of U.S. rates. If we use time and motion estimates of the tasks performed by ring spinners, then given the staffing levels in India in the 1920s workers were working only 18–23 percent of the time.[14]

Why Is Labor Quality So Low in Poor Economies?

While it seems clear from the above that the cause of the overstaffing in poor countries resides principally in the workers, explaining why so many surplus workers are employed in production in low-wage economies is not easy. Even

13. In Japan in 1929 Pearse describes doffing squads of five to eight workers who would doff a frame in about one minute. In India in 1930 the doffing of the whole frame seems to have taken longer (two to three minutes), but we do not know the size of the gangs; Pearse, 1929, 55, 65; Pearse, 1930, 129, 133, 138.

14. Wolcott and Clark, 1999, 400.

in cases for which we have considerable information, such as the textile mills of Bombay from 1890 to 1938, an explanation is not obvious. Bombay mill workers seemingly worked at low intensity and in a slapdash manner, so that employers were forced to assign many workers per machine to achieve full output from their invested capital.

The managers in Bombay in the 1920s knew that, by the standards of Britain and the United States, their mills were overstaffed. And after 1924 the industry was under severe stress, with many mills suffering losses. Why didn't they get rid of the excess workers?

The proximate answer is that reducing staffing had no benefits in terms of costs and profits. Some firms did move aggressively to reduce staff levels in the 1920s and 1930s. But these firms' profits were no higher than those of the firms that took no such steps. There was no obvious market signal that this was the right direction in which to move.

We can divide the firms into two groups—the *rationalizers,* who made some significant reduction in the numbers of workers per machine during the interval 1924–38, and the *non-rationalizers,* who did not change worker numbers. On average the rationalizers reduced worker numbers by 35 percent. But in 1935–38 the average gross profit rate of the rationalizers was 1.7 percent, while that of the non-rationalizers was 2.0 percent. There was nothing in the experience of the Bombay industry to suggest that shedding surplus labor led to higher profits.

Bombay Dyeing and Manufacturing was the most profitable of the rationalizers. But its average profit rate for 1935–38 was still only 6 percent. Even this mill was not a great success, at least in the eyes of its managers. According to the minutes of the meetings of its board of directors, the profits of the company were sufficient to induce replacement of some worn-out equipment. Between 1930 and 1938 the board authorized average annual expenditures on equipment of 374,469 rupees, approximately 1.3 percent of the value of their fixed capital stock. But on a net basis the number of their spindles and looms declined. And during these years the board also authorized large investments of profits in government bonds. By 1938 the market value of the company's government bonds was 8 million rupees—an amount sufficient to extend their capital stock by 25 percent, had they regarded investment in the cotton industry as profitable.[15]

15. Wolcott and Clark, 1999, 409.

Shedding labor did not increase profits mainly because firms which shed workers paid higher wages to the remaining workers. Thus in 1935–37 the average day wage in rationalized mills was 1.26 rupees compared to 1.11 rupees for non-rationalized mills. This disparity was entirely a creation of the rationalization process. From 1924 to 1935–38 rationalized mills' nominal day wages fell 6 percent, while non-rationalized mills' wages fell 21 percent. Furthermore, the increase in machinery could not be simply foisted upon the workers. Preparations were undertaken to minimize the effort requirements per machine, despite the apparently minimal tasks of the workers before rationalization. There were also ongoing costs. These included better machine maintenance and better cotton quality, both improvements designed to reduce the breakage rate.

In a competitive labor market workers can be employed under terms that would imply different levels of effort per hour. Firms that demand greater effort will have to pay higher wages. Thus it could well be that firms in Bombay had on average chosen the optimal wage-effort combination, given the capacities and inclinations of the workers. Those that tried to extract more effort from their workers had to pay more to retain them.

It was claimed by many observers, for example, that the reason for low labor productivity in places like Bombay was that Indian workers clung to outdated work norms, such as one worker per side of a ring frame. Thus "Before independence, work allocation was purely on an ad hoc basis and was dependent on the tradition of that particular region. If a worker attended to 200 spindles in one mill, he did the same in all the mills in the locality."[16]

But if labor resistance based on outdated work norms in the declining center of Bombay was the problem, rationalizing managers would have had enormous incentive to move to new locations. The day wages of workers were generally cheaper outside the established textile centers. In fact, there was significant growth in the interwar period in such places as Cawnpor, Coimbatore, Delhi, Madras, and Nagpur. But while employment and the amount of machinery in place expanded in these cities, productivity remained at its prewar levels. If staffing levels in the main centers of the industry were purely conventional, why did the managers of new mills in isolated locations not train their workers to operate eight hundred spinning spindles each, as should have been feasible?

16. Sreenivasan, 1984, 172.

Manufacturers were clear in their belief that light assignments were made for fear of reduced output per machine if workers looked after more machines. Thus one manufacturer testified to the Factory Commission in 1908 that "They had one man to each loom, because if they gave two looms to one man it would mean a loss of three-eighths of the loom's capacity. They would prefer to stop a loom altogether rather than hand it over to a man working another loom."[17]

The Buckingham and Carnatic mills in Madras, one of the largest and most profitable textile enterprises in India, introduced automatic looms in the 1920s. The staffing of ordinary looms at this time in India was still often one worker per loom, compared to one worker per eight looms in the United States. There would be twenty to thirty automatic looms per worker in the United States, but only three automatic looms were assigned to each weaver in the Buckingham and Carnatic mills. Since the looms were new to the workers, since they had no reason to expect a level of three looms per weaver any more than ten looms per weaver, if the previous staffing limitation had been based solely on convention—why not choose this moment to establish a more profitable convention?

Another sign that outdated work norms were not the problem was that between 1890 and 1929 the managers of Indian mills moved toward purchasing new machines that used less labor. One way of using less labor was to make the input and output packages larger so that they had to be changed less often. Thus the average size of the output bobbins spinning 20s yarn went up from 14 cubic inches circa 1890 to 16 cubic inches circa 1929. Similarly the average size of the input bobbins on 20s yarn moved up from 80 cubic inches circa 1890 to 115 cubic inches circa 1929. Managers were choosing machines that occupied more floor space but saved on labor. Why would they do this if they were constrained to have a fixed number of spindles per worker?

It is clear from the detailed experience of the Bombay industry in the 1920s and 1930s that problems in the employment of labor were the key difficulty. A further sign that there really were differences in the attitudes and behaviors of Indian workers compared to workers in high-wage economies was the conditions of employment in Indian mills.

The cotton mills in England were noted for the early introduction of strict systems of factory discipline. Workers, even those who were on piece rates,

17. Parliamentary Papers, 1909b, 315.

were expected to appear at opening time each morning, to work all the hours the mill was open, to stay at their own machines, and to refrain from socializing at work.[18] Indian mills by comparison were undisciplined. This lack of discipline and high absenteeism continued at least into the 1960s.

The Indian Factory Labour Commission report of 1909 is full of testimony by employers regarding conditions in the mills. A substantial fraction of workers were absent on any given day, and those at work were often able to come and go from the mill at their pleasure to eat or to smoke. Other workers would supervise their machines while they were gone, and indeed some manufacturers alleged that the workers organized an informal shift system among themselves. The mill yards would have eating places, barbers, drink shops, and other facilities to serve the workers taking a break.[19] Some mothers allegedly brought their children with them to the mills. Workers' relatives would bring food to them inside the mill during the day. "There was an utter lack of supervision in the Bombay mills." One manager even stated that the typical worker "washes, bathes, washes his clothes, smokes, shaves, sleeps, has his food, and is surrounded as a rule by his relations."[20]

There are few reliable estimates of the fraction of time workers were absent from their machines: the manufacturers put the figure at 10–30 percent of total work time. To partially control this absenteeism some employers used a pass system, under which a worker could leave the mill only with a pass or token from his or her department. Each department was allotted passes equal to 10–25 percent of the staff. But workers sometimes successfully resisted even this modest control.[21]

This lack of discipline persisted throughout the free market period of the industry under the British until 1947, and probably beyond. Thus R.K.P. Mody, a lecturer at the Victoria Jubilee Textile Institute in Bombay who had worked in both English and Indian mills, in a 1951 article giving "practical hints to jobbers [room bosses]," assumes that even a good jobber will allow workers to leave the mill rooms during work, as long as they have tokens.[22]

Mody condemns—but apparently recognizes as common—supervision practices that allowed workers to go out without tokens in groups of two or

18. Clark, 1994.
19. Parliamentary Papers, 1909b, III, 170; Morris, 1965, 114–15.
20. Parliamentary Papers, 1909b, 21, 27, 78, III, 204; quotations on pages III and 204.
21. Ibid., 25, 35, 72, III, 139, 148–49, 170, 181, 197, 200.
22. Mody, 1951.

Table 17.2 Absenteeism in Indian Mills, 1965

Period	Urban (%)	Rural (%)
Average (1955)	8.0	5.7
Average	10.6	8.9
First day after wage payment	11.0	6.1
Second day after wage payment	10.8	—
Third day after wage payment	10.2	—
First six days after twice-yearly bonus payment	12.4	7.7
First day after a holiday	10.5	7.9

Source: Rudraswamy, 1957, 1967.

more, "leaving machines and other work unattended." He also criticizes the customs of allowing workers to read newspapers inside departments, allowing them to sleep inside departments, and allowing children within the departments.[23] By the mid-nineteenth century in England no textile mill would have allowed any of these practices.

Absenteeism was still common as late as the 1960s. In 1939–44 daily absenteeism in Bombay averaged 10.7 percent, and in Ahmedabad, 4.5 percent.[24] Table 17.2 summarizes a study of sixteen South Indian mills which found high absenteeism rates that were apparently tolerated by mills in the 1950s and 1960s. In 1955, for example, 7 percent of the workers were absent for 25 percent or more of the work days. Absenteeism also increased on days after wage payments, on days after bonus payments, and on days after holidays. Yet management continued to employ such workers, even though a relatively small and identifiable group was responsible for many of the days lost from work.

This irregularity was not solely a product of the annual movement of workers back to their villages at the wedding season or for harvest. Mills often had formal leave systems that covered such occasions. Instead there was considerable day-to-day absenteeism.

23. Mody, 1951, 720.
24. Deshpande, 1946, 8.

Many mills made attempts to limit absenteeism, but by rather weak methods. Thus the rules of the Madura Mill Company in 1946 specified that any worker who was absent from the mill without permission for *eight days or more* was subject to suspension or dismissal.[25] More commonly the mills relied on modest bonuses offered to workers for good attendance.

Beyond their relatively liberal attitude toward absences, Indian mills even allowed workers to effectively subcontract their work for periods where they were absent. At least in the 1920s weavers in Bombay, a relatively skilled group of workers, were allowed to hire their own substitutes (*badlis*).[26] The weavers were paid on piece rates, so they would get the payment for whatever output the substitute produced. The substitute was paid by the weaver with no intervention or supervision by the firm.[27]

The evidence presented above strongly supports the idea that labor problems were at the root of India's failure to industrialize under British rule in 1857–1947 and subsequently under independent Indian governments. The socially induced lethargy that afflicted Indian labor may have extended throughout the society: had the deficiency been limited to the ranks of Indian managers and entrepreneurs, these inputs could have been relatively easily imported, as we saw in chapter 15 in the case of the Sassoon family enterprises.

Why Divergence?

If the fundamental cause of the income differences between economies is variation in the quality of the labor force across those economies, then why are the differences in income today so much greater than in 1800? After all, the variation in social capabilities between societies now is presumably no greater than it was in 1800.

There are three reasons why the same differences across societies now would lead to far greater divergence in income per person—the so-called Great Divergence.

The first is that in the preindustrial world, because of the Malthusian Trap, differences in labor effectiveness had no consequences for the average

25. Deshpande, 1946, 8.
26. Newman, 1981.
27. In some of the firms there does seem to have been a limit on how many consecutive days a *badli* could be employed by a weaver.

level of output per person across societies. Leisurely societies were just as well off as hard-working ones. Since the Industrial Revolution income per person has no longer been constrained by Malthusian mechanisms. So existing differences in capabilities between societies could now express themselves through income per person rather than population densities. The escape from the Malthusian era is one factor in the Great Divergence.

The second is that modern medicine has substantially reduced the subsistence wage in such areas as tropical Africa, allowing populations to continue growing at incomes which are substantially below the average of the preindustrial world. Even at wages that were low by preindustrial standards life expectancy in some of the poorest countries in Africa is still above the average preindustrial level.

The third reason, more tentatively, is that the new production techniques introduced since the Industrial Revolution have raised the wage premium for high-quality labor.[28] In the preindustrial world production processes tended to be "shallow," meaning that they did not involve a large number of steps. In addition they were typically tolerant of error and inattention along the way. Consider the production of wheat in preindustrial agriculture. The ground was plowed, the seed sown, the grain reaped, and finally it was threshed and winnowed. If too much seed was sown then some of it was lost; if too little, then some land input was not fully utilized. If the threshing was done poorly then some grain remained with the straw, which in any case was fed to the farm animals, so only part of the value was lost. But errors or poor performance at each step of the process tended to have only modest costs.

Poland in the early nineteenth century, for example, was a major supplier of wheat to Britain, and so its agricultural practices were of interest to the British. The Englishman William Jacob, who made an inspection tour of Polish farms in the 1820s, noted the generally poor performance of agricultural workers there. Of threshers he states, "a much greater proportion of the grain was left among the straw, than in that which has passed under an English flail." His data implied that Polish threshers, even with less care, threshed only half as much per day as English threshers. The grain exported from eastern Europe was also imperfectly winnowed, and it had to be rescreened on arrival to exclude large amounts of foreign material.[29] The grain from the

28. This idea is due to Kremer, 1993a.
29. Clark, 1987b, 425, 427.

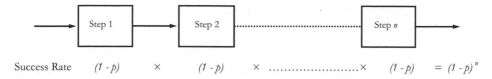

$$\text{Success Rate} \quad (1-p) \quad \times \quad (1-p) \quad \times \quad \dots\dots\dots\times \quad (1-p) \quad = (1-p)^n$$

Figure 17.2   A modern production process?

interior of Poland was floated down to the Baltic Sea on wooden barges un-protected from the rain and sun, so that by the time it arrived the top layer would have sprouted and begun to grow. This sprouted layer was simply peeled off on arrival.

The production system was fairly tolerant to the slapdash work ethic of the Polish workers. If threshers did not work hard, more could be added to complete the task. If the grain was not winnowed well, it could be screened further. If some grain sprouted, it could be discarded.

But the new technologies of the Industrial Revolution involved a more extensive division of labor and were less tolerant of errors along the way. In pottery factories in Britain by the nineteenth century, for example, there were twenty-nine different steps in the division of labor. In making cups the four-teenth was attaching the handle.[30] If this was not done correctly, then the finished cup was worthless. There could be no rescreening as with Polish wheat. In such a situation, Kremer argues, mistakes by the labor force will have a multiplicative effect.[31] As portrayed in figure 17.2, if there is a chance p of a mistake in each of n steps in the production process, and each is fatal to producing a saleable product, then the chance of getting a saleable product will be $(1-p)^n$. If, for example, the chance of a failure at each stage in the pot-tery works was $p = 0.1$, and there were 29 stages, then the fraction of success-ful cups made would be 0.05.

In this situation manufacturers might find the current African labor force, even offered at extremely low wages, not cost effective. Or, when confronted with a workforce with low work rates or high error rates, manufacturers might find it cost effective to add more workers at each stage of the process in order to ensure workflow and prevent errors. This could lead to the situation found in the empirical results of chapter 16: large amounts of extra labor in low-wage

30. Clark, 1994, 153–54.
31. Kremer, 1993a.

Table 17.3 Cloth Production in India by Sector, 1900–98
(square meters)

Year	Mill	Decentralized power loom	Handloom
1900–03	483	0	793
1936–39	3,630	0	1,420
1980–81	4,533	4,802	3,109
1997–98	1,948	20,951	7,603

Sources: Mazumdar, 1984, 7, 36; Office of the Textile Commissioner, 1997, 1998.

countries, but the same output per unit of capital as in the richer countries. Workers are given extremely easy work assignments in order to minimize the chance of mistakes.

Technology in successful, high-income economies thus evolves toward production processes that, developed in the work environments of these economies, give a high premium to regular and meticulous completion of work tasks. In economies in which the labor force is more relaxed and less disciplined, these technologies can only be utilized with extravagant amounts of extra labor to compensate for the characteristics of the labor force.

A further empirical implication of this idea would be that the productivity of modern techniques compared to their handicraft precursors would be much less in low-wage economies.

India, for example, has seen an extraordinary persistence of handlooms in the textile weaving sector. By the 1830s in England handloom weaving of cottons had largely been superseded by power looms in factories, even though the wages of handloom workers were only about half those of factory workers.[32] Yet some 175 years later the handloom sector in India is still large, particularly in cottons. Indeed the output of the handloom sector has grown steadily since statistics were first gathered in 1900. In 1997–98, as table 17.3 shows, output of woven cloth from handlooms in India was about ten times that in 1900. In 1997–98 25 percent of cloth production in India was still from handlooms.

32. Bythell, 1969.

Cloth production in India is in fact divided into three segments: the mill sector, consisting of large power loom plants as in the United States; the decentralized power loom sector, consisting of workshops of one to fifty power looms outside the formal regulation of the mill sector; and the handloom sector, consisting of looms in houses and workshops. The survival of the handloom industry in India is often attributed to government protection. Since independence the government has levied excise taxes on mill output while keeping the handloom sector tax free. Thus even in 1997–98 most fabrics were subject to an excise duty of 10–20 percent, but handloom cloth was still exempt. However, the decentralized power loom sector has largely avoided paying these excise taxes.[33] So the tax advantages serve mainly to explain why smaller power loom operations could outcompete large mills. They do not explain why handlooms can still compete against untaxed power loom operations. Power looms produce 2.5 times the hourly output of handlooms, and one weaver should be able to operate between four and eight power looms at a time, based on labor requirements in Britain and the United States circa 1900. Day wages per worker in the handloom and power loom sectors are about the same, implying that power loom labor costs per meter of cloth should be 5–10 percent of handloom labor costs. Since capital costs for power looms per meter of cloth are estimated to be only about 20 percent higher than those for handlooms, interest rates would have to be extraordinarily high before handlooms had any cost advantage.

But in practice power looms in India require much more labor than even machine-powered looms in England in the nineteenth century. Power loom weavers typically supervise only 1.5 looms each.[34] This level of staffing drastically reduces the labor cost advantages of the power loom. The high staffing levels for power looms might be explained by the low wages of the operators, but Indian wages now are as high or higher than those in England in the 1830s, when a more primitive power loom easily swept aside the competition of handlooms.

The competitive advantage of the handloom in modern India is consistent with the idea that differences in labor quality are more significant when more modern technologies are in use.

33. Misra, 1993, 89–119.
34. Mazumdar, 1984, 93.

Why the Differences in Labor Quality?

Regarding the underlying cause of the differences in labor quality, there is no satisfactory theory. Economies seem, to us, to alternate more or less randomly between relatively energetic phases and periods of somnolence. We saw above that India experienced declining income relative to the United States and the United Kingdom for 120 years since 1870. Recently—coinciding with modest economic reforms that did no more than partially return its economy to the free-market period of British rule—the country began to grow again. But growth in India is actually confined to only select states, including Gujarat, Maharashtra, and the Punjab. Others within the same political framework, such as Bihar and Uttar Pradesh, have continued to perform poorly. British income relative to France and Germany declined substantially from 1950 to 1980, but it has since returned to equality. Ireland, whose income per person was only about two-thirds that of Britain from 1800 to 1980, has since then seen its per capita income grow to one of the highest in Europe, exceeding that of Britain. New Zealand in the past twenty years has seen significant slippage in its income relative to other OECD countries.

This pattern of alternating periods of energy and somnolence extends far back in history. The Golden Age of the Netherlands in 1550–1650, for example, was followed by 150 years of economic stagnation. William Jacob, in his accounts of his tour of eastern Europe in 1826, remarked on the low energy of even free laborers: "some rare instances of perseverance in economy, industry and temperance, are to be found."[35] It is only the magnitude of the swings, the reversals in fortune, that seem greater in the post-Malthusian world.

35. Jacob, 1826, 65.

18   Conclusion: Strange New World

All Nature wears one universal grin.   —Henry Fielding (1731)[1]

God clearly created the laws of the economic world in order to have a little fun at economists' expense. In other areas of inquiry, such as the physical sciences, there has been a steady accumulation of knowledge over the past four hundred years. Earlier theories proved inadequate. But those that replaced them encompassed the earlier theories and gave practitioners greater ability to predict outcomes across a wider range of conditions. In economics, however, we see instead that our ability to describe and predict the economic world reached a peak around 1800. In the years since the Industrial Revolution there has been a progressive and continuing disengagement of economic models from any ability to predict differences of income and wealth across time and across countries and regions. Before 1800 living conditions differed substantially across societies, but the Malthusian model developed within classical economics successfully analyzes the sources of these differences. We know how climate, disease, natural resources, technology, and fertility shaped material living conditions. The Malthusian era described in chapters 1–9 is thus, though counterintuitive, perfectly comprehensible. Differences in social energy across societies, which have probably existed for all time, were translated by the Malthusian mechanism into variations in population density. In economics the known world thus stretches from the original foragers of the African savannah until 1800.

1. Fielding, 1731, 2.

Since then economics has become more professional. Graduate programs have expanded, pouring out a flood of talented economists armed with an ever more sophisticated array of formal models and statistical methods. But since the Industrial Revolution we have entered a strange new world in which the rococo embellishments of economic theory help little in understanding the pressing questions that the ordinary person asks of economics: Why are some rich and some poor? In the future will we all be among the lucky? In this book I have suggested ways in which the Malthusian era, through differential survival of individuals, can predict success or failure for modern societies, and also predicts a continuing future of economic growth. But even if that hypothesis is correct, it still leaves unexplained much of the variation in modern incomes across countries. In the modern world local social interactions that determine the attitudes of people toward work, and cooperation in work, are magnified by the economic system to generate unprecedented extremes of wealth and poverty.

Our economic world is one that the deluge of economics journal articles, working papers, and books—devoted to ever more technically detailed studies of capital markets, trade flows, tax incidence, sovereign borrowing risk, corruption indices, rule of law—serves more to obscure than to illuminate. For the economic history of the world constructed in these pages is largely innocent of these traditional staples of the discipline. The great engines of economic life in the sweep of history—demography, technology, and labor efficiency—seem uncoupled from these quotidian economic concerns. (And of course it is another divine irony that it is in precisely this world, where the bulk of the activity of economists has the least value for the material fate of mankind, that the combination of ever more rigorous training, limiting supply, and a booming demand for economists from business schools, central banks, and international agencies has driven up the salaries of even academic economists to unprecedented levels.)[2]

The modern age began with the conquests by the Europeans of the fifteenth century and later. The newly discovered societies of Africa, America, and the Pacific sought in vain to stem the invasions of the Europeans. The obsidian blades of the Aztecs were no match for Spanish steel, the war clubs of the Maori of no avail against British muskets, the mud walls of Timbuktu

2. The University of California, Davis, seems to be the sole exception to this salary inflation.

scant bulwark against French artillery. There followed the great age of imperialism, when Westerners imposed themselves in all corners of the globe. For a while the West conquered all. It shaped the political geography of much of the world; it transplanted Africans and Asians to different continents. Territory, technology, music, culture: as a consequence of the Industrial Revolution the West seemed to have it all.

But a visitor to the planet, innocent of its history, might have a very different impression. For such a visitor would see, ringing the modern West, a series of fortifications protecting it from invasion by the poor societies of South America, Africa, and South Asia. In the Mediterranean and South Atlantic naval patrols try to intercept desperate boatloads of migrants headed to the glittering cities of Europe. The U.S.-Mexico border is increasingly lined with rusting iron battlements, walls of concrete, and fences of wire. In the gaps, across the harsh Sonoran Desert, a trail of empty plastic gallon jugs demarcates the march of an invading army of desperately poor migrants from El Salvador, Guatemala, Honduras, and Mexico. Patrols in the Caribbean intercept sailing boats packed with Haitians trying to escape the violence and filth of Cité Soleil.

History shows, as we have seen repeatedly in this book, that the West has no model of economic development to offer the still-poor countries of the world. There is no simple economic medicine that will guarantee growth, and even complicated economic surgery offers no clear prospect of relief for societies afflicted with poverty. Even direct gifts of aid have proved ineffective in stimulating growth.[3] In this context the only policy the West could pursue that will ensure gains for at least some of the poor of the Third World is to liberalize immigration from these countries. We know a good deal about the economic consequences for migrants from the historical record of countries like Britain, the United States, Canada, Australia, and New Zealand, which had large flows of immigrants in the modern era. That record shows that migrants, particularly those from very-low-income countries, have been able to achieve enormous income gains through migration.[4] Aid to the Third World may disappear into the pockets of Western consultants and the corrupt rulers of these societies. But each extra migrant admitted to the emerald cities of the advanced world is one more person guaranteed a better material lifestyle.

3. Easterly, 2006.
4. See Clark, 1987a, table 8, for example.

Another irony is that the achievement of mass affluence in much of the world—the decline in child mortality, the extension of adult life spans, and the reduction in inequality—have not made us any happier than our hunter-gatherer forebears. While I have emphasized that income alone has been a profound shaper of how we live in the modern world, the one thing that income has not brought is happiness.

The evidence on this issue is simple. It consists solely of questionnaires put to people, both within individual societies over time and across societies, asking them how happy they are or how satisfied they are with their lives. This may seem an absurdly crude tool with which to measure happiness, but how else would we assess such a thing? And responses to such questionnaires within any society correlate well with characteristics we expect to be associated with happiness. In western Europe and the United States the married, the rich (including recent lottery winners), the healthier, the employed, the educated, and the thin all report greater happiness. The divorced and separated, the widowed, the poor, the less healthy, the unemployed, the uneducated, and the fat are less happy.[5] Furthermore, people who report greater happiness demonstrate physical correlates within the brain: more electrocortical activity in the left prefrontal cortex than in the right.[6]

Within any society the association between income and happiness is strong. Ranking by income per person, the top 10 percent in income is the happiest group, and the bottom 10 percent is the least happy.[7]

The association of income with happiness observed within societies might lead us to believe naïvely that another profound effect of the Industrial Revolution was to spread happiness and good cheer around the globe. Unfortunately there is little evidence of gains in happiness from gains in income, life expectancy, or health by societies as a whole. This can be observed in two ways. First, for some societies, such as Japan and the United States, we have survey measures of happiness that extend back over fifty years or more, a period

5. Easterlin, 2003; Blanchflower and Oswald, 2004, tables 4–7; Gardner and Oswald, 2007, table 2; Oswald and Powdthavee, 2007, tables 1–3. It must be noted that the amount of variation in reported happiness explained by all such observable features of people's lives is small, typically less than 5 percent. Thus the rich are happier than the poor *on average,* but many poor people are much happier than the average rich person, and many rich people are more miserable than the average poor person.

6. Kahneman et al., 2004, 429.

7. See, for example, Frey and Stutzer, 2002, table 1.

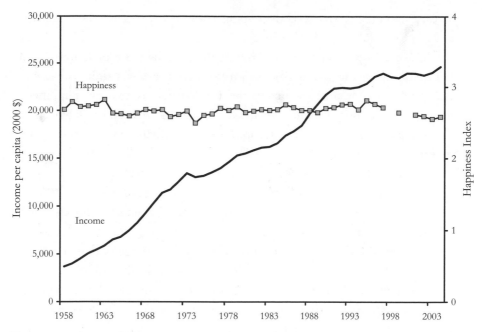

Figure 18.1 Average income per capita and average happiness, Japan, 1958–2004. Data from Veenhoven, 2005, and Heston et al., 2006.

during which these countries became much richer as a result of modern economic growth. Yet, as Richard Easterlin first pointed out in 1974, there has been no increase in average happiness with the growth of incomes.[8] Figure 18.1 shows the average reported happiness in Japan from 1958 to 2004, as well as income per capita measured in prices for the year 2000. Over the nearly fifty years from 1958 to 2004 income per person rose nearly sevenfold, while reported happiness, if anything, declined slightly.

The second set of evidence is derived from administration of the same survey questions across contemporary societies in which average income varies significantly. People in contemporary countries as poor as those of the world before 1800 on average report little difference in happiness from those in very rich countries such as the United States.[9] Average happiness at an income level per person of $20,000 and above is only modestly greater than that at incomes of $4,000 per person and less, the level of hunter-gatherer

8. Easterlin, 1974; Blanchflower and Oswald, 2004.
9. Frey and Stutzer, 2002, 416–17.

societies. At the national level the response of happiness to income is modest at best.

There has been much discussion of the appropriate interpretation of the failure of higher income to produce greater happiness over time and across countries. The key problem here is the ample evidence that our happiness depends not on our absolute level of well-being, but instead on how we are doing relative to our reference group. Each individual—by acquiring more income, by buying a larger house in a nicer neighborhood, by driving a more elegant car—can make him- or herself happier. But happier only at the expense of those with less income, meaner housing, and junkier cars. Money will buy happiness, but that happiness is transferred from someone else, not added to the common pool.

The finding that relative income is crucial also suggests that the poor countries of today may not be a good guide to the likely happiness of the mass of humanity before 1800. These poor nations, through the medium of television, can witness almost firsthand the riches of successful economies. If this helps set the point of reference about their economic position for the people in these poor societies, then possibly there is no absolute effect of income on happiness even at the lowest incomes. That would imply further that the people of the world of 1800, in which all societies were relatively poor, and in which communities were much more local, were likely to have been just as happy as those of the wealthiest nations of the world today, such as the United States.

Since we are likely mainly the descendants of the strivers of the pre-industrial world, the people driven to achieve greater economic success than their peers, these findings perhaps reflect our biological heritage from the Malthusian era. Perhaps we are not designed to be content, but instead to forever compare our lot with that of our competitors, and to be happy only when we do better. The contented may simply have died out in the Malthusian era.

Does this imply that the incredible advances in technology over the millennia, and the consequent gains in income per capita and in general living conditions, have all been for naught? Some, such as Robert Frank, have argued that, since the gains in happiness from higher income and consumption come only at the expense of the reduced happiness of those who lose out in such status races, much of the energy devoted to achieving higher incomes in any society is socially wasteful. The rich, the winners of the status races, should be heavily taxed to reduce such socially costly activity.[10] But happiness studies so far do not support any such policy conclusion. Greater taxation of the rich might reduce income inequality, but it would not make societies as a whole happier. We lack trustworthy evidence that societies with greater income equality are on average happier.

Happiness research does suggest one interesting parallel between taxation policy in our world and that in the Malthusian era. We saw in chapter 2 that taxes to fund the wasteful lifestyles of the rulers actually had no social cost in the Malthusian era. The glories of Versailles were not purchased at the price of the misery of the poor—whatever public relations problems Marie Antoinette may have had. Happiness research suggests that the same holds true for the modern era. If we value such collective goods as scientific research, space travel, public art, and fine architecture, then we should tax to fund them, whatever the economic cost. The consequent reduction of our material consumption will have little psychic cost.

World economic history is thus full of counterintuitive effects, surprises, and puzzles. It is intertwined with who we are and how our culture was formed. No one can claim to be truly intellectually alive without having understood and wrestled, at least a little, with these mysteries—of how we arrived at our present affluence only after millennia in the wilderness, and of why it is so hard for many societies to join us in the material Promised Land.

10. Frank, 1999.

Technical Appendix

In this appendix all the formulas used in the book are derived using simple algebra.

1. The Fundamental Equation of Growth

In all economies, if y is output per person, k capital per person, z land per person, and A the level of efficiency, then

$$g_y = ag_k + cg_z + g_A, \tag{1}$$

where g_x denotes the growth rate of a variable, a is the share of output paid to capital owners, and c the share paid to landowners.

To show this assume a general relationship between output and the other variables of the form

$$y = AF(k, z). \tag{2}$$

A now is interpreted as measuring how well the economy translates inputs into output. The exact nature of the function $F(k, z)$ is unspecified, and it does not need to be.

A small change in efficiency, ΔA, changes output by $\Delta AF(k, z)$. Thus a 1 percent increase in efficiency increases output by 1 percent. A small change in capital per person, Δk, changes output by $r\Delta k$, where r is the rental payment per unit of capital. This is because in a competitive economy the amount paid to each input equals the amount the last unit used adds to output.

379

Similarly Δz changes output by $s\Delta z$, where s is the rental per unit of land. Adding up these effects, we can divide small changes in output per person into

$$\Delta y = r\Delta k + s\Delta z + \Delta AF(k, z). \tag{3}$$

Dividing both sides of equation (3) by y and rearranging gives

$$\frac{\Delta y}{y} = \frac{rk}{y}\frac{\Delta k}{k} + \frac{sz}{y}\frac{\Delta s}{s} + \frac{\Delta AF(k, z)}{AF(k, z)}, \tag{4}$$

and equation (1) follows from equation (4).

2. Efficiency Growth Rates

Equation (1) implies that we can measure the rate of efficiency growth as

$$g_A = g_y - ag_k - cg_z.$$

Equivalently we can measure efficiency growth as the weighted average rate of the growth of payments to labor, capital, and land. That is,

$$g_A = ag_r + bg_w + cg_s. \tag{5}$$

To derive this note that the value of the output equals the sum of payments to owners of labor, capital, and land. So

$$y = w + rk + sz. \tag{6}$$

Equation (6) implies that, again for small changes,

$$\Delta y = \Delta w + \Delta rk + r\Delta k + \Delta sz + s\Delta z$$

$$\Rightarrow \qquad \Delta y - r\Delta k - s\Delta z = \Delta w + \Delta rk + \Delta sz.$$

Dividing everything above by y and rearranging gives

$$\frac{\Delta y}{y} - \frac{rk}{y}\frac{\Delta k}{k} - \frac{sz}{y}\frac{\Delta s}{s} = \frac{w}{y}\frac{\Delta w}{w} + \frac{rk}{y}\frac{\Delta k}{k} + \frac{sz}{y}\frac{\Delta s}{s}$$

$$\Rightarrow \qquad g_A = g_y - ag_k - cg_z = ag_r + bg_w + cg_s.$$

3. The Fundamental Equation in the Malthusian Economy

Before 1800 we have a special case of equation (1) in which in the long run $g_y = g_k = 0$. In addition $g_z = -g_N$, where N is the level of population. Thus if population was growing at 1 percent per year then land per person was falling at this rate. Substituting these values into equation (1) gives, for the long run,

$$g_A = cg_N.$$

Since income per person does not change over the long run in the Malthusian economy, and since to a first approximation wages and the return on capital should be constant, then equation (5) implies that

$$g_A = cg_s.$$

Hence the growth rate of real land rents in the Malthusian world, absent changes in real interest rates, should be the same as the growth rate of population.

4. The Sources of Efficiency Growth

If there are j sectors in an economy, the overall efficiency growth rate of the economy can be decomposed into the contribution from each sector through the equation

$$g_A = \sum \theta_j g_{A_j},$$

where θ_j is the value of output of sector j relative to the value of all final outputs produced in the economy.

5. Modern Growth

In the modern era the share of land rents in national incomes for industrialized economies has declined sharply, to typically 4 percent or less (see figure 10.3). This implies that for the modern era we can simplify the fundamental equation of growth even further:

$$g_y \approx ag_k + g_A.$$

Furthermore, growth in efficiency induces more physical capital investment. The amount of this induced capital accumulation can be estimated from the fact that

$$a = \frac{rk}{y}.$$

Since in the modern era a has been relatively constant at about 0.25 and the real interest rate r has also been relatively constant, by implication

$$g_k \approx g_y.$$

Thus

$$g_y \approx \frac{g_A}{(1-a)}.$$

In the modern era the products $a g_r$ and $c g_s$ are both close to 0, because g_r and c are each close to 0. Thus

$$g_A \approx b g_w.$$

Thus almost all the gains from growing efficiency in the modern economy have flown to wage earners. And we can approximate the rate of efficiency growth in the modern era just by looking at the growth of real wages.

6. Generalizations

The above results for the sources of growth in per capita income are derived for an economy with only one output, one type of labor, one type of land, and one type of capital (which is just stored-up output). But all these results generalize easily into analogous expressions for an economy with many types of output, labor, land, and capital. Thus in an economy with i types of output the growth of output becomes

$$g_Y = \sum \theta_i g_{Y_i},$$

where θ_i is the share of the commodity or service i in the value of output. The growth of the labor input becomes

$$g_L = \sum \frac{b_j}{b} g_{L_j},$$

where b_j is the share in the total payments to the factors of production paid to workers of type j. And the growth of the capital stock is similarly

$$g_K = \sum \frac{a_j}{a} g_{K_j}.$$

References

Abernathy, Frederick H., Anthony Volpe, and David Weil. 2005. "The Apparel and Textile Industries After 2005: Prospects and Choices for Public and Private Actors." Working Paper, Harvard Center for Textile and Apparel Research, Cambridge, Mass.

Abramovitz, Moses. 1956. "Resource and Output Trends in the United States since 1870." *American Economic Review* 46: 5–23.

Acemoglu, Daron, Simon Johnson, and James A. Robinson. 2001. "The Colonial Origins of Comparative Development: An Empirical Investigation." *American Economic Review* 91(5): 1369–1401.

———. 2002. "Reversal of Fortune: Geography and Institutions in the Making of the Modern World Income Distribution." *Quarterly Journal of Economics* 118: 1231–1294.

———. 2005a. "The Rise of Europe: Atlantic Trade, Institutional Change, and Economic Growth." *American Economic Review* 95(3): 546–579.

———. 2005b. "Institutions as the Fundamental Cause of Long-Run Growth." In *Handbook of Economic Growth,* eds. Philippe Aghion and Steve Durlauf. Philadelphia: Elsevier, pp. 385–471.

A'Hearn, Brian. 2003. "Anthropometric Evidence on Living Standards in Northern Italy, 1730–1860." *Journal of Economic History* 63(2): 351–381.

Alam, M. Shahid. 1987. "Some European Perceptions of Japan's Work-Ethos in the Tokugawa Era: A Limited Survey of Observations from the West's First Encounters Offers Parallels to Today's." *American Journal of Economics and Sociology* 46(2): 229–243.

Allen, Marion E. 1989. *Wills of the Archdeaconry of Suffolk, 1620–24.* Woodbridge, Suffolk, U.K.: Boydell Press.

Allen, Robert C. 2001. "The Great Divergence in European Wages and Prices from the Middle Ages to the First World War." *Explorations in Economic History* 38(4): 411–448.

———. 2005. "Capital Accumulation, Technological Change, and the Distribution of Income during the British Industrial Revolution." Working Paper, Nuffield College, Oxford.

Angel, J. Lawrence. 1971. *The People of Lerna: Analysis of a Prehistoric Aegean Population.* Athens: American School of Classical Studies.

Arnold, A. J., and Sean McCartney. 2005. "Rates of Return, Concentration Levels and Strategic Change in the British Railway Industry, 1830–1912." *Journal of Transport History* 26(1): 41–60.

Austen, Jane. 1957. *Sense and Sensibility.* New York: Heritage Press.

Bagnall, Roger S., and Bruce W. Frier. 1994. *The Demography of Roman Egypt.* Cambridge, U.K.: Cambridge University Press.

Balke, Nathan S., and Robert J. Gordon. 1989. "The Estimation of Prewar Gross National Product: Methodology and New Evidence." *Journal of Political Economy* 97: 38–92.

Banks, Joseph. 1962. *The Endeavour Journal of Joseph Banks, 1768–71,* Vol. 1, ed. J. C. Beaglehole. Sydney: Angus & Robertson.

Bassino, Jean-Pascal, and Debin Ma. 2005. "Japanese Wages in International Perspective, 1741–1913." *Research in Economic History* 23: 229–248.

Beaglehole, John C. 1974. *The Life of Captain James Cook.* Stanford, Calif.: Stanford University Press.

Becker, Gary. 1981. *A Treatise on the Family.* Cambridge, Mass.: Harvard University Press.

Becker, Gary, Kevin Murphy, and Robert Tamura. 1990. "Human Capital, Fertility and Economic Growth." *Journal of Political Economy* 98: S12–37.

Bekaert, Geert. 1991. "Calorie Consumption in Industrializing Belgium." *Journal of Economic History* 51(3): 633–655.

Benedict, Carol. 1988. "Bubonic Plague in Nineteenth Century China." *Modern China* 14(2): 107–155.

Bennett, Charles F. 1962. "The Bayano Cuno Indians, Panama: An Ecological Study of Livelihood and Diet." *Annals of the Association of American Geographers* 52(1): 32–50.

Bennike, Pia. 1985. *Paleopathology of Danish Skeletons.* Copenhagen: Akademisk Forlag.

Bergman, Roland W. 1980. *Amazon Economics: The Simplicity of Shipibo Indian Wealth.* Syracuse, N.Y.: Department of Geography, Syracuse University.

Biddick, Kathleen. 1987. "Missing Links: Taxable Wealth, Markets, and Stratification among Medieval English Peasants." *Journal of Interdisciplinary History* 18(2): 277–298.

Blainey, Geoffrey. 1975. *Triumph of the Nomads: A History of Ancient Australia.* Melbourne: Macmillan.

Blanchflower, David G., and Andrew J. Oswald. 2004. "Well-Being over Time in Britain and the USA." *Journal of Public Economics* 88(7–8): 1359–1386.

Blanshei, Sarah R. 1979. "Population, Wealth and Patronage in Medieval and Renaissance Perugia." *Journal of Interdisciplinary History* 9(4): 597–619.

Boag, George L. 1912. *Manual of Railway Statistics.* London: Railway Gazette.

Boaz, Franz. 1891. "Physical Characteristics of the Indians of the North Pacific Coast." *American Anthropologist* 2(4): 321–328.

———. 1899. "Anthropometry of Shoshonean Tribes." *American Anthropologist New Series* 1(4): 751–758.

Boix, Carles, and Frances Rosenbluth. 2004. "Bones of Contention: The Political Economy of Height Inequality." Working Paper, University of Chicago, Department of Political Science.

Borgerhoff-Mulder, Monique. 1987. "On Cultural and Reproductive Success: Kipsigis Evidence." *American Anthropologist* 89: 617–634.

Bougainville, Lewis de. 1772. *A Voyage Round the World,* trans. John Reinhold Forster. London: J. Nourse.

Brassey, Thomas. 1879. *Foreign Work and English Wages.* London: Longmans, Green.

Brennan, Lance, John McDonald, and Ralph Shlomowitz. 1997. "Towards an Anthropometric History of Indians Under British Rule." *Research in Economic History* 17: 185–246.

Broadberry, Steven, and Bishnupriya Gupta. 2006. "The Early Modern Great Divergence: Wages, Prices and Economic Development in Europe and Asia, 1500–1800." *Economic History Review* 59: 2–31.

Broadberry, S., and D. Irwin. 2004. "Labour Productivity in the US and the U.K. during the 19th Century." Discussion Paper 4596. Centre for Economic Policy Research, London.

Brown, Roger L. 1981. "The Rise and Fall of the Fleet Marriages." In *Marriage and Society: Studies in the Social History of Marriage,* ed. R. B. Outhwaite. London: Europa Publications, pp. 117–136.

Bruland, Kristine. 1989. *British Technology and European Industrialization: The Norwegian Textile Industry in the Mid-Nineteenth Century.* Cambridge, U.K.: Cambridge University Press.

Brunt, P. A. 1971. *Italian Manpower, 225 B.C.–14 A.D.* London: Oxford University Press.

Buck, John L. 1930. *Chinese Farm Economy.* Shanghai: University of Nanking.

Bureau of Railway Economics. 1915. *Comparative Railway Statistics: United States and Foreign Countries, 1912.* Washington, D.C.: Bureau of Railway Economics.

Burnette, Joyce. 1997. "An Investigation of the Female-Male Wage Gap during the Industrial Revolution in Britain." *Economic History Review* 50(2): 257–281.

————. 2006. "How Skilled Were Agricultural Labourers in the Early Nineteenth Century?" *Economic History Review* 59(4): 688–716.

Bythell, Duncan. 1969. *The Handloom Weavers: A Study in the English Cotton Industry during the Industrial Revolution.* Cambridge, U.K.: Cambridge University Press.

Campbell, Bruce, James Galloway, Derek Keene, and Margaret Murphy. 1993. *A Medieval Capital and Its Grain Supply: Agrarian Production and Distribution in the London Region c. 1300.* London: Institute of British Geographers.

Chagnon, Napoleon. 1983. *Yanomamo: The Fierce People,* 3rd ed. New York: Holt, Rinehart and Winston.

————. 1988. "Life Histories, Blood Revenge, and Warfare in a Tribal Population." *Science* 239: 985–992.

Chibi, Andrew A. 1998. "The Social and Regional Origins of the Henrician Episcopacy." *Sixteenth Century Journal* 29(4): 955–973.

Cipolla, Carlo M. 1972. "The Diffusion of Innovations in Early Modern Europe." *Comparative Studies in Society and History* 14(1): 46–52.

————. 1993. *Before the Industrial Revolution: European Society and Economy, 1000–1700,* 3rd ed. London: Routledge.

Clarence-Smith, William Gervase. 2005. "The Cotton Textile Industries of Southeast Asia and 'Bantu' Africa, 1840s to 1950s." London: London School of Economics, Global Economic History Network.

Clark, Gregory. 1987a. "Why Isn't the Whole World Developed? Lessons from the Cotton Mills." *Journal of Economic History* 47: 141–173.

————. 1987b. "Productivity Growth Without Technical Change in European Agriculture Before 1850." *Journal of Economic History* 47: 419–432.

————. 1988. "The Cost of Capital and Medieval Agricultural Technique." *Explorations in Economic History* 25: 265–294.

————. 1992. "The Economics of Exhaustion, the Postan Thesis, and the Agricultural Revolution." *Journal of Economic History* 52(1): 61–84.

————. 1994. "Factory Discipline." *Journal of Economic History* 54: 128–163.

————. 1996. "The Political Foundations of Modern Economic Growth: England, 1540–1800." *Journal of Interdisciplinary History* 26: 563–588.

————. 1998. "Land Hunger: Land as a Commodity and as a Status Good in England, 1500–1910." *Explorations in Economic History* 35(1): 59–82.

————. 2001a. "Markets and Economic Growth: The Grain Market of Medieval England." Working Paper, University of California, Davis.

————. 2001b. "Farm Wages and Living Standards in the Industrial Revolution: England, 1670–1869." *Economic History Review* 54(3): 477–505.

————. 2002a. "Farmland Rental Values and Agrarian History: England, 1500–1912." *European Review of Economic History* 6(3): 281–309.

————. 2002b. "The Agricultural Revolution? England, 1500–1912." Working Paper, University of California, Davis.

————. 2003. "Agricultural Wages." In *The Oxford Encylopedia of Economic History*, Vol. 1, ed. Joel Mokyr. Oxford: Oxford University Press, pp. 59–65.

————. 2005. "The Condition of the Working-Class in England, 1209–2004." *Journal of Political Economy* 113(6): 1307–1340.

————. 2007a. "Farm Wages, Population and Economic Growth, England, 1209–1869." *Economic History Review* 60(1): 97–135.

————. 2007b. "The Economic Aggregates for England, 1209–1869." Working Paper, University of California, Davis.

Clark, Gregory, and Gillian Hamilton. 2006. "Survival of the Richest: The Malthusian Method in England, 1585–1638." *Journal of Economic History* 66(3): 707–736.

Clark, Gregory, and David Jacks. 2007. "Coal and the Industrial Revolution." *European Review of Economic History* 11(1).

Clark, Gregory, and Patricia Levin. 2001. "How Different Was the Industrial Revolution? The Revolution in Printing, 1350–1869." Working Paper, University of California, Davis.

Clark, Gregory, and Alan McGinley. 1989. "Selective Pressure and Economic History: Economics in the Very Long Run." Paper presented to the Berkeley-Stanford Economic History Seminar, May 25.

Clark, Gregory, and Ysbrand van der Werf. 1998. "Work in Progress? The Industrious Revolution." *Journal of Economic History* 58(3): 830–843.

Clark, Gregory, Michael Huberman, and Peter Lindert. 1995. "A British Food Puzzle, 1770–1850." *Economic History Review* 48(2): 215–237.

Clark, W. A. Graham. 1907. *The Cotton Industry of British India and the Philippines.* Washington, D.C.: U.S. Government Printing Office.

Cockburn, J. S. 1977. "The Nature and Incidence of Crime in England, 1559–1625: A Preliminary Survey." In *Crime in England, 1550–1800,* ed. J. S. Cockburn. Princeton, N.J.: Princeton University Press, pp. 49–71.

————. 1991. "Patterns of Violence in English Society: Homicide in Kent 1560–1985." *Past and Present* 130: 70–106.

Cohen, Mark Nathan. 1977. *The Food Crisis in Pre-History.* New Haven, Conn.: Yale University Press.

Condorcet, Jean-Antoine-Nicolas, Marquis de. 1795. *Esquisse d'un tableau historique des progrès de l'esprit humain (Sketch for a Historical Picture of the Progress of the Human Mind).* Paris: Agasse.

Cotton Spinning Productivity Team. 1951. *Cotton Spinning.* London: Anglo-American Council on Productivity.

Cotton Yarn Association. 1929. "Statistics Concerning Cotton Spinning in India." *Journal of the Textile Institute. Transactions* 20: T10–T20.

Cousin, Victor. 1854. *Lectures on the True, the Beautiful, and the Good.* New York: D. Appleton.

Crawcour, Sidney. 1961. "The Development of a Credit System in Seventeenth-Century Japan." *Journal of Economic History* 21: 342–360.

Cressy, David. 1980. *Literacy and the Social Order: Reading and Writing in Tudor and Stuart England.* Cambridge, U.K.: Cambridge University Press.

Cronk, Lee. 1991. "Wealth, Status, and Reproductive Success among the Mukogodo of Kenya." *American Anthropologist* 93: 345–360.

Curtin, Philip D. 1989. *Death by Migration: Europe's Encounter with the Tropical World in the Nineteenth Century.* Cambridge, U.K.: Cambridge University Press.

Darwin, Charles. 1859. *On the Origin of Species.* London: John Murray.

———. 1965. *The Voyage of the Beagle.* London: J. M. Dent and Sons.

———. 1969. Autobiography. In *The Autobiography of Charles Darwin, 1809–1882: With Original Omissions Restored,* ed. Nora Barlow. New York: W. W. Norton, pp. 17–146.

———. 1998. *The Descent of Man.* Amherst, N.Y.: Prometheus.

Davis, Lance E., and Robert A. Huttenback. 1986. *Mammon and the Pursuit of Empire: the Economics of British Imperialism.* Cambridge, U.K.: Cambridge University Press.

Deane, Phyllis, and W. A. Cole. 1967. *British Economic Growth, 1688–1959,* 2nd ed. Cambridge, U.K.: Cambridge University Press.

Deaux, George. 1969. *The Black Death.* London: Hamilton.

Deshpande, S. R. 1946. *Report on an Enquiry into Conditions of Labour in the Cotton Mill Industry in India.* Simla: Government of India Press.

De Vries, Jan. 1984. *European Urbanization, 1500–1800.* London: Methuen.

———. 1985. "The Population and Economy of the Pre-Industrial Netherlands." *Journal of Interdisciplinary History* 15(4): 661–682.

———. 1994. "The Industrial Revolution and the Industrious Revolution." *Journal of Economic History* 54: 249–270.

De Vries, Jan, and Ad van der Woude. 1997. *The First Modern Economy: Success, Failure, and Perseverance of the Dutch Economy, 1500–1815.* Cambridge, U.K.: Cambridge University Press.

De Wever, F. 1978. "Rents and Selling Prices of Land at Zele, Sixteenth to Eighteenth Century." In *The Agricultural Development of the Low Countries as Revealed by the Tithe and Rent Statistics, 1250–1800,* eds. Herman van der Wee and E. van Cauwenbere. Leuven: Leuven University Press, pp. 1–23.

Diamond, Jared M. 1987. "The Worst Mistake in the History of the Human Race." *Discover,* May, pp. 64–66.

———. 1997. *Guns, Germs, and Steel: The Fates of Human Societies.* New York: W. W. Norton.

Dickmann, Nicola. 2003. "Fertility and Family Income on the Move: An International Comparison over 20 Years." Working Paper 360, Maxwell School of Citizenship and Public Affairs, Syracuse University.

Divekar, V. D. 1989. *Prices and Wages in Pune Region in a Period of Transition, 1805–1830 AD.* Pune: Gokhale Institute of Politics and Economics.

Doraiswamy, Indra. 1983. "Scope for Increasing Productivity in Spinning Mills." In *Resume of Papers, Twenty-Fourth Technological Conference.* Ahmedabad Textile Research Association, Bombay Textile Research Association, Northern India Textile Reseach Association, South India Textile Research Association. Coimbatore: SITRA.

Dore, Ronald P. 1965. *Education in Tokugawa Japan.* Berkeley: University of California Press.

Dove, Michael R. 1984. "The Chayanov Slope in a Swidden Society." In *Chayanov, Peasants and Economic Anthropology,* ed. E. Paul Durrenberger. Orlando, Fla.: Academic Press, pp. 97–132.

Duncan-Jones, Richard. 1990. *Structure and Scale in the Roman Economy.* Cambridge, U.K.: Cambridge University Press.

Durand, John. 1977. "Historical Estimates of World Population: An Evaluation." *Population and Development Review* 3(3): 253–296.

Dutta, Pratap C. 1984. "Biological Anthropology of Bronze Age Harappans: New Perspectives." In *The People of South Asia: The Biological Anthropology of India, Pakistan, and Nepal,* ed. John R. Lukacs. New York: Plenum Press, pp. 59–76.

Dyer, Christopher. 1988. "Changes in Diet in the Late Middle Ages: The Case of Harvest Workers." *Agricultural History Review* 36(1): 21–37.

Easterlin, Richard A. 1974. "Does Economic Growth Improve the Human Lot? Some Empirical Evidenc." In *Nations and Households in Economic Growth: Essays in Honour of Moses Abramowitz,* ed. Paul A. David and Melvin W. Reder. New York: Academic Press.

———. 2003. "Explaining Happiness." *Proceedings of the National Academy of Sciences of the United States of America* 100(19): 11176–11183.

Easterly, William. 2001. *The Elusive Quest for Growth: Economists' Adventures and Misadventures in the Tropics.* Cambridge, Mass.: MIT Press.

———. 2006. *The White Man's Burden: Why the West's Efforts to Aid the Rest Have Done So Much Ill and So Little Good.* New York: Penguin.

Easterly, William, and Ross Levine. 2001. "It's Not Factor Accumulation: Stylized Facts and Growth Models." *World Bank Economic Review* 15(2): 177–220.

Edelstein, Michael. 1982. *Overseas Investment in the Age of High Imperialism. The United Kingdom, 1850–1914.* New York: Columbia University Press.

Eden, Frederick M. 1797. *The State of the Poor.* London: J. Davis.

Eichengreen, Barry. 1984. "Mortgage Interest Rates in the Populist Era." *American Economic Review* 74(5): 995–1015

Eltis, David. 1982. "Nutritional Trends in Africa and the Americas: Heights of Africans, 1819–1839." *Journal of Interdisciplinary History* 12: 453–475.

Emmison, F. G. 2000. *Essex Wills,* Vol. 12. Chelmsford: Essex Record Office.

Engerman, Stanley L., and Kenneth Sokoloff. 2002. "Factor Endowments, Inequality, and Paths of Development among New World Economics." Working Paper 9259. Cambridge, Mass.: National Bureau of Economic Research.

Epstein, S. R. 1998. "Craft Guilds, Apprenticeship, and Technological Change in Preindustrial Europe." *Journal of Economic History* 58(3): 684–713.

Evans, Nesta. 1987. *The Wills of the Archdeaconry of Sudbury, 1630–35.* Suffolk Records Society, Vol. 29. Woodbridge, Suffolk: Boydell Press.

———. 1993. *The Wills of the Archdeaconry of Sudbury, 1636–38.* Suffolk Records Society, Vol. 35. Woodbridge, Suffolk: Boydell Press.

Everett, Daniel. 2005. "Interview." *Your Manchester,* May, pp. 10–11.

Farber, Howard. 1978. "A Price and Wage Study for Northern Babylonia during the Old Babylonian Period." *Journal of the Economic and Social History of the Orient* 21: 1–51.

Farris, William Wayne. 2006. *Japan's Medieval Population: Famine, Fertility, and Warfare in a Transformative Age.* Honolulu: University of Hawaii Press.

Federico, Giovanni, and Paolo Malanima. 2004. "Progress, Decline, Growth: Product and Productivity in Italian Agriculture, 1000–2000." *Economic History Review* 57(3): 437–464.

Feinstein, Charles. 1972. *National Income, Expenditures and Output of the U.K., 1855–1965.* Cambridge, U.K.: Cambridge University Press.

———. 1998. "Pessimism Perpetuated: Real Wages and the Standard of Living in Britain during and after the Industrial Revolution." *Journal of Economic History* 58(3): 625–658.

Feng, Wang, James Lee, and Cameron Campbell. 1995. "Marital Fertility Control among the Qing Nobility: Implications for Two Types of Preventive Check." *Population Studies* 49: 383–400.

Feuerwerker, Albert. 1984. "The State and Economy in Late Imperial China." *Theory and Society* 13(3): 297–326.

Fielding, Henry. 1731. *The Tragedy of Tragedies, or, The Life and Death of Tom Thumb the Great.* London; J. Roberts.

Filmer, Sir Robert. 1653. *An Advertisement to the Jurymen of England. Together with A Difference between an English and Hebrew Witch.* London: Richard Royston.

Finlay, Robert. 1992. "Portuguese and Chinese Maritime Imperialism: Camoes's Lusiads and Luo Maodeng's Voyage of the San Bao Eunuch." *Comparative Studies in Society and History* 34(2): 225–241.

Fitton, R. S. 1989. *The Arkwrights: Spinners of Fortune.* Manchester: Manchester University Press.

Flinn, Michael W. 1981. *The European Demographic System: 1500–1820.* Baltimore: Johns Hopkins University Press.

Fogel, Robert W., and Stanley Engerman. 1974. *Time on the Cross: The Economics of American Negro Slavery.* Boston: Little, Brown.

Frank, Robert H. 1999. *Luxury Fever: Why Money Fails to Satisfy in an Era of Excess.* New York: Free Press.

Frey, Bruno S., and Alois Stutzer. 2002. "What Can Economists Learn from Happiness Research?" *Journal of Economic Literature* 40(2): 402–435.

Galley, Chris. 1995. "A Model of Early Modern Urban Demography." *Economic History Review* 48(3): 448–469.

Gallup, John Luke, and Jeffrey D. Sachs. 2000. "Agriculture, Climate, and Technology: Why Are the Tropics Falling Behind?" *American Journal of Agricultural Economics* 82(3): 731–737.

Galor, Oded, and Omer Moav. 2002. "Natural Selection and the Origin of Economic Growth." *Quarterly Journal of Economics* 117: 1133–1191.

Galor, Oded, and David N. Weil. 2000. "Population, Technology and Growth: From Malthusian Stagnation to the Demographic Transition and Beyond." *American Economic Review* 90: 806–828.

Gardner, Jonathan, and Andrew J. Oswald. 2007. "Money and Mental Wellbeing: A Longitudinal Study of Medium-Sized Lottery Wins." *Journal of Health Economics* 26(1): 49–60.

Garrett, Eilidh, Alice Read, Kevin Schurer, and Simon Szreter. 2001. *Changing Family Size in England and Wales: Place, Class and Demography, 1891–1911.* Cambridge, U.K.: Cambridge University Press.

Gat, Azar. 2002. "Why City-States Existed? Riddles and Clues of Urbanization and Fortifications." In *A Comparative Study of Six City-State Cultures,* ed. Morgens H. Hansen. Copenhagen: Danish Royal Academy, pp. 125–138.

Geary, Frank, and Tom Stark. 2004. "Trends in Real Wages during the Industrial Revolution: A View from Across the Irish Sea." *Economic History Review* 57: 362–395.

Ghersa, C. M., M. L. Roush, S. R. Radosevich, and S. M. Cordray. 1994. "Coevolution of Agrosystems and Weed Management." *BioScience* 44(2): 85–94.

Given, James B. 1977. *Society and Homicide in Thirteenth Century England.* Stanford, Calif.: Stanford University Press.

Godwin, William. 1793. *Enquiry Concerning Political Justice, and Its Influence on Modern Morals and Happiness.* London: J. Robinson.

Goldstone, Jack A. 1987. "Cultural Orthodoxy, Risk, and Innovation: The Divergence of East and West in the Early Modern World." *Sociological Theory* 5(2): 119–135.

Gordon, Peter. 2004. "Numerical Cognition without Words: Evidence from Amazonia." *Science* 306: 496–499.

Government of India, Ministry of Labour. 1954. *Report on Intensive Survey of Agricultural Labour,* Volume 1: *All India.* New Delhi.

Government of India, Ministry of Statistics and Programme Implementation. 2004. *Housing Stock and Constructions (July-December 2002).* New Delhi.

Gransden, Antonia. 1964. *The Chronicle of Bury St. Edmunds, 1212–1301.* London: Nelson.

Greif, Avner. 2006. *Institutions and the Path to the Modern Economy: Lessons from Medieval Trade.* Cambridge, U.K.: Cambridge University Press.

Griliches, Zvi. 1996. "The Discovery of the Residual: A Historical Note." *Journal of Economic Literature* 34(3): 1324–1330.

Gross, Daniel R. 1984. "Time Allocation: A Tool for the Study of Cultural Behavior." *Annual Review of Anthropology* 13: 519–558.

Guilaine, Jean, and Jean Zammit. 2005. *The Origins of War: Violence in Pre-History.* Oxford: Blackwell.

Guppy, H. B. 1886. "On the Physical Characters of the Solomon Islanders." *Journal of the Anthropological Institute of Great Britain and Ireland* 15: 266–285.

Hadeishi, Hajime. 2003. "Economic Well-Being and Fertility in France: Nuits, 1744–1792." *Journal of Economic History* 63(2): 489–505.

Haines, Michael R. 1995. "Socio-economic Differentials in Infant and Child Mortality during Mortality Decline: England and Wales, 1890–1911." *Population Studies* 49(2): 297–315.

Hair, P. E. H. 1971. "Deaths from Violence in Britain: A Tentative Secular Survey." *Population Studies* 25(1): 5–24.

Hajnal, John. 1965. "European Marriage Patterns in Perspective." In *Population in History: Essays in Historical Demography,* eds. D. V. Glass and D. E. C. Eversley. London: Edward Arnold, pp. 101–143.

Hamilton, Gillian, and Gregory Clark. 2006. "Economic Status and Reproductive Success in New France." Working Paper, University of Toronto.

Hanawalt, Barbara A. 1976. "Violent Death in England in the Fourteenth- and Early Fifteenth Centuries." *Comparative Studies in Society and History* 18: 297–320.

———. 1979. *Crime and Conflict in Medieval England, 1300–48.* Cambridge, Mass.: Harvard University Press.

Hanley, Susan B. 1997. *Everyday Things in Premodern Japan: The Hidden Legacy of Material Culture.* Berkeley: University of California Press.

Harley, C. Knick. 1998. "Cotton Textile Prices and the Industrial Revolution." *Economic History Review* 51(1): 49–83.

Harris, Rivkah. 1968. "Some Aspects of the Centralization of the Realm Under Hammurapi and His Successors." *Journal of the American Oriental Society* 88(4): 727–732.

Harvey, Barbara. 1993. *Living and Dying in England 1100–1540: The Monastic Experience.* Oxford: Clarendon Press.

Hauser, William B. 1974. *Economic Change in Tokugawa Japan: Osaka and the Kinai Cotton Trade.* New York: Cambridge University Press.

Hawkes, Ernest William. 1916. "Skeletal Measurements and Observations of the Point Barrow Eskimo with Comparisons with Other Eskimo Groups." *American Anthropologist, New Series* 18(2): 203–244.

Headrick, Daniel. 1988. *The Tentacles of Progress: Technology Transfer in the Age of Imperialism, 1850–1940.* Oxford: Oxford University Press.

Helps, Arthur. 1874. *Life and Labours of Mr. Brassey, 1805–1870.* Boston: Roberts Brothers.

Henderson, W. O. 1965. *Britain and Industrial Europe, 1750–1870: Studies in British Influence on the Industrial Revolution in Western Europe.* Leicester: Leicester University Press.

Herlihy, David. 1967. *Medieval and Renaissance Pistoia; The Social History of an Italian Town, 1200–1430.* New Haven, Conn.: Yale University Press.

Heston, Alan. 1983. "National Income." In *The Cambridge Economic History of India,* Vol. 2: c. 1757–c. 1970, eds. Dharma Kumar and Meghnad Desai. New York: Cambridge University Press, pp. 376–462.

Heston, Alan, Robert Summers, and Bettina Aten. 2006. Penn World Table Version 6.2. Philadelphia: Center for International Comparisons of Production, Income and Prices at the University of Pennsylvania.

Hill, Kim, and A. M. Hurtado. 1996. *Ache Life History: The Ecology and Demography of a Foraging People.* New York: Aldine de Gruyter.

Ho, Jun Seong, and James B. Lewis. 2006. "Wages, Rents and Interest Rates in Southern Korea, 1700–1900." *Research in Economic History* 24: 217–283.

Ho, Ping-Ti. 1959. "Aspects of Social Mobility in China, 1368–1911." *Comparative Studies in Society and History* 1(4): 330–359.

Hobbes, Thomas. 1651. *Leviathan.* London.

Hollingsworth, Thomas H. 1965. *The Demography of the British Peerage.* London: Population Investigation Committee, LSE.

Homer, Sidney, and Richard Sylla. 1996. *A History of Interest Rates,* 3rd ed. New Brunswick, N.J.: Rutgers University Press.

Hopkins, Keith. 1966. "On the Probable Age Structure of the Roman Population." *Population Studies* 20(2): 245–264.

Houghton, Philip. 1996. *People of the Great Ocean: Aspects of the Human Biology of the Early Pacific.* Cambridge, U.K.: Cambridge University Press.

Houston, R. A. 1982. "The Development of Literacy: Northern England, 1640–1750." *Economic History Review* 35: 199–216.

Hudson, Michael. 2000. "How Interest Rates Were Set, 2500 BC–1000 AD: Máš, Tokos, and Foenus as Metaphors for Interest Accruals." *Journal of the Economic and Social History of the Orient* 43(2): 132–161.

Hunter, Richard A., and Ida Macalpine. 1963. *Three Hundred Years of Psychiatry, 1535–1860.* London: Oxford University Press.

Hurtado, A. Magdalena, and Kim R. Hill. 1987. "Early Dry Season Subsistence Ecology of Cuiva (Hiwi) Foragers of Venezuela." *Human Ecology* 15(2): 163–187.

———. 1990. "Seasonality in Foraging Society: Variation in Diet, Work Effort, Fertility, and Sexual Division of Labor among the Hiwi of Venezuela." *Journal of Anthropological Research* 46(3): 293–346.

Hutchins, John, Richard Gough, and J. B. Nichols. 1796. *The History and Antiquities of the County of Dorset,* Vol. 1. London: J. Nichols.

Ingram, Martin. 1985. "The Reform of Popular Culture? Sex and Marriage in Early Modern England." In *Popular Culture in the Seventeenth Century,* ed. Barry Reay. Kent, U.K.: Beckenham, pp. 129–165.

International Labour Organization, Bureau of Statistics. 2006a. *Occupational Wages and Hours of Work and Retail Food Prices: Statistics from the ILO October Inquiry.* Geneva: International Labour Organization.

———. 2006b. *Yearbook of Labour Statistics.* Geneva: International Labour Organization.

Jackson, Stanley. 1968. *The Sassoons.* London: Heinemann.

Jacob, William. 1826. *Report on the Trade in Foreign Corn and on the Agriculture of the North of Europe.* London: James Ridgeway.

Jannetta, Ann Bowman. 1992. "Famine Mortality in Nineteenth Century Japan: The Evidence from a Temple Death Register." *Population Studies* 46(3): 427–443.

Jannetta, Ann Bowman, and Samuel Preston. 1991. "Two Centuries of Mortality Change in Central Japan: The Evidence from a Temple Death Register." *Population Studies* 45(3): 417–436.

Jeans, James. 1884. "On the Comparative Efficiency and Earnings of Labour at Home and Abroad." *Journal of the Statistical Society of London* 47(4): 614–665.

Jenike, Mark R. 2001. "Nutritional Ecology: Diet, Physical Activity, and Body Size." In *Hunter-Gatherers: an Interdisciplinary Perspective,* eds. Catherine Panter-Brick, Robert H. Layton, and Peter Rowley-Conwy. Cambridge, U.K.: Cambridge University Press, pp. 205–238.

Jevons, F. B. 1895. "Work and Wages in Athens." *Journal of Hellenistic Studies* 15: 239–247.

———. 1896. "Some Ancient Greek Pay Bills." *Economic Journal* 6(23): 470–475.

Johnson, A. 1975. "Time Allocation in a Michiguenga Community." *Ethnology* 14(3): 310–321.

Johnson, Allen C. 1936. *Roman Egypt to the Reign of Diocletian: An Economic Survey of Ancient Rome,* Vol. II, ed. Tenney Frank. Baltimore: Johns Hopkins University Press.

Jones, Charles I. 2002. *Introduction to Economic Growth,* 2nd ed. New York: W. W. Norton.

Jones, Rhys. 1977. "The Tasmanian Paradox." In *Stone Tools as Cultural Markers,* ed. R. V. S. Wright. Canberra: Australian Institute of Aboriginal Studies, pp. 189–204.

———. 1978. "Why Did the Tasmanians Stop Eating Fish?" In *Explorations in Ethno-archaeology,* ed. R. A. Gould. Albuquerque: University of New Mexico Press, pp. 11–48.

Jun, By Seong Ho, and James B. Lewis. 2006. "Labor Costs, Land Prices, Land Rent, and Interest Rates in the Southern Region of Korea." *Research in Economic History* 24: 217–283.

Kahneman, Daniel, Alan B. Krueger, David Schkade, Norbert Schwarz, and Arthur Stone. 2004. "Toward National Well-Being Accounts." *American Economic Review* 94(2): 429–434.

Kalas, Robert J. 1996. "Marriage, Clientage, Office Holding, and the Advancement of the Early Modern French Nobility: The Noailles Family of Limousin." *Sixteenth Century Journal* 27(2): 365–383.

Kamps, Christophe. 2004. "New Estimates of Government Net Capital Stocks for 22 OECD countries 1960–2001." IMF Working Paper 04/67. Washington, D.C.: International Monetary Fund.

Kaplan, David. 2000. "The Darker Side of the 'Original Affluent Society.'" *Journal of Anthropological Research* 56(3): 301–324.

Kaplan, Hillard, and Kim Hill. 1992. "The Evolutionary Ecology of Food Acquisition." In *Evolutionary Ecology and Human Behavior,* eds. E. Smith and B. Winterhalder. New York: Aldine de Gruyter, pp. 167–202.

Kelly, Robert L. 1995. *The Foraging Spectrum: Diversity in Hunter-Gatherer Lifeways.* Washington, D.C.: Smithsonian Institution Press.

Kirkaldy, Adam W. 1914. *British Shipping: Its History, Organization and Importance.* London: Kegan Paul, Trench, Trubner.

Knauft, Bruce M. 1987. "Reconsidering Violence in Simple Human Societies: Homicide among the Gebusi of New Guinea." *Current Anthropology* 28(4): 457–500.

Koepke, Nikola, and Joerg Baten. 2005. "The Biological Standard of Living in Europe during the Last Two Millennia." *European Review of Economic History* 9(1): 61–95.

Komlos, John. 1993. "A Malthusian Episode Revisited: The Height of British and Irish Servants in Colonial America." *Economic History Review* 46: 768–782.

———. 1998. "Shrinking in a Growing Economy? The Mystery of Physical Stature during the Industrial Revolution." *Journal of Economic History* 58(3): 779–802.

———. 2004. "On British Pygmies and Giants: The Physical Stature of British Youth in the 18th and 19th Centuries." Working Paper, University of Munich.

Krause, Kate, and William T. Harbaugh. 1999. "Economic Experiments That You Can Perform at Home on Your Children." Working Paper, University of New Mexico.

Kremer, Michael. 1993a. "The O-Ring Theory of Development." *Quarterly Journal of Economics* 108(3): 551–575.

————. 1993b. "Population Growth and Technological Change: One Million B.C. to 1990." *Quarterly Journal of Economics* 108(3): 681–716.

Landers, John. 1993. *Death and the Metropolis: Studies in the Demographic History of London, 1670–1830.* Cambridge, U.K.: Cambridge University Press.

Landes, David. 1998. *The Wealth and Poverty of Nations. Why Some Are So Rich and Some So Poor.* London: Little, Brown.

Larsen, Clark Spencer. 1995. "Biological Changes in Human Populations with Agriculture." *Annual Review of Anthropology* 24: 185–213.

Larsen, Jakob A. O. 1938. "Roman Greece." In *An Economic Survey of Ancient Rome,* Vol. IV, ed. Tenney Frank. Baltimore: Johns Hopkins University Press, pp. 259–498.

Lee, James Z., and Cameron Campbell. 1997. *Fate and Fortune in Rural China: Social Organization and Population Behavior in Liaoning, 1774–1873.* Cambridge, U.K.: Cambridge University Press.

Lee, James Z., and Wang Feng. 1999. *One Quarter of Humanity: Malthusian Mythology and Chinese Realities, 1700–2000.* Cambridge, Mass.: Harvard University Press.

Lee, Ronald D., and R. S. Schofield. 1981. "British Population in the Eighteenth Century." In *The Economic History of Britain since 1700,* Vol. 1: *1700–1860,* eds. Roderick Floud and Donald McCloskey. Cambridge, U.K.: Cambridge University Press, pp. 17–35.

Le Roy Ladurie, Emmanuel. 1981. "History That Stands Still." In *The Mind and Method of the Historian.* Brighton, Sussex:: Harvester Press, pp. 1–27.

Levine, Ruth, and the What Works Working Group with Molly Kinder. 2004. *Millions Saved: Proven Success in Global Health.* Washington, D.C.: Center for Global Development.

Lindert, Peter H. 1986. "Unequal English Wealth since 1670." *Journal of Political Economy* 94(6): 1127–1162.

————. 2004. *Growing Public: Social Spending and Economic Growth since the Eighteenth Century,* Vol. 1. Cambridge, U.K.: Cambridge University Press.

Lindert, Peter H., and Jeffrey G. Williamson. 1983. "English Workers' Living Standards during the Industrial Revolution: A New Look." *Economic History Review* 36(1): 1–25.

————. 1985. "English Workers' Real Wages: Reply to Crafts." *Journal of Economic History* 45: 145–153.

Lizot, J. 1977. "Population, Resources and Warfare among the Yanomame." *Man, New Series* 12(3/4): 497–517.

Long, Pamela. 1991. "Invention, Authorship, 'Intellectual Property,' and the Origin of Patents: Notes Towards a Conceptual History." *Technology and Culture* 32: 846–884.

Lucas, Robert. 1988. "On the Mechanics of Economic Development." *Journal of Monetary Economics* 22: 3–42.

Lucas, Robert E. 2002. "The Industrial Revolution: Past and Future." In *Lectures on Economic Growth*. Cambridge, Mass.: Harvard University Press, pp. 109–188.

Macfarlane, Alan. 1978. *The Origins of English Individualism: The Family, Property, and Social Transition*. Oxford: Blackwell.

———. 1987. *Marriage and Love in England: Modes of Reproduction 1300–1840*. Oxford: Blackwell.

———. 2003. *The Savage Wars of Peace: England, Japan and the Malthusian Trap*. Basingstoke, Hampshire: Palgrave Macmillan.

MacGregor, John. 1850. *Commercial Statistics, A Digest*, Vol. 4. London: Whittaker.

Maddison, Angus. 2001. *The World Economy: A Millennial Perspective*. Paris: OECD.

Malthus, Thomas Robert. 1798. *An Essay on the Principle of Population*, ed. Anthony Flew. Aylesbury, Buckinghamshire: Penguin Books, 1970.

———. 1830. *A Summary View of the Principle of Population*. Aylesbury, Buckinghamshire: Penguin Books, 1970.

Marx, Karl. 1904. *A Contribution to the Critique of Political Economy*, trans. N. I. Stone. Chicago: C. H. Kerr.

———. 1990. *Capital*, Vol. 1, trans. Ben Fowkes. New York: Penguin Classics.

Marx, Karl, and Friedrich Engels. 1967. *The Communist Manifesto*, trans. Samuel Moore. Baltimore: Penguin.

Masali, M. 1972. "Bone Size and Proportions as Revealed by Bone Measurements and Their Meaning in Environmental Adaptation." *Journal of Human Evolution* 1: 187–197.

Mauro, Paolo, Nathan Sussman, and Yishay Yafeh. 2006. *Emerging Markets and Financial Globalization: Sovereign Bond Spreads in 1870–1913 and Today*. Oxford: Oxford University Press.

Mazumdar, Dipak. 1984. "The Issue of Small versus Large in the Indian Textile Industry: An Analytical and Historical Survey." World Bank Staff Working Paper 645. Washington, D.C.: World Bank.

McCloskey, Donald. 1981. "The Industrial Revolution 1780–1860: A Survey." In *The Economic History of Britain since 1700*, eds. Roderick Flood and Donald McCloskey. Cambridge, U.K.: Cambridge University Press, pp. 103–127.

McCulloch, J. R. 1881. *The Works of David Ricardo*. London: John Murray.

McDaniel, Antonio. 1992. "Extreme Mortality in Nineteenth-Century Africa: The Case of Liberian Immigrants." *Demography* 29(4): 581–594.

McEvedy, Colin, and Richard Jones. 1978. *Atlas of World Population History*. London: A. Lane.

McGhee, Robert. 1994. "Disease and the Development of Inuit Culture." *Current Anthropology* 35(5): 565–594.

McIntosh, Marjorie. 1980. "Land, Tenure and Population on the Royal Manor of Havering, 1251–1352/3." *Economic History Review* 33(1): 17–31.

McNeill, William H. 1976. *Plagues and Peoples.* New York: Anchor Books.

Mduma, Simon A. R., A. R. E. Sinclair, and Ray Hilborn. 1999. "Food Regulates the Serengeti Wildebeest: A 40-Year Record." *Journal of Animal Ecology* 68(6): 1101–1122.

Meiklejohn, Christopher, and Marek Zvelebil. 1991. "Health Status of European Populations at the Agricultural Transition and the Implications for the Adoption of Farming." In *Health in Past Societies: Biocultural Interpretations of Human Skeletal Remains in Archaeological Contexts,* eds. Helen Bush and Marek Zvelebil. British Archaeological Reports International Series 567. Oxford. Tempus Reparatum.

Mellink, Machteld J., and J. Lawrence Angel. 1970. "Excavations at Karatas-Semay U.K. and Elmali, Lycia, 1969." *American Journal of Archaeology* 74(3): 245–259.

Minge-Klevana, Wanda. 1980. "Does Labor Time Increase with Industrialization? A Survey of Time-Allocation Studies." *Current Anthropology* 21(3): 279–298.

Mischel, Walter, Yuichi Shoda, and Monica L. Rodriguez. 1989. "Delay of Gratification in Children." *Science* 244: 933–938.

Misra, Sanjiv. 1993. *India's Textile Sector: A Policy Analysis.* New Delhi: Sage.

Mitchell, Brian R. 1995. *International Historical Statistics: Africa, Asia and Oceania, 1750–1988.* New York: Stockton Press.

———. 1998a. *International Historical Statistics: Europe, 1750–1993.* New York: Grove's Dictionaries.

———. 1998b. *International Historical Statistics: The Americas, 1750–1993.* New York: Stockton Press.

Mitchell, B. R., and Phyllis Deane. 1971. *Abstract of British Historical Statistics.* Cambridge, U.K.: Cambridge University Press.

Mody, R.K.P. 1951. "Maximising Mill Output and Efficiency: Practical Hints to Jobbers and Mukadams." *Indian Textile Journal* 61(731): 718–721.

Mokyr, Joel. 1988. "Is There Still Life in the Pessimist Case? Consumption during the Industrial Revolution, 1790–1850." *Journal of Economic History* 48(1): 69–92.

———. 1990. *The Lever of Riches: Technological Creativity and Economic Progress.* New York: Oxford University Press.

———. 2002. *The Gifts of Athena: Historical Foundations of the Knowledge Economy.* Princeton, N.J.: Princeton University Press.

———. 2005. "The Intellectual Origins of Modern Economic Growth." *Journal of Economic History* 65(2): 285–351.

———. 2006. "Mobility, Creativity, and Technological Development: David Hume, Immanuel Kant and the Economic Development of Europe." In *Kolloquiumsband of the XX. Deutschen Kongresses für Philosophie,* ed. G. Abel. Berlin, pp. 1131–161.

Moore, Ray A. 1969. "Samurai Discontent and Social Mobility in the Late Tokugawa Period." *Monumenta Nipponica* 24(1–2): 79–91.

————. 1970. "Adoption and Samurai Mobility in Tokugawa Japan." *Journal of Asian Studies* 29: 617–632.

Morgan, Stephen L. 2006. "Height, Health and Welfare in South China over the Past Two Centuries." Working Paper, Melbourne University.

Morris, Morris D. 1965. *The Emergence of an Industrial Labor Force in India.* Berkeley: University of California Press.

Morris, Morris D., and Clyde B. Dudley. 1975. "Selected Railway Statistics for the Indian Subcontinent (India, Pakistan and Bangladesh), 1853–1946/7." *Artha Vijnana* 17(3): 202–204.

Murray, Alexander. 1978. *Reason and Society in the Middle Ages.* Oxford: Clarendon Press.

Nakamura, James I. 1981. "Human Capital Accumulation in Pre-Modern Japan." *Journal of Economic History* 41(2): 263–281.

Newman, Richard. 1981. *Workers and Unions in Bombay 1918–1929: A Study of Organisation in the Cotton Mills.* Canberra: Australian National University Monographs.

Nicholas, Stephen, and Richard H. Steckel. 1991. "Heights and Living Standards of English Workers during the Early Years of Industrialization, 1770–1815." *Journal of Economic History* 51(4): 937–957.

Nordhoff, Charles. 1934. *Pitcairn's Island.* Boston: Little, Brown.

North, Douglass C. 1981. *Structure and Change in Economic History.* New York: W. W. Norton.

————. 1994. "Economic Performance through Time." *American Economic Review* 84(3): 359–368.

North, Douglass C., and R. P. Thomas. 1973. *The Rise of the Western World.* Cambridge, U.K.: Cambridge University Press.

North, Douglass C., and Barry Weingast. 1989. "Constitutions and Commitment: Evolution of Institutions Governing Public Choice in Seventeenth Century England." *Journal of Economic History* 49: 803–832.

Obstfeld, Maurice, and Alan Taylor. 2004. *Global Capital Markets: Integration, Crisis, and Growth.* Cambridge, U.K.: Cambridge University Press.

Office of the Textile Commissioner, Mumbai. 1997. *Compendium of Textile Statistics, 1997.* Mumbai, India.

————. 1998. *Basic Textile Statistics for 1997–8.* Mumbai, India.

Ogden, Cynthia L., Cheryl D. Fryar, Margaret D. Carroll, and Katherine M. Flegal. 2004. *Mean Body Weight, Height, and Body Mass Index, United States 1960–2002.* Advance Data from Vital and Health Statistics 347. Hyattsville, Md.: National Center for Health Statistics.

Ó Gráda, Cormac. 1999. *Black '47 and Beyond: The Great Irish Famine in History, Economy, and Memory.* Princeton, N.J.: Princeton University Press.

Oliver, Douglas L. 1974. *Ancient Tahitian Society,* Vol. 1: *Ethnography.* Honolulu: University Press of Hawaii.

Olson, Mancur. 1993. "Dictatorship, Democracy and Development." *American Political Science Review* 87(3): 567–576.

O'Rourke, Kevin, and Jeffrey G. Williamson. 2001. *Globalization and History: The Evolution of a Nineteenth-Century Atlantic Economy.* Cambridge: Mass.: MIT Press.

———. 2002a. "When Did Globalization Begin?" *European Review of Economic History* 6: 23–50.

———. 2002b. "After Columbus: Explaining the Global Trade Boom, 1500–1800." *Journal of Economic History* 62(2): 417–456.

Oswald, Andrew J., and Nattavudh Powdthavee. 2007. "Obesity, Unhappiness and *The Challenge of Affluence:* Theory and Evidence." Working Paper, University of Warwick.

Oulton, Nicholas. 2001. "Measuring Capital Services in the United Kingdom." *Bank of England Quarterly Bulletin,* Autumn, pp. 295–307.

Overton, Mark. 1996. *Agricultural Revolution in England: The Transformation of the Agrarian Economy 1500–1850.* Cambridge, U.K.: Cambridge University Press.

Pack, Howard. 1987. *Productivity, Technology and Industrial Development: A Case Study in Textiles.* New York: Oxford University Press.

Palumbi, Stephen R. 2001. "Humans as the World's Greatest Evolutionary Source." *Science* 293: 1786–1790.

Pamuk, Sevket. 1987. *The Ottoman Empire and European Capitalism, 1820–1913: Trade, Investment, and Production.* Cambridge, U.K.: Cambridge University Press.

———. 2005. "Urban Real Wages around the Eastern Mediterranean in Comparative Perspective, 1100–2000." *Research in Economic History* 23: 213–232.

———. 2006. "Evolution of Financial Institutions in the Ottoman Empire, 1600–1840." Working Paper, Bogazici University.

Parliamentary Papers. 1834. *Royal Commission on the Employment of Children in Factories, Supplementary Report.* Vol. XIX.

———. 1870. *Annual Statement of Trade.* Vol. LXIII.

———. 1909a. *Royal Commission on Shipping Rings.* Vols. XLVII, XLVIII.

———. 1909b. *Report of the Indian Factory Labour Commission,* Vol. 2: *Evidence.* Vol. LXIII.

Parthasarathi, Prasannan. 1998. "Rethinking Wages and Competitiveness in the Eighteenth Century: Britain and South India." *Past and Present* 158: 79–109.

Passin, Herbert. 1965. *Society and Education in Japan.* New York: Teachers College Press.

Pearse, Arno S. 1929. *The Cotton Industry of Japan and China.* Manchester.

———. 1930. *The Cotton Industry of India: Being the Report of the Journey to India.* Manchester: Taylor, Garnett, Evans.

Pelletier, David L., Jan W. Low, and Louis A. H. Msukwa. 1991. "Malawi Maternal and Child Nutrition Survey: Study Design and Anthropometric Characteristics of Children and Adults." *American Journal of Human Biology* 3(4): 347–361.

Penn World Tables. http://www.bized.ac.U.K./dataserv/penndata/penn.htm.

Pennington, Renee. 2001. "Hunter Gatherer Demography." In *Hunter-Gatherers: An Interdisciplinary Perspective,* eds. Catherine Panter-Brick, Robert H. Layton, and Peter Rowley-Conwy. Cambridge, U.K.: Cambridge University Press, pp. 171–204.

Pepys, Samuel. 2000. *The Diary of Samuel Pepys,* ed. Robert Latham and William Matthews. Berkeley: University of California Press.

Perkins, Dwight. 1969. *Agricultural Development in China, 1368–1968.* Chicago: Aldine.

Pitt, David C. 1970. *Tradition and Economic Progress in Samoa: A Case Study of the Role of Traditional Social Institutions in Economic Development.* Oxford: Clarendon Press.

Pomeranz, Kenneth. 2000. *The Great Divergence: China, Europe, and the Making of the Modern World Economy.* Princeton, N.J.: Princeton University Press.

Powell, Marvin A. 1990 "Identification and Interpretation of Long Term Price Fluctuations in Babylonia: More on the History of Money in Mesopotamia." *Altorientalische Forschungen* 17(1): 76–99.

Power, Chris, Orly Manor, and Leah Li. 2002. "Are Inequalities in Height Underestimated by Adult Social Positions? Effects of Changing Social Structure and Height Selection in a Cohort Study." *British Medical Journal* 325: 131–134.

Prados de la Escosura, Leandro. 2000. "International Comparisons of Real Product, 1820–1990: An Alternative Data Set." *Explorations in Economic History* 37(1): 1–41.

Prescott, Edward C. 2004. "Why Do Americans Work So Much More Than Europeans?" *Federal Reserve Bank, Minneapolis–Quarterly Review* 28(1): 2–14.

Prestwich, Michael. 1996. *Arms and Warfare in the Middle Ages: The English Experience.* New Haven, Conn.: Yale University Press.

Psacharopoulos, George. 1994. "Returns to Investment in Education: A Global Update." *World Development* 22(9): 1325–1343.

Rajamanickam, R., and R. Ranganathan. 1997. *Labour and Machine Productivity in Spinning,* Part 1. Coimbature: SITRA.

Ramsay, James H. 1903. "Chroniclers' Estimates of Numbers and Official Records." *English Historical Review* 18(72): 625–629.

Rastall, Walter H. 1922. *Asiatic Markets for Industrial Machinery.* Special Agent Series 215. Washington, D.C.: U.S. Department of Commerce, Bureau of Foreign and Domestic Commerce.

Rathbone, Dominic. 1991. *Economic Rationalism and Rural Society in Third-Century A.D. Egypt.* Cambridge, U.K.: Cambridge University Press.

Ratnam, T. V., and R. Rajamanickam. 1980. "Productivity in Spinning: Growth and Prospects." In *Resume of Papers: Twenty-First Technological Conference.* Ahmedabad Textile Research Association, Bombay Textile Research Association, Northern India Textile Reseach Association, South India Textile Research Association. Bombay: BTRA.

Rawski, Evelyn Sakahida. 1979. *Education and Popular Literacy in Ch'ing China.* Ann Arbor: University of Michigan Press.

Rayner, J. L., and G. T. Crook. 1926. *The Complete Newgate Calendar,* Vol. 5. London: Navarre Society.

Razi, Zvi. 1980. *Life, Marriage and Death in a Medieval Parish: Economy, Society and Demography in Halesowen, 1270–1400.* Cambridge, U.K.: Cambridge University Press.

———. 1981. "Family, Land and the Village Community in Later Medieval England." *Past and Present* 93: 3–36.

Razzell, Peter. 1994. *Essays in English Population History.* London: Caliban.

Rhode, Paul W. 1995. "Learning, Capital Accumulation, and the Transformation of California Agriculture." *Journal of Economic History* 55(4): 773–800.

Ricardo, David. 1821. *The Principles of Political Economy and Taxation,* 3rd ed. London: John Murray.

Richerson, Peter J., Robert Boyd, and Robert L. Bettinger. 2001. "Was Agriculture Impossible during the Pleistocene but Mandatory during the Holocene? A Climate Change Hypothesis." *American Antiquity* 66(3): 387–411.

Robertson, George. 1955. *An Account of the Discovery of Tahiti. From the Journal of George Robertson,* ed. Oliver Warner. London: Folio Society.

Robinson, Eric H. 1974. "The Early Diffusion of Steam Power." *Journal of Economic History* 34(1): 91–107.

Rodrigues, Joao. 1973. *The Island of Japon,* trans. and ed. Michael Cooper. Tokyo: Kodansha International.

Rogers, Alan R. 1994. "Evolution of Time Preference by Natural Selection." *American Economic Review* 84(3): 460–481.

Roy, Subrata K. 1995. "Comparative Study of Physiological and Anthropometric Characteristics of High and Low Productivity Workers in Northern West Bengal, India." *American Journal of Human Biology* 7(6): 693–699.

Rubinstein, W. D. 1981. *Men of Property: The Very Wealthy in Britain since the Industrial Revolution.* London: Croom Helm.

Rudraswamy, V. 1957. *A Study of Absenteeism in Textile Mills.* Research Reports 2(5). Coimbatore: Southern India Textile Research Association.

———. 1967. "Absenteeism in South Indian Textile Industry." In *Proceedings of the Conference on Human Factors in Industry.* Bombay: Bombay Textile Research Association, pp. 109–125.

Rundall, Thomas. 1850. *Memorials of the Empire of Japon in the XVI and XVII Centuries*. London: Hakluyt Society.

Russell, Josiah C. 1948. *English Medieval Population*. Albuquerque, N.M.: University of New Mexico Press.

Russell, M. J. 1959. "Hired Champions." *American Journal of Legal History* 3(3): 242–259.

Rutnagur, S. M. 1927. *Bombay Industries: The Cotton Mills*. Bombay: Indian Textile Journal.

Sachs, Jeffrey D. 2001. "Tropical Underdevelopment." Working Paper 8119. Cambridge, Mass.: National Bureau of Economic Research.

Sahlins, Marshall. 1972. *Stone Age Economics*. Chicago: Aldine-Atherton.

Scaglion, Richard. 1986. "The Importance of Nighttime Observations in Time Allocation Studies." *American Ethnologist* 13(3): 537–545.

Schama, Simon. 1987. *The Embarrassment of Riches: An Interpretation of Dutch Culture in the Golden Age*. London: Collins.

Schneider, Friedrich, and Dominik H. Enste. 2000. "Shadow Economies: Size, Causes and Consequences." *Journal of Economic Literature* 38(1): 77–114.

Schofield, Roger. 1973. "Dimensions of Illiteracy, 1750–1850." *Explorations in Economic History* 10: 437–454.

Shannon, Fred A. 1927. "The Life of the Common Soldier in the Union Army, 1861–1865." *Mississippi Valley Historical Review* 13(4): 465–482.

Schulze-Gaevernitz, G. von. 1895. *The Cotton Trade in England and on the Continent*. London: Simpkin, Marshall, Hamilton, Kent.

Schumpeter, Elizabeth B. 1960. *English Overseas Trade Statistics, 1697–1808*. Oxford: Clarendon Press.

Sharma, R. S. 1965. "Usury in Early Mediaeval India (A.D. 400–1200)." *Comparative Studies in Society and History* 8(1): 56–77.

Shindo, Takehiro. 1961. *Labor in the Japanese Cotton Industry*. Tokyo: Japan Society for the Promotion of Science.

Shirras, G. Findlay. 1923. *Report of an Enquiry into the Wages and Hours of Labour in the Cotton Mill Industry*. Bombay: Labour Office, Government of Bombay.

Shiue, Carol, and Wolfgang Keller. 2007. "Markets in China and Europe on the Eve of the Industrial Revolution." *American Economic Review*, forthcoming.

Singer, H. W. 1941. "An Index of Urban Land Rents and House Rents in England and Wales, 1845–1913." *Econometrica* 9(3/4): 221–230.

Siskind, Janet. 1973. *To Hunt in the Morning*. Oxford: Oxford University Press.

Smits, Jan-Pieter, Edwin Horlings, and Jan Luiten van Zanden. 2000. *Dutch GNP and Its Components, 1800–1913*. Groningen Growth and Development Center.

Snell, Daniel C. 1997. *Life in the Ancient Near East, 3100–332 B.C.E.* New Haven, Conn.: Yale University Press.

Solow, Robert M. 1956. "A Contribution to the Theory of Economic Growth." *Quarterly Journal of Economics* 70: 65–94.

Sreenivasan, Kasthuri. 1984. *India's Textile Industry: A Socioeconomic Analysis.* Coimbatore: SITRA.

Steckel, Richard H. 1995. "Stature and the Standard of Living." *Journal of Economic Literature* 33: 1903–1940.

———. 2001. "Health and Nutrition in the PreIndustrial Era: Insights from a Millennium of Average Heights in Northern Europe." Working Paper 8542. Cambridge, Mass.: National Bureau of Economic Research.

Steckel, Richard H., and Joseph M. Prince. 2001. "Tallest in the World: Native Americans of the Great Plains in the Nineteenth Century." *American Economic Review* 91(1): 287–294.

Stein, Burton. 1960. "The Economic Function of a Medieval South Indian Temple." *Journal of Asian Studies* 19(2): 163–176.

Stiner, Mary C. 2001. "Thirty Years On: The 'Broad Spectrum Revolution' and Paleolithic Demography." *Proceedings of the National Academy of Sciences* 98(13): 6993–6996.

———. 2005. *The Faunas of Hayonim Cave, Israel.* Cambridge, Mass.: Harvard University Press.

Stinson, Sara. 1992. "Nutritional Adaptation." *Annual Review of Anthropology* 21: 143–170.

Stuart, William. 1902. "The Value of Chinese as Compared with White Labour." In *Proceedings of the Society and Report of the Council, 1901–2.* Shanghai: Engineering Society of China, pp. 75–97.

Sussman, Nathan. 2005. "Income Inequality in Paris in the Heyday of the Commercial Revolution." Manuscript, Hebrew University, Department of Economics.

Tann, Jennifer, and M. J. Breckin. 1978. "The International Diffusion of the Watt Engine." *Economic History Review* 31(4): 541–564.

Temple, Robert. 1986. *The Genius of China. 3,000 Years of Science, Discovery, and Invention.* New York: Simon and Schuster.

Textile Council. 1969. *Cotton and Allied Textiles.* Manchester.

Thompson, F. M. L. 1976. "Nineteenth Century Horse Sense." *Economic History Review* 29(1): 60–81.

Thrupp, Sylvia. 1957. "A Survey of the Alien Population of England in 1440." *Speculum* 32(2): 262–273.

Tomasson, Richard F. 1977. "A Millennium of Misery: The Demography of the Icelanders." *Population Studies* 31(3): 405–427.

Trevor, J. C. 1947. "The Physical Characteristics of the Sandawe." *Journal of the Royal Anthropological Institute of Great Britain and Ireland* 77(1): 61–78.

Truswell, A. Stewart, and John D. L. Hansen. 1976. "Medical Research among the

!Kung." In *Kalahari Hunter-Gatherers,* eds. Richard B. Lee and Irven DeVore. Cambridge, Mass.: Harvard University Press, pp. 166–194.

Trut, Lyudmila N. 1999. "Early Canid Domestication: The Fox Farm Experiment." *American Scientist* 87(2): 160–161.

Tucker, Bram. 2001. "The Behavioral Ecology and Economics of Variation, Risk and Diversification among Mikea Forager-Farmers of Madagascar." Ph.D. dissertation, Department of Anthropology, University of North Carolina, Chapel Hill.

United Kingdom, Department of Communities and Local Government. 2007. *Live Tables on Housing Market and House Prices,* http://www.communities.gov.uk/.

United Kingdom, Department of Education and Skills. 2003. *The Skills for Life Survey.* Research Brief RB490. London: The Stationary Office.

United Kingdom, Department of Environment, Food, and Rural Affairs. 2005. *Agriculture in the UK 2005.* London: The Stationary Office.

United Kingdom, H.M. Revenue and Customs. 2007. *Distribution of Personal Wealth, 2003,* http://www.hmrc.gov.uk/stats/personal_wealth.

United Kingdom, Office of National Statistics. 2003. *UK 2000 Time Use Study,* http://www.statistics.gov.uk/statbase/.

———. 2006a. *Annual Survey of Hours and Earnings,* http://www.statistics.gov.uk/pdfdir/ashe1006.pdf.

———. 2006b. *Trends in ONS Longitudinal Study Estimates of Life Expectancy, by Social Class 1972–2001.* London: The Stationary Office.

United Nations. 2006. *2003 Demographic Yearbook.* New York: United Nations.

United Nations, Development Program. 2005. *Human Development Report, 2005.* New York: Palgrave Macmillan.

United States, Census Bureau. 2002. *Statistical Abstract of the United States.* Washington, D.C.: US Government Printing Office.

United States, Department of Commerce. 1915. Bureau of Foreign and Domestic Commerce, Special Consular Reports 72, *British India.* Washington, D.C.: U.S. Government Printing Office.

United States, Department of Energy, Energy Information Administration. 2004. *2001 Residential Energy Consumption Survey,* http://www.eia.doe.gov/emeu/consumption.

United States, Department of Labor, Bureau of Labor Statistics. 2006. "Hourly Compensation Costs for Production Workers in Manufacturing, 32 Countries or Areas, 22 Manufacturing Industries, 1992–2004." Washington, D.C.: U.S. Government Printing Office.

United States, Economic Report of the President. 2001. Washington, D.C.: U.S. Government Printing Office.

United States, House of Representatives. 1912. *Report of the Tariff Board. Cotton Manufactures.* Washington, D.C.: U.S. Government Printing Office.

United States, Naval Oceanographic Office. 1965. *Distances between Ports.* Publication 151. Washington, D.C.: U.S. Government Printing Office.

Usher, Abbott Payson. 1929. *A History of Mechanical Inventions.* New York: McGraw-Hill.

Van Zanden, Jan Luiten. 1995. "Tracing the Beginning of the Kuznets Curve: Western Europe during the Early Modern Period." *Economic History Review* 48(4): 643–664.

———. 1999. "Wages and the Standard of Living in Europe, 1500–1800." *European Review of Economic History* 2: 175–197.

———. 2004. "The Skill Premium and the Great Divergence." Working Paper, University of Utrecht.

Veenhoven, Ruut. 2005. *World Database of Happiness, Distributional Findings in Nations.* Rotterdam: Erasmus University, www.worlddatabaseofhappiness.eur.nl.

Von Moschzisker, Robert. 1922. "The Historic Origin of Trial by Jury. III." *University of Pennsylvania Law Review and American Law Register* 70(3): 159–171.

Voth, Hans-Joachim. 2001. "The Longest Years: New Estimates of Labor Input in England, 1760–1830." *Journal of Economic History* 61(4): 1065–1082.

Waddell, Eric. 1972. *The Mound Builders: Agricultural Practices, Environment, and Society in the Central Highlands of New Guinea.* Seattle: University of Washington Press.

Walker, Robert, Kim Hill, Hillard Kaplan, and Garnett McMillan. 2002. "Age-Dependency in Hunting Ability among the Ache in Eastern Paraguay." *Journal of Human Evolution* 42: 639–657.

Walmsley, Herbert E. 1893. *Cotton Spinning and Weaving. A Practical and Theoretical Treatise.* Manchester: Heywood.

Ward, Marianne, and John Devereux. 2003. "Measuring British Decline: Direct versus Long-Span Income Measures." *Journal of Economic History* 63: 826–851.

Wasson, E. A. 1998. "The Penetration of New Wealth into the English Governing Class from the Middle Ages to the First World War." *Economic History Review* 51(1): 25–48.

Weir, David. 1984. "Life Under Pressure: France and England, 1670–1870." *Journal of Economic History* 44(1): 27–48.

Werner, D. W., N. M. Flowers, M. L. Ritter, and D. R. Gross. 1979. "Subsistence Productivity and Hunting Effort in Native South America." *Human Ecology* 7(4): 303–316.

White, Lynn. 1962. *Medieval Technology and Social Change.* Oxford: Clarendon Press.

Will, Pierre-Etienne, and R. Bin Wong. 1991. *Nourish the People: The State Civilian Granary System in China, 1650–1850.* Ann Arbor: University of Michigan, Center for Chinese Studies.

Williamson, Jeffrey G. 1984. "Why Was British Growth So Slow during the Industrial Revolution?" *Journal of Economic History* 44(3): 687–712.

Winterhalter, Bruce. 1993. "Work, Resources and Population in Foraging Societies." *Man* 28(2): 321–340.

Wolcott, Susan, and Gregory Clark. 1999. "Why Nations Fail: Managerial Decisions and Performance in Indian Cotton Textiles, 1890–1938." *Journal of Economic History* 59(2): 397–423.

Wood, George Henry. 1910 "The Statistics of Wages in the Nineteenth Century. Part XIX–The Cotton Industry. Section V." *Journal of the Royal Statistical Society* 73(6/7): 585–633.

Woodburn, James. 1980. "Hunters and Gatherers Today and Reconstruction of the Past." In *Soviet and Western Anthropology*, ed. E. Gellner. London: Duckworth, pp. 95–117.

World Health Organization. 2002. *World Report on Violence and Health*. Geneva.

Wrigley, E. A. 1990. *Continuity, Chance and Change: The Character of the Industrial Revolution in England*. Cambridge, U.K.: Cambridge University Press.

Wrigley, E. A., R. S. Davies, J. E. Oeppen, and R. S. Schofield. 1997. *English Population History from Family Reconstitution: 1580–1837*. Cambridge, U.K.: Cambridge University Press.

Yamamura, Kozo. 1974. *A Study of Samurai Income and Entrepreneurship*. Cambridge, Mass.: Harvard University Press.

Yasuba, Yasukichi. 1986. "Sandard of Living in Japan Before Industrialization: From What Level Did Japan Begin? A Comment." *Journal of Economic History* 46(1): 217–224.

Young, Arthur. 1792. *Travels in France and Italy during the Years 1787, 1788, & 1789*. London: W. Richardson.

Zaccagnini, Carlo. 1988. "On Prices and Wages at Nuzi." *Altorientalische Forschungen* 15(1): 45–52.

Zelin, Madelaine. 1986. "The Rights of Tenants in Mid-Qing Sichuan: A Study of Land-Related Lawsuits in the Baxian Archives." *Journal of Asian Studies* 45(3): 499–526.

Index

Page numbers followed by *f* indicate figures, those followed by *n* indicate notes, and those followed by *t* indicate tables.

birth rates (*continued*)
in England, 243; in Malthusian equilibrium, 20; relationship to living standards, 20, 26; schedules, 26, 26*f*, 123–24, 123*f*. *See also* fertility

Black Death: effects on life expectancies, 95, 101–2; effects on living standards, 99–102; transmission of plague, 100, 101

Bombay (Mumbai): cotton textile industry in, 318, 322, 346, 347*t*, 357, 358, 360, 361, 363–65; plague deaths in, 100; transport costs to, 309

bonds, rates of return on, 329, 330*f*, 330–31, 331*t*

British Empire, 314, 315–16, 331

bubonic plague. *See* Black Death

building laborers: real wages of, 41, 41*t*, 276–77, 276*f*; skill premium for, 180–81, 180*f*, 225; work hours of, 63, 63*t*, 65

calories, 50*t*, 50–52, 284–85

capital: divergence and, 329–33, 335; efficiency growth and, 204–7, 205*f*, 206*f*, 335; gains from productivity improvements, 296–99; as input to growth, 197–98, 200; as input to production, 8, 24, 231–32, 355*f*, 355–57; labor substitutions for, 356–57, 358–59; output per worker and, 335, 335*f*; physical stocks of, 202, 203*t*, 204–7, 275, 329; in preindustrial societies, 167–68; share in costs, 231–32. *See also* interest rates

capital, human. *See* human capital

capital goods: cost of, 333, 333*f*; English exports of, 313, 337, 338

capital markets, 331–33

Catholic Church: Inquisition, 145; views of usury, 215–16, 217

children: as consumption item, 291–92; death rates of, 294–95; employment of, 339; quality of, 223–24, 291–92. *See also* birth rates; reproductive success

China: agriculture in, 25; cotton textile industry in, 337–38, 358; differences from England, 260–62; education in, 262, 266; European involvement in, 314–15, 317; female infanticide in, 76, 77–78, 95, 110; fertility rates in, 75, 76–77, 77*t*; grain markets in, 261, 261*f*; hygiene standards in, 106; individualism in, 188; land rents in, 138; life

expectancies in, 95; literacy in, 265–66; living standards in, 31–32, 69, 70; male stature in, 58; market development in, 260; marriage patterns in, 75–76, 78; migration to frontier areas of, 267; population density in, 141–42; population of, 31–32, 267, 267*t*; Qing imperial lineage, 269–70, 270*f*; reproductive success of elite in, 11, 269–70, 270*f*; sex ratio in, 77, 78, 110; social mobility in, 162; tariffs of, 315; taxation as share of national income, 154, 154*t*; technological advance in, 133, 134; technological regression in, 143–44; wages in, 337–38

Christianity. *See* Catholic Church; Church of England; Protestantism

Church of England: tithe collections, 153; views of usury, 217

cities. *See* urban areas

cleanliness. *See* hygiene standards

coal: as energy source, 256, 285, 308, 338; English output of, 236, 237*f*; European reserves of, 260; prices of, 237, 237*f*, 338; technological advance in industry, 236–37; transport costs of, 309–11, 310*f*, 334, 334*f*

colonies, European, 104–5, 260, 305, 313–16. *See also* British Empire

consumption: of calories, 50*t*, 50–52, 284–85; children as goods, 291–92; of dairy products, 69–70; effects of rising incomes, 195–96; Engel's Law and, 52–55; of food, 43, 50*t*, 50–52, 195–96; possibilities, 67; proportion of income spent on food, 52–55; of protein, 50*t*, 50–52; real purchasing power and, 254–55, 255*f*; standard bundle of goods, 41–42, 42*t*; time preference in, 171–72; variety of diets, 51–52

contraception, 73, 74, 293. *See also* fertility limitation

cotton textile industry: beneficiaries of innovation in, 236; British managers and skilled workers in other countries, 357–58; in China, 337–38, 358; comparative costs in, 337–40, 338*t*, 340*t*; costs of mills, 333, 333*f*, 337, 338; female laborers in, 311, 339; gender differences in wages, 278; in India, 346, 347*t*, 356, 357, 358–59, 360–65, 364*t*, 368*t*, 368–69; inefficiencies in poor countries, 337, 340–42, 346–49, 356; international trade, 315, 316*t*, 322; in Japan, 262, 311, 346; labor costs and wages in, 13, 340, 342f; labor discipline in, 15, 362–65, 364t; labor intensity in, 353–54; labor productivity in, 13, 360–65; management decisions, 357–59, 359t; manual production, 319, 368–69; output per worker, 342, 343f, 346, 347, 347t, 348f; productivity growth in, 233–34, 296–97; profits in, 203, 235–36, 296, 346, 347t, 358, 360; returns on capital in, 296–97; ring spinning, 311–12, 313, 314t, 340–42, 343f, 355–56; technological advances in, 203, 233–36, 235t, 368–69; technological diffusion in, 296, 304, 313, 337, 338; transport costs in, 309, 310t; unskilled laborers in, 311–12, 337, 340–42; wages in, 337–38, 340, 342f, 353–54; work hours in, 339, 340t

culture: influence on growth, 11; institutional influences on, 208–9; lack of surplus for producing, 55; middle-class values, 8, 11, 132, 166, 183–84, 185, 262; selective pressures on, 10, 186

Darwin, Charles, 112, 186

death rates: of children, 294–95; definition of, 21; equal to birth rates, 21, 22–23, 22f; of European military abroad, 108, 109t; incomes and, 89f, 90, 96–99, 97f, 98f; of infants, 92, 96–99, 98f; of pregnant women, 244–45, 245t, 295; in preindustrial societies, 6, 91–92; reductions in modern world, 44–45; relationship to living standards, 20, 99–102; in rural areas, 104; schedules, 26–27, 27f, 123–24, 123f; urban, 93, 104

debt. See bonds; interest rates; public debt

democracy, 219–20

demographics. See birth rates; death rates; fertility; population

demographic transition, 8, 11, 225, 226f, 289–96, 290f

developing countries. See poor countries

Diamond, Jared, 13, 37, 187

disease: AIDS, 45–47; in cities, 93; death rates from, 58–59; plague, 95, 99–102; White Death, 110–11

division of labor, 367

economic growth. See growth

economic history of world, basic outline of, 1, 2f

education: in Asia, 262, 263, 266; returns on, 224–26. See also human capital; literacy

efficiency: of English economy, 232; estimates of, 231–32, 380; output per worker and, 336, 336f; in poor countries, 336–51

efficiency growth: accelerating rates after 1800, 228, 231–34, 240; as cause of income divergence, 334–36; in England, 232–33, 232f, 233t, 240–42, 240f, 241f; as input to economic growth, 200–201, 202–3, 204–7; measurement of, 135; population growth and, 227–28, 227f; in preindustrial societies, 257–58; relationship to physical capital growth, 204–7, 205f, 206f; sources of, 232–33, 233t; wage increases and, 272–77

efficient institutions hypothesis, 212–13

Egypt, Roman: fertility rates in, 77t, 78–79; infanticide in, 110; life expectancies in, 93; numeracy in, 176; price stability in, 156–57; returns on land rents in, 169; speed of information travel to, 305–6, 306t

endogenous growth theories, 210, 226–29

energy: human labor, 284–85; periods of, 370; yields of labor, 67–69, 68t. See also coal

Engel curves, 53, 53f

Engel's Law, 52–55

England: agriculture in, 25, 247–49; famines in, 69; fertility rates in, 71, 72, 81–82, 243; government expenditures in, 148, 149, 149f; hygiene standards in, 106–8; inflation in, 156, 156t; living standards in, 38–39, 41; male stature in, 58; manufactured exports of, 246, 248, 337, 338; mortality sources in, 126–28, 127f, 128f; Poor Laws of, 31, 34, 41, 50–51; population density in, 141; population growth in, 193, 194f, 243, 245–46, 247, 267, 267t; population in preindustrial period, 29–30; public debt, 157, 158f; social mobility in, 130–31, 131t, 160–62; subsistence incomes in, 23; taxation in, 148–54; technological advance in, 29–30, 30f, 136–40; urbanization in, 104; work hours in, 63t, 63–65. See also British Empire; wills

Enlightenment, 209

Europe: coal reserves in, 260; fertility rates in, 72–75, 73t, 76t; hygiene standards in, 6, 102, 105; living standards in, 69–70, 89–90; male stature in, 58, 60f, 60–62; marriage patterns in, 71–72, 74–75, 76t, 81–84, 105;

Europe (*continued*)
population growth in, 20, 21*t. See also* Black Death; colonies; France; Netherlands
evolution. *See* natural selection
exogenous growth theories, 209, 210–17

famines, 69
farm laborers: food expenditures of, 53–54, 54*t;* lifetime earnings of, 187*f,* 188; real wages of, 41, 41*t,* 272; work hours of, 63, 65
farmland: output of, 25; prices relative to output, 158, 159*f;* rents of, 274–75, 274*f;* in United States, 249, 250*t. See also* agriculture
female infanticide, 76, 77–78, 95, 110
fertility: in Asia, 267–70; decline in modern economies, 289–96, 290*f;* demographic transition, 8, 11, 225, 226*f,* 289–96, 290*f;* gross, 289–90, 291; Hutterite standard of, 72–73, 73*t;* by income group, 85–89, 267–70, 292–93, 292*t,* 293*f;* increase in England, 243; within marriage, 72–73, 73*t,* 76*t,* 76–77, 77*t,* 78–79, 82, 87–89, 292–94, 292*t;* in modern forager societies, 79, 80*t;* net, 290; relationship to life expectancies, 71; relationship to living standards, 71. *See also* birth rates; reproductive success
fertility limitation: absence of conscious control, 73–74, 80, 82, 87–89; in Asia, 76–78; with contraception, 73, 74, 293; in England, 81; in Europe, 71–72, 73–74; factors in, 74–75, 75*f;* in forager societies, 79; mechanisms of, 80–81; in preindustrial societies, 5–6, 79
Flanders: farmland prices in, 158, 159*f;* returns on landholding in, 175, 176*f*
food: composition of diets and income, 52–54, 54*t;* English imports of, 248, 249*t;* famines, 69; influence on stature, 56; production in preindustrial societies, 54–55; proportion of income spent on, 52–55. *See also* agriculture; consumption
forager societies: egalitarian consumption in, 36; energy yields of, 67–69, 68*t;* fertility limitation in, 79; food consumption in, 50, 52–53; labor income in, 280; leisure time in, 68; lifetime output in, 187–88, 187*f;* living standards in, 68–69; work hours in, 65
forager societies, modern: calorie production in, 68*t;* ethnographies of, 186; fertility rates

in, 79, 80*t;* food consumption in, 50*t,* 51; life expectancies in, 92, 93*t,* 96; male stature in, 59*t,* 59–60; mortality sources in, 124–25, 125*t,* 129; reproductive success in, 129, 130*t;* time preference rates in, 171–72; work hours in, 64*t,* 65–66
France: agriculture in, 196; colonies of, 314; fertility rates in, 72, 75, 78–79, 294; life expectancies in, 92; per capita incomes in, 321; population growth in, 243; social mobility in, 162
French Revolution, 230
fundamental equation of growth, 197–204, 379–82

Galor, Oded, 8*n,* 167*n,* 210*n,* 228–29
garment manufacturing, 347–50, 349*f,* 350*f. See also* cotton textile industry
Germany: colonies of, 314; per capita incomes in, 195, 321; reproductive success of rich in, 132
Glorious Revolution, 148, 149, 241, 242
gold standard, 331
government bonds, rates of return on, 329, 330*f. See also* public debt
government expenditures, 148, 149–50, 149*f,* 150*t*
grain markets, 261, 261*f*
Great Divergence. *See* income divergence
Greece, ancient: interest rates in, 169; slavery in, 221
gross reproduction rate (GRR), 289–90, 291
growth: alternation of energetic and slow periods, 370; explanations of modern, 197–207; fundamental equation of, 197–204, 379–82; incentives and, 145–47; Malthusian model and, 29–32; modern rates of, 200, 200*t,* 381–82; since 1800, 319–27; transition to modern rates of, 249–56, 257
GRR. *See* gross reproduction rate
guilds, 164, 218

happiness: relationship to income, 15–16, 374–77, 375*f;* relative to reference groups, 16, 376; surveys on, 374–75
Hawaii, 29, 143
health. *See* disease
heights. *See* stature
Hobbes, Thomas, 19–20

homicide: infanticide, 76, 77–78, 95, 109–10; in medieval England, 126, 127f, 160; in modern forager societies, 124–25, 125t; in modern societies, 160

human capital: increase in, 223–26; as input to growth, 201–2; returns on education, 224–26; value of, 201–2, 201t

hunter-gatherer societies. *See* forager societies

Hutterite standard of fertility, 72–73, 73t

hygiene standards, 6, 102, 105, 106–8

illegitimacy rates, 74, 82, 243

immigration, 105, 303, 373

imperialism. *See* colonies, European

incentives: economic, 147; growth and, 145–47; in medieval England, 147, 148t; in modern England, 148t

income divergence, 3, 12–15, 319–27; efficiency growth and, 334–36; explanations of, 13–15, 328–29, 352–53, 354–55, 372; increase in, 365–69; low subsistence wages and, 45; per capita incomes, 320–27, 321f; role of labor quality, 352, 353–54. *See also* poor countries; rich countries

income inequality: compared to wealth inequality, 279–80, 279t; decrease in, 11–12, 272–73, 299; effects of Industrial Revolution, 11–12, 278–83; in forager societies, 280; in preindustrial societies, 2, 36, 279. *See also* income divergence

incomes: association with happiness, 15–16, 374–77, 375f; birth rates and, 81f, 81–82, 84–89, 89f; comparison of English and Dutch, 247, 248f; consumption and, 195–96; death rates and, 89f, 90, 96–99, 97f, 98f; differences across countries, 320–27, 321f; increases since 1800, 2f, 2–3, 8, 195, 195f, 247, 248f; population growth and, 1, 245–46, 246f; proportion spent on food, 52–55; real, 193–94, 194f, 195f; real national in 2000, 44, 46t; real purchasing power of, 254–55, 255f; relationship to marginal tax rates, 152, 153f; subsistence, 22–23, 25, 136; variations across preindustrial societies, 91; world distribution of, 323–25, 325t. *See also* reproductive success, relationship to income; wages

India: building technology in, 265; cotton goods imported by, 315, 322; cotton textile industry in, 346, 347t, 356, 357, 358–59,

360–65, 364t, 368t, 368–69; farm laborer food expenditures in, 53, 54t; growth in, 370; imports and exports of, 322, 323t; incomes in, 44, 322–23, 324f; interest rates in, 170; labor productivity in, 354, 356, 360–65; literacy in, 264–65; living standards in, 69, 264, 319; male stature in, 55, 57, 61; plague outbreaks in, 100; poverty in, 325–27; railroad construction in, 313, 342–45; railway interest costs in, 330–31; wages in, 264. *See also* Bombay

Industrial Revolution: effects on income inequality, 11–12, 278–83; English advantages in, 10–11, 260–62; explanation of timing of, 8–10, 208; major events of, 231–39; as product of gradual evolution, 10, 208–9, 231; seen as sudden shock, 9, 231, 239, 242–49; timing of transition, 239–42

Industrial Revolution, theories of, 9, 208–10; endogenous growth, 210, 226–29; exogenous growth, 209, 210–17; institutionalism, 146–47, 210–17, 218–23, 224, 234, 238, 241; multiple equilibrium, 209, 218–26

industrious revolution, 62–66

inequality: in life prospects, 283–84, 283t; wealth, 279–80, 279t, 281–82, 281t. *See also* income divergence; income inequality

infanticide, 76, 77–78, 95, 109–10

infant mortality rates, 92, 96–99, 98f

inflation, 154–57; in England, 156, 156t; in preindustrial societies, 156–57; social costs of, 155, 155f

inflation tax, 155–56

information, speed of travel, 305–7, 306t, 307t

innovation: demand and supply of, 224, 224f, 237–38; external benefits of, 203, 207; in market economies, 185–86. *See also* technological advance

inorganic production systems, 256–57

institutionalism, 146–47, 210–17, 218–23, 224, 234, 238, 241

institutions: endogeneity of, 212–13, 226–28; human behavior changed by stability of, 11, 167, 208–9; influence on growth, 10; intellectual property rights, 163–64, 203, 237, 238; legal, 173–74; in medieval England, 147, 148t; personal security, 159–60; political economy of, 218–20, 219f; in preindustrial societies, 145–47; price stability,

institutions (*continued*)
154–57; public debt, 157; security of property, 158–59, 173, 174; taxation, 148–54. *See also* markets
intellectual property rights, 163–64, 203, 237, 238
interest payments, religious prohibitions and exceptions, 215–17
interest rates: decline in, 166, 168–69, 169*f*, 171–75, 175*t*; default risk premium in, 172; in early societies, 169–70; on government bonds, 329, 330*f*; growth premium in, 172–73; in medieval Europe, 168–69, 170*t*, 173; nominal, 154, 168; real, 168, 172; return on rent charges, 168, 169*f*, 174, 175*t*; in United States, 332–33; usury laws and, 215–17
Ireland: agriculture in, 25; per capita incomes in, 322, 370; population of, 246; potato famine in, 257; real wages in, 246, 247*f*
iron and steel, 236–37, 256
Iron Law of Wages, 31
Islam, views of usury, 215, 216–17
Italy: age declarations in, 177; real wages in, 47, 47*f*, 103–4; urbanization in, 103–4. *See also* Roman Empire

Japan: adoption frequency in, 268; agriculture in, 25; birth rates in, 89, 89*f*; cotton textile industry in, 262, 311, 346; differences from England, 261; education levels in, 262, 263; famines in, 69; farm laborer food expenditures in, 53, 54*t*; female infanticide in, 110; fertility rates in, 75, 76–77, 77*t*, 78; happiness reported in, 16, 375, 375*f*; hygiene standards in, 6, 105, 106, 107; incomes in, 16, 89, 89*f*, 375, 375*f*; interest rates in, 263; life expectancies in, 95; literacy in, 263; male stature in, 58, 61; marriage patterns in, 76; population density in, 141; population growth in, 267, 267*t*; reproductive success of samurai, 11, 268, 269*f*; social characteristics of, 262–63

knowledge: as asset, 202, 204; growth of and population size, 227–28. *See also* intellectual property rights; technological advance
Korea, return on land ownership in, 266. *See also* Asia
Kremer, Michael, 226–28, 367

labor: energy yields of, 67–69, 68*t*; as input to production, 24–25, 197–98, 231–32, 355*f*, 355–57; marginal product of, 24–25; productivity differences, 352; productivity of, 67; quality differences across countries, 352, 353–54, 357, 359–65, 369, 370; relationship to output, 24–25, 25*f*; share in costs, 231–32; as share of national income in England, 280, 280*f*; substituting for capital, 256–57, 258–59. *See also* building laborers; farm laborers; unskilled laborers; wages; work hours
labor markets, 162–63, 285–89
land: as input to growth, 197–99; as input to production, 24, 231–32; markets, 163; share in costs, 231–32; titles, 173. *See also* farmland
Landes, David, 11
land rents: decline in, 198; of farmland, 274–75, 274*f*; returns on, 168, 169*f*, 173, 174–75, 175*t*, 176*f*, 266, 284–85; as share of national income in England, 138, 138*f*, 198, 199*f*, 275, 280; urban, 198, 275
Law of Diminishing Returns, 24–25, 68
legal systems, 173–74, 214–15. *See also* intellectual property rights
life expectancies: adult, 92, 94*t*, 94–95, 95*t*, 97, 98*f*, 101–2; at birth, 21, 92; income differences and, 87, 97, 98*f*, 122, 283, 283*t*, 284; as inverse of death rate, 21, 27; in medieval England, 95, 101–2, 122, 122*t*; in modern forager societies, 92, 93*t*, 96; in modern world, 44–47, 46*t*, 366; in preindustrial societies, 1, 27, 91–96, 94*t*, 95*t*; relationship to fertility, 71; in urban areas, 93–94
literacy: in Asia, 263, 264–66; increase in, 166, 175–76, 178–79, 179*f*, 183, 226; relationship to wealth, 86, 184, 184*f*, 283, 283*t*, 284; rewards for, 180–81; of women, 295–96
living standards: comparisons of 1800 to early societies, 19–20, 38–39, 40; comparisons of Europe and East Asia, 69–70, 89–90; definition of, 21–22; divergence in, 319–20; effects of Black Death, 99–102; Engel's Law and, 52–55, 53*f*; increased work hours and, 66–69; in poor countries, 43*t*, 43–47; population growth and, 20; in preindustrial societies, 1–2, 5, 90; relationship to birth

rates, 20, 26; relationship to death rates, 20, 99–102; relationship to fertility, 71; stature as indicator of, 55–62

London: death rates in, 93; fertility rates in, 162; as financial center, 331; grain trade in, 163; infant mortality rates in, 96–97; legal system in, 173–74; migration to, 162, 163; speed of information travel to, 306, 307t; work hours in, 64

machine-building firms, 305, 312–13, 338
machinery question, 286–87
Malawi: effects of AIDS in, 45–47; male stature in, 55–56, 56f; wages and prices in, 43t, 43–44
Malthus, Thomas Robert, 5, 31–33, 34, 58, 80–81, 89, 243; *Essay on the Principle of Population,* 31, 33, 72, 75, 112
Malthusian equilibrium, 4–8, 20–25, 22f
Malthusian model: in animal economies, 32–33; assumptions of, 20–25, 22f; comparison of England and Asia, 267; economic growth and, 29–32; variations in wages and living standards, 47, 48; "virtues" and "vices," 36, 37t
Malthusian scissors, 123–24
management, quality of, 354–59
marginal product of labor, 24–25
markets: capital, 331–33; in China, 260; efficiency and capital growth in, 204–7; goods, 163; grain, 261, 261f; innovations stimulated by, 185–86; labor, 162–63, 285–89; in medieval England, 147, 160–61, 162–63
marriage patterns: in Asia, 75–76, 78; changes in, 243–45; economic factors in, 82–83; in Europe, 71–72, 74–75, 76t, 81–84, 105; fertility limited by, 74–75, 75f, 80–81; men's average ages, 76, 83, 244f; proportion of never married women, 74, 105, 243; women's average ages, 74, 75, 76t, 81, 82–83, 243, 244f, 245t
Marx, Karl, 272, 353–54
material living standards. *See* living standards
mechanized factories, 311
men: ages at marriage, 76, 83, 244f; wages compared to women's wages, 277–78. *See also* stature
Mexico: cotton textile industry in, 339; garment manufacturing, 350; power costs in, 338

middle-class values, 8, 11, 132, 166, 183–84, 185, 262
military death rates, 108, 109t. *See also* wars
modern economies: demand for unskilled labor, 285–89; life expectancies in, 44–47, 46t, 366; mortality sources in, 125–26; production functions of, 206, 206f; simple model of, 197–204. *See also* growth; poor countries; rich countries
Mokyr, Joel, 51n, 181n, 183n, 209
money, use of, 184. *See also* gold standard; inflation
mortality: sources of, 124–28, 125t, 129, 159–60; war deaths, 126–28, 128f. *See also* death rates; homicide
multiple equilibrium theories, 209, 218–26
Mumbai. *See* Bombay
murders. *See* homicide

nails, productivity growth and prices of, 252–53, 254f
Native Americans: exposure to European diseases, 111; male stature of, 59
natural economy, 5, 19
natural selection, 6–8, 10, 112–13, 167, 186–87
Neolithic Revolution: effects on inequality, 280; effects on work hours, 65, 69; living standards and, 37–38; population estimates, 139; social change after, 6–7, 186–87. *See also* agrarian societies
Netherlands: colonies of, 104–5, 314; fertility rates in, 102–3; growth in, 370; interest rates in, 175; male stature in, 55; marriage patterns in, 105; per capita incomes in, 247, 248f, 321; real wages and population in, 102–3, 103f; real wages in, 47, 47f; sex ratio in, 105; urbanization in, 104
net reproduction rate (NRR), 290
North, Douglass, 209, 212, 219, 242
NRR. *See* net reproduction rate
numeracy: age declarations and, 176–78, 177t; in forager societies, 186; increase in, 166, 175–78; in Japan, 263; rewards for, 180–81; vagueness of, 179–80

ocean transport, 307–9, 315–16
organic production systems, 256–57
organizational change, machine-building firms, 305, 312–13, 338

Ottoman Empire: interest payments in, 217; interest rates in, 170; taxation as share of national income, 154, 154t

Pacific islands, 108, 217. *See also* Polynesia
patents, 202, 237, 238. *See also* intellectual property rights
Pepys, Samuel, 4, 73–74, 105, 106, 182
personal security, 159–60
plague. *See* Black Death
Platt Brothers firm, 313–14, 342
Poland, agriculture in, 366–67
political economy: of institutions, 218–20, 219f; in Malthusian era, 33–35
poll taxes, 148–49, 163
Polynesia: death rates in, 62, 108; fertility rates in, 109; infanticide in, 109–10; male stature in, 62; value of metals in, 29. *See also* Tahiti
Pomeranz, Kenneth, 69n, 260–62
poor countries: explanations of poverty in, 13–14, 350–51; labor costs in, 347–49; labor quality in, 15, 359–65; life expectancies in, 45, 46t; living standards in, 43t, 43–47; management quality in, 354–59; output per worker in, 325, 345–47, 350, 350f, 354, 355; production inefficiencies in, 336–51; wages in, 12, 43t, 43–44, 347–49, 349f. *See also* income divergence
Poor Laws, 31, 34, 41, 50–51
population: densities of, 140–42, 141f, 184, 227–28; migration of, 105, 303, 373; stationary, 21, 23; world distribution of, 323–25, 325t
population growth: in Africa, 366; in Asia, 267, 267t; efficiency growth and, 227–28, 227f; in England, 193, 194f, 243, 245–46, 247, 267, 267t; global, 139, 139t; income growth and, 1, 245–46, 246f; relationship to living standards, 20; until 1800, 20; in Western Europe, 20, 21t
poverty: effects of poor laws, 33–34; food consumption and, 50–51. *See also* living standards; poor countries
pregnancy, deaths in, 244–45, 245t, 295
preindustrial societies. *See* agrarian societies; forager societies; Malthusian model
prices: evidence of, 41; grain, 261, 261f; productivity growth and, 252–53, 254f; stability of, 154–57

printing industry, 250–52, 263
production functions: effects of technological advance, 134–36, 136f; for England, 136–37, 137f; in modern economies, 206, 206f
production inputs, 8, 24–25, 197–98, 231–32, 355f, 355–57
productivity: in book production, 252, 253f; in cotton textiles, 233–34, 296–97; human capital investments and, 201–2; labor, 67; measurement of, 135; in nail production, 252–53, 254f. *See also* efficiency
profits: in cotton textile industry, 203, 235–36, 296, 346, 347t, 358, 360; international comparisons of, 332; of railroads, 298, 299t
property: ownership of, 184–85; security of, 158–59, 173, 174; transfers of, 184–85. *See also* land
property values. *See* land rents
Protestantism, 183. *See also* Church of England
public debt, 157, 158f. *See also* government bonds

railroads: capital goods exports, 313; construction of, 297, 298f, 307, 308t, 313, 342–45; debentures, 330–31, 331t; locomotives, 342, 344f, 345; output per worker-hour, 343–45, 345f; productivity differences, 343–45, 345f, 346f; profits of, 298, 299t; returns on capital, 297–98, 299t; technological advance in, 236–37, 304
real wages. *See* wages, real
reproductive success: of aristocracy, 122–23, 122t; of Chinese imperial lineage, 11, 269–70, 270f; in earlier societies, 128–29, 130t; of Japanese samurai, 11, 268, 269f; of literate men, 184, 185; urban-rural differences, 161–62. *See also* fertility
reproductive success, relationship to income, 113, 114f; comparison of modern and preindustrial England, 283, 283t, 284; differences between agrarian societies, 188; in England, 7–8, 113–23, 131–32, 132t, 292–93, 293f; evidence in wills, 113–20; literacy and, 185; social effects of, 11, 132, 167, 183–84, 185
Ricardo, David, 24, 31, 34, 274, 286
rich countries: capital growth in, 205, 205f; efficiency growth in, 205, 205f; government expenditures in, 149–50, 150t; per capita in-

comes in, 321–22; public debt of, 157; work hours and marginal tax rates in, 151–52, 152f. *See also* income divergence; modern economies

Roman Empire: age declarations in, 178; infanticide in, 110; life expectancies in, 94–95; speed of information travel in, 305–6, 306t. *See also* Egypt, Roman

rural populations: death rates of, 104; in preindustrial societies, 54, 196; reproductive success of, 161–62

samurai, reproductive success of, 11, 268, 269f

sanitation. *See* hygiene standards

Sassoon family, 316–18

Scientific Revolution, 183

security: personal, 159–60; of property, 158–59, 173, 174

selection pressures. *See* natural selection

serfdom, 220–23

shifting cultivation societies: calorie consumption in, 51; calorie production in, 67, 68t; ethnographies of modern, 186; leisure time in, 68; mortality sources in, 124, 129; time preference rates in, 171; work hours in, 64t

shipping. *See* transportation

skeletal remains: estimates of ages at death, 96; evidence of violent deaths, 125, 126f; stature of, 57, 60f, 60–62, 61t

skill premium, 180–81, 180f, 225, 276–77

slavery, 220–23, 222f

Smith, Adam, 35, 145, 146

social mobility: downward, 7–8, 113, 130–31, 131t; in England, 130–31, 131t, 160–62; in preindustrial societies, 162

Solow, Robert M., 198n

stature: income differences and, 283–84, 283t; as indicator of living standards, 55–62; influence of diet and health, 56; living, 55–60, 57t, 59t; in modern forager societies, 59t, 59–60; in preindustrial societies, 1, 56–62, 57t; skeletal evidence of, 57, 60f, 60–62, 61t

steamships, 307–9, 311

subsistence incomes, 22–23, 25, 136

subsistence wage, 45, 353, 366

Sumer, interest rates in, 170

survival of the richest. *See* reproductive success, relationship to income

survival of types, differential, 112–13

Tahiti, 29, 60, 66, 108, 109. *See also* Polynesia

taxation: in England, 31, 148–54, 160; marginal rates of, 149, 150, 150t, 151–52, 152f, 153f; in modern economies, 149, 150t, 377; poll taxes, 148–49, 163; share in all income, 154, 154t

technological advance: before 1800, 29–30, 30f; benefits to consumers, 236, 237, 246–47, 296–97; in cotton textile industry, 203, 233–36, 235t, 368–69; delayed effects of, 250–52; effects of isolated, 28–29, 28f; effects on unskilled labor, 285–89; in England, 29–30, 30f, 136–40; in Industrial Revolution, 31, 140, 237–38; in information transmission, 306–7; lack of incentives in Malthusian economies, 164–65; in market economies, 185–86; measuring from consumption, 254–55, 255f; measuring from population, 136–40, 139t; mechanized factories, 311; in nineteenth century, 305–19; population densities and, 140–42; in preindustrial societies, 5, 133–35, 136–40, 136f, 144, 249–56, 251t; rates of, 134–35, 140; in transportation, 307–11

technological diffusion: of British innovations, 303–5, 313; in cotton textiles, 296, 304, 313, 337, 338; inefficiency of labor use as barrier to, 345–47; restrictions on, 303; time lags in, 304t, 304–5

technology: definition of, 136n; inorganic production systems, 256–57; regression, 142–44

technology schedule, 24–25, 28–29

telegraph, 307

tenants, royal, 121, 122

textiles. *See* cotton textile industry

time preference rates, 171–72

tithe collections, 153

trade: in cotton textiles, 315, 316t, 322; effects of innovation, 185–86; English food imports, 247–49, 249t; English manufactured exports, 246, 248, 337, 338; international, 246, 248, 315, 322, 323t, 349–50; tariffs, 315. *See also* transport costs

transportation: productivity growth in, 233; steamships, 307–9, 311. *See also* railroads

transport costs: of coal, 309–11, 310f, 334, 334f; of cotton goods, 309, 310t; decline in, 307–11, 315–16, 334

United States: farm acreage in, 248, 250*t;* garment industry in, 349–50; housing in, 327; human capital in, 201–2, 201*t;* interest rates in, 332–33; male stature in, 55, 56; per capita incomes in, 321

unskilled laborers: in cotton textile industry, 311–12, 337, 340–42; demand for, 285–89; female, 277–78; gains from efficiency growth, 272–77; gains from Industrial Revolution, 11–12; wages of, 12, 23, 31, 47–48, 48*t,* 225, 272, 277–78; wages relative to average incomes, 282–83, 282*t*

urban areas: death rates in, 93, 104; land rents in, 198, 275; life expectancies in, 93–94; populations of, 54; real wages in, 103–4, 104*f;* reproductive success in, 161–62. *See also* Bombay; London

urbanization, 103–4, 104*f,* 163, 196

usury, 215–17

violence: deaths caused by, 124–25, 129; decline in, 166, 182–83; judicial, 182–83; threat of, 159–60; war deaths, 126–28, 128*f. See also* homicide

wages: in cotton textile industry, 337–38, 340, 342*f,* 353–54; effects of new production processes, 14–15, 366–69, 367*f;* of female workers, 277–78; in garment manufacturing, 347–49, 349*f;* Iron Law of, 31; marginal product of labor and, 24–25; in poor countries, 12, 43*t,* 43–44, 347–49, 349*f;* premium for physical strength, 277–78; skill premium, 180–81, 180*f,* 225, 276–77; standard bundle of goods purchased with, 41–42, 42*t;* subsistence, 45, 353, 366; of textile workers, 278; of unskilled laborers, 12, 23, 31, 47–48, 48*t,* 277–78, 282–83, 282*t;* wheat-equivalent, 23, 47–49, 48*t,* 49*t*

wages, real: before 1200, 47–48, 48*t;* before 1800, 40–49, 47*f,* 49*t,* 264; of building laborers, 41, 41*t,* 276–77, 276*f;* of farm laborers, 41, 41*t,* 272; increase in, 272–73;

in Ireland, 246, 247*f;* national variations in, 47, 47*f,* 48, 49*t;* in Netherlands, 102–3, 103*f;* of unskilled workers, 48*t,* 272; in urban areas, 103–4, 104*f*

wars, deaths in, 126–28, 128*f*

wealth: birth rates and, 87, 88*f,* 88*t;* inequality in, 279–80, 279*t,* 281–82, 281*t;* literacy rates and, 86, 184, 184*f,* 283, 283*t,* 284; living standards and, 3–4; relationship to life expectancies, 97, 98*f. See also* bequests; reproductive success

White Death, 110–11

wills: ages at death of testators, 92, 178; evidence of fertility by income group, 85–89, 88*f,* 88*t;* evidence of life expectancies, 97, 98*f;* evidence of reproductive success of rich, 113–20; evidence of social mobility, 130–31, 131*t;* evidence of wealth inequality, 282; fraction of surviving children, 97, 99*f;* number of grandchildren, 118–19, 119*f;* number of surviving children, 82, 115*t,* 120, 121, 121*f;* number of surviving children by asset level, 115–17, 116*f,* 292–93, 293*f;* number of surviving sons, 161–62, 161*f,* 294, 295*f;* social ranks of testators, 86, 87*t;* son-daughter ratio, 113–14, 115*t;* testators with no surviving sons, 161–62. *See also* bequests

women: ages at marriage, 74, 75, 76*t,* 81, 82–83, 243, 244*f,* 245*t;* deaths in childbirth, 244–45, 245*t,* 295; increased social status of, 277–78, 295–96; literacy rates of, 295–96; marriage patterns of, 74, 75, 76*t,* 81, 82–83; never married, 74, 105, 243; textile workers, 311, 339; wages of, 277–78

workers. *See* building laborers; farm laborers; labor; unskilled laborers; wages

work hours: effects of increases on living standards, 66–69; in England, 63*t,* 63–65; increase in, 62–66, 64*t,* 166, 181; in pre-industrial societies, 64*t,* 65; relationship to marginal tax rates, 151–52, 152*f;* in textile mills, 339, 340*t*

Wrigley, E. A., 116, 131, 256

Figure Credits

Figure 1.2 Courtesy Gustavo Politis

Figure 1.3 Courtesy Fitzwilliam Museum, Cambridge, England

Figure 2.7 Courtesy Anthony Clark

Figure 3.2 Courtesy Jean Louis Venne

Figure 3.5 Courtesy Ron Miller, www.rontravel.com

Figure 6.8 Courtesy Musée de Millau, Millau, France

Figure 7.1 Courtesy Philip Greenspun

Figure 8.1 Private collection, New York; photograph Erich Lessing, Art Resource, New York

Figure 8.3 Courtesy Anthony Clark

Figure 9.6 Courtesy the Science Museum of Minnesota

Figure 11.1 Courtesy Jürg Wittwer

Figure 11.3 © The New Yorker Collection 2005. Bruce Eric Kaplan from cartoonbank.com. All rights reserved.

Figure 12.2 Courtesy Lancashire County Museum Service, Preston, England

Figure 13.2 Courtesy Pratheep P S, www.Hampi.in

Figure 14.1 From the *Illustrated London News,* February 15, 1868; courtesy Peter Higginbotham

Figure 14.5 Courtesy Chris Knittel

Figure 15.7 Courtesy Arun Ganesh

Figure 15.8 Courtesy Chris Knittel

Figure 16.7 From the papers of Carter D. Poland of Anniston, Alabama; courtesy Special Collections and Archives, Auburn University

Figure 16.10 (*top*) Photograph by Lindsay Buck, courtesy Stephen Buck

Figure 16.10 (*bottom*) Photograph by Kenneth O'Bryen Nichols, courtesy Mike Nichols